The Great Tanganyika
Diamond Hunt

This book is dedicated with love to my dear wife Maria

The Great Tanganyika
Diamond Hunt

James Platt

All rights reserved; no part of this publication may be reproduced or transmitted by any means, electronic, mechanical, photocopying or otherwise, without the prior permission of the publisher.

First published in Great Britain in 2007 by Creighton Books
Email: jim.platt@planet.nl

© 2007 James Platt

ISBN-10: 90 807808 4 7
ISBN-13: 978 90 807808 4 2

The moral right of James Platt to be identified as the author of this work has been asserted by him in accordance with the Copyright, Designs and Patents Act 1988

British Library Cataloguing in Publication Data
A catalogue record for this book is available from the British Library

Designed in the UK by Special Edition Pre-Press Services

Printed and bound in Great Britain by Lightning Source UK Ltd

Also by James Platt and published by Creighton Books

East of Varley Head – Stories from Port Isaac, North Cornwall 1945–1950
(Published in 2003, ISBN 90807808 1 2)

Your Reserves or Mine? (Published in 2004, ISBN 90 807808 2 0)

South of Lobber Point – More stories from Port Isaac, North Cornwall 1945–1950
(Published in 2005, ISBN 90 807808 3 9)

www.creightonbooks.nl

Foreword

I stopped an old man along the way,
Hoping to find some old forgotten words or ancient melodies.
He turned to me as if to say,
"Hurry boy, it's waiting there for you!"
I blessed the rains down in Africa.

Africa—TOTO

Oh, take a trip to Africa,
Take any ship to Africa,
Come on along and learn the lingo
Inside a jungle bungalow!

Skokiaan—AUGUST MUSAREWA

We're foot-slog-slog-slog-sloggin' over Africa—
Foot-foot-foot-foot-sloggin' over Africa—
Boots-boots-boots-boots—movin' up and down again!
There's no discharge in the war!

Boots—RUDYARD KIPLING

So bongo, bongo, bongo, I don't wanna leave the Congo, oh no no no no no!
Bingo, bangle, bungle, I'm so happy in the jungle, I refuse to go!
Don't want no jailhouse, shotgun, fish-hooks, golf clubs, I got my spear,
So, no matter how they coax me, I'll stay right here!

Civilization—BOB HILLIARD AND CARL SIGMAN

Map of Tanganyika in 1960
showing the key locations of the book's narrative

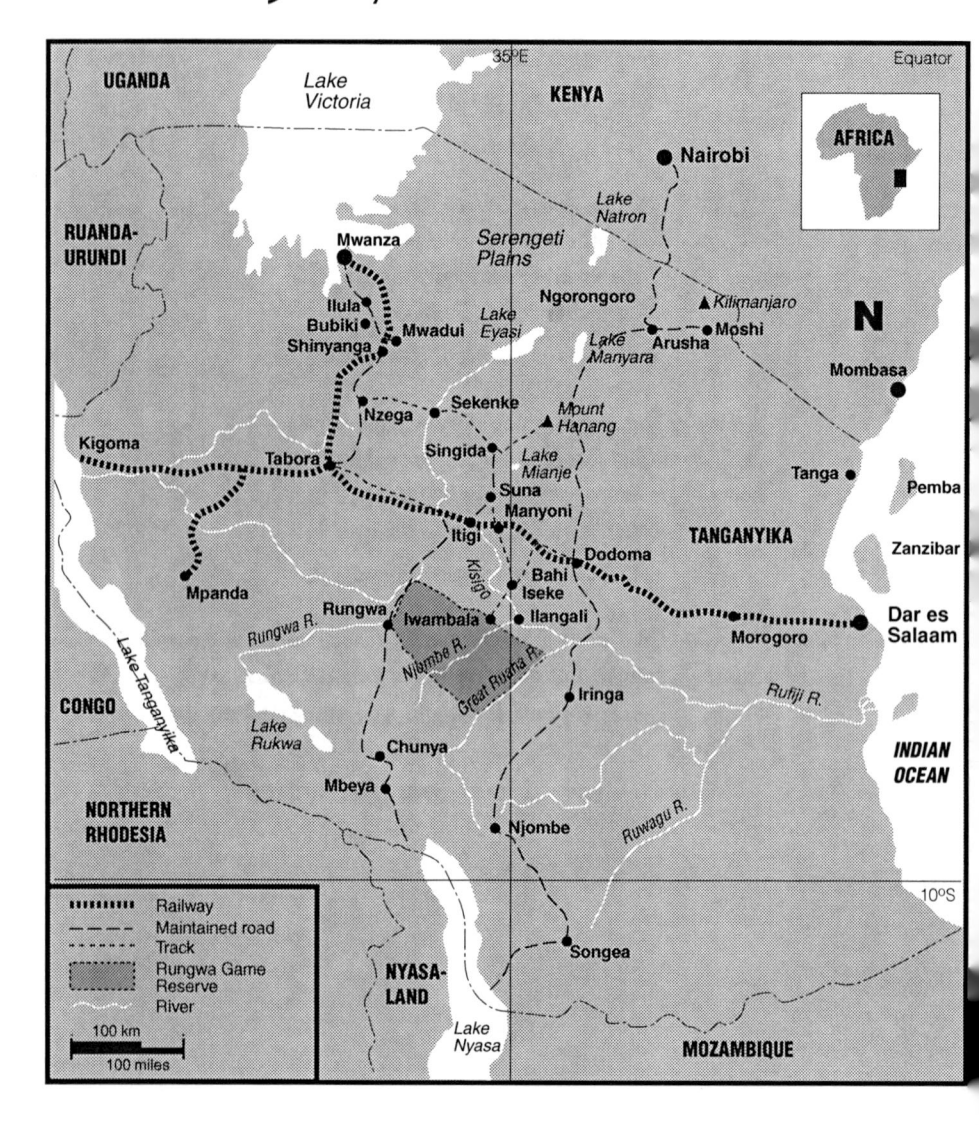

Contents

Foreword — v
Location map — vi
Acknowledgements — viii

1 Mzungu bila fedha A white man without money — 1
2 Endesha pole pole Drive slowly — 21
3 Kitabu elimu ya mawe porini The geologist's field manual — 45
4 Kazi yangu My work — 67
5 Safari porini kwanza First journey into the bush — 85
6 Ndani na nje ya kambi In and out of camp — 105
7 Habari za uvumbuzi? How goes the exploration? — 123
8 Tayare, thabiti, Ugogo Ready, steady, Ugogo — 143
9 Iwambala — 165
10 Maji a kunywa Water to drink — 189
11 Dodoma — 209
12 Mwindaji The hunter — 241
13 Tembo! Elephant! — 263
14 Kalismasi Christmas — 279
15 Iseke — 301
16 Mianje-Mungaa — 317
17 Matata mingi sana Lots of trouble — 339
18 Nchi ya Mbuga mkubwa Big Mbuga country — 363
19 Njia ya kutoka The exit road — 391
20 Kwa heri Good bye — 403
Glossary — 409
Plates — Before pages 143, 241, 317, 363

Acknowledgements

This book was designed and prepared in all details by Corinne Orde and Romilly Hambling who together form Special-Edition Pre Press Services. The kindness, level of style, expertise and patience that they put into the work were exemplary. Corinne's skill in editing and improving the book and its contents added so much to the finished work that it could not have been of greater benefit.

The book was digitally set and registered for print-on-demand orders with key trade and Internet booksellers and distributors by Lightning Source UK Limited of Milton Keynes. LSUK's total commitment to Creighton Books showed a consistent professional excellence and personal consideration that could not be bettered.

I am very much in the debt of everyone who appears in the pages of the book as well as many who for reasons of space and shortcomings of my memory do not. It was a privilege to have known them all and a pleasure to be able to recall them in print.

Special tribute is due to both Tom Molyneux and Bill Campbell-Whalley for the value of advice they gave and information they supplied. Under Tom I could not have wished to work for a better mentor in the bush. Bill very kindly provided me with a copy of the "Bible of the Bush", otherwise known as the "Williamson Diamonds Limited Geologists Field Manual" without which anyone who took part in the Great Tanganyika Diamond Hunt would never have known what rules it was that he was usually breaking.

Finally I would like to thank my dear wife Maria for her unfailing support.

Any qualities that the book has are to the credit of all those who are mentioned above. Any shortcomings are my *shauri* entirely.

1
Mzungu bila fedha
A white man without money

The porter carried my single suitcase on his right shoulder with a practised deftness. The suitcase was made of hard leather. Each of its corners was reinforced with a thick leather patch that served as a notice signifying that it was in order for the suitcase to be dropped heavily on any one of them.

I tailed along behind the porter as he led the way towards a waiting aircraft. Once there he fulfilled the key obligation of his profession by flipping the suitcase forward by means of a neat shrug of both shoulders and a rapid backward shuffle of his bare toes as one corner of it struck the ground hard just in front of him.

Slouching alongside the porter, a man that I assumed was the porter's aide stood with arms akimbo. He was loose-bodied, ready to share the burden if ever the weighty demands of the porter's job became too much for one man to manage.

I could easily have carried the suitcase myself and had attempted to do just that when the call for me to proceed to the aircraft came over the public address system. However, I quickly came to learn that in the place where I was, a white man carrying anything at all was not how things were done. The date was mid-September 1960, the time was early morning, and the place was in Kenya at Nairobi's international airport, named Embakasi.

My possession of the suitcase was therefore forcibly yielded up to the most insistent member of a riotous band of porters whose jointly expressed level of eagerness to take it away from me left me with the alternatives of either giving it up or fighting to retain it. The latter of the two options seemed unattractive to one who, like me, was brand new to the ways and wiles of Africa.

Selecting that one porter from the host before me was carried out by means of a Kenyan variety of Hobson's choice. I was in Africa for the first time. My feet had thus far been on Africa's ground for less than a day. Black faces looked all alike to me—it would require another month or so to engage the jumbled gears of my mind sufficiently to permit the wonderful individuality of black features to register bright and clear.

My knowledge of Africa was strictly related to the "Dark Continent" and "White Man's Grave" schools of thought. The little that I had picked up came in equal parts from reading, hearsay, and attending motion picture epics typified by *Sanders of the River* and the "Tarzan" series (starring the unforgettable Johnny Weissmuller) at the once-weekly cinema in the village of Port Isaac in Cornwall when I was growing up in the post-war years.

I was therefore conditioned to be well aware that in Africa a savage crocodile might lurk in wait for me in any given stretch of water; that a man-eating lion was more than likely to jump out on me from behind any bush; and that any one of a number of terrible diseases (involving a lot of sweating) could come along unexpectedly at any time to strike me down. I knew that I was set to encounter vast numbers of flying and crawling insects wanting to sting me; that there would be a great variety of snakes slithering up to bite me wherever I went; that I would surely run foul of rampaging herds of elephants intent on trampling me to a pulp; that savage natives dressed in leopard skins and armed with spears would be peering at me with ill intentions from behind rocks and trees; and that soaring circles of vultures up above the ground-based drama were looking down on me for the main chance of a feed to come along.

My association with black men of any nationality hitherto had taken place only with gentlemen of that colour who stood on station platforms of the London Underground exhorting boarding passengers to "Lettemofffirstpleez" and "Minededorzpleeze", together with other tribal chants of equivalent ilk couched in the most strident of tones.

A close encounter with an ambitious porter on his home ground at the Nairobi airport filled me with a feeling of deep insecurity. In both mind and spirit I was no Tarzan.

The porter was dressed in a pair of voluminous khaki shorts, a short-sleeved tunic-like shirt of similar dimensions and hue, and not much else. His unshod feet looked durable enough to walk across a pit filled with either broken glass or red-hot coals (or both simultaneously) and to attain the far side unscathed.

I stood with him and his companion at the foot of a short set of steps leading up to the aircraft's open rear door. The aircraft was a Douglas DC3 (better known as a Dakota); blunt nosed, with twin engines and a grey-silvered body that leant back at a characteristic angle, relying on a surprisingly small back wheel for support. The porter turned and said something to me in a language that I already knew to be Kiswahili (the famed *lingua franca* of East Africa) but of which I understood barely a word. I looked at him in bafflement as he again gave voice to what I assumed to be a repetition of his original words.

His companion, whom I re-cast in the role of interpreter, then took up the conversation in English. "He says," he told me, "that he wants some money."

I searched my pockets to show that I was willing to comply with the demand, while at the same time knowing that there was nothing in them that would satisfy the porter's desires. I was *en route* to Tanganyika to take up my first job after graduating from London University a couple of months previously, and I was about as impecunious as it was possible to be.

In the lower recesses of the back pocket of my trousers, however, my fingers located a forgotten coin. I drew it out. It was an English sixpenny piece. Thankful for the small mercy, I offered the tanner to the porter, who took it, looked at it, and uttered a kind of laugh that was best described as sardonically hollow. He spoke again.

"What did he say?" I asked the interpreter.

"He says he wants more!" came the response.

All I could do was to let the pair of them know that I was deeply sorry, but sixpence was all that I was able to give them. The parable of the Widow's mite came to mind, but under the circumstances it didn't bear relating to the porter and his companion. I also had the feeling that if I were to advise the porter that sixpence provided him with tuppence to lend, tuppence to spend, and tuppence to take home to his wife if he had one, it also wouldn't go down very well.

The porter cut to the heart of the matter with a further comment. "He asks," went on his companion, "how can it be that a white man in Kenya has no more than this"—he gestured in the direction of the sixpence—"to give to the Kikuyu?"

I didn't know how to respond to that, especially insofar as I sensed that being named a white man by one who was presumably a member of Kenya's Kikuyu tribe was hardly intended to be a compliment. The citing of a tribal affiliation came with a flavour of his challenging me and knowing that he could get away with doing so.

I had heard of the Kikuyu tribe, the name of which had featured much in British newspapers in recent years with reference to Kenya's Mau Mau "insurrection". The Kikuyu and the Mau Mau movement were allegedly so closely linked that the names were virtually interchangeable. The Mau Mau was a secret society that bound its members to one another with both perverse oath-taking ceremonies and the pursuit of objectives that included the overthrowing of the existing colonial regime and the attainment of full independence for Kenya based on Kikuyu supremacy.

Although the Mau Mau campaign and its bloody excesses were to all intents and purposes at an end when I arrived in Kenya, they remained sharply etched on to the national consciousness. The Kikuyu tribe had gained a reputation that made it greatly feared by almost all of the other tribes of Kenya. The Masai tribe was a notable exception to the rule, as the Masai were known not to fear anyone or anything. For myself, I lined up with the majority view.

The Mau Mau perpetrated murder and mayhem principally on the people of Kenya's other tribes. Anyone who was not held under oath to be for the Mau Mau was by definition considered to be an enemy and fit only for elimination. Mau Mau attacks on the white settlers and colonial administrators in Kenya garnered most of the newspaper headlines; however, to put this in perspective it was reported that during the insurrection more whites were killed in traffic accidents in Nairobi than were murdered by the Mau Mau—even if such a statistic was maybe beside any point at issue.

Moving on as a nation in the immediate post-Mau Mau period was proving to be a halting process for the people of Kenya. Although in principle the Mau Mau was defeated and Mr Jomo Kenyatta (the presumed mastermind behind the movement) was currently in prison preparing to graduate with honours, the British colonial regime (whether or not it knew that it was clinging to power by no more than the skin of the teeth that lay beneath its stiff upper lip) was still in place.

A popular song of the time that I heard on a KBC (Kenya Broadcasting Corporation) radio programme, sung to the tune of "Daddy Wouldn't Buy Me A Bow-wow", included the words: "Daddy wouldn't buy me a Mau Mau, Mau Mau, daddy wouldn't buy me a Mau Mau, Mau Mau—I've got a strangled cat and I'm very fond of that, but I'd rather have a Mau Mau Mau!"

As another sign of the changing times, a white man named Mr Peter Poole was executed by judicial hanging (or so it was reported) in Nairobi only a few days prior to my arrival. The hanging was in its way a historic first. Mr Poole had been convicted of the crime of murdering one of his black employees, something that many of his white contemporaries appeared to regard as no crime at all. Social tensions related to the execution remained high. Even I sensed them in the buzz of conversation around the bar at the Norfolk Hotel in Nairobi, where I stayed on the night of my arrival. A subsequent rumour suggested that the news of Mr Poole's execution might have been greatly exaggerated inasmuch as, the rumour went, Mr Poole had been spirited out of the country and was living elsewhere in secret under another name. Or maybe the rumour simply reflected wishful thinking by white die-hards, white and die-hard being titles that were essentially as synonymous in Kenya as were Kikuyu and Mau Mau.

In the light of Kenya's recent history it was clearly not an ideal time for me to be presenting a Kikuyu porter with an English sixpenny piece. I couldn't help but regard any member of the Kikuyu tribe (colloquially referred to as "Kiukes" in the security of the white man's watering holes) as posing a potential threat. Of course, for me at the time of those first steps in the Dark Continent, similar considerations pretty much applied to anyone with a black face. My porter, I thought, must have at least a passing association with the Mau Mau. He might not have been an oath taker, although as he departed he showed me that he was quite proficient in oath giving.

I was not unhappy to board the Dakota and buckle myself into the seat I was allocated. In spite of the imprecations expressed by the porter, he left with the sixpenny piece in his hand, bearing away all my worldly wealth in cash terms.

*

Everything was so novel and so different. I began to think about how I came to be in such an exotic land full of so many sounds, sights, smells, tastes and wonders that were absolutely new to me.

It all began with Latin.

If I hadn't chosen to take the subject of Latin instead of Physics when I was presented with the alternative options on entering the fourth form at Sir James Smith's Grammar School in Camelford in Cornwall in 1954, the examination subjects that I went on to take at "A" Level in the sixth form in 1957 would probably have been Chemistry, Maths and Physics rather than Chemistry, Maths and Geography. In that event, my onward path of studies through university would not have worked out as it did, and nor would the nature of my first job that had thereafter dropped me into a Dakota aircraft on the way to a destination in Tanganyika have been what it was.

Since someone has to be blamed for what happened, the blame might just as well be set at the feet of the Sir James Smith's Grammar School Physics master, Mr E. J. (Joe) Jeal. I didn't much care for either Joe or the subject he taught, and it is only fair dues to him that he also didn't seem to be enamoured with me. Joe was a small, thin scuttling man, with a great shock of wiry hair that rose on his head in a shape symbolic of the wedge that stood between us. The prospect of getting away from Joe by dropping the subject of Physics in favour of taking Latin therefore seemed rather attractive.

The Latin teacher was a diminutive lady named Miss Quick. She didn't always live up to her name. As with Robert Burns' mouse, she was a "wee, sleekit, cow'rin' tim'rous beastie". Her classes seemed to me to be calm havens in an otherwise heaving sea of unreasonable scholastic demands.

When it came to making an application to enter a university, I dropped by default into going for a course in Applied Geology since I was excluded from more conservative scientific pursuits by virtue of my dearth of qualification in Physics. I was offered a place in the Mining Geology faculty of the Royal School of Mines at Imperial College,

University of London, which I accepted as gladly as if it were a "Get Out of Jail Free" card.

My Mining Geology course ran from 1957 to 1960. In the early July of 1960 I received word that I had actually graduated with a BSc (Special) degree in Mining Geology with third-class honours, and had additionally been awarded the Associateship of the Royal School of Mines (ARSM). Success was much to my surprise, as I had confidently expected to fail. I could only assume that the gentlemen (and perhaps ladies) who marked my final year examination papers were filled with the milk of human kindness when they did so, and were moreover totally untouched by the shadow of Mr Joe Jeal.

With regard to the subject discipline of Mining Geology, the Mining part was one thing, the Geology part was another, and the two in combination were something else again. What the greater practical implications of my newly won qualifications in the profession of applying the science of Geology to the practice of Mining were seemed to be something that I wasn't sure anyone involved in teaching the course had reliably informed me about.

One thing was certain—I needed a job to suit my degree. When (or if) I got such a job, I would be able to find out what was expected of me through the trial and error of doing it.

Fortuitously, it so happened that in the time leading up to my graduation the Anglo American Corporation of South Africa, one of the world's great mining companies, was (while wearing the hat of its subsidiary De Beers Corporation) in the process of recruiting recent Geology and Mining Geology graduates for work on a major programme of field exploration aimed at the discovery of diamonds in the country of Tanganyika in East Africa.

The De Beers Corporation, through its Tanganyika-based operating subsidiary Williamson Diamonds Limited (WDL), held diamond exploration rights over most of the territory of Tanganyika and was required to work towards meeting a deadline a few years hence at which a great deal of those rights were scheduled by government statute to be surrendered to the state for reallocation to third parties.

Self-government for Tanganyika was seen in 1960 as a vague near-term possibility, although the attainment of full independence (famously enshrined in the Kiswahili word *uhuru*) was considered to be so far off as to be to all intents and purposes not worth bothering about. The concept of *uhuru* was regarded by white men who knew about such things as a myth that existed only in the minds of a few black troublemakers.

The WDL diamond exploration campaign was designed to comprehensively cover the territory of Tanganyika prior to the surrender deadline and, in doing so, to define the "best bits" to be held on to and the worthless bits to be given up.

The great recruitment drive took place both in South Africa and in Great Britain. It was envisaged that a total complement of around two hundred and fifty white staff would be hired, ranked in descending order as Graduate Geologists (mostly straight out of university and decidedly raw in terms of experience); so-named Field Officers (shorter on academic achievement than graduates, but longer on know-how); Field Assistants (tough characters, generally of the Afrikaans-speaking persuasion from South Africa and cowboys in all but name); and Prospectors (ageing men of steely character forged over many years spent in Africa, whose key attribute, I was to learn, lay in their ability to attract vast arrays of employees and camp followers associated with their bush-based activities).

All in all, the hiring brought together and put in place a melting pot of variegated opportunists. It promised to everyone involved the chance to live in interesting times. It favoured the brave whose intention was to swim at all costs and ignore the option of sinking.

My application to be considered for a job in Tanganyika with WDL was favourably received by the company and I was called for interview at the Anglo American Corporation's head office in London. My interviewer was a high-powered Personnel Officer named Mr Roberts. I met him for the interview in a suite of offices so opulent that I found it quite intimidating to begin with. I got used to the decor, however, as I was brought back for talks on two further occasions as I made my way into and up through the short list for engagement.

The main thrust of the interview that I had with Mr Roberts dealt with the poetical works of Mr Robert Burns, with which I fortunately had both a familiarity and a deep affinity. My attachment to the peerless Scottish Bard was made during the period of compulsory vacation work that I undertook during the summer of 1959 at a couple of small Scottish barite-producing mines, one of which was located in Renfrewshire and one in Ayrshire.

If Latin and Mr Joe Jeal were responsible for the success of my graduation, it was the great Robbie Burns who undoubtedly got me a job offer with WDL. Mr Roberts, a self-confessed fan of Robbie's works, appeared to pursue me with vigour as if to ensure that I took the job.

*

And so it came to pass that my journey to become a field geologist in Tanganyika commenced when I boarded a train at the Port Isaac Road railway station in north Cornwall in early September 1960. I travelled up the line to Waterloo Station in London; spent one night in that fair city; repaired to the Heathrow airport on the following day; and there joined a BOAC flight with the intended destination of Nairobi's Embakasi airport.

My itinerary called for me to spend one night only in transit in the city of Nairobi before flying onward to Mwadui in Tanganyika. Mwadui was WDL's home base associated with the company's office headquarters and celebrated mining operations of the same name.

The BOAC flight from London to Nairobi was the first flight that I ever took. My experience of flight was consistent with the shaky nature of my career to date, which seemed to have consisted of getting into almost too many situations about which I knew little or nothing of what ripples of consequence awaited me.

The BOAC aircraft was a Vickers Viscount, a turboprop airliner (whatever that meant) of true blue British design. It was capable of carrying forty-eight passengers plus crew at a cruising speed of three hundred and fifteen miles per hour and had a maximum range of fourteen hundred miles. Nairobi was, as the crow flew without getting lost on the way, about four thousand seven hundred miles away from London. I surmised that it was a done deal not only that *en route* to Nairobi the Viscount would need to make more than one landing to refuel but also that the overall flight would last a long time between start and end.

The fuselage of the Viscount looked like a huge, fat, blunt-nosed shiny cigar, relieved on both flanks with a sequence of ten small oval windows. The great wings on either side epitomised elegance, each one supporting a pair of impressive-looking propeller-mounted engines.

I was assigned a seat next to one of those windows. The Viscount departed from London, presumably on time, although I never gave the departure time any thought. The announced duration of the flight was to cover the best part of two days, allowing for touching down on the way at airports in Malta, Benghazi (Libya), Khartoum (Sudan), Entebbe (Uganda), and finally Nairobi.

I remembered little of the progress of the flight. An intense nervousness and a solid feeling of disorientation swamped any memories. I wasn't even sure if there was any particular aspect of the flight that I enjoyed. I didn't have a fear of flying—a heartfelt concern at being in the air replaced that—and the flight impressed itself on me as a means to an end rather than as a personal adventure in progress. Each time we landed my mind blanked out the retained experiences of the preceding leg of the journey. It was as if I had stepped into a capsule at one airport and stepped out of it at another, with nothing to mark the stage in between. The same principle of travel could have been applied to a time machine.

The Viscount landings in both Malta and Benghazi occurred during the hours of darkness. We were permitted to disembark from the aircraft for a short while at each airport. There was heat to feel but nothing to see.

The Viscount's approach to Khartoum airport passed almost directly over the legendary confluence of the White Nile and Blue Nile rivers, from where the unified River Nile was sent flowing north to its delta on the Mediterranean sea through a land saturated by the blood of millennia that took in both the greatest pinnacles and the sorriest depths of human endeavour.

The Blue Nile came tumbling down into Khartoum from the fabled mountain kingdoms of Abyssinia. The White Nile originated far away to the south of Khartoum in the great lakes of East Africa, and arrived to join the Blue Nile after a tortuous journey through forests, deserts and the vast and barely navigable reed-choked Sudd in the Sudan. When they met at Khartoum, the two Niles appeared at first reluctant to merge. Before they ran out of individuality their respective waters flowed alongside one other as if divided by a tight seam stitched by a master tailor.

The best description of Khartoum that I ever heard was provided to me a couple of years later by a certain Mrs Dennis Kent. She was the better half of the bluff and burly Mr Dennis Kent, who ran a general store in the little desert-edge town of Kanye in the Bechuanaland Protectorate. According to Mrs Dennis, Khartoum as a transit stop on the way to somewhere else was "As hot as hell!" I couldn't disagree with her. When I stepped out of the Viscount the oven-like blast of heat that greeted me was like nothing else I had ever before encountered. By contrast the ambient temperature at Nairobi when I got there was almost temperate.

As if to assuage the impact of Khartoum's elevated temperature on me, a steward with a jet-black visage that shone as if it had been polished came along to present me with a small glass almost full of viscous yellow liquid. He wore a robe (of the type known as a *kanzu*) that was not only blindingly white but also long enough to sweep the ground around his feet as he walked. He completed his attire with a tall and rakish red fez on the head.

The steward grinned at me and in doing so disclosed the fact that what he lacked in incisors he made up for in canines and molars. His cheeks were marked by a geometrical arrangement of small scars. He put the glass in my hand and simultaneously placed tremors in my heart. Under his scrutiny I swallowed what was in the glass since I wouldn't have dared not to, and found the liquid so sweet that any flavour it might have been meant to contain was expertly masked.

It was much to my relief that I boarded the Viscount for its departure from Khartoum for Entebbe. A lady in the seat beside me was clearly an "Old Africa" type. She told me how wonderful it was to fly with BOAC and know that the "B" stood for "British". She made no secret of the fact that she subscribed to a dictum that Mr Cecil Rhodes offered to some of his student scholarship beneficiaries, "Remember that you have been born British, and have therefore already won first prize in the lottery of life!"

The lady said that there was so much comfort to be drawn from knowing that a British pilot sat at the forward controls in the cockpit of the Viscount. Where the British went, she said, proper standards were assured. They were the standards of what she called "home", but exactly what they were or where home was she didn't say. I knew of standards back at my version of "home" in Cornwall that wouldn't have fitted into the social circles in which that lady moved, from which I could only judge that I was going to have to revise what was proper and what was not so that I too could assure the appropriate standards.

"Can you imagine", she said to me in a tone carrying with it a slight element of incredulity, "that there are aircraft flying around the skies with Indians at their controls?"

Since to date I had met even fewer Indians than black men, I couldn't respond to her in kind, so I nodded sagely as if her remark had struck a chord with me. The type of Indian that I was most familiar with was usually seated firmly in a saddle, feathers in his hair, a quiver of arrows on his back, and a bow in his hand. Beyond that, all I knew was that if a cowboy fired a gun at a bunch of such mounted Indians at least half a dozen would fall from their horses at the same time. The prowess of such Indians in flying aircraft was never depicted in any cinematic offering concerning them that I had seen.

The stopover at Entebbe was blessed with moderate temperatures befitting the proximity of the airport to Lake Victoria. We were again allowed to leave the Viscount to stretch our legs in what was a rather Spartan terminal building. A few years later that same drab spot would acquire a legendary status throughout the world following a daring raid on it by Israeli soldiers who successfully rescued a large body of hostages who were being held in the terminal at the behest of the infamous then Ugandan President Idi Amin.

While waiting at Entebbe airport to depart for Nairobi, I was provided with a bottle of cold beer brewed by the East African Breweries. The brand name "IPA" stood on the bottle's label in all its glory. The three countries that made up the economic confederation known as East Africa were Kenya, Uganda and Tanganyika. Each was governed by its own separate British colonial regime, but in the more common-interest matters such as currency, postage, air transport, railways, other infrastructure and, not least, the brewing of beer, the three functioned more or less as one.

The dark green bottle of IPA was much more of a drink than the yellow syrup of Khartoum had aspired to be. The bottle was of a size that was more than impressive, holding liquid contents that must have been heading in the direction of a couple of pints. I was to find that there was a problem with IPA when the sun was out and the days were as hot as they not infrequently were, since that quantity of exposed beer did not remain cold in the bottle for very long. I concluded that the contents of a refrigerated bottle of IPA were designed either for sharing with others or for downing rapidly, the latter option being the preferred one.

My personal record for IPA consumption would be set at the contents of twenty-four bottles in the space of the same number of hours within a number of outlets in the town of Dodoma in central Tanganyika. However, I knew several people who were able to imbibe a lot more IPA than I could—and in a much shorter time as well.

The flight to Nairobi from Entebbe made a relatively short hop over Lake Victoria to reach Kenyan airspace, crossed the so-called White Highlands and descended above enormous spreads of rolling savannah. The Viscount landed at Nairobi's Embakasi airport in the late afternoon.

I travelled from the airport into the city of Nairobi as one of a number of passengers in a small transit bus. The road, which was paved, ran for a long distance adjacent to a very high wire mesh fence enclosing what appeared to be an extensive reach of scrubland. At one point during the journey I was thrilled to see two giraffes loping along in the bush on the far side of the fence, keeping pace with the bus as if they were the vanguard of a welcoming committee.

The streets of Nairobi were, if not quite teeming then appreciably busy. The sights from the bus were as alien to me as if I was travelling on a far-off planet. The flow of people in the streets seemed disciplined. Each person gave an impression of knowing where he or she was going and of being keen to get there before the creatures of the night came out. The city might have been a pressure cooker controlled by a tight lid of weighty lessons of the recent past.

The bus drove past a modern, impressive-looking building which appeared ultra-tall in the context of the generally low-lying city sprawling all around it. It was the New Stanley Hotel, a prized icon of the city. There was even a nightclub within the walls of the New Stanley to test the limits of local sophistication, although the nightclub facility would almost certainly be patronised exclusively by whites.

The Norfolk Hotel where I was to spend the night was further on, up at the head of a slight rise. The Norfolk, much older than the New Stanley, was another of Nairobi's gems and traditionally renowned as the city's prime watering hole for both landed white gentry and members of the white hunter fraternity, many of whom were living legends, visiting the city between safaris.

To a large extent Nairobi's reputation was built from activities associated with big game hunting safaris. Hunting, trophy processing and conservation were the strange bedfellows that went hand in hand. The Rowland Ward Company of Nairobi was famous all over the world for taxidermy and trophy-mounting services, supplying hunting gear, equipping safaris, and keeping formal records of big game as manifested by such measurements as weight of elephant ivory or length of antelope horns.

My accommodation at the Norfolk was in one of a number of round-walled cabins set under individually high-pointed thatched roofs and located in behind the main body of the hotel. The cabin was known as a *chumba* in Kiswahili, although I preferred the Afrikaans name of *rondavel*, which was a lot more evocative of the true character of the accommodation.

The bed in my *rondavel* stood beneath a great enveloping cone of mosquito netting suspended from above by a big hook sunk into a crossbeam. A steward clad in what I was coming to believe was the standard uniform of his kind—a white *kanzu* set off by a great red sash at the waist and a jaunty fez of the same colour on his head—brought my suitcase along to the *rondavel*. I looked at him and felt a hefty touch of trepidation. I knew I was behaving irrationally, but it was much too soon for me as a newcomer to feel comfortable about singing a fraud's song in a strange land.

The feelings of uncertainty regarding the great unknown that I had experienced in London prior to boarding the BOAC Viscount and departing for Nairobi were held more or less in abeyance for the duration of the flight. When I stood alone in the *rondavel* at the Norfolk Hotel they came flooding back, and I could only think about just how much I didn't want to be there.

I resolved that when I retired to bed I would lock the *rondavel* door and remain awake and vigilant for the whole night ahead. I could hopefully then avoid being slaughtered when my guard was down. In any case I was too much on edge to be able to contemplate sleep. The thought of having to install myself on a bed within the flimsy shroud-like folds of the mosquito net offered me an additional deterrent to repose.

I went to have a look around the Norfolk Hotel. From what I could see it was open for the reception of guests of any skin colour at all, provided that the skin colour was classed as white. White people in Africa appeared to speak of themselves as "European", irrespective of whether they came from Europe or not.

English was the common language of the white patrons of the

Norfolk Hotel. It was clear to me as an observer that the said patrons' preferred method of addressing the black bar stewards was in loudly toned English rising to the level of an indignant shout when, as was all too often the case, an instruction needed to be repeated.

The white patrons took various words of Kiswahili to scatter in the manner of seeds through the barren ground of their discourse and thereby demonstrate to their drinking companions that they were old Africa hands and insiders entirely to their own satisfaction.

*

Kiswahili was to become an essential foundation stone of the fifteen subsequent months that I was to spend in Tanganyika, so much so that it is worth diverting momentarily from my narrative to bring attention to some of the merits of this wonderful language.

The Kiswahili word for "Europe" was *Ulaya*. The word stem *laya* denoted a national or tribal root and the prefix *u* signified "the country of". *Ulaya* was the country of the Europeans.

One European was an *mlaya*, a number of Europeans together were *walaya* (*m* being the singular and *wa* the plural prefix), and moreover the *walaya* would be expected to speak *kilaya* (*ki* being the prefix denoting a spoken language). It was only a passing curiosity that the Kiswahili word for "prostitute" was *malaya*.

Be that as it may, it was extremely rare to hear of white persons being referred to by the indigenous people of East Africa (one of whom was an *mtu* and several of whom were *watu*) as *Walaya*. The accepted Kiswahili word used to describe a white man was *mzungu*, and naturally when there were several of the same to be considered the word was *wazungu*. The *wazungu* as a rule did not speak *kizungu* (which didn't really exist as a generic language) but rather *Kiingereza* (English).

I always suspected that, irrespective of whether one *mzungu* or many *wazungu* were considered, the titles (both singular and plural) had their origins in well-directed humour—few peoples could beat the *watu* of East Africa in the game of devising nicknames to exploit the unedifying personal characteristics of the luckless individuals (both black and white) to whom the nicknames were awarded.

I was told that a report to a District Commissioner about a tribe in Tanganyika named the *Ha* noted that, "the *Waha* come from *Uha* and speak *Kiha*", and caused the DC to comment "Ha ha!" The story sounded funny enough when I heard it recounted in the bar of the Dodoma Hotel, but to appreciate the joke at its best perhaps you had to have been there at the time.

Kiswahili, translating roughly as the "language of the coast", was a spoken and written language with its origins in Arabic. The Arabic association with East Africa was traditionally rooted in links to the former slave trade. In its purest form as spoken in the coastal communities of East Africa, where it was not unnaturally known as coastal Kiswahili, the language was used with expressive articulation.

The crudest form of Kiswahili was the "up-country" version, which was basic, stripped to its fundamentals, and intended to serve purely as a general medium of communication between the host of indigenous tribes and the few other races that dwelt among them — in other words between servants and masters.

A good knowledge of up-country Kiswahili was mandatory for an *mzungu* like me who would be assigned to work in remote bush conditions in the company of a gang of *watu*, none of whom would speak English for the simple reason that they wouldn't have been hired for the work if they did. *Watu* who spoke English were fortunately found to be few and far between. They were all reckoned (naturally enough by *wazungu*) to be "bush lawyers". It was tough enough for any of us living and working out in the bush without any bush lawyers in the camp, let alone with them in residence.

Up-country Kiswahili was spoken all over the East African confederation and had gone on from there to permeate to the west and to the north along the respectively mighty courses of the Congo and White Nile rivers.

Armed with a reasonable understanding of up-country Kiswahili, any *mzungu* could converse with *Waharabu* (Arabs), *Wahindi* (Indians) and members of most of Tanganyika's tribes. The great *lingua franca* was an essential means of promoting good communication between many different types of people who generally didn't like each other all that much, but you couldn't have everything.

Following my eventual arrival at Mwadui I was given an up-country Kiswahili phrase book and basic grammar to study, and I found it to be replete with interesting things to learn to say in Kiswahili, such as, "Make tea!" and "Who broke this dish?" and "Why have you not swept this floor?" and "I have no work for you!" The phrase book also instructed me as to how I could, if required, pose the question, "Do you have a venereal disease?"

On such a basis the well-tempered *mzungu* could direct the activities of menials all through the livelong day, commencing with being brought tea in bed in the early morning through to the ultra-critical necessity of being served sundowners on the veranda whether or not the sun was yet over the yardarm.

The Arabs and the Indians of Tanganyika were, almost exclusively when I was among them, traders and shopkeepers. The Arabs came voluntarily to East Africa in dhows from across the Indian Ocean in centuries past as masters of the long defunct slave trade. The Indians were originally transported to East Africa from their sub-continent in the nineteenth century to work on the construction of railways, in the course of which rather a lot of them appealed to the taste of man-eating lions.

Neither Arabs nor Indians were celebrated for their ability to integrate into East African society at large, which was a characteristic shared in spades (no pun intended) by *wazungu*. The relationships of Arabs and Indians with the indigenous population were rarely good, and little or no effort seemed to be put by either side into trying to make them better.

In the town of Singida in Tanganyika an Indian trader named Mr Manji Dhanji, whom I was to get to know quite well, asked an elderly Prospector of WDL for advice on what kind of goods he might stock if (horror of horrors) the day of Independence (*uhuru*) should ever dawn —not that it ever would, but you never knew really and it was as well to be prepared. The Prospector suggested to Mr Manji Dhanji that he might get in a large stock of running shoes, since, he went on, every Indian and Arab and more than a few *wazungu* in the locality would be in dire need of a pair.

Many of the Prospectors were former cronies of the late Dr John Williamson, the discoverer, founder and thereafter the virtual tribal chief in his own right of the township and diamond mine at Mwadui. Dr Williamson's death a couple of years prior to my arrival left the cronies unprotected and motivated the new WDL regime installed by De Beers to banish a lot of them from the comfort of town by putting them to work out in the bush. The Prospectors established and managed vast semi-permanent exploration and development camps as personal fiefdoms with a *watu* workforce of hundreds, plus many more camp followers.

A Prospector of Swiss origin, Mr Albert Künzler, married a tribal chief's daughter, and the entire population of her home village followed him around the country wherever his work took him. He was immensely fat, a Chaka or Lobengula in all but name. Albert had a legendary capacity for IPA, but was most famous for his artistic talent. He produced paintings of landscapes, game animals and traditional tribal portraits of exquisite quality. I bought a study of a tribeswoman's head from him for forty East African shillings. A small collection of his works was reputedly hanging on display in the United Nations Building in New York.

*

I never knew if any of Albert's paintings graced the inner walls of the Norfolk Hotel—had they done so they would have had to fight for precedence with a vast array of stuffed heads of big game that hung from the walls almost anywhere that I cared to look, no doubt courtesy of the services of Messrs Rowland Ward.

The bar room of the Norfolk was replete with such hanging heads. It was a long, hardwood panelled room, a favoured haunt of the kind of people who no doubt contributed regularly to keeping the taxidermists in business. The bar dress code appeared to run to shirts (short sleeved), shorts (to half way down the thigh), and socks (up to the knee). The dominant colour of the attire on offer was khaki. Some of the khaki shirts (or tunics) that I saw draped on the shoulders of certain comfortable habitués of the bar were fitted with bullet loops (with not a bullet in sight) crossing the upper breast. On their feet they wore dun ankle-length boots of soft leather uppers and crepe soles that were generally referred to as *velskoon* from the Afrikaans language word for "skin shoes".

The style of *velskoon* made by the Bata shoe company eventually became my favourite type of footwear, with or without socks. Those shoes fitted my feet like gloves and were ideal for working in bush conditions.

Faces of the *wazungu* congregated in the Norfolk Hotel bar were ruddily veined, bellies were variably pendulous, and hands both raised and lowered glasses of beer with well-accustomed metronomic frequency.

I listened to a drift of conversation touching on the recent hanging of Mr Peter Poole, although the principal topic under (not unrelated) discussion seemed to cover issues involved with the shortcomings of *watu* in general and domestic servants in particular. There was no more popular subject chosen to exercise the minds and mouths of colonial *wazungu* than that one.

In the East African convention of the time, *wazungu* normally referred to *watu* as "boys". The use of the term "boy" to characterise an *mtu* was in such common currency that I picked it up and adopted it right away.

All through my time in Tanganyika I thought of the black people that I worked with in the bush as "the boys", and even as "my boys". We depended on one another and in most of the situations we encountered together my fate was far more in their hands than theirs was in mine. We got used to being with one another and made a good thing of it as a rule, each one of us complying with what was an unwritten code of conduct.

Yet that was then and now is now, and in the interim social conventions, unwritten or not, have rightly changed. In the subsequent chapters of my narrative and in conjunction with twenty-first century norms, those with whom I worked will therefore always be referred to as *watu*.

They were indeed men. Many of them were good men, a few of them were bad men, and among them there were some men who were a privilege to know, whatever generic title might be assigned by *wazungu* to categorise them.

2
Endesha pole pole
Drive slowly

I boarded the Dakota aircraft bound for Mwadui from Nairobi airport having swapped my one and only sixpenny piece for the undoubtedly lasting disdain of a Kikuyu porter. In spite of his unforgiving attitude I felt a fair amount of sympathy for him. However, this finer feeling was diluted with nervous anticipation for what lay ahead.

The night that I had just spent in a rondavel of the Norfolk Hotel had boosted my spirits a little in that it had not turned out to be nearly as much of an ordeal as I expected. In fact I was surprised to discover that I slept well under the pleated cone of the mosquito net for a number of hours during the night. The principal benefit that I got from the experience was a firm conviction that not only was the cover of a mosquito net at night a comfort but it also provided a sense of genuine security.

Among the personal effects enclosed in my leather suitcase reposing in the hold of the Dakota was a four-inch thick bound compilation of the lecture notes that I had taken down with various degrees of painstakingness during my thankfully concluded university studies. I packed the notes in the suitcase in a moment of unthinking enthusiasm. I knew well, as did every student, that following graduation such notes had served their purpose as a means to end and would in all likelihood never need to see the light of day again. The notes made a significant contribution to the overall dead weight of the suitcase contents, however, as the Kikuyu porter must have discovered.

In addition to the great slab of lecture notes my suitcase also contained a small Bible bound in red leather. It was a present received from my paternal grandmother on the occasion of my birth. As far as plans for its future consultation went, the Bible would make a good companion to be ignored alongside of the lecture notes.

When I was finally sent out from Mwadui to work in the bush, both the lecture notes and the red leather-covered Bible resided at the bottom of a large, heavy-duty tin trunk, a standard-issue piece of WDL equipment. What I didn't know was that there was a tiny hole in a bottom corner joint of the tin trunk. Since the tin trunk remained static in one place in the far rear of my tent for a considerable period of time, a colony of termites managed to find the tiny hole and use it to enter the tin trunk to set up home inside. The termites ate only a small proportion of the lecture notes, but found the India paper pages of the Bible much more to their taste, succeeding in consuming about a third of the Good Book before their presence was discovered. I admired the termites for getting far more out of the written words of God than I ever did.

*

Following its departure from Nairobi and once it had reached its cruising altitude, the Dakota followed an approximately due southwest flight path to its destination at Mwadui, two hundred and fifty miles away. Periodic turbulence bounced the aircraft up, down and sideways, causing the fuselage to groan at its seams in protest. The aircraft was old enough to have seen war service in the 1940s, a probability also signified by the Spartan, bare-bones nature of the cabin fittings.

As the Dakota rattled across the border between Kenya and Tanganyika, Mount Kilimanjaro thrust its truncated white cap above the early morning haze out to the east of us. We flew over the vast grassy expanse of the Serengeti plains. Away to the west, Lake Victoria shone like an immense mirror as its surface caught the glance of the rising sun. I thought of the Rubaiyat of Omar Khayyam in which lo, the hunter of the east hath caught the Sultan's turret in a noose of light.

Poorly drained and lightly vegetated flatlands underlain with silt and pimpled by rounded hills of bald grey granite stretched in a gigantic swathe for a hundred miles south of the southern fringe of Lake

Victoria. This type of silt, I discovered later, was known in English as "black cotton soil" and in Kiswahili as *mbuga*. Its presence signified the all too sluggish rudiments of a drainage system. *Mbuga* soil was both glutinous and cloying to the least touch in the wet season; iron hard and split by desiccation cracks in the dry.

Mwadui was located down towards the southern limit of the Lake Victoria associated *mbuga* country. Whatever the status of Mwadui might have been prior to the discovery of diamonds in its vicinity, it had subsequently evolved to give its name to a township constructed specifically to serve the WDL mining operations. The greater township area was encircled by a high, heavy-duty wire mesh security fence, which was said to be electrified. Set well within the major area contained by this primary fence a second security fence enclosed a well-defined restricted area in which those mining and diamond recovery operations were carried out.

Entry to the restricted area was tightly controlled, the key objective being to prevent the clandestine removal of diamonds from the property. The measure of success was the extent to which the theft of diamonds could be minimised. In matters concerning the theft of diamonds it seemed that human ingenuity knew no bounds. One way or another, a few diamonds would always fall into the wrong hands. With a receptive body orifice into which a diamond or two could be inserted for concealment, or with the provision of a means of forcibly slinging or catapulting a stolen diamond over the wire fence (electrified or not) for collection by an accomplice, the unauthorised appropriation of some diamonds was more or less a sure thing.

Bernie McBride, a brittle-edged Australian geologist who ranked at Number Three in the Mwadui-based exploration hierarchy and who had previously worked for the De Beers Corporation on beach-alluvial diamond deposits in South West Africa, said to me once, "As long as diamonds are being mined, some bastard will always find a way to steal a few!"

A trade in illicit diamonds, some taken out of Mwadui and others coming in from the diamond fields of the neighbouring republic of the Congo, was reckoned to flourish throughout Tanganyika. The bare feet of couriers trod little-known tracks that wove through the bush like a spider's web homing in on Dar es Salaam, the capital city on the Indian Ocean coast.

As far as *wazungu* were concerned, the principle governing the theft of diamonds was that dishonesty was a black thing—*watu* and only *watu* were the criminals. By contrast, *wazungu* were paragons of virtue by their own cognisance, all of them as honest as the day was long—for were they not appointed by divine right to keep a keenly supervisory eye on the *watu* so as to nip the latter's nefarious practices in the bud and punish the guilty?

As I learned from my fellow passenger on the BOAC Viscount on the way out to Nairobi, the *wazungu* were the guardians of all that was good in the way of proper standards in Africa. ("Ha, ha!" said the DC). Juvenal knew best what made such guardians tick: "*Sed quis custodiet ipsos Custodes?*" (But who is to guard the guards themselves?)

*

Some background information on Dr John Williamson, the discoverer of the diamond mine to which he gave his own name and the founder of the Mwadui town and mining complex, may be appropriate at this point in my story.

Dr Williamson was a Doctor of Geology, a graduate of McGill University in Montreal, Canada. He died from cancer of the throat in January 1958 at the far too young age of fifty years.

When I reached Mwadui in September 1960, the De Beers regime was already well established within WDL. By all accounts De Beers seemed to have done its level best both to eradicate as many traces of Dr Williamson's rule as it reasonably could and instil a hitherto unaccustomed rigour in local management practices.

Dr Williamson was justly famed for his qualities of persistence, dedication, faith and the courage of belief in his own convictions—all of which characteristics typified a professional geologist at the top of his game.

Perhaps Dr Williamson should have gone on to stick at doing what he did best, since in his self-appointed later role as paramount Chief of WDL and all that therein was he came to be variously described as "a difficult man to work with", "a man who did not suffer fools gladly" and other such euphemisms reflecting the less admirable traits of a domineering personality. He was said to be chaotic in his decision-making, given to frequently undermining the authority of his senior staff, countermanding their orders and all too often working at cross-purposes to them from a position behind their backs.

My assessment of Dr Williamson, derived from both written and anecdotal evidence, was that his Mwadui-based lifestyle was characterised by excess in all things. He owned an excess of riches, he imbibed an excess of alcohol, he smoked an excess of cigarettes and he filled his court with an excess of sycophantic cronies. The cumulative product of the excess formed the weight that ultimately crushed him.

It is probable that Dr Williamson's monarchic aspirations were marked by mildly psychopathic tendencies bubbling along beneath a shell of overly acute paranoia. Although his actions inspired no mutiny in the good ship "WDL" that he mastered, Dr Williamson could easily have served as a model for Herman Wouk's Captain Queeg of the "USS Caine".

In short, Dr Williamson was a victim of both success and excess, and while there was no stain (yellow or otherwise) on his achievements, he eventually went the punch-drunk way of a champion boxer who failed to hang up his gloves in time.

It was Dr Williamson's faith in the occurrence of diamond deposits in Tanganyika that helped to carry him through what must for him have been a barely tolerable stretch of disappointing years. His dream of discovering diamonds went long unfulfilled, but it seemed that his belief in ultimate success did not waver. On one momentous day, as I heard the story recounted at the bar of the Mwadui club by a couple of members (only *wazungu* needed apply), the weight of frustration finally seemed to reach the point of bringing the great man to his knees. He sank beneath the shade of a tree to contemplate his options. One of the Mwadui club members said that the tree was a baobab, but the other declared that it was an acacia. Irrespective of the species of the tree above him, Dr Williamson's geologically inspired hands instinctively commenced picking up and crumbling lumps of soil from around the place at which he sat. A diamond emerged from a dusty handful of dirt, liberated to fall at Dr Williamson's feet, ablaze with light.

The rest was history.

If the story wasn't true, then it surely ought to have been.

Dr Williamson's newly found riches drew opportunists to his side in the way that the garbage dump behind the Mwadui staff canteen attracted platoons of imperiously strutting marabou storks and flapping squads of vultures intent on consuming the discards on open display.

His drone-like acolytes buttered him up with both flattery and constant reassurances that his feelings of insecurity demanded of them. They might not all have attended Dr Williamson's court for personal gain, yet every crumb that fell into their eager hands from his groaning table helped to keep them on station.

*

With Dr Williamson's endeavours by now fresh in the mind of readers who have made it this far, and before proceeding further with my tale, it may be worth taking this opportunity to set out a broad overview of the geological characteristics of diamonds together with the nature of diamond exploration practice, as this will have a direct bearing on some later chapters.

The host rock in which diamonds occur is named "kimberlite" in honour of its type-location near the city of Kimberley in the Cape Province of South Africa. Kimberlite is, according to those ill-fated Mining Geology notes that were destined to be partially eaten by termites, an igneous rock (a variety of mica-peridotite) of ultra-basic (iron-rich) composition formed at great depths in the earth's magmatic core from where it gets intruded up into the shallower younger rocks of the earth's crust. The typical shape assumed by a solid body of kimberlite in the ground is that of a vertically extensive standing pipe.

A kimberlite pipe is, on account of the incorporation and assimilation in its mass of blocks of younger rock (known as xenoliths) both great and small, quite heterogeneous in composition and varied in texture. The xenoliths represent pieces of rock torn away from its walls by an ascending pipe undergoing the violent process of intrusion.

Kimberlite is moreover a relatively "soft" and chemically reactive rock—twin characteristics that make it an easy prey to alteration by meteorological weathering. The effect of weathering on kimberlite is to break the primary rock down into a mass of secondary clay minerals containing resistant residual minerals—inclusive of diamonds of course. The clay products are manifested in a superficial zone of so-called "yellow ground" and a deeper underlying zone of the more famous "blue ground". The latter is transitional at a relatively shallow depth into primary kimberlite.

During the weathering process the diamonds contained in primary kimberlite are liberated to rest within both the yellow and the blue grounds. Fabulous riches are often extracted from the clays prior to pressing on with the less lucrative but much longer-term option of mining and processing the primary kimberlite.

A diamond, chemically consisting of pure carbon, normally occurs in octahedron-shaped crystals related to the cubic system of crystal classification. A high refractive index makes a natural diamond appear to possess an inner fire. The diamond holds the pinnacle position in Moh's standard scale of mineral hardness, and what with its virtual indestructibility, its historical significance, its legendary reputation and its rarity in nature, it is no wonder that it is among the commodities of the world most prized by both its owners and the thieves who have designs on it.

Diamonds, although chiefly clear white in colour, may also be found in any one of a range of other shades including pink, yellow and green. The depth of colour is a function of the impurities held in the crystal lattice. Dark shades do not appear to feature much in gem-quality diamonds. Of course, not all diamonds that emerge from kimberlite are of gem quality. Non-gem diamonds, known as "boart", are commonplace. Boart is mainly used for industrial applications, as in the facing of cutting tools.

It fell to the lot of very few indeed of those of us who worked on the WDL diamond exploration programme in Tanganyika to encounter even a single example of a diamond, whether of gem or of industrial quality, in the course of our work. For any of us to have found an actual diamond under bush working conditions would be reckoned as a monumental *coup*. It was therefore fortunate that none of us entertained the expectation of such a happy state of affairs coming to pass.

Diamonds are always associated with kimberlite and its clay alteration products, although unfortunately not every kimberlite pipe is diamondiferous. Dr Williamson could easily have attested to that particular truth. However, when kimberlite is subjected to weathering and surface erosion, certain of its more resistant and heavy constituent minerals (referred to as "indicator" minerals) are released into the natural environment to reside in locally overlying and immediately surrounding soil and sub-soil. Indicator minerals tend to work their way into drainage systems by virtue of processes such as down-slope soil creep or the runoff effects of rainfall. Once into a stream and river network, the indicator minerals may be transported downstream for distances commensurate with their relative resistance to abrasion.

The surface expression of a kimberlite body is roughly circular—as befits its cited pipe-like morphology. A pipe offers a virtual bull's-eye as a target for exploration. The indicator minerals radiate outwards along drainage channels falling off the halo-like hub of kimberlite as if they were the ever-extending spokes of a gigantic wheel.

The indicator minerals critical to diamond exploration are three in number. They are a holy trinity respectively named ilmenite, pyrope garnet and chrome diopside. As indicators they are infinitely less elusive to discover through sampling soils and stream beds than diamonds are.

Ilmenite, an oxide of iron and titanium, is a shiny, metallic black mineral. Its high specific gravity allows it to be easily concentrated, on the assumption that there is water available for that purpose, by manual processes such as panning or jigging of samples. However, water, not least in the dry season, can be as difficult to find as actual diamonds. (The availability of water was a lot more relevant to our wellbeing in the bush than finding a diamond ever was.) As an indicator mineral, ilmenite typically occurs in small rice-like grains that are streaked or coated in part with a durable white product of secondary oxidation known as leucoxene. Just like good wine, grains of ilmenite travel well and can be found in stream-bed sediments a long way downstream from their primary source.

Pyrope garnet, a member of the garnet family of minerals and crimson in colour, is a magnesium aluminium silicate by composition. Under certain conditions of size, depth of colour and clarity, a pyrope garnet crystal can be classified as a semi-precious gemstone. The ability of this indicator mineral to travel along an active drainage system is much less than that of its more durable compatriot ilmenite. It will normally be destroyed by abrasion and attrition at a comparatively closer juncture to its primary source, which greatly enhances the importance of its role as a definitive indicator for kimberlite.

The third of the indicator minerals, chrome diopside, is by chemical composition a calcium magnesium silicate characterised by chromium impurities. Bright green in colour, it wears even less well on the move than does pyrope garnet. If chrome diopside is found to occur in soil or stream samples, the location of the kimberlite from which it was liberated could be expected to be not far off.

The economic value of a kimberlite pipe is vested in its containing gem diamonds that are not only plentiful but also of good size and quality. Such criteria were more than amply associated with Dr Williamson's world-class discovery at Mwadui and were instrumental in promoting his meteoric rise and subsequently creeping fall.

*

There were so many high-quality gem diamonds extracted from the WDL mine during Dr Williamson's time that if a few of them went missing it didn't really seem to matter. The mine was so rich it couldn't avoid generating riches for its owners. It was reliably rumoured that Dr Williamson kept a galvanised metal bucket full of gem-quality diamonds in his personal office, and that sometimes when the drinks had flowed along their customarily copious course he and his cronies were apt to pick up the bucket and pour the stones over one another in a literal shower of glittering opulence.

A field manager named Mr Merle McKeown that I worked for on a De Beers diamond exploration programme in the eastern province of Northern Rhodesia in 1963/64 provided some credence to the bucket of diamonds rumour when he told me about an experience he had when he held the position of Chief Geologist for WDL at the height of Dr Williamson's reign. On one occasion, he said, he was called into Dr Williamson's office for the purpose of inspecting a few diamonds laid out for his attention on a desktop. During the inspection one of the diamonds accidentally fell to the floor from his fingers and promptly sank out of sight into the thick pile of the carpet underfoot.

In retrieving the fallen gem, Mr McKeown (who was never known to be addressed by his Christian name) said that he discovered an additional four diamonds lying deep in the carpet pile. It was as if he had created a high-stakes re-enactment of Tom Sawyer's "brother go find your brother" game of using a deliberately discarded marble to find a lost counterpart.

Mr McKeown told me that one Friday morning Dr Williamson handed him a huge fifty-four carat uncut rose-pink gem-quality diamond that he wanted photographed to best advantage against a tasteful backdrop drape of velvet. (The diamond was eventually cut down to a twenty-three carat brilliant and set into the centrepiece of an Alpine rose-styled brooch. It was presented to Princess Elizabeth on the occasion of her marriage in 1947 and was at the time the largest pink diamond ever discovered.)

On completion of the photographic task Mr McKeown took the future Crown jewel back to Dr Williamson's office for replacement in the office vault, only to find that Dr Williamson had shut up shop for the weekend and, together with a band of his close disciples, had repaired to the Mwadui club bar from where he was to all intents and purposes inextricable.

Mr McKeown's entreaties to have the vault opened so as to secure the pink diamond within fell on unreceptive ears. Dr Williamson, he said, told him to hang on to the great gemstone, look after it for the weekend and bring it back on Monday morning. Mr McKeown told me that he went around all weekend with the diamond weighing down one of his trouser pockets, afraid to take his hand off it and too nervous to even attempt to sleep.

With the untimely demise of Dr Williamson and the subsequent arrival at WDL of De Beers, the careless handling of diamonds was dispensed with—or at least that was the general idea. A number of Dr Williamson's cronies were reassigned as prospectors and were dispersed out into the bush.

The Great White Recruitment Drive for Geologists, Field Officers and Field Assistants then went on to pull together a cast of younger and unseasoned characters and cast them to the four winds of the unsuspecting territory of Tanganyika.

Incidentally, the name "Tanganyika" was derived from a combination of the Kiswahili words *tanga*, meaning "sail", and *nyika* meaning the type of open savannah bush of the great upland plateau (standing at an altitude of 3,500 to 4,500 feet above sea level) that occupied much of the country to the west of its littoral region. "Tanganyika" thereby depended on the proud traditions of both land and sea, in connection with which it was not all that easy to dismiss visions of slave caravans crossing the *nyika* on land, while at sea the *tanga* of a dhow bearing cargoes of slaves away to Arabia across the Indian Ocean from the primary slave market on the island of Zanzibar flapped and bellied out at the touch of a favourable trade wind.

*

To return to my tale, however, a welcoming committee of two South African Field Officers was there to meet me on my arrival at the Mwadui airstrip in the Dakota from Nairobi. Both of them seemed to express an air of supreme confidence in their own abilities. I was immediately convinced that they had experienced far more than I ever could or ever would with respect to working in Tanganyika. I took to both of them right away. One of them was of the South African Afrikaans-speaking persuasion and the other owed his allegiance to the English language. Their names were, respectively, Derek Visagie and Gerry Wilson. In the fluent manner of so many South Africans, Derek and Gerry were able to switch between the two languages at will, sometimes using both in the course of a single spoken sentence.

They were both warm-hearted, down-to-earth men who were good at their jobs and gave an impression of taking on life on with panache. I found that many other white South Africans who worked on the diamond exploration programme were people with similar qualities. The only *contretemps* that I had with any of them arose in the few instances in which Afrikaans-speaking individuals seemed intent on blaming me for the fact that it was their side that allegedly lost the Boer war.

As far as the Boer war went, I had heard all about the relief of Mafeking, the relief of Ladysmith and a contemporary popular song entitled "Goodbye Dolly Gray". The need to cope with the scarred minds of Afrikaans speakers focused on what I saw as a rather pointless war was a not infrequent feature of my ongoing education in matters South African.

Derek and Gerry were Field Officers by job grade and vehicle mechanics by profession. They were based at Mwadui from where they ventured out into the bush on occasional forays. They bore a large measure of the responsibility for the wellbeing of the huge fleet of WDL Land Rovers that were the mainstay of the nation-wide diamond exploration programme. However, since the majority of the Land Rovers in the fleet were located in remote bush camps a long way away from Mwadui and as a consequence were out of sight and out of mind, the working pressures on the pair of mechanics were not always as great as they could have been.

The nerve centre of their vehicle maintenance empire was a long, barn-like service garage clad on its walls and roofed over its top with corrugated metal sheets. It was situated not far from the white staff canteen. The garage acted as an oven in the grip of the sun and as a comparative sieve in the rain. A sign over its broad, slide-mounted entry door proclaimed that the establishment was named *Badu Kidogo* Motors. *Badu* in Kiswahili translated as "not yet" and *kidogo* meant "little". Together the two words formed a popular local expression somewhat akin to the Spanish *mañana*, if not rather more so.

Derek provided the brains behind *Badu Kidogo* motors, whereas Gerry supplied a wide range of key mechanical skills.

Gerry was well known in all the exploration camps as a bullshitter's bullshitter, not least when it came to assertions concerning his previous experience. An evening pastime in camps sometimes involved *wazungu* attempting to work out how old the youthful-looking Gerry would have to be in order to have accomplished everything he claimed to have done to date. It was possible to reach a required age of eighty years without any necessity to commence digging deeper.

There were few of Gerry's personal reminiscences that failed to gain something in the telling. Gerry fine-tuned his powers of hyperbole as he spread himself around in a most engaging manner.

The trips that Gerry made out of Mwadui to exploration camps normally involved his taking a serviced Land Rover on the outward journey and bringing back a Land Rover requiring service and/or repairs on his return. Such visits were popular in the camps as, apart from a talent for bullshit, Gerry brought along personal and company mail, fresh vegetable and dairy produce from Nairobi (courtesy of the Dakota flight schedule), other supplies and spare parts as needed, and numerous items of insider gossip. The freight he took with him from camp on the return journey consisted chiefly of personal mail for posting, exploration sampling reports and soil and river- or stream-bed sample concentrates (the final product of the diamond exploration process) for analysis.

It was Derek who took primary charge of me. He shepherded me around Mwadui; guided me through the initial administration formalities that involved me signing a confusing plethora of forms; took me to get my mug shot photograph taken; introduced me to a great many *wazungu* whose faces I remembered but whose names I promptly forgot as always; and installed me in my assigned place of accommodation.

My accommodation quarters were contained in a room in a building specifically allocated to white field staff in transit. Those who stayed on the premises included newcomers like me and older hands who were either in Mwadui for a couple of days or simply travelling through and taking an overnight break between bush assignments.

The building was a large thatch-roofed bungalow known as the Pink House owing to the fact that, as it would have been described back home in Cornwall, the outside walls were painted with pink whitewash. The Pink House stood in a state of grand isolation on the outer edge of the Mwadui township. Behind the Pink House both an experimental livestock farm (some cattle and pigs) and a market garden were located, each of them bold ventures in a hostile environment.

Inside the Pink House the walls were made stark by the application of conventionally coloured whitewash. The floors were paved with intensely polished red terracotta tiles. The furnishings were basic in the best barrack-room tradition. Guests came and went both frequently and unannounced during the approximately three weeks that I spent in residence at the Pink House prior to my being released into the bush, although unfortunately the presence of other guests didn't apply to the first three days and nights of my stay, when I had the place all to myself.

At the immediate rear of the Pink House the black custodian of the property lived with his family in a minuscule hut constructed of red brick and capped by no more than a few essential sheets of corrugated metal. A fire, surrounded by pots made from both clay and cast iron, smouldered steadily on a patch of dusty ground located midway between the front door of the brick hut and the back door of the Pink House. The custodian, an *mtu* whose official title was "house boy" invariably made his appearance dressed in a singlet that might once have been white (which my mother would have described as "more holey than righteous"), and a lightly chequered wrap-around sarong-like garment that begged to be washed even more than the singlet did. He squatted on the doorstep of his hut, staring gloomily at the fire as if the engendering of cheerful flames was beyond his control.

My close juxtaposition to him did nothing for my peace of mind. When I was alone in the Pink House at night I thought of the custodian back there perhaps reckoning that I was well within easy spearing range. Sleep eluded me to the extent that I was never sure if I slept at all during any one of those first three nights at the Pink House, even though logic told me that I must have done. A state of foreboding was easily able to erase the power of rational thought.

For a start there was the isolated location of the Pink House, which seemed to offer an open invitation to nocturnal marauders, the security of a mosquito net over my bed notwithstanding. Close to hand was the fierce-looking custodian, with whom my conversation was restricted to the few polite fundamentals of Kiswahili that I was picking up such as yes (*ndio*), no (*hapana*), hello (*jambo*), goodbye (*kwa heri*), please (*tafadhali*), thank-you (*asante*), may I come in (*hodi*) and come-in (*karibu*).

I once heard the come-in word emphasised at the Dodoma Hotel by an *mzungu* who, following three loudly expressed *karibus* that elicited no response from the *hodi* supplicant at the door of his room, bellowed out "*Ka*-fucking-*ribu!*" Sadly, I couldn't find that particular term in my Kiswahili phrase book.

Lizards drifted around on the inner walls of the Pink House with a nonchalance that suggested they believed that they were the only genuine residents. Some of the lizards were big and blue-bodied with scary looking red heads. Continuous sounds of things that rustled, scrabbled and scurried came down from the thatched roof as whatever it was that was up there in the thatch demonstrated an unwillingness to move in silence as it went about its business. I lay in bed beneath the mosquito net and trembled in counterpoint to the percussive rhythm of tiny claws skittering, clicking and slipping on the polished terracotta tiles. It did me no good at all to try and imagine what the owners of the claws looked like.

A sound of some distant and some not so distant drumming pulsed regularly in the external night. It seemed that as well as standard drums a number of empty jerry cans were also being pounded out there with a manic sense of purpose. A lot of the drums were homemade by stretching and tightly drawing an appropriately sized piece of wet rawhide (cattle or game) over the open top of a five-gallon tin can by means of thin rope or sinews and allowing the rawhide to dry in place. Such resonant drums were used with skill by the *watu* in every exploration camp that I worked out of.

The five-gallon tins, which were square in cross-section, were a universal standard in Tanganyika. Known as *debes*, when full they either contained cooking oil (*mafuta ya kupika*) or lamp oil (*mafuta ya taa*). Empty *debes* were greatly prized by the indigenous people in their villages not so much as a basis for making drums, but more for use as storage containers for domestic water and key dry food staple items such as sprats (*dagaa*), peanuts (*njugu*), and sugar (*sukari*).

*

At the front of the Pink House, a narrow dirt track rambled off to the left towards the administration office blocks and a gathering of *wazungu* staff bungalows that stood a few hundred yards away. Further on still lay the staff canteen where I went to take all my meals, plus the staff club and bar and last, but by no means least, *Badu Kidogo* Motors.

Derek took me to the staff canteen to have lunch following my arrival. The menu on offer would not have been unremarkable in a Lyons Corner House back in London. A highlight was the surprising availability of quantities of ice cream, a dish that in Kiswahili was referred to as *isicleem*. Derek told me of me a useful Kiswahili word *iko*, which depending on the inflexion given to it could be made to mean either "there is" or "is there?"

I was then able to place an order—"*Iko isicleem?*" The steward knew what to bring me, and would bring it provided other *wazungu* diners hadn't already beaten me to it. By rights the steward should have answered my question with either a yes or a no and left it to me to follow up by saying that I would like to have some *isicleem*; however, the *iko* factor always seemed to work its magic and that was good enough for me.

Given the innate courtesy of the peoples of Tanganyika, it was something of an anomaly that the Kiswahili word for "please" (*tafadhali*) was very rarely heard in conversation. Its absence was more than made up by an almost compulsive need for expressions of thanks to be issued as profusely as possible in accordance with a scale that built to an ultimate crescendo:

Thank you!	*Asante!*
Thank you very much!	*Asante sana!*
Thank you very very very much!	*Asante sa-a-a-a-a-na!*

And so on and so forth.

Gratitude knew no limits, as if by a majority verdict it was considered much better to receive than to give. It can be seen that the extent of appreciation was emphasised by endowing key vowels with as much elasticity as the circumstances called for. The same principle was also vested in specifying distances. *Kule* meant "just over there". *Ku-u-u-u-u-u-le* could be used to signify somewhere out in the far reaches of the country.

A sign alongside the track that led away from the front of the Pink House advised anyone who was able to read it, "*Endesha pole pole, watembeaji wako mbele*" (Drive slowly, there are pedestrians ahead). Whatever its intention, it offered a lesson in deception as I never saw anyone looking anything like a pedestrian anywhere along the said stretch of track. In addition, *pole pole* didn't appear to be a key characteristic of most of the driving habits I saw practised by exploration personnel both within and without the Mwadui precincts.

A year or so after my arrival I read a report that during the commission of the WDL national exploration campaign to date, no fewer than two hundred and forty-five Land Rovers had been totally written off before their time. The score was at least one Land Rover wrecked for each and every *mzungu* Geologist, Field Officer, Field Assistant and Prospector who passed in and out and on and off the payroll. Inexperience, carelessness, over-consumption of alcohol, *shauri ya Mungu* (will of God) and some occasionally nefarious activities were all involved in creating the litany of mechanical mayhem and delighting the hearts of Land Rover salesmen everywhere. Incredibly (with *shauri ya Mungu* providing full cover) none of the accidents had resulted in fatal consequences.

Tony Knowles and "Joker" McKenzie (whose Christian name was never made known to me) were a pair of geologists who worked for some time out of a camp near a place named Suna in the southern part of the Singida District. Suna was a well-known location where two roads heading north from Itigi and Manyoni respectively came together in an acute "V" and continued as one towards the town of Singida. Tony and Joker presided over the write-off of three Land Rovers in the space of a single afternoon, thereby creating an all-time record that endured in spite of the efforts that were put by others into breaking it.

The first of the three Land Rovers to fall was driven by Tony and Joker's *mtu* driver. He allegedly lost control of his Land Rover on the crest of a high embankment on the Itigi road to the south of Suna, which resulted in the vehicle rolling over and over down the embankment from top to bottom. When news of the accident reached their camp, brought in by a passing motorist, Tony and Joker took a Land Rover each and roared off down the road to investigate the scene of the reported accident.

Tony led the way. He brought his Land Rover to an abruptly

skidding halt in a cloud of dust at the mid-point of the embankment. Joker, who was hot on Tony's tail, roared through the dust and stopped his Land Rover by slamming it into the back of Tony's vehicle. The write-off tally rose from one to three in a single instant.

It was a sad moment for Tony as he took great pride in the Land Rover he habitually drove. He named his vehicle the "White Rose" in honour of his Yorkshire origins, and had that very name painted on the outside of the Land Rover's side door on the driver's side. On a certain dark night in Dodoma, someone (possibly a Lancastrian) painted out the "Rose" portion of the legend and replaced it with "Nacker". This affront to Yorkshire pride had fortunately been remedied when the Land Rover prang times three took place.

Tony and Joker named their camp at Suna the "Drop Inn". They strung a rope across the road at the famous "V" junction in between a couple of tall trees, and on the rope they hung a wooden sign with the camp name painted large on it. In their camp they maintained a substantial stock of bottled beer, which together with the exhortation on the sign, induced many passers-by to drop in at the camp to partake of refreshment.

I stayed overnight at the Drop Inn on a couple of occasions when I was working from a camp located up in the northern part of the Singida district, and discovered that a good skin full of IPA was an essential requirement if sleep was to be obtained. Joker had got hold of a tame bush baby from somewhere or other, and its nocturnal movements, which ranged far and wide around the campsite, were not only noisy but also very intrusive.

*

A principal reason for my spending three weeks in Mwadui following my arrival from Nairobi was that I needed to obtain a local driving licence prior to my being allocated a Land Rover and assigned to a bush camp. I possessed no other driving licence for the simple reason that I couldn't drive.

On each day during those three weeks other than at weekends, I was privileged to receive driving lessons in Mwadui from a Senior Officer of the WDL Security Department. The fact that he eventually arranged for me to be awarded a Tanganyika driving licence was probably due less to my driving skills (dubious at best) than to his heartfelt desire to do whatever it took to get rid of me.

With my driving instructor in the passenger seat I ground the gears of a Land Rover all around the Mwadui residential compound to start with, taking the words on the sign outside the Pink House very much at face value. According to the security officer, *pole pole* was the be-all and end-all of recommended driving practice, with or without the inducement of pedestrians to avoid.

Ultimately I went out of Mwadui with my instructor to drive north along the main road that crossed the great expanse of *mbuga* to reach the town of Mwanza at the south end of Lake Victoria, a distance of about ninety miles. The road was dirt-surfaced and well maintained.

Mwanza, when we got there, seemed to glimmer with lake-reflected light. Neat buildings lined the lakeside, small craft slid across the sparkling waters, and a yacht club, into which the likes of me would be unlikely to gain permission to ever set foot, gave a fair impression of the trappings of civilisation.

I drove the Land Rover all the way up to Mwanza. On the strength of this performance my instructor drove the vehicle all the way back to Mwadui. I assumed that enough had been enough as far as he was concerned.

He shouted at me only twice while I was driving, and as I had expected a little more vituperation than that to come my way it began to look as if things might not have been as bad as they could have been. The first shout came during an encounter with a number of pedestrians on a narrow bridge crossing a wide gully a few feet deep. The bridge, unfenced on either side, consisted of two parallel tracks of wooden boards separated by a shallow central well. The pedestrians assumed that they had the right of way. It was only fortunate that they weren't willing to contest their claim, since they demonstrated a readiness to jump off the bridge to save themselves from being run down instead.

The second shouting incident involved a close encounter with a cyclist, who was wobbling his bike around in the middle of the road with even more uncertainty than I was managing with the Land Rover. He was totally oblivious to me driving up behind him.

The previously mentioned Mr Dennis Kent, the storekeeper at Kanye in the Bechuanaland Protectorate whose wife was so perceptive about the ambient temperature at Khartoum airport, once told me that, "the most dangerous thing on the roads of Africa is a *kaffir* on a bicycle". (*Kaffir*, an ultimately disparaging word that, in the southern

Africa of the time was in universal use by white people to characterise black people, had no Kiswahili equivalent that I knew of.)

Words apart however, Dennis was right. The *mtu* on a bicycle ahead of me was a creature whose next move was sure to be utterly unpredictable. As far as he was concerned the entire road was his. I sounded the Land Rover's horn, and he promptly swerved his bike to one side and fell off onto the road. Such a reaction, I understood, was normally the way it went.

Coming into sharp contact on the road with a cyclist or a pedestrian or for that matter a domestic animal was, as my driving instructor told me, to be avoided at all costs. It seemed pretty obvious really, but he went on to say that in the event of a vehicle accident involving people or animals, standing instructions were that the driver should not stop his vehicle but should take steps to proceed immediately to the nearest police station to report the accident.

An accident always generated a crowd. Even in the most remote localities, if a passing vehicle knocked someone down an angry mob would gather at the scene as if it had sprung from the ground by magic. Stopping the vehicle at the place of an accident would give rise to the very real possibility that the driver, especially if he was an *mzungu*, might be lynched by the mob.

Additional hazards that I had to contend with on the road to Mwanza involved wandering domestic animals, both four legged and feathered; the outer edges of vending stalls and the piled up goods of roadside traders; PWD (Public Works Department) road maintenance gangs and their carelessly parked equipment; the great clouds of hanging dust that trailed behind every passing vehicle; and transverse corrugations on the road surface.

The latter gave the road what was sometimes known as a "washboard effect", although washboard hardly did justice to the dramatic nature of some sequences of corrugated ruts that I came across.

It was claimed that corrugations developed as a natural consequence of the skipping action of vehicular tyres on the texturally variegated surface of dirt roads. Once they were formed the corrugations deepened and migrated along roads (*pole pole* of course), pushed like crawling waves on the face of the Indian Ocean. Corrugated stretches of road were prolific and could be met up with on any journey with little or no advance warning. Encountering a set of corrugations in a vehicle travelling at a speed that was *upesi sana* (the opposite of *pole pole*) was akin to slamming head on into a course of cemented bricks.

I once ran unexpectedly into a group of four severe corrugations on the road adjacent to the railway track linking Itigi and Tabora. At the time I was driving a defective diesel-powered Land Rover back to Mwadui to exchange it for a petrol-driven replacement. The consequence of my sudden impact with the corrugations was that the front wheels of the Land Rover became misaligned. Thereafter the Land Rover was still possible to drive (just) on dirt roads, but it proved to be a major trial on the paved road through Tabora, which set the front tyres squealing like stuck warthogs.

There was reputed to be an optimum driving speed for tackling corrugations that would permit a vehicle to skim over the crests rather than whacking up and down from trough to trough. That being so, I was forever denied the pleasure of finding out what that speed was, as no matter how much I tried I never managed to catch it. If I wasn't the worst driver of a WDL Land Rover, I must at least have vied for the honour.

The wheel alignment damage caused by the set of four deep corrugations on the Itigi to Tabora road shook me up considerably, to the extent that I wasn't sure if I was able to continue with the journey there and then.

By a stroke of fortune there was a PWD road camp not very far on from where my encounter with the corrugations took place. It was ironic that the PWD gang (about fifteen *watu* altogether) was working on grading the road and would probably have eliminated those deadly corrugations on the following day. They graded the road using a process involving felling a bushy tree, attaching it by the trunk to a tractor with the help of a lengthy chain, and then dragging the tree up and down the road all day. It was a surprisingly effective means of erasing corrugations, giving results that were a definite improvement on mechanical grading.

I pulled my Land Rover into the PWD camp, and since the hour was late thought it best that I should spend the night there and continue onwards in a better state of mind on the following day. The PWD *watu* were most welcoming, gave me a place to park the Land Rover on one edge of their camp and left me to my own devices. The single item of consumable food that I had brought along with me was a small tin of peaches. I opened it, ate and drank the contents, and tried to make myself as comfortable as I could for the night ahead on the Land Rover's front seat.

There came a tapping on the side of the Land Rover, and a voice advising me, "*Chakula tayare, bwana*". (Food is ready, sir!) The PWD *watu* were showing me the best of bush hospitality, and although I was not exactly enthusiastic about dining with them I could do no less than accept their kind invitation. I accompanied mine host across a patch of open ground to where a ring of *watu* were waiting for me, some squatting on their haunches and others sitting on logs and rocks strategically placed around a healthy looking fire.

*

Bwana was the universal form of address used by an *mtu* towards an *mzungu*. Vice versa didn't apply. *Bwana* meant "mister" or "sir" depending on the context, and implied a level of respect that came without any guarantee that the respect was merited. In the exploration camps the practice was to attach the Christian name of the *mzungu* to the title—as for example in *Bwana* John. To associate *bwana* with a surname was felt in the camp context to be a formality taken too far.

Sometimes *Bwana Mkubwa* (Big *Bwana*) might be invoked. This address implied a desire to flatter, bolstered by it being inevitable that a request for a favour was coming up afterwards. The converse of *Bwana Mkubwa* was *Bwana Mdogo* (Little *Bwana*), a classic example of the skill with which *watu* were able to damn with faint praise.

The scale of obsequiousness was cranked up further when an *mtu* chose to address a comparatively young *mzungu* (like me) as *mzee*. This was a title of great respect that was typically applied to elderly tribesmen with the dignified presence that came from generations of traditionally acquired wisdom. *Mzee* didn't ring at all true when I heard it directed at me. The geologist I was to work for in the first exploration camp I joined particularly disliked being addressed as *mzee*. A cheery "*Jambo mzee!*" delivered to him in the early morning fell on his ears as "Hello, old man!" which he took exception to as being a Wodehousian informality that sat ill on his shoulders.

Comparatively speaking, *wazungu* were often reckoned by the *watu* to be men of wisdom irrespective of the tenderness of their age. The mistake made by the *watu* was to confuse the expression of general knowledge with wisdom. Many *wazungu* knew a lot about the world at large, but as to an average *mzungu* being particularly wise, a chance would be a fine thing.

On one occasion I was addressed as *Mheshimiwa* (Exalted One) by an *mtu* who exhibited all the unctuousness of Uriah Heep blended with serf-like grovelling. As *Mheshimiwa* was a title exclusively reserved for application to Mr Julius Nyerere (the father-to-be of Tanganyika's *uhuru* movement and the post-*uhuru* architect of the destruction of the nation's social fabric and economy), the title as handed to me meant that something major was about to be requested. The one and only *Mheshimiwa* Julius was at that time on the early slopes of his ascent to unjustified international fame. *Nyerere* translated as "little ants" so perhaps Julius needed a grandiose title to compensate for his other name's shortfall.

*

The fire at the PWD camp flared and glowed at the juxtaposed inner ends of four dry logs laid out in the form of a cross. Where the incendiary ends of the logs came together, a moderately sized rounded boulder placed at each of the four right-angled junctions made a tight fireplace styled enclosure to contain the glowing coals. With the aid of an occasional handful of dry twigs, the fire was kept going by means of pushing the logs in towards the centre as their ends were consumed.

At the side of one of the boulders stood a cast-iron three-legged cauldron, black on the outside, and dark crusty brown all around its rim. The cauldron was almost filled up with steaming off-white maize meal (*posho*) porridge of the stiff unsweetened variety known as *ugali*. (A more fluid counterpart, sweetened with sugar if any sugar was going, was called *uji*).

I was well aware of *ugali* in its role as a staple diet of the gang of *watu* I worked with back at my camp, but I had yet to sample its delights.

Propped up against another boulder were two long green sticks on each of which, open to the attention of the fire, was assembled a ladder-like arrangement of small fish. The fish (*samaki*) had an ugly appearance that was enhanced by the fact that they had been cooked without the benefit of either decapitation or gutting.

They were catfish. The most interesting habit of catfish, as the dry season got ever closer and the river and pond water that they lived in dwindled away by the day, was that they buried themselves in bottom mud as deeply as possible just before the last of the water disappeared.

Encased in the ever-hardening mud they survived (or "estivated") in a state of suspended animation until the next wet season came along to revive and release them back to their natural environment.

The *watu* in one camp with me once dug up a veritable shoal of catfish from the bed of a dry river, and brought them back to camp to be eaten. A few of the catfish were huge creatures, at least three feet long. It took no more than a slight taste of a cooked fragment of one of them to convince me that whatever the taste of catfish meant to the *watu*, it meant a lot less to me.

Since at the PWD camp I was gazing for the first time on a culinary array of catfish I entertained no firm opinion one way or the other as to the acceptability of how one of them would taste. As a guest invited to the feast it was indicated to me that mine was the honour of being the first to select a catfish of my choice and to lift from the cauldron a handful of *ugali* to accompany it. I hesitated a little to begin with and then realised that no one could commence eating until I acted. I pulled the smallest of the catfish away from one of the sticks, noting that it parted company with an unpleasant sucking sound, and then dug my hand into the *ugali* to remove a portion of it from the cauldron as best I could without burning my fingers.

The easy part of the formalities was then over. The PWD *watu* dug in to their meal with vigour. I was faced with the daunting prospect of consuming my share of catfish and *ugali*. The smell of the catfish was remarkably unsubtle, and the taste provided substance to a quality of exceptional fishiness. What the *ugali* lacked in flavour it made up for in the abrasive influence of the sand and grit that were such a feature of its texture.

I pushed a fragment of catfish into a small ball of *ugali*, placed the combination in my mouth, and chewed on it with vigour until sufficient time had elapsed for me to express my *asante s-a-a-a-nas*, bid *kwa heri* to the PWD *watu*, and, with honour satisfied, steal away into the night to find a bush under which I could both spit out the well-masticated mouthful and dump the remains of the feast that I still held in my hand.

3
Kitabu elimu ya mawe porini
The geologist's field manual

The Tanganyika driving licence that I obtained at Mwadui entitled me to drive a Land Rover—and for that matter to get behind the steering wheel of any other motor vehicle of comparable size not only anywhere in the country but as far as I knew all over East Africa as well. The award of a driving licence was a miracle equivalent to the one in which five thousand people were allegedly fed on five barley loaves and two small fishes. It wasn't difficult for me to imagine that, had those two small fishes been catfish, most of the five thousand would have preferred the five barley loaves.

The critical aspect of the miracle of a driving licence was vested in my actually getting one; to ensure the miracle's completion the inevitability of an accident waiting to happen that my having a driving licence implied would have to be avoided.

In between driving lessons I spent my working days in the Exploration Department's offices in the WDL administration block under the mentorship of the Chief Draughtsman. That worthy, who went by the name of Jack, gave me a basic grounding in precisely what my field duties were likely to entail.

Jack, who was probably in his early forties, was as helpful to me as he was genial in his manner. He took great pains to show me that there was a right way to do things and that that way was "by the book".

There was a fussy fastidiousness about Jack that didn't tolerate much in the way of flexible interpretation of the written rules and that regarded initiative takers with dismay.

Jack gave me tuition in basic requirements for monthly reporting and keeping of camp accounts; in the maintenance of sampling and other exploration records; and in the mystic arts of bush camp administration. He managed his job—with the assistance of a secretary named Barbara, a lovely lady ever ready to assist newcomers and old hands alike—entirely to his own satisfaction.

The "Book" to which Jack owed his allegiance and to the dictates of which he adhered in accordance with an expression used by certain South African Field Officers, "like shit to a woollen blanket", was the *Geologist's Field Manual—Prospecting for Diamonds in Tanganyika* (the *GFM*), a fifty page long mimeographed document originally published by WDL and amended by regular updates.

A copy of the *GFM* was issued to all *wazungu* members of the WDL exploration staff. Each of us signed on the dotted line for our personal copy of the document, and we were expected to read, mark, learn and inwardly digest it and to conduct ourselves at all times in accordance with the letter of its every edict. *GFM* updates were issued from time to time in the form of "Instructions to Field Staff", which were thereafter incorporated into the *GFM* as essential regulations in their own right.

The *GFM* was a feast of rules and snippets of advice compiled over a period of years. It contained contributions both reactive and proactive from the three most recent holders of the title of WDL Chief Geologist. In chronological order (oldest first) the respective names of this trio were Mousseau Tremblay, a French Canadian nicknamed "Moose" who left WDL to take up work with the Geological Survey of Quebec; Louis Murray, a South African who was promoted to hold the eminent position of Consulting Geologist with responsibility for diamonds at the Anglo American Corporation head office down in Johannesburg; and Gus Edwards, the incumbent at the time of my arrival and an Australian ascetic who enjoyed a reputation of having a limited capacity for fun after working hours.

The fundamental importance of the *GFM* in directing the expected conduct and practices of those of us who worked on exploration out in the bush was at once obvious from even a limited perusal of its pages.

For this reason alone an examination of its salient features at this point in my story will be well worthwhile, and in the telling will take up the balance of this chapter and a little of the next one.

Great credit was due from its readers to all those involved in the compilation of the *GFM*, some of whose names were given in the document. Unfortunately, most of the contributors remained anonymous, yet the results of their efforts and the incisive nature of their insights were ever alive in the *GFM*'s pages.

*

The *GFM* was prepared primarily for the benefit and instruction of the Senior Geologists in charge of exploration camps, although that intention by no means exempted the document from receiving the attention of those whom the Senior Geologists thought they led. It was the responsibility of the Senior Geologists to ensure that their assistants (Junior Geologists, Field Officers and Field Assistants) followed the regulations contained within the *GFM* to the letter.

Additional reasons were offered for the compilation of the *GFM*: it would provide its readers with an appreciation of the history of exploration for diamonds in Tanganyika; it would set out the fruits of the experiences of many who worked on the exploration programme over the preceding years; it would ensure that the understanding of Senior Geologists with respect to the kind of information that they were expected to report back to the Chief Geologist in Mwadui was completely in accord with requirements; and it would stress to all involved in exploration that the ultimate objective of the programme was to obtain an economically viable outcome.

*

With respect to any area of the country designated for exploration it was obligatory for the *wazungu* assigned to it to commence their work by collecting and compiling whatever information on the area was available. Important features of the information gathering process were to establish both the nature of the infrastructure and the options for maintaining communications with the exterior. It took an act of faith to believe that a reasonable amount of information to pull together would be found to actually exist.

It was also considered essential to establish in advance as much knowledge as possible for the area about the customs of the local indigenous population; the opportunities for obtaining food and equipment supplies for the camp; the location of a good water supply; and any factors of significance that were likely to either help or hinder the work to be carried out.

Prior to moving into a new area, the Senior Geologist was required to make contact with the District Commissioner under whose aegis the area fell in order to brief that gentleman on the plan in hand for the proposed exploration programme. The DC would be able to provide the Senior Geologist with a letter of introduction to the principal chief in the area to be explored (on the assumption that the chief would be able to read the letter or find someone to read the letter to him). In addition the DC would be expected to offer the Senior Geologist some general advice on the area (although he might well disappoint on that score); highlight known pitfalls to be avoided; and perhaps have one of his people suggest locations for some suitable camping sites.

The next step for the Senior Geologist was to visit the said chief and his disciples on their home ground in order to commence forming friendly relations. Under the chief's direction the wheels of success rolled at their smoothest when they were greased with ample gifts. The chief and his self-appointed representatives always formed the first line of consultation on matters as vital as campsite locations; road and (if necessary) airstrip construction needs; general considerations involving the temporary occupation of land; the engagement of local labour; and the settlement of any disputes between WDL personnel and the chief's subjects, otherwise known as the local population. According to the *GFM* it was essential that disputes should always be referred to the chief in the first instance.

There was nothing that a chief couldn't sort out if the price in his hand was right. The *GFM* did not provide that snippet of advice to its readers of course.

Adherence by *wazungu* based in the bush to the list of regulations set out in the *GFM* was mandatory in the view of WDL management. Following the rules was, it was declared, sure to work to the ultimate benefit of working conditions in any given exploration area. Provided that all involved, *wazungu* and *watu* alike, kept themselves in the chief's good graces and gave him the respect he was entitled to (as distinguished from the respect he deserved), the *GFM* pointed out that the chief would prove to be an instrumental figure in aiding the effective pursuit of the exploration programme.

Working relationships with a gang of *watu* in camp and in the bush were something with which an *mzungu* coming fresh into Tanganyika would be most likely to encounter difficulty. Recent university graduates could find themselves totally unprepared to cope with what faced them in this regard. *Watu* and *wazungu* stood figuratively facing one another on either side of a flimsily constructed bridge spanning a great rift-like array of cultural, political, racial and social differences. It was only by exercising the most careful steps that the parties could expect to advance along the bridge and come together in a shared compromise somewhere around its mid-point.

Any *mzungu* who developed a decent appreciation of the personal qualities of the *watu* with whom he worked—in bush that was often just as wild as it was remote—made a major advance forward. Out in the bush all of us both needed and depended on one another. When we were together we had much more in common than we might have believed possible, and as a consequence our whole was greater than the sum of its black and white parts.

The GFM bade us as its readers to follow a whole host of administrative norms relating to matters concerning the organisation and welfare of the *watu*.

Reference was made to a so-called muster roll book that was designed to provide a reference at all times to the current status of the labour employed. A muster roll book was to be kept in every camp and reviewed daily, since there was little in the way of a predictable pattern about employee (*watu*) turnover. At the end of each month a fresh muster roll was prepared in the book of the same name, taking into consideration all of the changes and corrections that had occurred during the previous month.

The muster roll, which could be kept up in either English or Kiswahili (or both for the more enthusiastic administrators among us), called for various personal particulars to be recorded for each and every *mtu* employed.

These included both an *mtu's* own name and (more definitively) his father's name; the all-important identity of his tribe (which to a large extent governed who and what he was and how he would be expected to behave under any given circumstances); his tax registration number (in the unlikely event that he had one); the type of work he was engaged to do and the rate of pay he would receive; the nature and duration of his contract of work; and whether he had opted to receive daily food rations or payment in lieu of the same.

Provision was made in the muster roll to record, on a monthly sheet ruled into daily columns, the actual days worked per employee so that the gross pay due could be reckoned up at any time in short order. The net pay due to an employee was calculated with allowance for advances received and deductions made against pay. In the event that an *mtu's* work was to be terminated, severance and repatriation allowances were payable in accordance with how good the employer's (*wazungu*) opinion was on the employee's work and conduct. Most terminations were of an honourable nature, but an occasional one wasn't.

The standard employee contract (or ticket) of work was known as a *kipandi* (the plural of which was *vipandi*). A *kipandi* was a legally binding contract covering a specific number of days of work—in the case of the GFM regulations the time was thirty days, which were not necessarily consecutively run.

The terms and conditions of a thirty-day *kipandi* were set out on the *kipandi* itself, which was essentially a pre-printed standard form made of stiff card on which the prescribed personal particulars were set out. The employer was then legally obliged to provide the thirty days of paid work unless prevented from doing so by events such as a trade dispute; vagaries of climate; technical shortfalls; and beyond that anything at all related to God's will (*shauri ya Mungu*).

During its currency a *kipandi* was normally retained in the possession of its holder. It was released back to the employer usually for the purposes of recording the successful completion of a day's work. Counting from the record of the first day worked, a thirty-day *kipandi* would normally need to be completed within a thirty-six day time frame for employees who resided in the camp. For other employees who lived outside the camp (typically employees hired locally) completion of a thirty-day *kipandi* needed to be made within forty-two consecutive days.

By permission of the employer the duration of a *kipandi* could be spread on either side of a period of non-paid leave of up to thirty days. Receipt of payment for work done, whether or not the payment was made for a full or partial *kipandi*, had to be acknowledged by the employee with a signature (if he could write) or otherwise by an inked impression of his right thumbprint.

*

All payments were made in cash. The money was either obtained directly from WMD in Mwadui (when it was convenient to do so) or drawn on WMD's account from the branch of the Standard Bank of South Africa Limited in the town located closest to the working area, in which camp supplies and services were also regularly procured.

Cash payments for work done meant that a large amount of cash had to be obtained, transported and held in camp pending its release to employees. Such a pile of cash made an inviting target for the attention of thieves. In camp the cash was secured in a large, well-nigh indestructible, heavy-duty cashbox, a sort of portable safe for which the single key was kept in the possession of the Senior Geologist of the camp. Hiding the key away could provide additional security as long as the hiding place did not get forgotten.

On its top, the cashbox was equipped with a stout "U"-shaped chrome-plated steel handle through which could be threaded a strong chain accessorised with an impressively large padlock.

When it was activated to fulfil its wage-paying function the cashbox was, by a WDL security mandate, to be locked up, chained and solidly padlocked to an immovable object, favoured examples of which were the central pole inside the Senior Geologist's tent, the gear lever of a Land Rover in transit, or the metal frame of a bed (as for example in a hotel). In compliance with the existing conditions of WDL's insurance for its contents, the cashbox was required to be in locked-down and chained-up status whenever it was left unattended.

*

Under the terms of a *kipandi* an employee could be dismissed without notice on completion of his statutory thirty days of work. He could also be fired prior to completing the thirty-days, although in that case his firing was subject to regulations prescribed in law. Through a process known as "Lawful Dismissal" the employee could be dismissed for any reason at all at any time during the currency of a *kipandi* on condition that his contracted period was paid out in full. On his own account he could break his *kipandi* at any time provided the grounds cited by him for doing so were within the scope of the law.

It sounded bewilderingly complicated to me.

A process of "Lawful Summary Dismissal", under which the employee would be paid only his wages due at the time of dismissal, dealt with the following cases: circumstances of misconduct (both on and off the job); wilful disobedience of lawful orders given by the employer; a lack of skills essential to the work that the employee originally claimed or implied he possessed; habitual or substantial neglect of regular duties; and absenteeism from work without the benefit of either the employer's permission or a good excuse.

Relying on the law to govern conditions of employment could well have placed a nice gloss on the work of camp administrators, but given the remote nature of many of the locations in which the work took place, leaning on legal considerations was something that served only to gladden the hearts of those euphemistically named bush lawyers. If difficult decisions had to be taken it was much more important that they were seen by everyone in camp to be fair and just rather than merely stuck on observing the letter of the law.

It was an absolute right of an employee, once he had completed three full *vipandi*, to be repatriated at his employer's expense back to the place at which he had been hired. Under certain circumstances the right to repatriation of any members of his family residing with him at the workplace by permission of the employer was also applicable.

Repatriation was also his right in cases of Lawful Summary Dismissal where the employer was unable to provide him with further work; where the employee was not able to complete a *kipandi* owing to sickness or accidental incapacity; where mutually agreed terms and conditions were set up; and where an order of court arising from an application from either the employer or the employee was involved.

The repatriation expenses included not only fares and subsistence rations for the journey home but also an issue of rations sufficient to cover any period of delay between the date of termination of a *kipandi* and the date of departure from camp. Under circumstances in which repatriation was held up by choice of the employee or for reasons of *shauri ya Mungu*, the employer was not liable to provide the employee with rations (although for obvious reasons the employee would most likely be given them).

Occasionally the employer's obligation to repatriate an employee could be set aside (although in practice it was inconceivable that it ever would be). If it so happened that the employee failed to exercise his right to repatriation within six months of the termination of his work, his rights would be deemed to have lapsed.

Exemptions to the obligatory payment of repatriation expenses could only be made under an order from an officially designated administration or labour officer (who was no doubt comfortably set up at district HQ). Such an order would be invoked by a written or verbal declaration by the employee that he did not wish to exercise his right to repatriation; by the employee electing to settle at or near the place of his former employment; by the termination of a contract of work by a court order consequent on misconduct of the employee; and when, in the case of employee misconduct, it could be shown by the employer that the employee was in possession of the necessary funds to repatriate himself (a tall order at best).

*

If an employee died in the course of his work his legal heirs were, assuming they could be located, entitled to receive all wages and benefits due to him at the date of his death, together with any of his personal property and effects that they could properly lay claim to. (Claimants chancing their arms and spouting tribal allegiances could spring up at the drop of a hat when the possibility of obtaining something for nothing was afoot.) It was the employer's duty to hand the said wages, benefits and personal property of the deceased over to the local government authorities for distribution by them to the eager heirs.

The *GFM* described both the characteristics and the application of a standard-issue form on which to report the death of an employee. The form, duplicate copies of which were to be submitted to the Labour Officer for the district in which the death occurred as well as to WDL at Mwadui, called for information on the employee's identity; his next of kin; the circumstances of the death; particulars of any injuries received; and the names and signed (or thumbprinted) statements of witnesses.

This reporting requirement (solely included for the attention of purists) was established under Section 3 (5) of the Accidents and Occupational Diseases (Notification) Ordinance, 1953, Cap. 330).

According to a regulation presented in the *GFM*, six death report forms were to be kept available in every camp against the occurrence of circumstances calling for their use. Six such forms made a rather ominous inclusion in a camp's inventory of administrative stationery.

*

Exploration camps were intended to be no more than temporary set-ups as a rule. Given the considerable geographical extent of the majority of areas assigned for exploration, related camps were forced to have a nomadic nature, subject to regular moves to make the most efficient logistical use of the area's infrastructure.

An employee who chose not to take part in a relocation further than four miles away (in practice few if any camp moves were made over a lesser distance) was entitled to receive payment up to the end of his current *kipandi*—unless notice of the pending camp move had been given to him when the *kipandi* commenced and he had not then demurred. The regulation applied principally to locally engaged labour.

*

As the labourer, wherever he was engaged, was always deemed to be worthy of his hire, the ability of the employer to make direct deductions of money from an employee's pay was restricted by law.

Deductions from pay, all of which needed to be recorded in writing, could be made in respect of unpaid taxes; contributions to an (unlikely) pension scheme; and the (much more likely) cost of loss or damage to Company property and equipment caused by the negligence of the employee. In the latter instance the employee's pay was normally garnished in accordance with the lesser of either the cost of the lost item or a day's pay.

In practice the rules were one thing, but getting money out of most of the *watu* was quite another. It would be substantially easier *kutoka damu kwa jiwe* (to take blood out of a stone).

Advances on wages of up to an amount of one half of a *kipandi's* rate of pay were permitted under the rules, and were in principle recoverable by deductions in instalments of no more than one third of the total pay due at the at the end of each *kipandi*. In practice the policy for making advances on pay was subjectively informal, related in individual cases to the total length of the employee's service and the trust placed in him by his employer.

*

The statutory rates of pay for the various classes of employees were sacrosanct institutions. Paying favoured individuals at rates in excess of those set up on the established scale invariably led to dissatisfaction among their less fortunate fellow employees and went on to cause problems at other camps where the statutory rates were more strictly applied. Work at the bush camps commonly took place on six days per week (Monday through Saturday). Sunday was typically a free day. No pay was due on free days, although the issue of rations on free days was guaranteed.

The pay scale for what was defined in the pages of the *GFM* as "outside prospecting" covered eleven categories of employee. These ranged from Category 1 (kitchen boy or *toto*) through to Category 11 (First-Grade Senior Headman). Promotions to levels above Category 8 required endorsement by either the Chief Geologist or the WDL Assistant General Manager.

The Category 1 pay rate commenced at twenty shillings per *kipandi* and rose by two shillings after the completion of six *vipandis* up to a maximum of twenty-four shillings per *kipandi*. In sharp contrast, the Category 11 pay rate began at two hundred and eighty shillings per *kipandi* and rose by ten shillings after completion of six *vipandis* up to a maximum of three hundred and fifty shillings per *kipandi*.

In between these two extremes lay all the other grades and conditions of camp employees, namely sample washers (including *watoto* and women); various "menials"; labourers; clerical assistants; storekeepers; artisans; compass runners; fully fledged clerks; lower-grade headmen; drivers; sampling supervisors; jig operators; and last but not least a few variations on a theme of senior headmen.

The bulk of the *watu* working at any given camp were classed as labourers—their pay structure was set to start at forty shillings per *kipandi* and to rise by five shillings on completion of six *vipandis* up to a maximum of fifty shillings per *kipandi*. In addition they could benefit from a defined scale of overtime rates. It was reasonable to manage overtime under relatively settled working conditions, but it was all but pointless to bother with overtime out in the remote bush.

An extra incentive (which under different circumstances could be referred to as a perk of the job) made provision for a bonus of fifteen cents (one shilling contained one hundred cents) for each day that the employee was involved in strenuous work such as pitting, trenching or labouring on underground tasks.

A retrospective bonus was payable to each of the members of a traverse gang involved in running a sampling line that could ultimately be shown to have had a direct bearing on the discovery of a kimberlite pipe. The not especially handsome bonuses (or is it *boni*?) awarded were fifteen shillings to the compass runner and three shillings to everyone else.

There was also a seasonal Christmas bonus comprising an extra day's pay that furthermore presented its recipients with the opportunity to select either festive fare (a couple of pounds of meat; two or three pounds of rice and a packet of cigarettes) or the equivalent of the same in cash.

Provision was made as well for paid annual leave and return travel expenses for employees completing not less than two hundred and eighty-eight days of work within a period of twelve months. Employees in Categories 1–8 received twelve days of paid annual leave with third-class return fares, whereas those in Categories 9–11 employees were granted fourteen days of paid annual leave with travel allowances applied to second-class facilities. Such travel expenses could, with the Senior Geologist's discretion ruling the day, be taken to include the employee's wife and up to four of his children.

*

One of the most important entitlements of *watu* employed at bush camps was a daily ration of food staples. Rations were not given out to accompanying dependants and camp followers, although as in all things tribal there were many ways and means of working around that particular rule.

The food rations were usually purchased in bulk from establishments of Indian or Arab traders located in the larger towns. *Wazungu* formed close commercial relationships with many of these traders. All purchases were made on the basis of written orders made out in a triplicate book. The original copy of the purchase order was given to the trader supplying the goods. He attached it to his invoice for goods supplied and submitted the same to WDL at Mwadui for payment. A second copy of the purchase order accompanied the Senior Geologist's monthly report, equally destined for the attention of WDL.

The quantities of rations provided to each employee were as follows:

Item	Kiswahili	Allocation
Ground maize meal	*Posho*	Twenty-four ounces daily, including Sunday
Meat	*Nyama*	Maximum of four pounds per week and absolute minimum of two pounds per week

Dried sprats	*Dagaa*	Used as a meat substitute in cases of meat supply difficulty
Sugar	*Sukari*	Half a pound per week
Salt	*Chumvi*	Four ounces per week
Ground nuts	*Njugu*	Half a pound per week (when available)
Oil (groundnut, cotton-seed, or red-palm)	*Mafuta ya kupika*	Three ounces per week
Vegetables*	*Mboga*	Two pounds per week (approximately)
Fruit*	*Matunda*	Two pounds per week (approximately)
Blanket	*Blanketi*	One issue after three months of employment and thereafter one issue every six months

*Fruit and vegetables were difficult to procure regularly. In the event of shortages of either, the lack was made up to the *watu* by increases in the allocations of some of the ration items that were distributed weekly.

*

The generally turgid nature of the contents of the *GFM*, a quality ably exemplified in many of the preceding pages of this chapter, was to some extent alleviated by an inclusion within the *GFM* of an article entitled "Hints to field men on how to make life more comfortable in the bush". The article was written by a Mr J. W. Higgs, who is herewith acknowledged not only for the contribution to the *GFM* but also for the most useful insights and advice to *GFM* readers that he set out in it.

In Mr Higgs' opinion, legal requirements relating to WDL providing accommodation in the bush (for the *wazungu* as well as the *watu*) were all but impossible to follow to the letter. It was necessary for WDL to ensure that bush living conditions were as comfortable as they could be by setting up the best possible arrangements for quality of life under canvas.

Mr Higgs declared that his article was not written for the benefit of hardened "old timers", but was rather aimed at young and essentially "green" men going into the bush for the first time. He set his article out in terms of four key essentials, namely: equipping for the field; correct maintenance of Land Rovers; setting up a camp; and guidance for "good eating".

It was WDL's responsibility to provide its field men with the proper equipment that they would need for exploration work, together with clear instructions for its use. "Remember", wrote Mr Higgs in addressing the readers of his article, "that you are probably being sent out to some distant area where roads will be bad, therefore take care to ensure that all your equipment is well packed. For example, flat objects should not be packed on top of angular ones, and everything should be strapped down thoroughly". I considered myself duly informed.

A useful tip when moving around with equipment, according to Mr Higgs, was to sew up as much of it as possible of it in what he called gunnysacks. Not only would this practice result in reducing wear and tear, not least on the edges of awkwardly shaped items such as camp furniture, it would also permit numerous small packages to be bound together into one large gunnysack-enveloped package that would be simple to handle. Gunnysacks, although perhaps not readily obtainable at Mwadui, were more easily got hold of from traders in the towns. Basic rations for the *watu* (their *posho* for example) were supplied in gunnysacks, which when empty could be retained in the camp store hut for use in support of camp moves. Mr Higgs recommended using a sail maker's needle and stout twine for sewing up the gunnysacks.

He was kind enough to point out that it would be extremely unlikely that readers of his article would play sporting games in the bush (not much!), therefore sports clothing and equipment could be safely left out of any inventory of personal effects. He reminded his readers that Tanganyika was located in the tropics, which eliminated any genuine need for packing warm clothing—unless of course the reader was being assigned to work somewhere down in the Southern Highlands.

The fundamental clothing needs for the well turned out *mzungu* in camp were set by Mr Higgs at two pairs of long khaki trousers and/or khaki shorts; a few shirts and/or bush jackets; one jersey; a raincoat; thick stockings, and at least two pairs of good boots. The latter could be obtained in Shinyanga at a price of sixty shillings per pair, according to Mr Higgs (although he didn't provide the name of the relevant trading outlet).

He did add, however, that it would be worth anyone's bother to get hold of some strips of durable cloth or pliable canvas to wrap around the legs during the wet season as a means of preventing socks and boots getting drenched on traverses through long grass. Mr Higgs advised in that regard that he had had a pair of leather puttees made at a cost of forty shillings—they helped him a bit, although evidently not too much. On the other hand, his puttees had proved invaluable in keeping grass seeds out of his socks in the dry season, which made any eventual success just a matter of swings and roundabouts.

For the amusement, and perhaps more importantly the peace of mind of his readers in bush situations, Mr Higgs recommended the personal acquisition of either a rifle or a shotgun. Good second-hand firearms, he wrote, could be obtained fairly cheaply from recognised suppliers to would-be hunters in both Tanganyika and Kenya. He favoured a .30-06 calibre rifle on the grounds that it was big enough to kill anything except an elephant and small enough not to "make a mess" of a small buck. (Both assertions could have benefited from informed debate.) The cost of such a rifle was about six hundred shillings. Ammunition for the same was widely available from general traders in most town centres.

If the reader could also afford to buy a 0.22 calibre rifle, Mr Higgs reckoned that lots more inexpensive amusement was possible. A twelve-bore shotgun was said to be a further asset to have, to be used for the dual purposes of shooting birds and self-defence (against what kind of threats the reader might well have wondered). The choice of the type of gun depended entirely, concluded Mr Higgs, on what the owner wished to do with it.

*

In spite of, or perhaps because of, their write-off rate it was Land Rovers that provided the WDL diamond exploration programme with both its mobility and flexibility. Land Rovers were the workhorses that guaranteed optimum momentum for bush-based activities. Each *mzungu* to whom a Land Rover was issued for use in connection with his work was responsible for keeping the said vehicle in good shape and efficient running order. Appropriate garages to which the vehicle could be taken from the bush for servicing and repairs were likely to be few and far away from camp. Essential maintenance requirements, including checks on fuel, battery fluid, brake fluid, engine and gear oil and grease levels, were, under the *GFM* regulations, considered to be an intrinsic part of camp routine. Spare parts for Land Rovers could be ordered from specialised traders located in the larger towns or otherwise directly from WDL at Mwadui.

Mr Higgs referred to a "recently" commissioned WDL training course that sought to instruct newcomers like me in simple Land Rover maintenance practice prior to sending us to the bush. It was to our advantage, wrote Mr Higgs, to learn all we could in the few days of time that were allocated to the course.

The course sounded to be very much to the advantage of those who undertook it, upon the list of whom my name did not appear.

In other sections of the *GFM* substantially more detailed advice on the use of and care for Land Rovers out in the bush was presented. A daily maintenance checklist for the vehicles was set out. It involved checks on tyre pressures (including the spare tyre); radiator water level; removal of grass seeds and leaves stuck in the radiator; battery fluid and oil levels; grease requirement; fan belt tension; tightness of nuts and bolts (not least on the wheels); status of the fuel filter; and the continuing good order of the jack and vehicle tools.

A monthly check list took in the following: engine oil change; cleanliness of battery terminals; condition of the air filter; efficiency of the spark plugs; security of throttle linkages; brake and clutch fluid levels; front and rear lighting; examination of the differential; front wheel alignment (or realignment) and greasing; and condition of the engine mountings.

In addition to this veritable cornucopia of information the *GFM* provided a "trouble shooting guide" listing commonly occurring problems of the Land Rover engine, transmission and electrical system, together with the steps to be taken to deal with them.

On reading through the checklists I had cause to wish, not for the first time, that I possessed even as much as a smidgeon of mechanical skills. The fair hand of *Badu Kidogo* Motors seemed to float over the information in the *GFM* relating to Land Rovers as if it was bestowing a benediction.

A *GFM*-appended instruction to field staff signed by Mousseau Tremblay insisted that Land Rover servicing must at all times be carried out in accordance with specifications—whether the vehicles were located out in the bush or not. This instruction went on to demand that Land Rovers be given all due care and attention consistent with good driving practice. Moreover, no vehicle was to be driven fast at any time. The penalty for anyone shown to be guilty of negligence in the handling of a Land Rover would be instant dismissal from his job, and this, the instruction went on, would be applied without hesitation.

Vehicle accidents were subject to a standard reporting format. The vehicle accident form was undoubtedly used on many more occasions than were either intended or anticipated when it was drawn up. Required criteria to be reported covered the "who" (the driver's personal details, specifications concerning his driving licence and information on his physical condition at the time of the accident); the "when" (date and time of the accident and the location of the police station where the accident was first reported); the "where" (the place of the accident with a sketch of the immediate scene); and the "what" (involvement of any other vehicles, animals or pedestrians, the weight and physical nature of the load carried by the vehicle, the driving speed immediately prior to the accident taking place, the damage incurred, the estimated cost of repairs, and the names of any witnesses).

The service document package for each Land Rover included a booklet of vehicle log cards on which the daily mileage travelled was entered in accordance with the mileage meter on the driver's control panel. Completed log cards were submitted as an attachment to regular monthly reports.

If the intention behind this booklet was to make sure that the distances travelled were consistent only with work-related mileage, it reckoned not with the ingenuity of some *wazungu* to juggle with both figures and mileage meters when needs must.

*

The effort that ought to be put into setting up a camp should, in Mr Higgs' view, be commensurate with the expected length of time that the campsite would be occupied. Mr Higgs wrote, "if you are not staying too long it is not worth going to any great trouble making yourself comfortable." Few *wazungu* in my experience would have agreed with that assertion.

According to Mr Higgs, the choice of a campsite had to be governed in the first instance by the availability of water for both domestic and exploration (sample washing) purposes. Flowing streams were likely to offer the best options in terms of available volume of water, but the quality of such water could be another matter, especially if a camp was located not far enough downstream from a large village.

The other side of the coin was that flowing water was merely a wet-season phenomenon in most parts of the country. However, water in the dry season could generally be located by digging deeply into dry riverbeds (incidentally a technique practised with great success by itinerant elephants).

A second tip by Mr Higgs for locating water for camp purposes was to look for water holes dug by the indigenous population and then to proceed to dig nearby in order to find water. The direct use of local water holes was likely to stir up trouble according to Mr Higgs. The cry sent up, he claimed, would be, "The white man is stealing our water!" (*Mzungu anaiba maji yetu!*)

With a suitable water supply secured, the camp would ideally be set up on an elevated stretch of ground blessed with some shady trees under which to pitch the tents. Depressions and hollows tended to attract heat and therefore made less attractive camping spots. It went without saying that permission to establish a camp must be sought from the local chief, with care taken not to infringe on any cultivated ground (*shambas*). Local chiefs, according to Mr Higgs, were normally most obliging men who were always ready to go out of their way to make things easy for the camp personnel.

And that was the way it worked for some of the time.

The first rule of comfort for an *mzungu* contemplating a place to set up the camp was to decide where he wanted to put his own tent. He would then follow up by ensuring that the *watu* were camped as far away from him as possible (a minimum distance of two to three hundred yards was recommended) since in Mr Higgs' opinion *watu* could be very noisy in the evenings.

If the plan was that the camp should be one of long duration, Mr Higgs recommended putting down concrete floors on which to site the accommodation facilities (including tents) and other essential constructions such as the store hut, the kitchen and a mess area. The GFM provided detailed specifications for the preparation of an acceptable form of concrete for this very purpose using cement, sand and pebbles in respective proportions of 1:4:3. The emphasis was on the incorporation of local materials, riverbeds being a prime source of sand and pebbles.

A latrine (referred to in English as a "shit house" and in Kiswahili as a *choo*) was not the least important of the facilities to be incorporated into camp design. Mr Higgs pointed out that a *choo* pit should be dug at least fifty yards away from the nearest *mzungu*-occupied tent or hut and should have minimum dimensions of six feet in depth, four feet in length and four feet in breadth.

With the pit excavated, an initial layer of covering poles should be placed lengthwise to cover the pit over, leaving only a one-foot wide gap in the middle. A transverse layer of poles should then be placed on top of the first layer with an equivalent width of gap left at the centre once again. In this way a one-foot square hole would present itself on a secure weight-bearing platform directly over the core of the excavated pit. Residual gaps between the so-arranged poles were then closed up with leaves, clumps of grass and small branches. A layer of soil, shovelled from the pile of excavated material, was spread over the platform to the extent that the only opening remaining was the central hole, ready for reception. It only needed a wall (*boma*) of cut thorn bush to be put up around the *choo* for the protection and privacy of any occupant. The *choo* seat was prepared by setting up two thick fork-ended poles—one standing on each side of the pit with the forks uppermost—and laying a straight pole of similar thickness on the forks to span the distance between them.

When a camp moved on, the *boma* enclosing the *choo* needed to be dismantled and the *choo* pit to be backfilled and levelled off. Similar considerations applied to all other pits and trenches dug to aid the comfort of camp life, not the least important of which was a refuse pit for the receipt of kitchen and other debris.

As something of an afterthought, Mr Higgs observed that a *choo* should also be excavated for the exclusive use of the *watu* in order to cut down on an alleged risk of hookworm infection that could result from large-scale defecation behind camp-fringing bushes.

Acceptable huts for camp use could be erected in a traditional manner by employing a framework of sticks and poles bound together with strips of bark. A mess hut and a self-contained kitchen, declared Mr Higgs, made a great deal of difference to the comfort of camp life. In areas where long grass was available for cutting it could be used for thatching the sides and roofs of such huts. In the absence of thatch, a plaster prepared from mud and animal dung (domestic cattle or game) made an adequate substitute. During the height of the wet season, however, a tarpaulin sheet cover was very much to be preferred as an alternative to thatch on the roof.

The expertise of the chief's local people in knowing what was practical under most circumstances that were likely to be encountered was generally available for tapping into and, according to Mr Higgs, would offer singular benefits when sought out. He additionally suggested that responsibility for messing (including the procurement of food and domestic supplies and the control of the cook and his acolytes) should be delegated to a specific *mzungu* in camp. Relevant duties would include regular inspections of the kitchen area to ensure that food was not left lying around to become contaminated; verification that all drinking water had been properly boiled; and seeing that the camp refrigerator (if there was one) was set up in the coolest possible location to allow it to work at maximum efficiency (it was normally paraffin-driven).

In a camp with a large complement of *watu*, a stick and thatch or stick and mud hut could make a convenient store. Mr Higgs suggested that such a store hut should be fashioned so that the *watu* could enter by one doorway, collect their due rations from the storekeeper as they passed through the hut, and leave by a second door. He noted how essential it was to have the ration collection process well organised so as to reduce the time committed to it.

*

Food for consumption in camp by the *wazungu* could be bought from, among others, members of the local population, village markets and shops, and traders in towns. In certain circumstances, as in the early part of the wet season when all vegetation grew with wild abandon, it was possible to forage for greens in the bush, and on top of that there was always the possibility of using a rifle or a shotgun to augment the meat supply under the terms of a legally issued shooting licence.

By eating such fruit and vegetables as could be obtained and by drinking plenty of milk (mixed from milk powder as a rule), the average *mzungu* in the bush would, in Mr Higgs' opinion, be able to remain healthy. If green vegetables were in short supply, Mr Higgs recommended the consumption of onions as these were always plentiful (he wrote) and were supposed to contain most of the key vitamins essential to good health.

A good tip offered by him was that a camp should acquire a number of chickens—say, four or five hens and a rooster. Not only would that ensure a regular supply of eggs but also, in an emergency, one or other of the birds could be sacrificed to make a meal or two.

At the initial contact with the local chief prior to setting up camp, it was considered good practice to inform the chief that the *wazungu* were interested in buying eggs, milk, vegetables and an occasional chicken from him and his people. The scarcity of fresh milk in the bush could be compared to the incidence of the teeth of chicken.

In the unlikely event that fresh milk was available a suitable receptacle to contain it should be provided from the camp, and the milk should be boiled before consumption. Fresh milk could be used to make butter by allowing it to stand in a receptacle for a day to let the cream rise and separate for skimming off and beating until the butter appeared. Such homemade butter was preferable to the tinned variety in normal use, as the latter tended to be rather unstable and became more than a little oily under the heat of the day.

Mr Higgs concluded his compilation of helpful hints with a number of food preparation recipes selected for the delectation of *wazungu*. He seemed to imply that an *mzungu* would perform the rites of cooking, although that was something never likely to happen in a well-ordered camp where all culinary and other domestic arrangements were held fast within the remit of an *mtu* cook. A good cook (*mpishi*) was an unsung hero worth his weight in gold to a camp.

The dishes for which detailed recipes were presented by Mr Higgs in the *GFM* were: bread (inclusive of instructions as to how to make an oven out of a biscuit tin, a hole in the ground, and a supply of red hot coals); banana fritters; pumpkin fritters; onion pie; game meat kebabs; and dried meat or jerky (known as *biltong* by the South Africans and *nyama kukausha* in Kiswahili).

Since a camp cook would be expected to know only too well how to prepare any of the said dishes and a whole host more besides, the details of the recipes could be left to the imagination of the reader of the *GFM* who not only wouldn't want to attempt to prepare any of them but wouldn't have dared to even try to interfere in the kitchen area for fear of incurring the wrath of the *mpishi*.

4
Kazi yangu
My work

As mentioned in the previous chapter, the Chief Geologist with responsibility for managing the WDL diamond exploration programme during my time on it was named Gus Edwards. Gus was Australian by nationality, as was not only his Assistant Chief Geologist, Trevor Rodger, but also the joint third in command stringer Bernie McBride.

Together they made up a cosy little Australian clan.

Gus possessed a sense of humour that was dry enough to have evaporated away well before I met him. He was a man of catholic tastes, with a keen interest in philately, wildlife photography, history and politics, all of which made him something of a fount of general knowledge. Gus would no more have wanted to sit in a bar slugging back IPAs with bush types than he would have chosen to wear his heart on his sleeve.

As I knew him, Gus had no small talk. Bullshit was anathema to him. Moral rectitude drove him, and in this he distinguished himself favourably by comparison with far too many of the rest of us who worked under him.

Gus was the author of another interesting "Instruction to field staff" incorporated into the *GFM*. The memorandum in question gave readers an interesting take not only on the social mores of those of us who lived out in the bush camps together but also on Gus's view of the same. It gleamed like an unsheathed sword in the slow march of the plodding *GFM*.

In it Gus pointed out that the WDL General Manager had been receiving an increasing number of complaints from sources outside Mwadui about our alleged misbehaviour. Featured among the complaints were numerous reported sightings of WDL Land Rovers being driven around in towns when they were supposed to be supporting exploration work out in the bush. It was therefore incumbent on Gus (who presumably took his instructions from the WDL GM) to bring to our attention the standards of conduct and discipline that were expected of us.

Gus reminded us that Land Rovers were not—repeat *not*—to be used by us for private purposes. Moreover, he went on to state, our visits to towns and other local centres from camp were only permitted for carrying out work-related business. As if that were not enough to let us know where we stood, the individuals among us who were recognised as offenders were advised that if we were reported to be present in major towns on days when we should have been working in the bush we would be called upon to explain ourselves. In the absence of our coming up with a satisfactory excuse we would be fined for personal mileage incurred in Land Rovers at the rate of 1.75 shillings per mile.

Our annual leave allowance, wrote Gus, was generous enough to preclude any necessity for us to take regular weekend "leaves" in town. He declared that the only bush-based "holiday" as such that was granted to us was Christmas Day.

In his opinion, camp supplies and rations did not need to be replenished any more often than fortnightly, and even for that purpose any trips out of camp to collect supplies could only be sanctioned by the Senior Geologist in charge, who was saddled with full responsibility for the behaviour of his subordinates.

Gus stated his belief that it was all too obvious that not enough care was being taken with regard to Land Rover maintenance. He reckoned that Sunday was an appropriate day for carrying out such maintenance in camp in compliance with checklists presented in the *GFM*. Should the careless attitude to maintenance continue (he went on), a system of fining the culprits would have to be put in place, since (he alleged) far too many major repairs to vehicles were attributable to neglect of maintenance, to speeding and to a general climate of pervading nonchalance.

In his instruction Gus reckoned that far too many of us out in the exploration camps were approaching our work as if it was a combined holiday and wide-scale hunting expedition. Gus declared that it was high time that we realised that we were paid to work and not to play.

Gus's most acerbically made observations related to our standards of behaviour in public places (inclusive of hotels, bars and social clubs) where *wazungu* gathered to raise a glass or two. He let us know that we were always being watched and we therefore needed to bear in mind that any misbehaviour would in all probability be reported back to WDL. The casual reader of Gus's instruction could have been forgiven for assuming that WDL had a network of paid informers spread all around the country.

Gus reminded us that social clubs in Tanganyika were run for the benefit of their members, and if any of us thought differently we were acting under a delusion. Such social clubs were recreational institutions with a membership that was exclusively *wazungu*. Most major centres could count on the existence of at least one club of this type. The clubs were referred to as "thorn bushes" by some of us, since whenever you went into them you were certain to be surrounded by a lot of pricks. None of the external social clubs enjoyed reciprocal arrangements with the Mwadui club in which all of us were automatically granted membership as a benefit of employment. What it meant, wrote Gus, was that we could only visit an external club when accompanied by one of its members or otherwise at the direct invitation of the club's committee.

According to Gus it was obvious that most social clubs would make any of us welcome if we approached them supported by a reputation of good conduct. Unfortunately too many social club committees had reported incidents involving us that were characterised not so much by that most desirable good conduct as by boorish and drunken behaviour. This had done considerable damage to the good name of WDL and had made unwelcome guests of its representatives. It all presupposed that boorishness and drunkenness were exclusive qualities that we of WDL brought to the party. The club members, like Caesar's wife, were presumed to be above suspicion. ("Ha, ha!" said the DC once again).

In addition to the emphasis on our behavioural shortfall, Gus went on to allude to the state of our general appearance and dress sense when we visited towns. We were not expected to turn ourselves out immaculately, but we should at least make an effort to look clean and neat, and for anyone of us to appear in public sporting a two or three days' growth of beard was in no way acceptable.

That was telling us, Gus!

*

Compared with Gus, Trevor Rodger was another kettle of fish altogether. He was as indecisive and pedantic as he was unhelpful when he was placed face to face with a genuine problem requiring resolution. Trevor was a typical "Mr Peter Principle"—his career path epitomised promotion through a hierarchy to attain a genuine level of incompetence.

Trevor's level of desire to head through the gates of Mwadui in a Land Rover and spend some time out in the bush had all the substance of a rumour of rain in the middle of the dry season. I suspected that Trevor was unwilling to sally forth and run the risk of exposing his inadequacies.

Not long after I arrived at Mwadui, Trevor and Mrs Rodger issued me with a formal invitation to join them for dinner at their bungalow residence. I let my true colours rest under no bushel since when seated at their table I first of all sniffed, in what was a genuine lifetime habit, at the food on my plate. There was no doubt that Trevor regarded my olfactory prowess as a social gaffe. My philistinism was confirmed when, following my being offered a bowl containing a number of potatoes that might almost have made a single serving for one back home in Cornwall, I thought it polite to remove only about two thirds of them. What I took was less than what I wanted to take—unfortunately, the bowl of potatoes was also intended to supply portions to the other four people with me at the table. I sensed that I had joined the ranks of the great uncouth in Trevor's book from that moment on. Be that as it may, I was never invited to dine with him again at any venue. This was not entirely to my displeasure, however, as Trevor's company was not, as far as I was concerned, something to revel in.

*

If the fates had conspired to put me on the wrong side of Trevor, they twisted back in my favour on the very next day. A stroke of great fortune came my way in the person of a Senior Geologist in from the bush and accommodated in the Pink House for two or three days. I was alone after hours no more.

The Senior Geologist was an Irishman, a graduate of Trinity College in Dublin. His name was Tom Molyneux. I took to him at once. Our personal relationship developed so rapidly that he went to the administration people in the Exploration Department and made arrangements for me to work for him in the bush once my Mwadui-based induction period was complete.

Tom told me that he was in the process of setting up a programme of reconnaissance exploration over a great swathe of the virtually uncharted Rungwa Game Reserve located some two hundred and fifty miles or so to the southeast of Mwadui along the Kisigo River. He said that his base camp was going to be established in very remote country, one of the few parts left, he said, of the "real Africa". I was delighted to find acceptance so soon. The association of "game reserve" with the intended work seemed intensely exciting.

Tom was a few years older than me, had completed a year on diamond exploration in the bush already. He was experienced, tall, of moderate build, bespectacled, bucktoothed and crop-haired. He wore his Irishness like a badge—it and a marked tendency to eccentricity of manner made being in his company invariably a pleasure.

During his previous year of service Tom told me that one of the camps he occupied was situated up in the north of Tanganyika on the fringes of the area known as the Serengeti Plains. During his sojourn in that area Tom said he had known Dr Bernhard Grzimek, the "father of the Serengeti National Park" and author of the famous book *Serengeti Shall Not Die*.

The borders of the Serengeti National Park were something of a moveable feast at the time, as they were still in the process of being finalised in order to most reasonably encompass the seasonal migration routes of the great herds of wildebeest that occupied the plains.

Under the authority of a type of game hunting licence familiarly known as a "pot licence", Tom shot a number of Thomson's gazelle (*tomi* in Kiswahili) in the vicinity of his Serengeti camp. *Tomi* were small antelope of very prolific distribution. The pot licence was valid, and the *tomis* were shot in accordance with its permitted quota.

The *tomi* skins were pegged out for drying around Tom's camp. They were on prominent display and were observed by a patrolling game ranger who was not at all happy with what he saw. The *tomi* were subsequently deemed to have been possibly shot inside the uncertain border of the national park. Tom was, on that basis, accused of poaching the *tomis* and was summoned to a court hearing at which he received a nominal fine and a ban on either owning or using a firearm for a period of three years. His inadvertent oversight relating to the positioning of the national park border worked in his favour. Tom went on to work for WDL with all the aplomb and distinction that would also characterise his later career as a professional geologist.

*

Those of us who owned firearms and took out licences to shoot for the pot sometimes trod a fine line between making what were legal kills and what was technically poaching. Shooting for the pot occasionally took in an off-licence or outside-quota species of game that happened to appear in the wrong place at the wrong time. In Gus's written description of our excessive behaviour patterns that notably included drunkenness and boorishness, poaching could also have featured, although in my experience I never knew of any instances of poaching being anything other than simply opportunistic.

For all that, it was probably nothing short of remarkable that, to my knowledge, only one of us ever ended up in jail, or at least in jail in Tanganyika. The character with that claim to fame was nicknamed "Tank". At the time when I arrived in Mwadui, Tank, who enjoyed a reputation for having a Gerry Wilson type of silver tongue and an anything-goes attitude, was languishing in the district prison at Morogoro, a pretty town located one hundred and twenty miles to the east of Dar es Salaam, surrounded by precisely aligned sisal plantations and backed by a range of blue serrated hills.

Tank drew his inside stretch for the unauthorised appropriation of one of WDL's Land Rovers. In the context of some of the less savoury aspects of the behaviour of exploration personnel, Tank's misdemeanour did not seem to be all that serious to some of us. Tank was reputed to take all his meals with the Morogoro prison governor and to be accommodated within the prison in the manner to which he was accustomed.

We remembered him best for comparing the taste in his mouth on the morning after a big boozing session with "an Indian shit house at the height of paw-paw season". The expression ranked him as a true poet—as anyone who had visited one of the cited establishments at the referred-to time of year would be aware.

*

As a likely consequence of question marks related to pot licence shooting a formal instruction to field staff dealing with exploration work in and around game reserves was issued. This instruction, written in March 1960 and signed by Louis Murray, was also incorporated in the *GFM*. It was an instruction of significant importance to one like me who, thanks to Tom's good offices, was destined to perform work in the Rungwa game reserve.

Louis Murray's instruction made it clear that permission for us to carry out exploration in a number of designated game reserves had only been granted to WDL under very specific conditions applied to the conduct of exploration staff. It was pointed out that a breach of any of the said conditions could lead to an annulment of the exploration rights, and it further emphasised that any offence committed against the Tanganyika Fauna Conservation Ordinance (the FCO) could lead to the immediate cancellation of WDL's authority to have its representatives enter any of the named game reserves.

Individual copies of the FCO, the instruction noted, were issued to all of us (although I have to acknowledge once again that I was not among those privileged to receive a copy). The conditions placed on our working in game reserves, declared the instruction, were under no circumstances to be infringed. Any deviations would be considered as constituting a serious breach of WDL regulations.

The FCO determined that no person other than the national Game Warden or his personally authorised representative(s) could undertake scientific research, conduct control measures, or hunt any animal (inclusive of fish) in a game reserve.

Permission for third parties to enter or reside in a game reserve therefore required the written authorisation of the Game Warden. Examples of these third parties mentioned in the FCO were a public officer on duty; a servant of a public officer on duty; a person whose place of ordinary residence was in the game reserve; a person travelling through a game reserve along a road; and a person engaged in forestry or water works (which could be assumed to include exploration activities) of any kind permitted by law.

The written authorisation of the Game Warden additionally covered the circumstances in which permission for anyone to be in the possession of a weapon (including a firearm, or a bow and arrow or a spear) in a game reserve could be granted.

The FCO demanded that no person should wilfully or negligently cause any bush or grass fire to occur; or fell, cut, burn, injure or remove any standing tree, bush, sapling, seedling (or any part of the same) in a game reserve unless (once again) the written authorisation of the Game Warden was obtained. In the event that a forest reserve was also named, the signature of the Conservator of Forests or his personally appointed representative was needed as well.

Naturally enough, however, the few people who actually dwelt in game reserves, plus those like us who were authorised to perform work in the same places, were permitted to fell trees for the purpose of building shelters for themselves and their dependants and servants (if they had any).

With regard to the ground rules for the conduct of our exploration practice in the Rungwa Game Reserve, the FCO gave us a few common-sense guidelines.

Some of the special conditions placed on the presence of properly authenticated and authorised employees of WDL in game reserves were: (a) that no permanent or semi-permanent camp could be erected; (b) fires were permitted to be lit for cooking purposes only; (c) as little disturbance as possible should be caused to game animals; (d) if a game scout (or scouts) was available to accompany us, no member of our party could carry an offensive weapon; (e) if no game scout was available then a weapon intended solely for the purpose of protecting human life could be carried by the person in charge of our party; (f) if it was necessary to use such a weapon, a detailed written report specifying the circumstances of the action, including time, place and game animal(s) involved should be submitted to the Game Department without delay; (g) prior to entering a game reserve, the person in charge of the party should report in person to the Game Ranger under whose jurisdiction the game reserve fell; (h) the permission granted was valid only for the duration of the planned work; and (i) at the conclusion of the planned work the Game Warden should receive formal notification that work had ended.

The instruction regarding our working in game reserves wound up with an expression of regret that WDL was unable to provide us with a nation-wide map showing the location of all game reserves and any other areas of restricted entry.

However (the instruction went on), for any given area the local DC could usually be relied on to give us an idea of where any game reserves under his jurisdiction were located, and if the DC didn't have this information, he would be at least be able to provide directions as to where the nearest Game Department official could be found.

So that was all right then!

*

There were very few *wazungu* among those of us who worked on exploration in the bush who didn't own either a rifle or a shotgun, or (for that matter) both of the above. Wherever any of us went, there also went our firearms. Obtaining an owner's licence for a small to moderate calibre rifle or twelve-bore shotgun was no more than a formality. You made an application, it was granted and that was that. The applicant's competency for bearing arms never seemed to be an issue. My obtaining both small-calibre rifle and shotgun owner's licences was proof positive of that point.

It was much less easy to obtain an owner's licence for either a large-calibre rifle or a handgun. The one implied an end use for specialist big game hunting, and the other suggested close-quarter combat of the worst kind. Licences for such firearms called for so much justification to be presented along with the application that they were not only all but impossible to get hold of but also really not worth the effort to pursue.

The calibres of the arsenal of rifles spread throughout the bush camps ranged from 0.22 up to 0.450. In Mwadui I bought at second hand both a 9 mm calibre bolt-action rifle (made at Brno in Czechoslovakia) and a Greener single-barrel twelve-bore shotgun. I took the two weapons and a large quantity of associated ammunition with me when I left to join Tom at his camp.

I wasn't sure that I really wanted to own firearms, although I was encouraged to exercise the right to bear them by the inducement of peer pressure to conform to what was reckoned to be normal practice. The first thing that owners of firearms had to ensure, come what may, was that their firearms should not get lost. The second thing was that if the firearms were lost then they should be lost for good, never to appear again in the hands of others, especially when the others were ranked as undesirables. Owning a firearm was therefore something of a liability. The authorities would take an extremely dim view of any loss of a personal firearm through owner negligence.

Self-protection as such was not a priority consideration where ownership of firearms was concerned. In the Tanganyika of the day there was no real feeling of social unrest and very little criminal activity of the kind that would justify shots being fired at perpetrators in fear or in anger. Proximity to big game animals was something else of course, yet unless big game was deliberately (or inadvertently) interfered with it posed no serious threat to us as the one wish of big game always appeared to be to give us as wide a berth as possible.

The main reason for our taking up arms was to shoot game "for the pot" and thereby augment and improve our camp food supply. The familiar "pot licence", valid for one year, could be picked up quite easily from any local government office. It gave the licensee the right to prey on specified quotas of game animals such as *tomis*, wildebeest, warthog, hartebeest, impala, waterbuck, and roan antelope, together with an unlimited number of game birds, among which the most important were guinea fowl, francolin and sand grouse. All kills were required to be recorded in terms of date, time and location of shooting.

I obtained my first pot licence from the authorities in Dodoma. All that it took for me to get it was that I turned up at the relevant office, handed in the application, paid the fee and received the licence across the counter in return. At the time, and since I already owned a couple of firearms, it seemed to be the natural thing to do. I had few if any thoughts of ever using the pot licence as an excuse to shoot anything—although, as it happened, those thoughts would have a rather temporary shelf life.

The validity of a pot licence ceased on its formal date of expiry, irrespective of whether or not its nominated quotas of game were shot out. If all of the game quotas were completed prior to the expiry date the pot licence was equally invalidated, but an application from the licensee for a replacement pot licence was not possible until the expiry date of his existing licence was reached and passed. An option to shoot game available from quotas on someone else's pot licence was then sometimes exercised by keen hunters. The legality of doing so was open to question but was never challenged by the authorities as far as I was aware. Gus's assertions on exploration for diamonds becoming confused with extended hunting trips were perhaps not lacking in substance.

A problem faced by those of us who hunted with pot licences was that there was no guarantee that the various species of game nominated for shooting would be available when meat for the pot was wanted. For example, *tomis* and wildebeest were found on the open plains—impala and waterbuck lived in denser bush. What we could shoot depended on the type of game habitat in which we worked. As a consequence, the fulfilment of pot licence quotas was approached with a certain amount of flexibility, and substitutions of what was available for what was not available were relatively commonplace.

In practice we rarely, if ever, referred to the creatures of the bush as "animals". They were always known as "game" in a fair reflection of the attitude of the time, which lumped them together in collective terms as meat on the hoof. The game appeared to exist in numbers that were so unlimited and so self-sustaining that shooting out all the quotas on a host of pot licences could not dent their multitude. As if to leave the connection between game and meat in no doubt, the Kiswahili word *nyama* could be taken to mean either "meat" or "animal".

It was possible to take out special hunting licences for the really big game such as buffalo or elephant. These licences were extremely tightly controlled and were issued subject to the approval of a senior official of the Game Department with all due consideration given to the experience, intentions and character of the applicant. The minimum calibre of rifle mandated for hunting buffalo and elephant was 0.450.

Buffalo and elephant were two members of big game's so-called "big five", the other three being lion, leopard and rhinoceros. For hunting any of this latter trio, licences were issued only (and no doubt conditionally) to professional white hunters.

*

In addition to my two firearms, among the other essential purchases that I made at Mwadui prior to departing to join Tom at his Rungwa Game Reserve camp was my bush apparel. Its exclusive colour was khaki. I obtained three pairs of shorts and one quite stiff-feeling safari jacket. I also got hold of a broad-brimmed hat and a pair of the ankle-high boots with crepe soles and soft leather uppers that the South Africans called *velskoon*. The boots (made by Bata of course) were extremely comfortable on the feet—I wore a pair steadily until they fell apart and then bought a new pair to run through the process all over again.

As if to make it clear that the good old days were dying hard, a pith helmet, otherwise known as a sola topee, was offered to me for headgear if I so desired, although I couldn't conceive of the circumstances that might have induced me to don such a colonial-styled relic. The only person I saw wearing a sola topee anywhere in Tanganyika was Tom's head *mtu*, Vincent by name. For Vincent, the sola topee served as his badge of authority. For his own headgear Tom favoured a Panama hat of the non-rigid variety.

Another important item that I was induced to buy in Mwadui was a 35 mm Agfa camera. A WDL photography society was highly active. Jack, the draughtsman who mentored me so ably, was one of its luminaries. He told me that my opportunities for taking photographs in the bush would be unparalleled.

Out in the bush we often walked over ground on which *wazungu* feet might not have previously trodden. We encountered situations that were as exciting as they were unusual. There was no shortage of spectacle for a camera to record. Most of us preferred to use 35 mm colour slide film for our photographs; exposed films were mailed to the Kodak processing laboratories in Johannesburg for development and slide mounting. There were those among us who complained bitterly that their "best" slides were lost through appropriation by processing laboratory technicians, although in all my dealings with Kodak, involving over a thousand 35 mm slides, I never lost a single one. I could have been lucky of course, or (more likely) I might not have photographed anything that the technicians thought worth stealing.

*

Someone at Mwadui, probably Trevor, decided that my induction would be incomplete unless I made at least one bush excursion before I was sent out to join Tom. I was therefore told that I had to accompany a geologist named Nimmo Reid, a South African with at least a full year of bush experience behind him, on a trip to deliver some essential supplies to a camp located about forty miles to the south of the town of Tabora near a village named Igalula. Tabora, a celebrated district centre town, was located approximately one hundred miles to the south of Mwadui.

Nimmo was either reticent or taciturn in nature. I couldn't decide which of the two qualities characterised him better. There was a Homeric "black browed" look about him. The art of conversation did not seem to feature too high on his list of social skills, but since I was equipped with a similar characteristic we managed to communicate well enough when we were together.

Nimmo had two genuine claims to fame. The chief of these was derived from the regular use from a camp that he headed of a PWD-constructed track leading around a hill. It was discovered at a later date that a cutting on the track went through the surface expression of a kimberlite pipe that was not recognised by anyone associated with the camp, including Nimmo. Dr Arnold Waters, the God-like Consulting Geologist for the entire Anglo American Corporation whose Olympian throne was sited in Johannesburg, was reported to have replied, when asked by someone why WDL was using graduate geologists to perform mundane (their word, not mine) sampling tasks in the Tanganyika bush, that "a geologist would recognise a copper deposit if he walked over it!" I wouldn't have wanted to include my own powers of observation within Dr Waters' confident generality and could well imagine that I would have done no better than Nimmo in the case of the drive-through kimberlite pipe.

Nimmo's second claim to fame was his inability to spell any two consecutive words correctly, irrespective of how many or how few syllables each word might possess. I was shown a short note written by Nimmo that advised: "I will meet McGinnis at the hotel". Four of the words were wrongly spelt. It very much begged the question as to how Nimmo had managed to pass examinations, but he obviously had and it took all sorts, presumably.

The bush excursion with Nimmo commenced early one afternoon. He was at the wheel of the Land Rover as I didn't yet have my driving licence. We took no *watu* along with us, which didn't make any impression on me since I didn't yet know enough to recognise bad practice when I saw it. A little experience of travelling around the backwaters of Tanganyika would show me that the *watu* knew the country and its hazards a lot better than the *wazungu* ever would. In Africa, the unexpected (whether two-legged or four-legged or dumped from the sky above) could come along more or less as the order of the day. The practice that I eventually adopted was to travel in the company of at least one *mtu*. Out on the roads and along the tracks two heads were infinitely better than one, especially when the one was white.

Our destination was a camp set up to carry out reconnaissance exploration, which meant comprehensively covering a large assigned area for the likely presence of kimberlite with a broad network of representative samples of both residual soil and of sediments lying in drainage channels. Reconnaissance camps were truly nomadic, moving about as necessary in order to optimise the distance travelled to sampling sites.

Positive indications from reconnaissance sampling programmes pointing to the presence of kimberlite within the area of influence of the samples taken were normally followed up by more focused exploration practice referred to as "detailed work", which involved an essentially settled camp dealing with a relatively restricted area of activities. Detailed work relied on "close-spaced" sampling within the framework set by the original reconnaissance sampling and took the objective of pinpointing the source for the positive indications.

Most of us started off by working on reconnaissance. After a suitable period of time many among us then aspired to graduate into the realms of detailed work. There were, however, rather a lot of us and, moreover, there was quite a lot of the country to cover with reconnaissance samples. What there was not a lot of were discoveries generating opportunities for detailed work. It seemed that assignments to detailed work were the prerogative of WDL's favoured few.

The fact that the final analysis of all reconnaissance samples taken in the bush in Tanganyika was carried out in laboratories down in Johannesburg offered an additional drawback to individual detailed work ambitions. The far-flung analysis placed several months of hiatus between the date on which a sample was taken in the bush and the date on which the results were known back in Mwadui. The *mzungu* and the gang of *watu* responsible for taking the original sample could well have been dispersed in the interim to any of the four winds and would be most unlikely to be still in the right place at the right time for follow-up detailed work to come their way. It never fell to my lot to be engaged in detailed work and as a consequence I didn't miss the experience.

An area assigned to a reconnaissance camp typically covered the catchment of a significant drainage system and was thereby bounded by the rim of the drainage system's watershed. Since the area was "self-contained" in this way, the place of origin of the sediments sampled by the reconnaissance team in drainage channels, streambeds or riverbeds would almost certainly be located somewhere in the area.

When the results of reconnaissance sampling eventually disclosed the presence of any of the three indicator minerals (ilmenite, pyrope garnet and chrome diopside) positive for kimberlite, detailed work clicked immediately into gear. In detailed work the indicator minerals were tracked back to their primary source through intensive sampling along streams and sampling residual soils on a close-spaced grid.

The advantage that detailed work held over reconnaissance sampling was that the analysis of its samples was carried out there and then. In detailed work there was none of the imposed delay that sending samples to Johannesburg for analysis placed on progress. In the process of analysis the samples were concentrated by being panned or jigged in water; the ensuing concentrates were separated and examined; indicator minerals (if any) were identified and their respective numbers were counted up; and the numerical counts for the individual minerals were plotted in their relative locations on a large-scale map of the detailed work area. As the plot of indicator mineral numbers built up it was contoured to provide a graphic representation of the distribution. The guiding principle was that the numbers were expected to increase in the direction of their source.

Identification of a primary source from the results of detailed work sampling was no better than a tentative outcome until exposure of bedrock was achieved. Pits were excavated as the principal means of exposing bedrock, dug down through a profile that hopefully intersected yellow ground, blue ground and finally kimberlite at no significant depth.

*

A sampling team working out of a reconnaissance camp usually consisted of one *mzungu* and up to a dozen *watu*, including a head *mtu*. A reconnaissance camp established in a reasonably "civilised" location could contain as many as four such teams under the direction of a Senior Geologist. Extra *watu*, pooled across the board, included the cook and his helper, Land Rover drivers and administrative types. However, four teams (or for that matter even three teams) in camp were unwieldy to manage in remote locations, and in those instances two teams only were normally preferred for optimum effectiveness.

Two *wazungu* in one camp might not necessarily like each other very much but would have no alternative other than to hang together if they weren't going to hang separately. When three *wazungu* were in camp together the inevitable result was that two ganged up on one. Four *wazungu* in camp created situations that were not much better. Daggers were all too often drawn as the inability of individuals to escape from the personal quirks and irritating habits of others assumed a significance on which decisions to go to war could easily have been based.

Those engaged in reconnaissance sampling lived under canvas, whereas for detailed work the accommodation tended towards being rather more fixed and comfortable. The accommodation was directly related to the nature of the work—to cover an assigned area a reconnaissance camp might need to move up to half a dozen times, whereas a detailed work camp would contemplate no moves at all once it was set up. Detailed work brought with it the implied cachet of superior status to those who undertook it. Reconnaissance versus detailed work was a situation of us against them, a class system in all but name.

When Tom went off to assume his first detailed work command post, he dumped his bush garb and took to wearing a long-sleeved white shirt set off at the neck with a green cravat. In addition he disposed of his small collection of long-playing records of popular music and obtained a set of classical music LPs. As one who was destined never to cross the detailed work divide, I looked on in wonderment.

*

Following any discovery of a kimberlite pipe through detailed work, the evaluation process, involving more extensive pitting with the support of core drilling, commenced. As a general rule it was the Prospectors who carried out such evaluations. They were tough and experienced individuals among whose numbers were to be counted former cronies (a fair sprinkling of whom were Canadians) of the late Dr Williamson. The Prospectors regarded the great intake of Geologists, Field Officers and Field Assistants with sceptically jaundiced eyes and made no secret of the fact that that they didn't at all like what they saw.

Since the evaluation of kimberlite was their game, hopefully with some association of diamonds, secrecy surrounded the work of the Prospectors. Visiting their operations was a privilege handed out only to the few they favoured who were either long-term drinking buddies or senior types out of Mwadui who could not be refused.

By choice the Prospectors did not work with *wazungu* assistants. They regarded the latter as useless—not without reason. However, the complement of *watu* that they employed was often quite enormous. It ran into hundreds and to it had to be added wives, children, a host of camp followers, dogs, domestic livestock and what have you.

The Prospector (and celebrated artist) Mr Albert Künzler, he who married a chief's daughter, held court in his bush camp with virtually an entire tribe backing him up. I met with him on a number of occasions at the bar of the Diamond Fields Hotel in Shinyanga and found that his social persona combined the more overt characteristics of the actors Brian Blessed and Oliver Reed.

I always looked on the Prospectors as being white chiefs in all but name. Their word in their own domains was law. As little as a crumb of approval from any one of them was something I greatly desired, although it was rarely forthcoming.

I got my chance when a small group of Prospectors gathered in a camp outside Dodoma for the purpose of holding a wake to commemorate the release from prison in Kenya of Mr Jomo Kenyatta. Ironically, Mr Kenyatta's surname translated in Kiswahili as "the light of Kenya".

The words the Prospectors used when raising their glasses to toast Mr Kenyatta could well have been based on some of the Mau Mau oaths that Mr Kenyatta was alleged to have had an association with. Whether the alleged association was a direct or an indirect one it didn't much matter to the Prospectors. What mattered was that the man was again (regrettably) on the loose.

As I chanced to be passing the camp at the time when the wake was being held, I got to attend the waning stages of the "ITMA" ceremony. I was unaware at the time of the significance of either the wake, or of Mr Kenyatta's release, or of the politics he espoused, or of the implications of his "*Uhuru!*" call on Tanganyika as well as Kenya.

Uhuru was indeed by then becoming a word that was being ever more frequently heard around Tanganyika. It was sometimes coupled with "nation", as in "*uhuru na nchi!*" but was heard much more frequently in connection with "work": "*uhuru na kazi!*"—freedom and work! It was as if a key to the future was being forged and all that was needed was the political strength to turn it in a lock in order to open a door.

The most vocal exponents of the *uhuru* call were what the Prospectors referred to as "bush lawyers"—*watu* whom they regarded as living representations of the adage that a little knowledge was a dangerous thing. As often as not bush lawyers were able to speak some English, which particular skill made them unemployable in any of our camps. An English-speaking *mtu* would not be touched with the proverbial barge pole, or even, to use a more appropriate local version of the same, with a sisal pole.

The cop-out excuse that we used to justify refusing employment to such people was that *watu* who spoke English were habitually lazy. The truth of the matter was that the risk of hiring a bush lawyer was considered unacceptable.

It wasn't even that work vacancies with us in camp were all that plentiful anyway. Any camp worth its salt erected a prominent sign close to the *wazungu* tents declaring "*Hakuna nafasi ya kazi hapa*" (There are no work opportunities here). The sign was always put up as a matter of course, whether or not it was needed. It served to ensure that quite a lot rather than a multitude of *watu* turned up seeking work, and as such it was a semi-useful screening tool.

One day a member of Mr Kenyatta's Kikuyu tribe ignored the sign posted at one of my camps and turned up looking for work. His entreaties were couched in English. Some of the *watu* who were with me when he appeared quite literally turned grey with fear at the sight of him. The reputation of his tribe, and perhaps of his leader as well, had preceded him. The then camp cook, Paulo Odhiambo, a member of another well-known Kenyan tribe named the Luo, was beside himself with anxiety.

I turned the Kikuyu applicant down as politely as possible, and for the rest of the day and the following night an atmosphere of dread that he might return to do us ill shivered over the camp, but we never saw him again.

5

Safari porini kwanza

First journey into the bush

The reconnaissance camp that I was to visit together with Nimmo was one of the larger of its type. It was a four-*wazungu* camp. The Senior Geologist in charge was a diminutive Scotsman named Bruno Brown who was more than adequately imbued with the prickly bombast that was so often an overt feature of small men with Caledonian roots.

The three wazungu who reported to Bruno were all ranking Field Officers. Personality-wise they were a mixed bag, although they shared common ground in South African nationality and down to earth likeability. Their names were Erhardt (Eddie) Kostlin (whose ancestral background was German); Leon Kritzinger (Afrikaans-speaking); and Neville Huxham (English-speaking). Eddie was the tallest of the three by far. Leon and Neville were of slightly less than average height, but even so they stood a good head and shoulders above Bruno, even when Bruno was standing on his tiptoes.

A few months after my visit Bruno was promoted to the job of manager of the extensive facilities of a WDL "service" depot set up just outside the town of Manyoni. Bruno's function was to oversee and direct services (both mechanical and supply) in support of an ever-increasing number of reconnaissance camps scattered about the surrounding region. In this high-profile role Bruno was happy to work himself into a steady state of near apoplexy as wrecked Land Rovers arrived one by one in his courtyard.

Leon and Neville comported themselves in the manner of two peas in a pod. They were a true double act. When one appeared in view, the other was sure not to be too far away. They were a perfect attraction of opposite poles, Leon being a country boy and Neville the scion of a family associated with publishing the *Rand Daily Mail*, a famous Johannesburg daily newspaper. The *RDM* had a relatively liberal editorial policy, in which capacity it was regarded as a thorn in the side of the ultra right-wing South African *apartheid* government under the then Prime Minister Dr Hendrik Verwoerd. Leon and Neville shared an uncanny understanding of one other that was almost telepathic. Of them it was said, with a certain amount of inevitability really, that "while Kritzinger fitzfinger, Huxham fuxham".

A couple of years subsequent to my meeting with Neville at Bruno's camp, I chanced to be in Johannesburg for a weekend visit. I went down to the city of gold with Tony Knowles (of Drop Inn fame) from Lobatsi in the Bechuanaland Protectorate where we were both then based. We spotted Neville talking with a small group of companions in a cinema foyer and lost no time in demonstrating great delight in greeting him like the long lost brother that our shared experiences in Tanganyika led us to believe he was.

Neville didn't reciprocate our enthusiastic approach, however. He shrank from us with the kind of urgently nervous despatch that was usually demonstrated by blue lizards on the Pink House walls. A mask of mortification instantly replaced the airy elegance that had hitherto gone into chatting to his companions as his eyes met ours. It seemed that Neville's much appreciated capacity for whooping it up was a personal trait that he must have discarded somewhere up in Tanganyika.

I heard a little later on that an article presenting an edited selection of Neville's experiences in Tanganyika had actually appeared in the pages of an edition of the *Rand Daily Mail*. My informant told me that the article presented a theme best summed up in terms of "It's hell up there!" There was no doubt that Neville's article impressed the readership of the *Rand Daily Mail*, even if it didn't do much for those of us who thought we knew him once.

*

The road from Mwadui to Tabora was dirt-surfaced, wide, open and of all-weather quality. There was very little traffic proceeding in either direction on it as we made our way to Tabora, but Nimmo drove carefully nevertheless. Near Nzega, Nimmo directed my attention to a distant group of whitewashed *rondavels* that he said were the accommodation quarters for a camp engaged in detailed work. As time was short and we still had some distance to travel to our destination, Nimmo decided not to call in at the camp and we passed it by, trailing dust.

The bush on either side of the road was of the light savannah type known as *miombo*. It stretched across a plain that receded into the far distance all around us. It consisted of grey twigged thorn punctured by green umbrella-capped acacia trees and underlain by sun-brittle yellow grass that might crumble at the slightest contact with hooves. Here and there a scatter of smoothly domed hills of bald granite just managed to raise their heads above the treetops. Nimmo described the well-nigh featureless bush as "the MMBA", meaning "the Miles and Miles of Bloody Africa".

I once visited a camp equipped with facilities that were rather more basic than usual, little of Mr Higgs' valuable advice having been heeded as far as a number of items of construction went. On seeking the *choo*, I was handed a shovel and a couple of sheets of toilet paper, and with a languid wave of the donor's hand was invited to step out into the MMBA. A further query from me as to where the *choo* was elicited the response, "You've got the biggest shit house in the world out there!"

It should be pointed out that the incidence of *wazungu* crapping on a regular basis in the MMBA was not marked. A camp *choo* was regarded as a high-priority essential. When we were away from camp on sampling traverses special measures were called for of course. Those who had to go had to go. Not only were there lots of bushes to go behind, but there were also useful scavengers like the spotted hyena (*fisi*) that were ready to accept any form of shit for their own consumption and thereby clean up after us. The presence of any *fisi* in the proximity of a camp was highly undesirable, however. *Fisi* were *hatari sana*! Very dangerous!

Occasional huddles of mud-walled huts seemed to be attracted to the proximity of the bigger trees as if they were tsetse flies homing in on human targets. *Watu* could be seen sitting, squatting or otherwise lounging in indolent conclave on communal areas of cleared ground inside the shadier encirclements of such huts. Perhaps the *watu* were waiting for the wet season, but it was more likely that they were anticipating the return of the women (*wanawake*) from their daily toil in the *shambas* so that the women could busy themselves in grinding maize kernels to prepare (and then cook) the *posho* for the evening meal. The *watu* could also have been discussing the advent of *uhuru*, although it was unlikely that the side issue of *kazi* was being given any consideration.

Scrawny fowls scratched at the dust around the *watu's* feet. Goats watched over by *watoto* (small boys) competed with one another for the few remaining scraps of greenery that they could reach down from the thorn bushes.

The historically famous (or, depending on one's point of view, notorious) town of Tabora was located at an important junction on the Central railway line where the Mwanza line came the one hundred and seventy miles down from Mwanza on Lake Victoria up in the north by way of Shinyanga. To the west of Tabora the Central line ran for some two hundred and twenty miles to its terminus at Kigoma on Lake Tanganyika. Kigoma was located close to the town of Ujiji where Mr Henry Morton Stanley found and presumed to greet Dr David Livingstone. Heading east from Tabora, the Central line covered five hundred miles via Itigi, Manyoni, Dodoma and Morogoro to reach its other terminus at Dar es Salaam, Tanganyika's capital city on the Indian Ocean coast.

To all intents and purposes the Central line followed a former slave trade route. Tabora, named Kazeh in the slave trading days, was an important staging post for Arab slavers.

"Tabora" was reputed to be a conveniently shortened form of a tribal word "*matabolwa*". This was the name of a famine food consisting of cakes made out of pounded-up sweet potatoes that was sold extensively in local markets at the time of the slave trade.

At a later stage Tabora, then equipped with the railway, served as a key centre for the German East African colonial administration. Tanganyika was, even in my time there, still referred to by some of its more elderly residents as "*Jalamani*" (German) in a sure demonstration that the power of German colonial administration was, once experienced, never forgotten.

Happily, the slave trade no longer existed within the scope of living memory. The former slaving routes were, it was said, clearly defined by an incidence of mango trees, thanks to the propensity of Arab slave traders in mango season to consume the fruit during their expeditions and to toss the flat core stones aside, where many of the stones took root, grew into seedlings and developed into impressive trees.

The Arabs of Tanganyika remained set in the business of trading, but human traffic no longer formed part of their stock. They specialised in supplying comestible goods in bulk from dusty outlets ensconced in the relative safety of town centres. A not insignificant proportion of the population of the island of Zanzibar, out in the ocean off Dar es Salaam, was of Arab origin. Zanzibar was the site of the principal slave market in the old days, a major port for the slaving dhows to dock and pick up their cargoes.

The Arab traders' security preferences consisted of adhering to the society of their own kind and travelling around in numbers. From my observations when I came to deal with Arabs for the purchase of camp supplies they treated their employees in a manner indicating that the extinguished furnace of the slave trade yet retained a few glowing embers within its ashes.

Of the various peoples that I associated with in the course of my work in Tanganyika, the Arabs were the least easy to appreciate. They were ever suspicious of the motives of *wazungu*; withdrawn in manner; popular with very few members of any other ethnic group, and barely tolerated by one and all among the non-Arabs. It seemed reasonably certain that, when *uhuru* finally managed to hit the streets, the Arabs of Tanganyika would need a lot more than a pair of Mr Manji Dhanji's running shoes to get them off the hook as the pot finally boiled over. Fortunately for them, for the time being the *uhuru* pot was no more than lukewarm and none of the King Canute-like officials of the current colonial administration expected it to even simmer in their lifetime.

*

The name of the village that we had to look out for in the vicinity of Bruno's camp in accordance with our directions was Igalula. It should have been simple enough to locate, although a glance at a map of the area immediately surrounding Tabora made it plain that the name was by no means unique as there were at least three Igalulas on display. One location that took this popular name was located just to the north of Tabora near the Mwanza railway line; another was a short distance to the east of the town alongside the Central line; and the third, evidently the one we were looking for, was down in the bush about forty miles to the south.

Tabora, with a population numbering about twenty thousand, was the third most populous town in the whole country. Only Dar es Salaam and Mwanza outranked Tabora on the population list—to which pair of towns Tabora was respectively connected by the both the railway and the roads that replaced former slaving routes.

Tabora occupied the heart of a great tribal area known as Unyamwezi, which was the homeland of the Wanyamwezi people. As I was to discover later on, members of the Wanyamwezi tribe were good workers in general and made very well regarded employees in bush camps.

Tabora was sparsely laced by an internal network of paved roads lined with neat shops, trading outlets and warehouses held under either Indian or Arab ownership. There was also a good service garage and a decent hotel adjacent to and associated with the railway station. The main body of the town sprawled in the midst of an immensity of big mango trees, overlooked from the top of a small hill by the placid redoubt of a former German fort.

Tabora's assembled array of government buildings looked clean and white (what else?) set in behind well tended lawns and bursts of bright flowers. They contained the seat of the District Commissioner (the DC) and the local branches of various Departments of government including Agriculture, Education, Tsetse Fly Control (about which I would get to know much more later at first hand), Forestry, Game and Wildlife, Labour, Public Works, Mines and so on—not forgetting the related Departments of Police, Judiciary and Prisons.

A DC was spoken of as God's representative in the district that he commissioned, although it was true enough that due reverence was not always paid to him to the extent that he might have desired. Insofar as I never managed even as much as to see let alone meet a real live DC anywhere in Tanganyika, I often wondered if the title of DC was set up only as a stick designed to be brandished at the population as an indication that a greater force could be brought to bear on it if it didn't behave itself—so watch out.

In the course of my work and travels I did, however, come across *wazungu* agents of government here and there, and from my experience of them (with the notable exception of members of the Game Department) I felt that they showed very little appreciation of the peoples of

Tanganyika and their immediate needs. Not to put too fine a point on it, they were, in a word, ineffectual. Their actions as I saw them were counter-productive to positive social progress. Moreover, without the touch of even the first faint zephyrs of the winds of change in the offing, they spoke Kiswahili with accents execrable enough to rival Mr Harold Macmillan trying out his spoken French on the ears of General De Gaulle.

*

In keeping with his practice back at Nzega, Nimmo didn't stop the Land Rover in Tabora either. The hour of sunset was approaching rapidly, and reaching Bruno's camp before darkness took over was a much greater priority for Nimmo—as it was for me as well. The road leading south from Tabora towards Bruno's camp was little more than a meandering sandy track threading through ever-increasingly thick bush that characterised the drainage basin of the Ugalla River. That particular river flowed to the west. Far downstream the Ugalla changed its name to Malagarasi and entered Lake Tanganyika just to the south of Kigoma.

The density of the bush became monotonous and prevented us from having any long-distance perspective at all. Bruno's camp, Nimmo told me, was not located beside the track that we were following—what we had to do was look out for what was supposed to be a well signposted junction somewhere or other on the left-hand side that would direct us to where we had to go. The "supposed" qualification left me with a few misgivings.

I encountered tsetse fly for the first time while we were driving on that track. Let the blood letting commence! Tsetse flies (normally referred to for convenience as "tsetse" although there was certainly nothing convenient about them) formed a profound deterrent to any form of domestic farming involving cloven-hoofed livestock. In tsetse country such livestock withered and died. Their owners often didn't fare an awful lot better.

The only solution for the eradication of the tsetse scourge was the wholesale cutting down and burning of the bush where the tsetse thrived. As a proposition this was neither sensible nor practical. The game was immune to tsetse, and the two—animals and insects—lived together in a state of irritated truce. Tsetse did sterling service in helping to protect the habitat of the game from commercially oriented external human depredations.

In Kiswahili tsetse were known as *wandorobo*, which translated as "bush dwellers". The name was also applied in a pseudo-tribal manner to the collective numbers of human misfits, outcasts, drifters and vagabonds who wandered around in deep bush, living on what they could either forage from the trees and ground or hunt down with bows and arrows. They were a disparate collection of wretched looking individuals who existed on their own terms far beyond the pale of Tanganyika's modest trappings of civilisation.

Now and then, usually when I was traversing with a team of *watu* in a remote location, we came across human *wandorobo*. I suspected that they saw us on many more occasions without our knowing it. However many facets their way of life counted on, poaching was a key feature of their vested interests. They tended to make themselves scarce when we spotted them, flitting away into the envelope of the bush like anxious game. Others came to us to seek, and always to get, both food and tobacco. As I knew them, the *wandorobo* were people without either guile or rancour.

The *wandorobo* were sometimes named *washenzi* by members of conventional tribes. *Washenzi* was a deprecatory form of address aimed at people allegedly lacking in sophistication by people who claimed to be as sophisticated as they came. In the English context an *mshenzi* would be born into a rural backwater and be classed as a village idiot, much in the way that I was when I went up from Cornwall to attend the Royal School of Mines in London. *Shenzi* was also used to name the archetypal breed of African dog that was characterised by a drawn and frowning face and a curled question mark of a tail. The *shenzi* canines were princes among underdogs and my sympathies were always with them.

Tsetse, constant companions and camp followers to the *wandorobo* tribe, lived on blood. They obtained the blood from itinerant game in the first instance, but human blood when it was available did them just as well. Not only that, humans were thinner-skinned than game, which made the human blood supply much easier for tsetse to tap into.

A typical tsetse was a little bigger than a common European housefly but was a lot more streamlined than the latter in its appearance. Its key features were a pair of large eyes, a sleekly ribbed abdomen and a wicked looking hypodermic syringe-styled proboscis. Once it had landed and settled on a patch of exposed skin, a tsetse proceeded to insert its proboscis into a selected pore with a high degree of instinctive expertise. If the insertion of the proboscis was not painless to the victim, it was at worst no more than mildly irritating. The tsetse then flexed its abdomen in the manner of a concertina to induce blood to be sucked through the proboscis, a process that stopped either when the abdomen was engorged red with blood to bursting point or when the tsetse was swatted flat by its victim, whichever came sooner. A realisation of just how much blood a single unchecked tsetse could draw out was demonstrated in full measure if a fully charged one was whacked against a forearm.

It was only fortunate that tsetse were not nocturnal insects. Unlike vampires, tsetse went down with the sun. The relief was offset in some places as mosquitoes were more than ready to arise in the dark and resume the tsetse's blood-sucking duties.

As the Land Rover driven by Nimmo rattled and bumped down the track towards the assumed locations of Igalula and Bruno's camp, a multitude of tsetse found a way to join us in the cab of the Land Rover. Closing doors and winding up windows offered no barrier to their ingenuity for penetration. The tsetse buzzed and droned around us, hazarding our safety in transit as our hands flurried, waved and slapped in a hopeless effort to prevent them from settling on us and feeding.

A section of the *GFM*, written by Dr A. W. Nurick who was a former WDL Chief Medical Officer, provided readers with information concerning tsetse and the tropical disease of sleeping sickness with which tsetse were associated. The good doctor advised that about eighty per cent of the land area of Tanganyika was infested with tsetse, which were, as I was discovering on the way to Bruno's camp, at their most prolific where thick bush and game co-existed.

This widespread distribution of tsetse offered a sure-fire guarantee that few of those of us who went into the bush were likely to avoid contact with these rapacious insects. The sole item of good news imparted by Dr Nurick was that the deadly sleeping sickness disease, caused by a parasite carried by tsetse entering the bloodstream of tsetse victims, was carried only by a rare species of tsetse which, moreover, was of limited incidence within specifically identified geographical areas.

Outside these areas tsetse were more or less harmless to man once the annoying aspects of their attentions had been discounted.

As outlined by Dr Nurick, a good deal of fear and superstition was associated with sleeping sickness in the minds of *wazungu*—largely as a heritage of the good old days before the nature and treatment of the disease were understood, when much of Africa was still regarded as the "white man's grave". To put his readers at their ease, Dr Nurick let us know that no *mzungu* death from sleeping sickness had taken place in East Africa for several years prior to his time of writing.

Dr Nurick did not recommend the use of prophylactic drugs, based on the model of anti-malarial drugs that we routinely took, as a counter to sleeping sickness. Any one of us who developed an illness that failed to respond to a course of anti-malarial drugs was instructed by him to proceed with the utmost despatch to the nearest medical establishment (a list of locations of a number of which was provided) at which trained technicians able to examine blood slides for evidence of the sleeping sickness parasite were employed.

*

The encounter with tsetse that Nimmo and I experienced on the way to Bruno's camp took our minds off the ominous fact that it was getting darker by the minute. There was also no indication of the supposed signpost on the left-hand side of the track to bring us a bit of relief.

As the tsetse disappeared into the gathering darkness, the cicadas that were massed in trees alongside the track ceased their communal piercing whistle, a sound best likened to that of a Land Rover wheel bearing approaching a state of collapse. Cicadas were beetle-like insects so prolific in numbers that they swarmed in trees for mile after mile, rarely failing to give a driver the impression that something mechanical in his vehicle could be about to give up the ghost, and soon.

With darkness fully upon us, Nimmo pulled the Land Rover off the track and drew it up under a tree. He declared that he didn't know where we were, but wherever it was we had to remain there at least until dawn broke. We weren't exactly lost, although to all intents and purposes we might as well have been, as our chances of finding Bruno's camp in the dark were negligible.

So began my first night in the bush in an unanticipated place. Nimmo lifted a canvas-cased rifle out from where it was lying behind the seats in the front of the Land Rover, took out the firearm, and fired two shots into the air, the one shot separated from the other by an interval of about two minutes. The principle he demonstrated was that if Bruno's camp was within the audible range of rifle shot—a range that would be aided by the enhanced carrying power of sound by night—someone in the camp would reciprocate with a couple of shots. After all, they were presumably expecting us and would be listening out for our approach. However, the subsequent silence from without was as marked as it had been when Sir John Moore's corse was hurried to the ramparts at Corunna.

There were so many stars blazing in the sky above us that they seemed to take up a greater proportion of the heavens than did the black bits in between. The starlight was hard, cold and white enough to justify life membership of the Mwanza yacht club.

Nimmo, clearly at home with the practice, opted to stretch out on top of the load in the back of the Land Rover for the night. I was as happy with his choice as the circumstances permitted me to be since they allowed me to repose in the front where, in the absence of enough room to actually lie down, I could recline on the seats, wind up the windows and lock the doors from the inside to keep the predators out. There was no doubt in my mind that there would be one or more predators of the two-legged or four-legged or scaly-bellied kind nearby and bearing me nothing in the way of good will. I was also hungry, but I could live without a meal. I just didn't want to be a meal.

We took up our respective positions, and as the night developed the bush around the Land Rover resonated steadily with rustling, clicking, cracking, whistling, bumping and shuffling sounds. Against this background there were occasional blood curdling screeches, gurgling whoops, distant bellows, the crash of a hurried passage of something big through a dry thicket, and a single cackle of demented glee thrown in for good measure.

An ever-increasing impulse to swat mosquitoes, which I found out were particularly attracted to the flavour of my blood, failed to distract me from a fearful imagination as to what was out there and closing in. (Mosquitoes knew exactly what they liked and ignored what they didn't like. I could sit out in the early evening in camp and have my wrists, ankles and ears prospected and bitten assiduously by mosquitoes while the others who sat with me would be totally unscathed.)

I was awake well before dawn and wondering why we hadn't gone back to Tabora for the night. We could surely have located a town of that size, even in the dark. Tabora would have brought along the possibility of obtaining a bite to eat. The line of least resistance was, however, not Nimmo's way. As Nimmo saw it, we had a destination to get to and we were going to keep heading towards it until we reached it.

It was a sound object lesson for me to take in. Anything could happen on a journey in the Tanganyika bush. Hazards in the way were as plentiful as opportunities. You never knew what you could drop into or what could drop on you. The only principle to adhere to was to keep going forward, without deviating from the understanding of your journey that you shared with those waiting for you at the other end. If night caught you in the bush, then you sat in the bush either until the night was gone or until those who were waiting for you came to find you.

When the first light of dawn touched the eastern sky the bush fell into a purity of silence that it retained until the sun broke cover. The mosquitoes departed and the tsetse commenced the day shift. A pair of guinea fowl (kanga) scuttled across the open track not far ahead of where the Land Rover stood.

Nimmo was ready to carry on as soon as there was sufficient light for one tree to be reliably distinguished from another, and in me he found a willing partner for his plan.

We continued heading south down the track, scouted around, backtracked a little, and finally discovered the turnoff to Bruno's camp that we had missed on the previous evening. It was a lot less obvious to spot than it should have been according to the information we were given in Mwadui, although perhaps in fairness we had entertained greater expectations of it than were justified.

The turnoff and its signpost were at best semi-concealed. It was probably not unkind to assume that the arrangement was intended to inconvenience the type of visitors from Mwadui who were more geared to finding fault than to offering constructive comment. Such visitors didn't always approve of reconnaissance camp lifestyle, as Gus's classic instruction in the *GFM* had made clear.

*

Getting lost in the bush was easy to do, and most of us did it at least once.

My main experience of becoming lost occurred when I set out from camp one morning to walk a few hundred yards of shortcut through the bush to reach and check on a local track used by our Land Rovers. The task was expected to take no more than fifteen minutes to complete. I finally returned to camp six hours later.

The bush in which I got myself lost was of a relatively thick savannah type. There was a good incidence of tall trees, filled in between with tightly crowded bushes and thorn scrub. Deviating around these natural obstacles resulted in my losing all sense of direction. During the height of the day the sun offered no assistance with shadows that were long enough to indicate which direction was west and which direction wasn't. Every tree and bush that I floundered around looked exactly like the next one ahead of me.

I lost count of the number of trees that I either climbed or attempted to climb to get an overview of the surrounding area, which in any case always managed to appear featureless. Shouting didn't help either, as I must have moved well out of earshot of the camp by the time I let out my first high-pitched halloo.

I fought off waves of panic at least twice and a rush of despair on one occasion. It was by pure good fortune that I eventually stumbled upon the track that I was originally looking for. I was shocked to discover that I was two miles away from where I had intended to go several hours previously. Trudging back to camp, where to my chagrin on arrival I found that I had yet to be missed, I marvelled at how easy it was for an attempt to walk through a short stretch of bush to go so wrong so quickly.

During the reconnaissance work I did with my traverse gang in the Rungwa Game Reserve, we always carried a compass and took our direct bearings from that. However, the all-purpose tool for ensuring that we maintained a general sense of direction in the bush was vested in what was known as a *panga*. A *panga* was a long-bladed, sword-like implement, broader at the tip than at the haft and honed to razor keenness on one edge. In other parts of the world the tool was known as a *machete*, but *panga* for me was a much more functional word with which to express the spirit of the blade. *Pangas* were in use all over the country. Few village huts would not have had a *panga* feature with distinction in their construction, and nor would a finished hut not have been likely to contain one or more examples of the same.

As well as being employed for cutting and chopping sticks and trees, not to mention for butchering meat, a *panga* was an effective weapon for both defence and offence, capable of removing a head from a pair of shoulders with a single stroke.

When out on traverse we used *pangas* for blazing trees, in which process a sliver of bark was lopped from both the side facing our advance and the diametrically opposite side to support our return journey. The stark white blazes, made with a frequency that permitted us always to see at least two consecutive blazes in sequence, signposted our way through trackless bush as if they were cats' eyes on a paved highway.

It was never too clear to me how the representatives of the Game Department regarded the practice of blazing trees, especially in game reserves. Game Rangers claimed not only that our blazing gave assistance to poachers (who were quite capable of making their own blazes) but also that it was detrimental to the wellbeing of trees.

On the other hand the damage caused to trees by blazing was negligible in comparison to the destruction wreaked on trees by elephants, who more often than not seemed intent on organising their day around flattening as many trees as they could in the time available.

*

It was with a sense of relief that we finally arrived at Bruno's camp, even if it was to find that we weren't expected at all. It provided another lesson for me to take on board: that whatever was planned in Mwadui was dependent for its transmission to the bush on a rather flimsy communications network working properly, which it rarely did. Bush telegraph, or a runner bearing a message held in a cleft stick, would have been more efficient.

For all that, what mattered was that we had arrived and were welcomed and set up for the day. We were treated to a very acceptable breakfast and remained for lunch as well. With the Land Rover unloaded, we departed in early afternoon to return to Mwadui and the Pink House. Following all the interruptions of the previous night I felt that even I might be able to sleep well in the Pink House for once.

Bruno's camp was built to be comfortable without any sense of ostentation. It was a typical example of a reconnaissance camp reliant on accommodation under canvas. The experience of visiting it was most valuable in the opportunity it gave me to appreciate the camp layout for future reference and to compare and contrast what was on display with Mr Higgs' advice as provided in the pages of the *GFM*.

The camp was set up in three distinctive sectors. These were the *wazungu* camp, the *watu* camp, and the services sector. The *wazungu* and the *watu* camps were separated by a good two or three hundred yards, well in line with Mr Higgs' recommendation. The services sector was located in between the two camps, much closer to the *wazungu*'s tents than to the *watu*'s.

Separation of *wazungu* and *watu* camps was a universally accepted practice that no one involved would have wanted to take effect in any other way. There was no suggestion of segregation involved, even though in the strict sense segregation, or *apartheid* by mutual choice, was what ruled the practice. *Apartheid* was an Afrikaans word signifying racial segregation that was instilling itself into the international vernacular, spreading like a plague out of South Africa where it was institutionalised in government policy.

*

Dr Hendrik Verwoerd, the South African Prime Minister, had only recently withdrawn his country from membership of the British Commonwealth in a knee-jerk reaction to international condemnation of South Africa's *apartheid* policy. The likely consequence of South Africa quitting the Commonwealth was widely believed to offer a murky future for the country; however, most of the South Africans that I met working for WDL appeared to view leaving the Commonwealth as no bad thing, irrespective of what they thought about Verwoerd himself in private.

In the bar of the Dodoma Hotel, a beefy English-speaking South African pulled an old-issue South African penny from his pocket, showed me the head of the coin with a long-haired portrait of Jan van Riebeck stamped into it, and flipped it over to expose the tail and its image of an outspanned Voortrekker wagon. He touched the wagon with the tip of his right index finger. "Where's Verwoerd?" he asked me. I didn't know where Verwoerd was, but I was keen to find out. "He's hiding behind the wagon shitting his pants!" came the answer.

The Verwoerd government was rarely the butt of any jokes, especially down in South Africa where the authorities were not renowned for tolerating humour at their expense. Verwoerd allegedly shitting his pants behind a wagon was as *risqué* a joke as could be imagined.

*

The services sector at Bruno's camp was an extensive patch of cleared ground on which the camp Land Rovers were parked. On the edge of the clearing furthest from the *wazungu* camp was the fuel and engine oil supply contained in an array of forty-four gallon drums standing on top of a raised table-like platform of *panga*-cut logs and saplings. Also on the platform could be seen a line-up of green jerry cans plus a manual fuel pump ready for insertion into any drum of choice. Adjacent to the near side of the services sector the kitchen facilities, mess hut and camp store were erected, and near them a portable water tank was drawn up for convenience.

Jerry cans were always used to carry an extra supply of fuel and water in the Land Rovers whenever they went out of camp. One unmarked jerry can could look identical to any other unmarked jerry can, on the strength of which great care was needed to make sure of the nature of the contained liquid before it was poured into anything else. There were many incidences in camps around the country of diesel fuel being poured from a jerry can into the tanks of petrol-driven Land Rovers and vice versa, as well as of water being poured into the fuel tanks of both types of engine.

The portable water tank was mounted on two wheels and fitted in front with a socket device that linked to a ball joint fixed at the back of a Land Rover that allowed the tank to be pulled around in the manner of a trailer. A water tank was an essential item of equipment in any camp that for some reason couldn't be set up in close proximity to a water source.

The nerve centre for *wazungu*-oriented domestic arrangements was the kitchen, built from a framework of poles covered with a green tarpaulin that served as a roof. Otherwise the kitchen was open to the elements on all four of its sides. The fireplace on which food was cooked formed an all-important feature at the front of the kitchen, where it was well outside the range of influence of the fuel storage platform. Under cover of the tarpaulin, the cook's utensils and other tools and paraphernalia of his trade were stored in no apparent order. It was assumed that the cook knew what was what and where it was when he wanted it. The fireplace was a three feet high "U"-shaped construction of mud bricks within the arms of which the fire blazed away. A cast-iron grille covered the top above the fire, and on it the cook (*mpishi*) performed the never-ending task of turning out culinary delights for the *wazungu*. With four *wazungu* to cater for, Bruno's cook had to have a load-sharing assistant that he could boss around—a privilege he might also have sought but probably wouldn't have got in a two-*wazungu* camp.

Having a quality cook in camp was vital to the maintenance of morale. Much care was devoted to his selection since his skills (or lack of the same) would have to be lived with and the consequences of an error of judgement in his hiring could be too terrible to contemplate.

A good cook in camp meant that whatever kind of adversity assailed the working day there would always be hot water and a decent meal for the *wazungu* to look forward to when the day drew to a close. A good cook was an asset with a price far above rubies, or for that matter even above diamonds. The rule of engagement was that the quality of a cook was directly proportional to the circumference of his waistline. In the context of the time, a thin cook was as much a contradiction in terms as was an incorruptible politician.

The mess at Bruno's camp was, in the style of the kitchen, tarpaulin roofed over a rigid frame of bush cut poles. The sides of the mess were closed up with bundles of dry grass thatch tied on to the poles with strips of bark. A broad space left open for entry faced towards the kitchen. The internal furnishings of the mess consisted of a long folding table and a number of collapsible green canvas chairs of the kind that film directors used. In one corner a small paraffin-powered refrigerator purred and rattled as it fought to keep its load of a few perishable items and as many bottles of beer as could be crammed into it as cool as it could.

The *wazungu* tents were pitched to the rear of the mess, and at a suitable distance further back behind the tents the *choo* and shower facilities were located, the one to the left, the other to the right. The operational part of the shower was a semi-rigid waterproof canvas bag, open at one end and closed around a small tap-fitted showerhead at the other. The unit was suspended, showerhead down, by a rope slung over a stout bough on a convenient tree at an appropriate height and tied to the lower trunk of the tree within easy reach. Underfoot, directly beneath the suspended bag, a platform of thin bark-bound poles was laid down for anyone using the shower to stand on. For privacy, the arrangement was surrounded by a high *boma* of cut thorn bush.

Charging the shower was an established part of the evening routine for the cook's assistant. He lowered the canvas bag, filled it with water at the desired temperature and then hoisted it back into position again. The *mzungu* entered the *boma* equipped with a bar of soap and a towel, undressed, turned the showerhead tap to the on position and was in business until either he was clean or the supply of hot water came to an end, whichever happened first.

Soap was guarded zealously as the *watu* were adept at removing unattended bars of the same for their own use, especially if the soap had any vestige of perfume about it. Such brands of soap as Lifebuoy, Imperial Leather and "fabulous pink" Camay were considered by the *watu* to be prizes indeed. The *watu* were masters of lifting just about any small item that wasn't either tied up or nailed down. They usually devoted their attentions to items of little consequence, and I couldn't blame them for it.

The opportunity to enjoy an evening shower was also a benefit to the general wellbeing of camp that could not be overstated. No matter whether there was a lot or only a little hot water available, showering in the evening with dinner to follow was seen as a privilege that always set the events of the preceding day in positive perspective.

The *choo* at Bruno's camp was deep and noisome, constructed in full compliance with the advice provided by Mr Higgs in his *GFM* article. The encompassing *boma* pressed so hard in around the horizontal pole on which a user of the *choo* parked his posterior that, when he was seated, his face was separated from the *boma* by no distance at all.

On two separate occasions when I was elsewhere sitting in a *choo* of similar design I was induced to move my bowels rather quickly when a snake slid through the thorns of the *boma* a few inches in front of my very eyes. To paraphrase the great Oscar Wilde, once was carelessness, twice a misfortune.

The *choo* for the *watu* was normally located in the bush behind their tents. Inspecting that particular facility was a task that each *mzungu* in camp assumed was being done by someone other than himself. It was only necessary to consider Tank's paw paw season image to be deterred from visiting the *watu's choo*. There was always the MMBA for them to bare their backsides to of course.

Bruno's camp store was constructed of prefabricated metal sheets that formed into a *rondavel* shape when they were bolted together. The roof was then shaped like a shallow cone. The construction was fitted with a metal door equipped with a lock. It was simple but effective and was capable of being erected in no more than an hour and dismantled in half that time.

Inside the store for safe keeping were recently taken samples reduced in volume by panning. They were packed and labelled in secure Kraft paper envelopes and ready for transport to Mwadui at the earliest opportunity, on which journey they would be accompanied by relevant location maps, records and reports. Once received and registered at Mwadui, the samples would be securely boxed up for despatch by air for their short hop to Nairobi and long onward connection to Johannesburg, where analytical technicians were waiting to receive them. The work of these technicians would determine whether or not follow-up detailed work was called for; however, a lot of figurative water would flow under a lot of equally figurative bridges before that actually happened.

The store also contained neat stacks of bulging gunnysacks containing prescribed non-perishable elements for the daily and weekly rations issue to the *watu*, with *posho* being in the ascendancy.

Fresh meat was never stored—it was portioned out immediately after it arrived in camp, whether or not it came from town or was shot by courtesy of a general game licence. It was up to the *watu* what they then did with their meat. The stipulation governing the butchering of the meat was that it must be in accord with the dictates of Islam. In order to be consumed by Muslim employees, the meat needed to have been properly *halalled* by someone qualified to perform the task.

Meat obtained in towns was always purchased from a Muslim butcher, on which basis it was assumed that the *halal* formalities had been carried out to the letter. Where shooting for the pot was concerned, it was necessary to have an appointed Muslim from among the *watu* make a fast run up to the kill (unless the kill was a warthog) in order to cut its throat, spill blood and perform the *halal* rites before the final spark of life was extinguished. It was a tall order, and it called for a lot more religious faith than I possessed to accept that it was always done correctly.

For a camp located outside the tsetse country, domestic cattle on the hoof could be purchased and ritually slaughtered to suit the culinary satisfaction of Muslims and infidels alike. I found the slaughtering to be a bloody process best not witnessed too often.

Each item of statutory rations was weighed individually for the *mtu* who was about to receive it in accordance with regulations, and meticulous records of issued rations were maintained. In spite of this it seemed that the *watu* were never truly thankful for what they were about to receive. They sometimes augmented their diet by foraging in the bush, coming up once in a while with windfalls such as wild honey; various species of wet season greenery known collectively as "spinach" or *mchicha*; estivating catfish; salvageable carrion from creatures abandoned by the predators that killed them and rescued by beating off the attentions of vultures; and once in my experience some absolutely gigantic mushrooms a couple of feet across which had exploded through the carapace of a large termite hill deep inside which the termites' fungus gardens had gone berserk.

6
Ndani na nje ya kambi
In and out of camp

Looking across the kitchen from the front of the mess at Bruno's camp, a number of small and rather shabby green canvas tents, although partly screened by the bush, could be observed in the middle distance. These were the *watu's* tents, set up around the perimeter of a clearing in the centre of which a communal fire smoked freely.

There were a dozen or more of these tents in the arrangement, each tent accommodating up to four *watu*. The tents were not fitted with flysheets. A single layer of canvas kept the weather out. Some well-patched stretches of the said canvas did not look to be particularly waterproof, as the approaching wet season would no doubt demonstrate. However, internal groundsheets were made available to the *watu* along with their standard blanket issue, thereby giving them due cause to be thankful for small mercies.

The *watu* put together items of furniture for their camp as only they knew how, utilising both bush and boulders to cobble together chairs, tables, and the containing structure of the fireplace associated with ingeniously arranged tripods and racks for cooking their rations.

Music was a life-enhancing essential within the radius of influence of the jolly flames of the *watu* camp fire after dark and was generally manifested in percussive rhythms beaten out on a homemade hide drum, or on an empty *debe* or a jerry can. It all depended on what was available at the time. The drumming was accompanied by closely harmonious vocal chants and counter chants. To add variety a tune might also be teased out of an instrument made from a small wooden box (of the kind that might once have contained cigars) fitted on top with a bristling fan composed of varied lengths of flattened bicycle spokes. The box was held in the hands and the spokes were plucked with the thumbs to produce notes that were hauntingly atmospheric.

It was exceptional to come across a non-smoker among the *watu*, irrespective of each one's religious orientation. A large stock of cigarettes was held in the store hut for doling packets out at a subsidised cost to craving smokers when they came for their issue of rations. There were two distinctive brands of cigarette held ready for disposal. Both brands, respectively named *Nyota* and "Crown Bird", were well-known standards of East African manufacture.

The "Crown Bird" brand was named after the national avian symbol of Tanganyika, the crowned crane. Such birds were often spotted standing in an attitude of tall and elegant aloofness, usually at a distance. A picture of a crowned crane appeared on the front of the cigarette packet that took its name. The popular name for "Crown Bird" cigarettes was *Ndege*, which was the Kiswahili word for a winged creature (including an aeroplane but excluding a bat).

In the unlikely event that cigarette quality should ever merit discussion, discerning *watu* reckoned that *Ndege* cigarettes were superior to those that went under the *Nyota* trademark. In spite of that, most *watu* preferred the latter, probably because they were cheaper.

Nyota translated as "star" in Kiswahili, and its packets did indeed feature a black star (and accompanying crescent) set against a biliously green background. The familiar name for the *Nyota* brand of cigarettes, however, was *Kali*, in which regard the unerring aim of the *watu* in hitting targets in compliance with vital characteristics had struck home once again. *Kali* was a word that had multiple meanings based on savagery according to the context in which it was used; among its connotations, fierce, angry, pungent, sharp and aggressive were not inapplicable to *Kali* cigarettes. The smell, and supposedly the flavour, of *Kali* cigarettes was thereby summed up in a single word.

As to the existence of alcohol in camp, in principle there was a "dry" camp policy that in practice was strictly ignored. The refrigerator in the *wazungu* mess was normally well stocked with bottles of IPA, occasional bottles of which were liberated by the *watu* when the *wazungu* weren't around.

According to WDL management, camp refrigerators were provided for the express purpose of protecting items of perishable food and were not intended for keeping beer cool. All that those of us who worked out in the bush could do was wish good luck to anyone back at Mwadui who was misguided enough to believe this.

As a rule, the *watu* preferred to drink locally brewed varieties of beer (*pombe*) when they could get it, as was normally the case when a village lay within walking distance of camp. Using fermented maize, *pombe* was brewed by village women. It was a grey and glutinous gruel that its fanciers liked to imbibe by the gallon. Downing a full *debe* of *pombe* posed no challenge at all to such *watu*.

I neither sampled local *pombe* nor regretted not sampling it. The penetratingly sour smell that enveloped any *mtu* who partook of a skinful of *pombe* on the previous night persisted like an almost solid aura through most of the following day.

The South Africans referred to local *pombe* as "*kaffir beer*"—in fact an *mtu* who told me that his name was Kaffir Beer turned up one day at one of my camps looking for work. Basic local *pombe* was sometimes enlivened (after which its name was transformed to *skokiaan*) by the inclusion in the brew of items such as strips of raw meat, fiery chillies, and (in a story I was told that might or might not have been true) dead rats and a handful of calcium carbide granules of the kind used in conjunction with a little water to power acetylene lamps.

The quantities of local *pombe* consumed in and around the *watu* camp were directly proportional to the intensity of the beat of nighttime drums and the actual number of drums involved. Local *pombe* created the kind of raucous laughter in the *watu* that a hyena might have envied; promoted the violent settlement of old scores; and gave rise to more familiarity than was desirable when *wazungu* and *watu* met in their cups.

There were no boy scouts in the *watu* camp.

On one occasion I was offered a drink poured from a bottle of locally distilled spirit, a gin-clear liquor named *moshi* (meaning "smoke"). *Moshi* could equally have been named liquid *kali*. One sip provided the kind of kick that a dinner-plate sized hoof of a giraffe at full lope would deliver. The smoke-infested aftertaste that assaulted the palate following a slug of *moshi* was a cruel and unusual punishment to be avoided for ever and ever and Amen to that.

*

In sharp contrast to the *watu's* tent accommodation, an *mzungu* tent accommodated only one person within its ample spread of stiff green canvas. A typical example of an *mzungu* inner tent, as seen at Bruno's camp, stood approximately six feet high at its apex and commanded a floor area with dimensions of about twelve feet by seven feet. The inner tent was set up beneath a tightly drawn and pegged-down all-embracing canvas flysheet. The flysheet projected some six feet in front of the tent's entry flap to provide an area of shade and shelter in which the *mzungu* could sit at a small folding table on his director's-type chair and work at his sampling records, his reporting and his reading.

The flysheet held off both the sun and the rain, and the interstitial gap between it and the inner tent canvas permitted a free through passage of breezes to both cool and ventilate.

Adjacent to the front pole supporting the flysheet, a canvas washbasin on collapsible scissor legs stood ready for use. A number of hooks screwed into the pole at appropriate heights facilitated, *inter alia*, the placement of a receptacle containing a sliver of soap; the hanging of a towel; the positioning of a small mirror; and the suspension of a Tilley lamp designed to hold back the night and attract incoming insects.

A Tilley lamp was powered by methylated spirits and looked something like a streamlined version of a good old hurricane lamp crossed with a primus. I always found hurricane lamps more reliable than Tilley lamps, but the march of progress was not to be trifled with. The base of a Tilley lamp was a fuel chamber that could be pressurised by manipulating a built-in plunger-like pump. Once the pressure was pumped high enough, the fuel outlet could be opened to allow vaporised fuel to rush to a meshed element and be brought to a hissing luminescence following ignition.

Bright light was then cast over a wide circle of influence, into which the insects zoomed as if they were *haj* pilgrims heading for Mecca. Homing insects caused particular aggravation in the early days of the wet season—enough could arrive to bury a Tilley lamp under a heaving mass of grub-like bodies and fluttering wings.

The items of furniture inside an *mzungu's* tent were, given the restricted space, few in number. A large tin trunk (of a type that I would eventually discover was not always termite-proof) was placed where it fitted best, usually at the back of the tent. In it were stored the *mzungu's* personal effects. A smaller tin trunk (more of a tin box really), which was much less secure in appearance than its bigger counterpart, stood just inside the front entry of the tent. It contained stationery, sample ticket books, reporting forms, files, and rules and regulations missives sent out by WDL.

A bed was erected alongside one of the tent's inner walls. The standard issue bed was of a type known as "Hounsfield". It could be assembled or dissembled by an expert in almost no time flat. The elements of a Hounsfield bed were: a sheet of canvas (brown for a change) with approximate dimensions of three feet by six feet and fitted with wide loops on the outer edges of its long axis; a set of thin yet tough steel rods that were linked with hard plastic sockets so as to make a rigid frame when threaded through the canvas loops; and three open "W"-shaped transverse "legs" of sprung steel that were inserted into the rod assembly sockets to both mount and stretch the canvas sheet tight.

Thus prepared, a Hounsfield bed, which on its legs stood only a few inches above the groundsheet, was able to support a considerable weight—which was just as well for ensuring the quality of repose of some of WDL's Afrikaans-speaking Field Officers.

The bedding issue for a Hounsfield bed consisted of an appropriately sized thin mattress plus three blankets, four sheets, four pillowcases and two pillows. Other than the standard mattress, the bedding could normally be selected for quality and quantity according to personal preference. We could live in the bush in as rough a manner as we wanted to, but most of us (and not least myself) believed in living rough only if or when there was absolutely no other alternative to doing so. An assembled Hounsfield bed replete with bedding was tastefully draped with a securely tucked in finely meshed mosquito net suspended from the apex of the tent. All was then reckoned to be ready for the ease of its intended occupant.

Every Hounsfield bed that I had the fortune to sleep on was extremely comfortable. I slept so much better on a Hounsfield bed than I ever did in any hotel bed around the country. One of the benefits of returning to camp after a visit to town came from my being able to get back into my Hounsfield bed again.

The beauty of a Hounsfield bed was that it was both light and easily portable—a sentiment that was hopefully shared by the *mtu* doing the porter's duty. The bed and bedding could be taken on extended foot sampling traverses through bush where Land Rover access was impracticable and on which the traverse team might be away from the main camp for several days. On such trips we spent the nights in what were known as "fly" camps—set up wherever we happened to be when daylight faded and a riverbed in which a water hole could be dug was available nearby.

An almost miraculous consequence of digging a hole in a riverbed to expose water was the gradual appearance of what went on to eventually become large numbers of butterflies. They settled to drink all around the perimeter of the water. The close association of butterflies with the existence of water in the bush was taken to offer a cast-iron guarantee that if butterflies were seen then water was unlikely to be far away. The link between the two must so often have saved the day for thirst-wracked travellers.

The Kiswahili word for butterfly was *kipepeo*. Tom came along one day and announced it to me. He said that he planned was to learn a new Kiswahili word every day and, as it happened, his word for that particular day was *kipepeo*.

Wazungu who chose to travel light when out on extended sampling safaris took no bed and only minimal bedding along with them. They slept on the ground beneath a canopy of stars. That kind of practice was not for me, however. Although I was conscious of imposing on the *watu* in their role as porters, my Hounsfield bed with mattress, a blanket, a mosquito net, and sometimes even a light tarpaulin sheet to spread over the eventual assembly in the fly camp always went wherever I went.

The mosquito net gave me a feeling of security in the night that I would not otherwise have had. Its flimsy presence stood like a solid wall between me on the Hounsfield bed and whatever nocturnal marauder was out there on the other side of the net. The roaring of lions (*simbas*) in the night eventually became familiar enough for it to pass without comment. The roaring was taken for granted until it began to appear that it was advancing in our direction.

I never had the experience of a lion getting uncomfortably close to either a fly camp or an established camp that I was in. Where established camps were concerned, lions naturally seemed inclined to give them a wide berth. However, one night a leopard (*chui*) came by and wandered in between the flysheet and the canvas wall of my tent. The leopard brushed along the canvas immediately adjacent to the side of my bed, mere inches away from me. It stopped for a moment at the rear of my tent to cough once or twice and then went on its way in search of better game.

I heard on good authority that no game animal, big or small, would be likely either to damage a tent or to violate the sanctity of a mosquito net. When they came along the essential thing to do was not to alarm them. A hippo (*kiboko*) or a rhino (*kifaru*) or a buffalo (*nyati*) would take no prisoners if alarmed into making a rapid beeline out of or through a camp.

I knew from personal experience that an elephant (*tembo*) was adept at picking its way over the stretched guy ropes of a tent with so much delicacy that it didn't impart as much as a shiver to the flysheet. I heard the great feet settling on the ground, and from above me at tent peak level came the sound of rumbling and gurgling as the elephant's stomach digested the foliage of what might have been as much as half a tree. On the morning after, I found a mound of fresh elephant dung left outside the front of my tent as if it was a gift of passage.

Tiny creatures entered my tent frequently at night. I could hear them scuttling and scratching on the groundsheet. I neither knew nor wanted to know what they were. One of them gnawed all the way through the left heel of my pair of *velskoon*. The gnawing seemed never ending. I wasn't brave enough to rise up and chase the rodent away for fear of it turning its attention to me.

The main danger for anyone sleeping in the bush while exposed under the open heavens was, as recounted by very many hotel bar *habitués*, an intrusive hyena (*fisi*). Hyenas wandered far and wide at night and were apt to snatch a bite at any tasty piece of flesh, living or dead, that presented itself to their powerful bone-cracking jaws. The hand or foot of a sleeping *mtu* or *mzungu* (hyenas didn't discriminate) could be easily removed in a single snap.

The horror of horrors lay in the legendary reputation of hyenas for scooping up the faces of sleepers in their jaws. I met people who claimed to have seen such face-stripped victims and was happy to take them at their word. Whatever the truth of the matter, the legend provided enough motivation for me to sleep under the cover of a mosquito net no matter what.

A WDL Field Officer named Bill Campbell-Whalley (who was known as Campbell) told a tale of an incident that occurred when he was fly camping at a bush location known as *Simba Nguru*, which translated as "the lion fish" or perhaps "the lion that fishes". As Campbell was one who travelled light, he stretched out on the ground to sleep with no more than a blanket and the stars for cover. That the location was not misnamed was ably demonstrated when a lion strolled through the fly camp, walked around Campbell's blanketed form a couple of times, reached out a front paw to prod him once, sniffed and licked (or rather rasped) his face and ambled away into the night again. A mosquito net over Campbell would have disadvantaged the lion, but that was not Campbell's way at all.

Campbell grew up in a house back in the UK that was once the property of Mr John Hanning Speke, the true discoverer of the source of the White Nile (notwithstanding that the expedition's leader, Mr Richard Burton, rather shamefully attempted to take most of the credit for the discovery). Burton and Speke didn't revel in one another's company in camp to the extent that they could well have exemplified the not uncommonly acrimonious relationships of many camp-sharing *wazungu* on the trail of diamonds.

A close identification with the spirit that drove Speke led Campbell to follow in the former's footsteps. Campbell spoke in the manner of one who was born to be a leader of men. His way was very much that of a man who (euphemistically) did not suffer fools gladly.

Since I had no problem in presenting myself to Campbell as a fool who should not be suffered gladly, I found him to be both impressive and slightly intimidating at the same time. Campbell undertook a roving brief around the area in which I worked under Tom's leadership, which meant that our personal contacts were fairly sporadic, taking place normally when our respective supply visits to Dodoma coincided.

During lunch in the dining-room of the Dodoma Hotel I once watched Campbell browbeat a waiter by demanding (in loud tones that were very much playing to the crowd) to be brought a copy of the current menu. A typed sheet of paper that masqueraded under the name of menu was brought to Campbell post haste. He appeared to study it in detail for a while before summoning the waiter once more. With the anxious waiter alongside him, Campbell pointed at both the menu and a small bug that was crawling on the edge of his plate and snapped at the waiter, over and over again, *"Anaandika dudu wapi?"* (Where is insect written?)

I didn't know how the waiter took the complaint. As for me, in the words of Mr Jimmy Durante, "I was mortified!" I wished I could have sympathised to the waiter in similar words but as was usual in Tanganyika it was always the *mzungu* who was right, and siding with an *mtu* against an *mzungu* was something an *mzungu* was never supposed to do.

When driving his Land Rover one day, Campbell ran over a bicycle belonging to an Indian resident of Dodoma and refused to accept responsibility for the accident on the grounds of the owner's carelessness in leaving his bicycle in the wrong place at the wrong time. The Indian owner of the bicycle was not of the same opinion, however, and even though he was up against the word of an *mzungu*, which by definition was vested with total integrity, he went ahead in pressing a claim for compensation. He came up to me one day when I was standing beside my Land Rover outside an Arab trader's warehouse in Dodoma town centre waiting for a number of gunnysacks of *posho* to be loaded.

I wasn't aware of the details of the situation regarding the accident to his bike, but he explained it to me, and as far as I was concerned compensation for his loss was something that a company like WDL ought to carry out in good heart. I said I would take my opinion back to Campbell, who was at the time with Tom over at the Dodoma Hotel.

I was in the process of joining Tom and Campbell in the hotel bar when I noticed that the Indian, who was clearly striking while the iron was hot, had preceded me and was in the act of addressing Campbell who looked as incandescent as a Tilley lamp element. As I reached them it was to find the Indian telling Campbell that I had agreed to process his compensation claim.

Campbell turned the force of his anger on to me. "Did you do that?" he kept shouting at me. I would have been happy to have had the ground open up and swallow me. I was totally cowed and could only think of how I might best throw in the towel. I tried to say well no, I hadn't exactly done that. Whereupon the Indian said nothing, but looked at me through the knowing eyes of one who was well used to the ways of perfidious Albion. He turned on his heel, and slowly walked away from us.

It was a moment that shamed us all. Campbell's declared ambition was to become a Ranger in the Game Department. I could easily imagine that game would fare much better at his hands than some people did, and I could envisage great success for him.

*

It was in Bruno's camp that I obtained my first sight, by virtue of glancing through the open front sheet of Bruno's tent, of one of WDL's illustrious cashboxes. In accordance with regulations the cashbox was attached to a tent pole by a securely padlocked chain.

As described previously, each *mtu* was paid what he was due on completion of his current thirty-day *kipandi*. I learned about the valiant attempts that were being made to streamline the schedule of payment so as to have as many *vipandi* as possible finishing on the same date. The large number of *watu* made it even more complicated. The anomaly was that a *kipandi* commenced on the date when the *mtu* was hired and was not tied to a monthly calendar. As a consequence, the payment of due wages had become something of a masterpiece of erratic disorganisation. This meant that a camp cashbox almost always had to contain a fair amount of hard cash ready for *ad hoc* wage settlements, purchase of supplies and rations, dealing with contingencies, and the availability of petty cash. Not only that, but the cashbox was often used as a combined bank and safe deposit facility for *watu* who handed some of their pay back to the Senior Geologist in charge for safe keeping in the cashbox against withdrawal at a later date. Certain personal documents and items of registered mail might also be held in the cashbox for them in the same way.

Each and every *mtu* was well aware of the near inevitability that the fate of any money in his possession was to be given away, lost or stolen in short order. It was a dictate of human nature in camp that an *mtu* whose money was stolen would probably go and steal the same amount from another *mtu*. An *mtu* known to be "in the money" would at once be certain to attract the attention of other members of his tribe who would put him under great pressure to be in the money no longer. He would have to wait his turn for the same tribal bonds to work similarly in his favour.

It was probable that no *mzungu* could or ever would understand just what it was that cemented together the members of a tribe. Perhaps John Donne came near to hitting the nail on the head when meditating on the subject of no man being an island, entire of itself. A tribe seemed to me to function as a collection of individuals formed into a single social entity, not entirely unlike the way of a termite colony.

WDL, as I knew, looked on cashbox banking for the *watu* with displeasure, although stopped short of banning it outright. My view was that anything that kept the *watu* happy in the bush could never be a bad thing. When I was given responsibility for a camp cashbox I had no hesitation in being the banker to the *watu* right up to the day on which I was given good reason to wish that I had toed the WDL line.

An *mtu* who was unable to write confirmed receiving his pay by means of a thumbprint. He normally dabbed the ball of his right thumb on an inkpad provided for that purpose. If the inkpad wasn't available for use (inkpads tended to dry out quite rapidly) then the fallback practice involved the *mzungu* scribbling on the ball of the *mtu's* thumb with a ballpoint pen and making the print on that basis. The nature of whatever was deeply engrained in some thumbs inevitably caused the biro to fail to write conventionally for some little time afterwards.

With the introduction of a little smudging and smearing, and in the full realisation that the average *mtu* thumb ball was so calloused and scarred that ridges and whorls were meaningless, it really didn't matter whose thumb was stuck down on paper for receipt of pay as long as the hand that the pay went into was the correct one.

It didn't take some *wazungu* very long to recognise the advantages of a system in which money could be issued on the basis of no more than an indeterminate thumbprint. In a few of the camps that held a big workforce it was rumoured that quite a number of illiterate ghost *watu* were on the payroll with dreamt-up names, allocated tribal fealties and thumbs that didn't originate in Tanganyika. The best that could be said about this type of nefarious practice was that it was (probably) not widespread. There were in any case much more lucrative scams than that one open to attract the interest of the discerning *mzungu*.

*

As well as the issue of pay, I was able to observe how a Senior Geologist like Bruno was required to provide medicine on demand to the *watu*. The nature of the demand for medicine could best be described as frequent—although where getting sick was concerned there was never a schedule to follow.

The generic Kiswahili word for medicine was *dawa*. The request worn thin by repetition was *"Ninataka dawa!"* (I want medicine!) A medicine chest containing some basic remedies was kept in camp for the purpose of treating minor ailments and common complaints only. In a case of serious affliction a patient needed to be taken to the nearest rural clinic or otherwise to a hospital in town.

On the basis of WDL's cumulative experience of administering medicine to *watu* engaged in exploration in the bush, that indispensable authority that was the *GFM* offered its readers a list of the twelve commonest ailments encountered, together with some additional advice on their treatment.

In order of the likely frequency of occurrence, here they are:

(1) TROPICAL ULCER (*kidonda*) Tropical ulcers were characterised by a circular sore surrounded by a raised rim of inflamed flesh, almost invariably found on the legs. They were likely to occur most commonly towards the end of the dry season and were caused by a vitamin deficiency due to the lack of fresh fruit and vegetables. Treatment with boracic acid powder covered with a dry dressing was recommended. Wet dressings and ointments were to be avoided. Since minor cuts and scratches often gave rise to tropical ulcers, care had to be taken to always disinfect such small wounds at the time of injury.

(2) HEADACHE (*kichwa nauma*) Headache was a symptom of several ailments, which included malaria. In circumstances in which a headache was not accompanied with chills and fever, it needed to be treated with one Aspirin tablet.

(3) MALARIA (*homa*) Despite the *watu* having acquired a certain amount of natural immunity, the incidence of malaria was common among them. Typical symptoms were chills (*baridi*); fever (*homa*); aches and pains; and a painfully swollen spleen. The recommended treatment was a course of one Totaquine tablet taken every four hours. In the event that the patient did not respond to treatment within three days he was required to be taken to the nearest hospital or clinic. The *watu* were not to be given anti-malarial prophylactics such as Camoquin or quinine as these tended to destroy natural immunity.

(4) CONSTIPATION (*tumbo nauma fungua*) In the event that an *mtu*

complained of *tumbo nauma*, he had to be asked if he needed to open (*fungua*) or close (*funga*) his bowels. The most commonly used remedy for opening the bowels was a solution of magnesium sulphate solution and castor oil, obtainable from any mission dispensary and given twice per day as one tablespoonful to a cup of water.

(5) Diarrhoea and dysentery (*tumbo nauma funga*) The recommended treatment for diarrhoea was one tablespoonful of kaolin taken in a cup of water twice daily. In the case of dysentery, involving blood (*damu*) in the stool, Thalazol pills were to be given. It had to be ensured that the patient always used a covered *choo* (and not the MMBA) to void his bowels into.

(6) Scabies (*upele*) The small skin sores associated with scabies caused considerable itching and discomfort. They could be appropriately treated with sulphur ointment. The affected area was first softened by scrubbing with soap prior to applying ointment and then not washed or made wet again until the ointment had had the time to take effect. Two or three such applications might be necessary. The patient's clothes were to be immersed in boiling water.

(7) Cough, cold, sore throat, and influenza (*kohoa*) These were to be regarded much more seriously in the case of *watu* than they were for *wazungu*. *Watu* could easily be vulnerable to pneumonia following on a heavy cold, and this was particularly so where the very young and the elderly were concerned. Typical symptoms of pneumonia were fever, problems with breathing and pains in the chest. When present such symptoms required a patient to be taken to hospital immediately. If a cold appeared simple, Aspirin and cough medicine were to be given as a remedy. Pains in the throat, laryngitis, pharyngitis and swollen tonsils were to be treated with sulpha pills as directed.

(8) Conjunctivitis (*macho nauma*) Red and inflamed eyes were frequently complained about. Eyewash and eye drops were readily available from most local shops and could be used to treat most such cases. However, any foreign object embedded in an eyeball could *under no circumstances* be meddled with in the bush, and the patient had to be taken at once to the nearest dispensary or hospital.

(9) Venereal Diseases—gonorrhea (*kisonono*) and syphilis (*tego*) If an *mtu* complained of open running sores, painful urination and mysterious aches and pains, he was likely to be suffering from

some kind of VD. No *mtu* ever admitted to contracting VD directly but normally elected to advise that he was sick (*magonjwa*) and wanted to have an injection (*sindano*). He needed to be sent to the nearest clinic for treatment. In some camps the practice was to deduct the costs of VD treatment from the wages of the person involved on the grounds that VD was not *shauri ya kampuni!* (the fault of the company!)

(10) EARACHE (*masikia nauma*) *Watu* working in open, windy areas often complained of earache. The pain could be relieved by treatment with Aspirin. If pus was issuing from the ear, or in other circumstances in which the pain did not ease within a day, a patient would again be sent to a clinic or hospital.

(11) WORMS (*wasusu ya tumbo*) When *watu* complained of bugs (*wadudu*) in the stomach they were best sent to a clinic for treatment. There were so many types of stomach worms that it was pointless to try to stock medicines for them in camp.

(12) BILHARZIA (*kichocho*) Bilharzia occurred only in specific areas and was caused by drinking or bathing in shallow, stagnant water containing the causative organism. With care exercised in recognising these conditions, any incidence of bilharzia could be prevented. If an *mtu* complained of blood in his urine he had to be sent to a hospital to be examined. Should the tests prove positive for bilharzia the treatment required a series of twelve to fourteen injections over a three-week to one-month period. It was mandatory for the patient to commit to the complete course of treatment. If he refused to commit he would be discharged.

In the light of this list of tropical diseases there was obviously more than enough to worry about in terms of maintaining a decent level of general health in camp. The list concluded on a positive note, however, by offering the sage advice that it was not only humane but also good business to observe all the necessary precautions to ensure that the *watu* were kept in the best possible state of health. A happy and healthy *mtu* would, it was advised, work far more efficiently and be much easier to get along with than a sick *mtu*.

If there was a religious mission clinic within reasonable reach of camp, it was recommended that a camp account should be opened there, with payment for services rendered and medicine provided being made on a monthly basis so as to avoid the need for making frequent small payments. Mission clinics were run on strictly commercial terms—government-run clinics didn't charge for standard referrals of minor complaints but were a lot less efficient than their mission counterparts.

According to the *GFM*, WDL *watu* referred to hospital were required to be supplied with their rations for the duration of their treatment. Nevertheless, in what was a mean-spirited rule best ignored, it was not obligatory to pay an *mtu* for any days on which he was sick provided that it could be shown that the cause of his sickness was not work-related. The lack of sympathy accorded to VD sufferers in the pages of the *GFM* suggested that the authors of the rather worrying list of the twelve common ailments and diseases could have shown a little more generosity of spirit. On the other hand they might have lacked experience in the ways of the world. Of course, the exact opposite could equally have been true.

The *GFM* followed up the listing with a few generalised suggestions, commencing with the observation that Sloan's Liniment (or an equivalent) could be a handy general cure for miscellaneous aches and pains.

In my eventual experience of treating allegedly sick *watu* in the bush with the contents of a not very comprehensively stocked camp medicine chest, never a day passed without at least a couple of *watu* coming along to me with a request for *dawa*. It was recommended that a specific time of day should be fixed in camp for the issue of medicine. Emergency cases had to be dealt with as and when they occurred, notwithstanding that, as far as *watu* thinking went, any situation requiring medicine to be issued was a personal emergency.

Symptoms complained about were legion, although fortunately mostly of a minor sort. The *watu* placed an enormous amount of faith in the curative powers of *wazungu* medicine. Indeed, their faith was greater than mine, and as often as not it made them whole. Aspirin was reckoned by them to be no more or no less than a miracle drug. As far as minor complaints and a pain here and there were concerned *wazungu* medicine worked to bring relief to the *watu* almost every time. They had faith in patent medicines being panaceas for all ills. It didn't seem to matter to them what kind of pills it was that they were taking—the pills did them good because they knew they would.

For a period of a couple of weeks the medicine chest in one of my camps contained only a large bottle of cough mixture. I used a spoonful of it to treat every patient that came along to me complaining of aches and pains, and I dripped it onto cuts, bruises and grazes. The cough mixture became a virtual elixir of life with its power of suggestion bringing satisfaction to all my patients.

Any *mtu* was of course either blessed or cursed, depending on his point of view, with traditional medicinal practices to fall back on if the supply of *wazungu dawa* ran out. However, most *watu* were quite reluctant to entrust their care to local medical practitioners. The latter were known as *wachawi*, which when translated became "witch doctors". A witch doctor (*mchawi*) could be a genuine force for good, although the reputation of the witch doctoring profession was vested more on the dark side of the long art of medicine. An *mtu* who consulted a witch doctor was reckoned to be less interested in improving his own health than he was in having the witch doctor make something unpleasant happen to a third party.

When all else failed the fallback classic medicinal remedy to bring relief was what was known as a *mafaa* pill. *Mafaa* translated as "utility" or "general purpose". Pills made under that name were sold on an individual basis all over Tanganyika. A *mafaa* pill looked like a giant gob-stopper. It was big, round, red and shiny and supposedly capable of healing or curing just about any medical complaint imaginable.

It would not have surprised me to learn that a witch doctor had been involved at some stage along the line that led to the generation of *mafaa* pills. Since these pills did their best to approximate the size of golf balls, a zebra would have been hard pressed to swallow one, let alone an *mtu*. Yet, whenever a supply of *mafaa* pills was brought into camp, the demand for them always exceeded the supply.

*

Among the most important items in a camp's inventory of medicinal remedies were snakebite kits. Each *mzungu* was issued with one, and received instructions (that were more or less comprehensive) on its use. The principal strength of a snakebite kit lay in the knowledge that it was ready for use if necessary. Neatly contained in its own tin, a snakebite kit was an essential accessory that went along with the team on every sampling traverse.

The elements of a snakebite kit were two sealed glass vials of antivenom serum; a hypodermic syringe and a supply of needles for the same; a strip of rubber to be used as a tourniquet; a razor blade; and a small rubber suction cup. It was claimed by some that the razor blade was there to permit a victim of snakebite to cut his throat once all other measures had failed.

Although I knew all about the way the snakebite kit ought to work, I never found out how effective the anti-venom serum might be in counteracting the effects of snakebite since fortunately I never had cause to use it or see it used. It was probably a fact that all over the country long-unused snakebite kits contained serum that was too far out of date to be effective. The snakebite kit was carried as a matter of both assurance and insurance, but no one would know how worthwhile it was until a snake actually bit someone and prompted its use.

In Kiswahili the word for snake was *nyoka*. All species of the same were no more anxious to make direct contact with us than we were to come across them. It was inevitable, however, that our respective paths would cross, and when they did the encounter almost always resulted in the death of the *nyoka* at the hands of the *watu*. It was exceptionally rare for vice versa to apply. No matter that the majority of the species of snake were utterly harmless to man, to the *watu* a *nyoka* was a *nyoka* was a *nyoka* and no chances were taken.

It was fortunate all round that the sighting of a snake was so uncommon. Snakes tended to make themselves scarce by taking appropriate evasive action once they picked up the ground vibrations of creatures approaching them on either two or four feet. It was only the more sluggish of the venomous snakes like the puff adder that we really needed to worry about. Such snakes held on to their position on the ground and were so well camouflaged that they were hardly ever noticed unless trodden on.

The first problem to be solved in the event of snakebite was what species of snake it was that did the biting. The person unlucky enough to be bitten would normally have his mind focused on matters other than species identification. Witnesses to the incident would be unlikely to help much beyond confirming that the bite was delivered by a *nyoka*.

The venom of some species of snake attacked the blood of the person bitten, whereas the venom from others acted on the nervous system. Of the two vials of serum in the snakebite kit one contained an antidote for haemotoxic venom and the other for neurotoxic venom. Injection of the wrong type of serum to match the species in question could have fatal consequences, provided that the venom itself hadn't already done that job.

When a team went out on a sampling traverse, a procession of its members in single file was preferred. The most expendable member of the team, who in the case of my team was me, led the way. Opinion was divided on which one among us would attract the first bite if our traverse line took us to a venomous snake. Some thought it would be whoever was in the lead, while others believed that the third in line was in the position of ultimate danger since it would need the passage of the first two to annoy the snake enough to induce it to take a bite.

Being bitten by a snake was neither the victim's nor the snake's fault. It was a matter of *shauri ya Mungu* and *bahati mbaya* (bad luck) rolled up together.

*

Nimmo and I left Bruno's camp for our return to Mwadui in the heat of the afternoon. Dust devils flitted hither and thither through the scanty bush to the north of Tabora (in which fair town Nimmo once again didn't stop) as we drove through.

Most of the dust devils that we saw were small. They were mere eddies accompanying the occasional thousand-foot-high giants that blasted across open land in whirling columns of sand, dust and scraps of dead vegetation. The great dust devils were avoidable with all due care taken, although sometimes they changed course on what seemed to be a sudden whim and caught travellers napping.

A tale was told of an *mtu* who was taken up in the vortex of a towering dust devil and impaled with a multitude of acacia thorns prior to being dumped on one side as the dust devil moved on. That may have been no more than a cautionary fable, but I did once see a Land Rover thrown onto its side in an encounter with a dust devil, an experience which taught me that *kali* was too kind a word to apply to dust devils in full flight.

The short stay in Bruno's camp that Nimmo and I had enjoyed (I assumed that Nimmo was also happy with it) made a wonderful learning experience for me. I knew that I had absorbed no more than a few rudiments of what was likely to be required of me when I joined Tom at his camp, but it had made a very good foundation for me to build on.

7
Habari za uvumbuzi?
How goes the exploration?

Having learned a little about what I might expect in terms of camp life and its supporting facilities when I joined up with Tom, I naturally went on to try to develop a more detailed understanding of the type of work I would be carrying out. I didn't imagine that Tom's camp was likely to be cast in the exact image of what I had seen during my visit to Bruno's set-up but assumed that there would be enough in common between the two for me to adapt constructively to any differences. A similar appreciation involving common ground principles could also, I thought, be profitably applied to my relationships with the various peoples of Tanganyika that I would meet.

WDL's nationwide campaign of exploration was executed on a platform of meticulous planning. That was what Jack told me when I was with him in Mwadui so it must have been true.

The regions designated for exploration were blocked out on a large-scale master plan. Each region was subdivided into a number of sectors ranked in terms of priority for attention. Sectors were individually assigned to Senior Geologists who were charged with forming teams of both *wazungu* and *watu* and planning for and executing an appropriate exploration programme. The overall size of the team was dependent on the extent of the sector to be explored and the quality of the existing infrastructure.

According to the *GFM*, the maps available for organising and controlling the exploration work in the bush were both imprecise and not necessarily all drawn up to an identical scale. The most comprehensive mapping coverage of Tanganyika at the time consisted of one set of 1:1,000,000 scale sheets and a second set of 1:500,000 scale sheets. The latter was commonly referred to as the "Military Series". A wealth of history lay in that particular title.

A fair amount of detailed surveying to produce maps supported by aerial photography had been carried out in some regions of the country, but even so, it was reckoned that the Military sheets were to be preferred. However, the *GFM* made it plain that use of the Military sheets was to be regarded as a last resort. Irrespective of any obvious inaccuracies they might contain, maps based on aerial photography were mandated by WDL to be used in the camps for plotting the location of reconnaissance samples.

We were assured that every effort was being devoted to the compilation of reliable mosaics, derived from available aerial photographic material, covering the ground to be explored. Sequences of overlapping aerial photographs, taken along what were known as "flight lines", were cut up into pieces that were fitted together like a jigsaw to make the mosaics. The flight line photographs were used for ground feature identification in instances where the mosaics were indefinite, as the former could be viewed in localised three-dimensional exaggerated relief with the aid of a portable stereoscope.

WDL's forward planning envisaged that a reliably assembled aerial photographic mosaic was to be a camp standard for the coordination and control of exploration practice. Instructions were set out that each mosaic issued was to be maintained in a dry and secure location in the camp it related to. The mosaic should never be taken out into the bush—for on the spot guidance of traverses, working maps showing essential features to be expected along the way were to be traced off the mosaics.

The fundamental use of a mosaic was to prepare an advance plan of action. Existing roads and tracks, new tracks that needed to be cut, locations of potential campsites, key topographical features, and priority areas for attention were marked on the mosaics in easily erasable Chinagraph (grease) pencil colours. It didn't form a particularly accurate plan at the outset, but as successive traverses were carried out, and as the knowledge and understanding of the area improved, the plan was regularly upgraded to become more and more real by the day.

In practice the situation on the ground rarely corresponded precisely with the expectations of forward planning. Tracings generated from the mosaics often contained more than a few discrepancies due to their being derived from a fallible mortal's interpretation of what he thought he saw on aerial photographs.

For all that, it was fair to acknowledge that most interpreters of aerial photographs were proficient. They did, however, make mistakes. Their work was a well-judged blend of art and science, and all too often the art overrode the science. The fit of the various pieces making up a mosaic might be less than jigsaw-perfect. The best that could be said of traced-off maps was that they were acceptable as general guides. They were not the gospel truth. A team out on a sampling traverse could well find thick bush, savannah, or hillocks, or gullies or even broad riverbeds appearing in locations that were at odds with what these maps indicated. In such cases the maps were changed accordingly and we moved on, adjusting to the moment. A good sense of direction, which took me some time to acquire, provided the best means of coping with an inaccurate map.

The distribution of the samples taken was dependent on the nature of the terrain. Forward planning as to what type of sample would be taken where was an essential feature of the design of any programme. It carried a built-in flexibility. The unexpected was never far away. We preferred it when there was a well-defined drainage system to sample as we could then cover the ground faster and more positively than sampling of residual soils allowed us to do. Soil sampling was carried out in poorly drained and extensively flat terrain, as well as over watersheds separating one drainage system from another.

The beds of rivers and streams provided the ideal conditions for the natural concentration of seasonally transported heavy minerals such as on the downstream side of rock bars, or in gravel traps, or at the bottom of potholes and on the outer edges of curves against the riverbank. The heavy mineral fraction could include any of the three indicator minerals (ilmenite, pyrope garnet and chrome diopside) that we were actively seeking as guides pointing to the upstream presence of kimberlite.

Black sand was so abundant in the base of some gravel traps that it could be shovelled out wholesale. Occasionally we saw red streaks and trails of garnet marking the swirl of eddy currents fossilised at the onset of the dry season. Garnet in such quantities was almost invariably of the common almandine variety, liberated by weathering and erosion from the very common garnet gneiss rocks in which it occurred.

The great advantage that rivers and streams gave us was that for much of the year their beds were dry and could be walked along as if they were open tracks through the bush. Of course the riverbeds were inclined to wind around a lot more than was desirable for a track to do, and walking on yielding sand did no favours to either our feet or our stamina. It was only the existence of sporadically encountered stagnant pools secreted under shaded jumbles of rocks that provided any indication that water had ever flowed in such rivers at all.

Riverbeds were inaccessible only during the early part of the wet season when the heavens opened and the long awaited downpour created foaming flash floods crested with broken trees, mud, thorn bush, elephant dung, and any creature (on two or four legs) unlucky enough not to have got out of the way in time.

The great danger of flash floods was that they could be triggered by remote cloudbursts a long way upstream from where we might be working under bone dry conditions. The flood would then arrive unexpectedly. Its harbinger was a flickering tongue of water seething over the surface of the sand. Behind the tongue soon came a wave-like torrent of churning water many feet deep. It raced at high speed, bearing a heaving cargo of debris. The rushing spate might easily endure for a day or two, but when it spent itself the flow of water slowed, the water cleared as its level fell, and we were back in business again until the next cloudburst decreed otherwise, hoping that gravel traps had been enhanced by the addition of a few more heavy minerals.

The game treated drainage channels as bush tracks in the dry season, just as we did. In their case the interest was as often as not directed towards either locating vestiges of standing water or otherwise sniffing out water at a shallow depth in the sand where a water hole could be comparatively easily scooped out.

As we walked along dry riverbeds, it was always exciting to contemplate what might be waiting for us around the next bend. A small herd of buffalo, a few itinerant elephants, or a group of impala—anything was possible. In the hottest part of the day big game usually liked to rest up in the shade of the bush, which made their presence in riverbeds not all that likely. Still, we never knew for sure.

Elephants were true experts in making water holes. They knelt down, swept away and heaped up the sand from side to side using their tusks as shovels. Impressively deep excavations could be the result. Other species of game, not forgetting us as well, all had good cause to thank elephants for finding water for our benefit.

*

A typical team walking up a riverbed on a sampling traverse might consist of one *mzungu* and as many as a dozen *watu*. Speaking on the basis of my own experience in such matters, it was debatable as to who among the team was doing the following and who was doing the leading. The *mzungu* looked after the traced map and the selection of sampling sites; the *watu* carried the gear, excavated the samples and demonstrated regularly that they knew a good deal more about working out in the bush than the *mzungu* ever would.

The *mzungu* would no doubt demonstrate his superiority by rising to the occasion should the team walk over one of Dr Arnold Waters' famous copper deposits. As a test of *mzungu* mettle the copper deposit identification needed to be taken as read. As far as I knew, no copper deposit was missed, although for that matter none was ever found either.

In principle, a sampling traverse was designed to occupy a full day of work between departure from and return to camp. Soon after dawn each morning the traverse team piled into a Land Rover to be driven out to a location as close as possible to its planned starting point in the bush. Later on the team would be picked up by Land Rover at a pre-arranged time and location for its return to camp

When the logistics required it for reasons of practicality, single traverses covering two or more days were run with the team fly-camping in the bush wherever they happened to be when night fell. The maximum number of days allocated to such traverses was four, the limitation being imposed by what the team was able to carry both to perform its work and to feed and accommodate its members.

A one-day traverse covered a minimum of eight miles over which samples were taken, together with any additional distance needed to either backtrack to the starting point or go on to another agreed pickup location. On a fly-camp traverse it was possible to cover ten or twelve sampled miles each day. The distances were not substantial, but thick bush took time to get through, there were many hazards to be negotiated, big game to be avoided and (by no means least) samples to be taken, bagged and either secured for collection or panned down to concentrates if water was available *en route*.

The sampling of rivers, streams and their associated network of drainage channels was carried out at a nominal interval between selected sample points of two miles minimum and three miles maximum. The distance between consecutive samples was a matter of judgement based on experience and was governed by the natural characteristics of sample sites and their capacity for trapping heavy minerals.

At tributary confluences a sample was taken in both the tributary and the main stream. The respective samples were taken at sites that were far enough upstream from the point of confluence to avoid any possibility of contamination from the backwash of wet-season flooding. Tributaries were sampled back to their sources in a precisely similar way to the sampling of the main stream.

Over areas on which soil sampling was deemed necessary to obtain optimum cover, the samples were taken on a nominal one-mile square grid pattern. The grid was established on a set of parallel baselines exactly eight miles apart, cut and cleared of obstacles through the bush to a width that allowed reasonable Land Rover access. Since line cutting was laborious work, not least in the thick bush, we tended to shy away from soil sampling as long as there was a vestige of a drainage channel to provide an alternative.

Precisely measured traverse positions were set up a mile apart along the length of the baselines, using either a stake of wood or a large blaze on a tree. The traverse positions were coordinated between baselines in accordance with the planned sampling grid. A traverse commenced from a position on one baseline and, controlled by compass bearing, ran the full eight miles to the next baseline, hopefully to end up in the near vicinity of the intended position on the latter.

We became quite proficient at extending compass bearings using three straight poles in alignment, and we only needed to check the bearing with the compass occasionally as the alignment of poles was carried forward, sparseness of the bush permitting. The intervals between samples were measured with the assistance of a surveyor's chain. Closure of traverses from baseline to baseline was rarely exact but was normally close enough to be acceptable. The penalty for inaccuracy was that the errant traverse would have to be repeated. We were quick to learn to do our best to avoid that kind of outcome. My experience of traversing was that of rocks I saw little, of bush and game I saw much.

The sampling gear consisted of a square sheet of canvas with sides of approximately four feet each; a foot and a half square box screen with an aperture of one eighth of an inch; a couple of shovels; a hoe (*jembe*) of the traditional kind that women swung to break ground in their *shambas*; a supply of freshly laundered large white canvas bags to contain the individual samples as they were taken; a traced map of the locality (hopefully accurate); and a sample report cum ticket record book.

At a selected sample site in a river or stream channel, a quantity of gravel and sand was shovelled up and manually shaken through the screen onto the spread-out canvas sheet until an undersize fraction of about twenty pounds by weight had accumulated. The oversize fraction was given a once-over inspection to check for anything of interest. If nothing of interest was seen then the oversize was rejected.

The undersize fraction was transferred to a sample bag, and a sample report was made out. A perforated ticket carrying the sample identity number, torn from the edge of the appropriate page in the sample report book, was inserted in a securely waterproof Kraft paper envelope and placed on top of the sample in the sample bag, after which the bag was closed using a pair of ties attached to its neck. For additional security of identification, the sample number was written on a luggage label-like tag, which was also tied around the neck of the bag.

A soil sample was cut to a depth of two inches over a standard measured surface area of one yard square. The cutting tool was a *jembe*. Screening of soil was seldom required as the material excavated was almost entirely of a fine grained nature. Care was exercised in ensuring that the soil sampled was residual, being derived from and therefore indicative of the geological characteristics of the underlying bedrock.

A bagged soil sample weighed up to twenty pounds. Eight soil samples were taken in the course of a regular eight-mile traverse. We developed a practice of leaving the samples at the sample sites for the first four miles out, following which the traverse team split into two—one group to complete the second half of the traverse and the other group to retrace the first half back to the starting point and pick up the bagged samples on the way.

The location of each sample was plotted as a small circle on the traverse map with its number written alongside. The sample report book contained the following information: date, time, sampler's names, map location reference, geological information (if any), and such other observations related to the site as were deemed relevant. Since we all too often came up short on any geology to report, we tended to fall back on the fruits of our local experience and record subjects such as the incidence of tsetse fly when they were too prolific, the type of game we encountered in the locality and sightings of various species of snakes. Most of what we wrote was true.

Each sample book contained fifty consecutively numbered sample reporting sheets with counterfoils. When a sample book was completed it was returned to Mwadui, from where it was sent for archiving at the analytical laboratory in Johannesburg. Once in a while we wondered about the reactions of technicians down in Johannesburg who might have chanced upon the pithier of the locality-related comments made in some of the sample report books.

A Field Officer told me he wrote "Fur queue!" and "Fur cough!" and "4Q!" on a number of sample report forms and succeeded in provoking not a single reaction. It was open to debate as to whether or not the fate of all completed sample books in what must have been a cast of thousands sent to Johannesburg, was to disappear into a black hole of disinterest.

Our feeling of not much happening at the laboratory wasn't helped by the customary lapse of several months between the day on which a sample was taken in the bush and the day on which the Johannesburg analytical results were received back at Mwadui.

Badu kidogo just about summed the whole thing up.

In camp we panned the bulky samples down into more or less optimally small volume concentrates before submitting them to Mwadui. "Optimally" implied that the panning was terminated well before the stage at which losses of indicator minerals could occur through over-panning.

Once in Johannesburg, the sample concentrates were examined, presumably with all due care and attention, for indicator minerals.

The indicator minerals were separated from the concentrates and the number of separate grains or fragments of any of the three types found to be present was counted. In addition, any evidence of abrasion, attrition and the preservation of crystal facets was assessed as a highly qualitative measure of how far from their source the indicator mineral grains under scrutiny might have travelled.

In reality all of the results of sample analysis were more qualitative than quantitative. When the results were comprehensively plotted on master maps and the indicator mineral counts were individually contoured, it was at once evident which areas were favourable for the discovery of kimberlite, which areas were worthless and which areas were anomalous and might swing either way with a bit more work. The plotted results of river and streambed samples were especially impressive in depicting trails of indicator minerals pointing towards opportunities to open up that elite province of those favoured by WDL management, namely detailed work.

*

The burden of carrying full sample bags over long distances was very much eased if a source of water was available in the bush. The samples could be panned down to manageable size there and then, and the range of a traverse could, with time permitting, even be extended to allow more samples to be taken in a day than would otherwise have been the case.

I worked with a number of *watu* who were capable of carrying three full sample bags piled one on the other on top of their heads. It was a feat to marvel at. *Wazungu* were unable to emulate the head balancing technique. I tried it and failed dismally. The best that I could do was to carry two bags, one on each of my shoulders. It was in no way easy. I tended to fall so far behind the three-bag head-toting *watu* that without a cut baseline to aim for and know where I was when I reached it they might never have seen me again.

Apart from his role in ensuring that a copper deposit would not be missed even if he had to fall face down on it, the *mzungu* served as the guarantor of fair play on soil sampling traverses. A team of trained *watu* was more than capable of covering eight miles of traverse correctly in all respects, but since none of them liked carrying a full sample bag any further than they had to, options for short cutting the prescribed process needed to be guarded against via *mzungu* supervision.

There were a number of cases of traverses undertaken by unsupervised *watu* that were performed impeccably both out and back. The samples were cut to precise specification at the appointed locations. The work was checked and determined to be in order. The number of samples, each one duly ticketed, was just what it should have been. The only problem was that all of the samples that were so well taken were found to have been discarded into the surrounding bush at their respective sampling locations. The sample bags had all been filled by random digging in the vicinity of the end of traverse baseline station.

It wasn't cricket, but it was understandable; as far as the *watu* were concerned, a sample was no more than a bag full of soil. One bag full of soil looked no different from another bag full of soil; therefore it was immaterial where the soil came from as there was plenty of soil wherever they cared to look. As long as the *wazungu* got the correct number of full bags, then the *watu* had done their job well by their own reckoning. In any case most of what the *wazungu* did or wanted to do made so little sense to the *watu* that it wasn't worth worrying about.

Wazungu supervision was supposed to impose ultimate integrity on the sampling process. As supervisors, the disparate bunch of greenhorns, grifters, chancers and opportunists that made up the bush establishment of WDL contained overtones of being blind in the country of the one-eyed.

*

Detailed work, essentially a process of intensive soil sampling, involved an incremental tightening up of the sampling grid around any reconnaissance samples that had tested positive for indicator minerals. The sampling grid interval was reduced by stages through a half of a mile, a quarter of a mile, a tenth of a mile, a twenty-fifth of a mile, a fiftieth of a mile (approximately one hundred feet) and so on. The ultimate dimension of the grid was commensurate with how positive the incoming results from the detailed work continued to be.

The beauty of detailed work was that samples were concentrated and assessed for indicator mineral on the spot very soon after they were taken. Johannesburg was not for them. The changing nature of favourable ground could then be reviewed daily, permitting priorities to be assigned, rapid decisions to be made and unfavourable sectors of the area subject to detailed work to be returned to the bush and its denizens.

Sample reduction to concentrates in detailed work camps was carried out through a standard practice of panning into a cut-down half of a forty-four gallon drum filled with water. A battery of such cut-down half drums was set up in the manner of a production line. Most of the *watu* were auditioned for panning—the technical expertise of some was better than that of others. The best of the bunch were retained for the job. Their contribution to the integrity of the overall process was of far more significance than they were normally given credit for.

Hand jigging was employed for sample concentration in instances when the sample material was relatively coarse. A hand jig was a fine-meshed circular screen about a foot and a half in diameter. The way the jigging procedure worked was as follows: a quantity of sample was placed in the jig to fill it to a depth of a couple of inches; with hands diametrically opposed the jigger held the jig in a flat and almost submerged position in the half drum of water; a rotation accompanied by a small up and down movement was then imparted to the material in the jig by an appropriate motion of the jigger's hands; and the heavy mineral fraction of the sample was induced by the vertical component of the motion to sink to the bottom of the jig and by the rotation to accumulate as a round "eye" at the jig's centre.

Once the jigger's experience allowed him to judge that the jigging was complete, the screen was removed from the water and allowed to drain for a short while before being flipped over and turned out on a canvas sheet to present the eye of heavy mineral concentrate for assessment.

*

When a detailed work sampling campaign produced a promising anomaly suggestive of underlying kimberlite (as happened now and then) the next step was that the bedrock had to be exposed and identified by a technique known as "pitting", which not unnaturally involved the excavation of exploration pits from surface down through the overburden and into bedrock.

The pits were small-scale shafts sunk on a square cross-section of four feet by four feet. The dimensions were controlled and kept even by excavating within an appropriately sized metal frame. Labour for pitting was cheap, plentiful and skilled.

The depth to bedrock might be no more than a matter of a few feet, although the penetrative characteristics of tropical weathering ensured that greater depths were necessary to reach bedrock more often than not. For depths of pit greater than ten feet a strong wooden "A" frame fitted with a block and tackle and bucket was erected over the collar of the pit for the purposes of raising and lowering the pit digger and his gear (it was a one-*mtu* show down there); lowering and raising the *mzungu* who had to go down to inspect the geological nature of the walls and floor of the pit, whether he liked it or not; and hoisting excavated material and associated samples up to the surface.

Some pits plumbed depths that were sufficient to frighten the life out of anyone standing at the top and looking down. It was only too easy to imagine how terrifying the view might be from the bottom up. I took comfort in never being put in a position of having to discover what that was like. The deepest pit that I saw went down sixty feet. It appeared to dwindle to infinity at its bottom and gave full meaning to the expression "the bowels of the earth".

The discovery of kimberlite was always an exceptional event when it happened. The vast majority of the pits that were sunk bottomed in barren rock.

Standing instructions called for all open pits in progress to be surrounded at the top by a secure *boma* to keep intruders at bay. When the pits were no longer needed, or otherwise when the detailed work programme that they were part of was terminated, the *boma* was dismantled and burned and the pit was backfilled and levelled off in true *choo* tradition.

There was no limit not only to what was able to fall into the maw of an open and unprotected pit but also to what sometimes did. The range of victims could include domestic animals, small game, serpents, rodents, *wandorobo* and all and sundry that went bump in the night, not forgetting Mr Dennis Kent's *kaffir* on a bicycle.

The presence of a snake at the bottom of a pit was capable of creating great excitement, not least in the heart of the *mtu* whose task it was to go down and start digging. The excitement was intensified in cases when the *mtu* in question didn't see a snake that was down there in a corner of the pit waiting for him until his feet touched the bottom. His immediate reaction was to rise to surface with all of the speed and none of the grace of a rocket, as if for him the laws of gravity had been temporarily repealed. Large rocks were then dropped into the pit in an attempt to kill the innocent snake. When the rock option failed, a shotgun (if available) might be brought along and fired vertically downwards to enter in the fray. Eventually an *mzungu* volunteer had to descend to finish the snake off with the help of a razor-edged *panga*. Unfortunately, volunteering for anything at all was not something that *watu* did. They appeared to believe that snakes were put on earth as creatures for them to kill on sight, except in cases when the killing ground was at the bottom of a deep pit.

*

When the existence of a kimberlite pipe was confirmed, the process of its evaluation, allegedly clicking at once into faultless gear, took over from detailed work. The evaluation process sought to determine whether or not diamonds were associated with the newly discovered kimberlite pipe.

If the kimberlite pipe was diamondiferous a reliable estimate of the quantity, quality and size range measured in carats of diamonds (gem and industrial) per unit volume of kimberlite was required. A few large gem-quality diamonds per unit volume could signify a better option than a greater number of smaller stones.

Responsibility for the evaluation process was normally assigned to one of the WDL Prospectors, who would move with his mighty tribal horde of *watu* and camp followers to establish an operational base in short order. A lot of excavation work was called for, and with a substantial and compliant labour force and a couple of mechanical diggers on the side it was easily managed.

The excavated material was stockpiled, when applicable, in distinctive geologically directed batches of yellow ground, blue ground and primary kimberlite. The respective batches were individually run through a pilot processing plant. As an ample supply of water was essential, the camp and the processing facilities were not necessarily located in the immediate vicinity of the pipe.

The stockpiles were created adjacent to the pilot plant. The material was brought in from the pipe to the stockpiles in five-ton trucks. The pilot plant flow sheet incorporated crushing, slurrying, concentrating and diamond recovery sections.

The dimensions of the excavations for evaluation were precisely controlled. The volume excavated was measured in individual units of five hundred cubic feet, referred to as "diamond loads". The weight of a diamond load was nine-twentieths of a long ton. As a long ton weighed 2,240 pounds, a diamond load weighed nine hundredweights—otherwise approximately one thousand pounds. A minimum of five hundred diamond loads of each of the geological subdivisions encountered was processed to provide assurance that the pilot plant results could be considered to be representative of the grade or value of the kimberlite pipe as a whole.

When pilot plant results were of economic interest an estimate of the *in situ* resources of kimberlite available for exploitation was made with the help of a standard technique known as diamond drilling, in which the diamond of the name referred to the industrial-quality stones with which the head of the hollow drilling bit employed was set.

Diamond drilling cut continuous cores of rock that were brought to surface in successive ten-foot increments (ten feet of core being the maximum length of core that filled an extractable tube in behind the drill bit) for examination and detailed geological logging and sampling. Depending on the type of drill rig used, holes as long as several hundred feet could be drilled. The factor governing the ultimate depth of hole that could be reached was the ability of the drill motor to cope with the ever-increasing weight of the string of drill rods.

The drill rigs were normally hired from specialist contracting outfits. The drill operators, *wazungu* one and all, were a far wilder bunch overall than any of their WDL counterparts could ever aspire to be, and that was saying something. They were immensely hard workers. Diamond drilling was a laborious, wet and greasy job that I decided was best observed from a position of comfort on the sidelines.

*

The work carried out from each camp in the bush was written up in a formal monthly report (the twenty-fifth day of the month being the closing date for reporting) that was signed off by the Senior Geologist in camp before being submitted to WDL in Mwadui.

My friend Jack the draughtsman was the first in line not only for the receipt of incoming monthly reports but also for chasing up any late submissions. When I was with him he showed me a pristine example, just in from the field, authored by a Senior Geologist named Hugh Rance. The report had been prepared in crisp typescript and was accompanied by neat, take-it-in-at-a-glance maps.

"This is what it's all about!" Jack told me, "This kind of thing gets noticed!"

To my regret I had the opportunity to meet Hugh Rance only once. He was a natural for assignment to detailed work: tall, languid, and carrying with him a superior presence sculpted from a public school and Oxbridge-type background. What I had in common with him would not have made a meal for a tsetse fly. He wrote one hell of a good report, though.

*

The fundamental sampling-related information that monthly reports were supposed to deliver was as follows: the location of all samples taken, plotted accurately on a traced map (or maps) and individually identified by their assigned numbers; a foolscap-sized index map (scale 1:250,000) showing the relative outline positions of both the currently submitted sample location maps and their counterparts as submitted with previous monthly reports; the results of geological interpretation and mapping, including lithology and structure (faulting, folding, jointing and any measured orientations of the same); an assessment of any differences picked up between the actual situation on the ground and the indications of the relevant aerial photographic mosaic; and the observed incidence of any alleged indicator minerals in sample concentrates (without prejudice to the final result that would come later, following a definitive analysis at the laboratory in Johannesburg).

The standing instruction was, as far as geological interpretation was concerned, that in the absence of outcrop "some idea" of the local geology should be generated. We were further instructed that geological information of one kind or another could be "obtained easily" by examining the physical characteristics of samples as they were taken. However, any getting involved in extra work (and thereby incurring extra expenses) to sort out the geology was off limits unless it could be clearly shown to be critical to the progress of the sampling programme, as the sampling programme was the priority.

The map (or maps) accompanying a monthly report had to follow certain basic formatting standards, including a clearly marked reference to the national (1:1,000,000 scale) sheet within which the area sampled was contained; a graphic (never written) scale; a north-pointing arrow; indications of prominent features of both geography and infrastructure such as baselines, roads, tracks, railway lines, rivers, streams, ponds, lakes, type of bush, clearings and open ground; and locations of *mbugas*, *shambas* and all encountered huts and buildings.

The use of either colour or graphic representation of reported features on traced maps was forbidden. Information could only be presented in black and white terms with the support of standardised alphanumeric codes.

The size of monthly report maps was a moveable feast that lay in both the lap of the gods and the hands of the Senior Geologist under whose auspices the maps were drawn up. The maps needed to be neither too big to be unwieldy nor too small to provide a reasonable overview of the work completed. Since the maps sent in to Mwadui from all over the country were coordinated in Jack's drafting office, it was left up to the coordinators to decide on the standard size of map that would be most practical for them—following which we in the camps would simply follow their orders. And that was where it was left, as a decision on the same remained perennially pending.

An option existed to plot and report the progress of grid sampling of residual soils on squared graph paper using a scale of one inch to one mile. The minimum size authorised for such plots was foolscap. If a month's work covered too much ground for showing on a single foolscap-sized sheet of graph paper, then increasing the size of the plot needed to be done in multiples of foolscap sheets.

Sample plots on graph paper for detailed work (foolscap or multiples thereof, please) were assigned a scale commensurate with the selected sampling grid. The ultimate dimensions of the map were required to be "chosen judiciously" with full consideration given to the likely area dimensions of the kimberlitic anomaly being investigated.

The Senior Geologist in charge of a detailed work programme was under instructions to put his best efforts into contouring (in black lead pencil only) any reported counts of indicator minerals on the monthly sample plots. Each anomaly was given a specific name or code number for identification. One Senior Geologist, in a rare burst of perception, named the anomalies in his area of responsibility for characters from *Alice's Adventures in Wonderland*.

All of the detailed work maps and sample plots were required to be marked with a "tie-in" point that allowed each one to be accurately cross-referenced to the original map(s) featuring the reconnaissance sample(s) that provided the motivation for the detailed work.

The maps associated with Prospector's monthly reports specifying progress in evaluation projects were also tied in to supporting detailed work and reconnaissance maps. They were drawn up (with the Mwadui office's abhorrence of colour on maps once again applicable) on standard sheets of tracing paper measuring thirty-two inches by thirty inches. Activities such as sampling, pitting, trenching, diamond drilling, geophysical work and geological mapping were to be highlighted. Vertical profiles of pits and drill-holes were also to be included.

In order to assist in the three-dimensional visualisation of the kimberlite body being evaluated, the geological information—inclusive of the results of excavation, pitting, trenching and diamond drilling—was required to be presented on as many separate cross-sectional profiles as was considered necessary.

*

The all-inclusive contents of a camp's regular monthly report consisted of the following: a descriptive report; remarks and supporting commentary relevant to the information presented; maps, plots and cross-sections; cash statements, expenditures and balances; purchase orders; completed *vipandis*; and Land Rover usage and maintenance figures.

All items of expenditure were allocated (as relevant) to one of a specific set of numbered activity operating accounts, which included reconnaissance exploration, detailed work, equipment use (exclusive of vehicle equipment), vehicle operation and vehicle maintenance.

Every *mzungu* in a camp led by a Senior Geologist prepared a personal monthly activity report in duplicate. He retained one copy and submitted the other to the Senior Geologist for review and approval prior to its incorporation into the latter's monthly camp report compilation. The monthly package was, in the absence of any direct transport, normally taken to the nearest town to be sent to Mwadui by registered surface post.

In what could be construed as an open invitation to the fraudsters among us, WDL was willing to have bulk submissions of *vipandis* posted to Mwadui at the cheapest mailing rate. The *vipandis* in this instance were to be securely tied into a package with both ends open. A note was to be included with the package naming the camp of origin, the date of submission and the total expenditure represented by the *vipandis*.

The camp cash disbursement was the sole responsibility of the Senior Geologist unless the responsibility was delegated elsewhere. It was interesting to note, however, that under the terms of a standing instruction, Field Assistants on reconnaissance teams were not authorised to handle WDL cash at any time. There was a telling message begging to be released from that particular instruction bottle.

Company cash was used in principle to pay the *watu* and to purchase consumable supplies (for example *watu* rations, cooking and lighting oil, petrol or diesel fuel, vehicle spare parts) and non-consumable supplies (such as camp furniture, kitchen equipment, sampling screens, shovels, pick heads and pick handles, ropes, corrugated metal sheets, canvas sheets, general hardware) for camp if, for any reason, a trader wasn't prepared to issue goods on the strength of a WDL purchase order.

Gus Edwards preferred that non-consumable supplies for camps should be obtained directly from stock held at Mwadui, believing that that was an effective means of regulating such transactions. He did his best to make our local purchases of these supplies untenable by demanding of us a written declaration to the effect that the supplies in question could be obtained locally at a competitive price. The Chief Geologist then consulted with either WDL's Chief Storekeeper or other interested heads of department as to whether or not permission to buy locally should be granted. It all made work for the working man to do, as Professor C. Northcote Parkinson could well have observed.

Local purchases of non-consumable items additionally needed the authorisation of the Chief Geologist other than in cases where "dire necessity or urgency" could be invoked as an excuse—many of us were experts in calling up that particular justification.

Among other WDL instructions printed on the same hymn sheet for us to read, mark, learn, inwardly digest and wonder about the logic of were: orders for fuel could not be combined with orders for tyres; orders for rations could not be combined with orders for picks and shovels; paraffin for camp use could be ordered in combination with rations; urgent telegrams sent to Mwadui needed to avoid being written in language that was too cryptic (shades of Nimmo Reid); and last but by no means least, we were strictly forbidden to buy any extra piece of standard-issue field equipment for our personal use at WDL's expense.

The way in which we stuck to prescribed standards for making out monthly cash statements was all too often a long way removed from the good old shit and woollen blanket analogy. In a hard-hitting instruction memorandum, Gus went on to offer his view that it appeared probable that very few of us were holding on to a personal copy of our individual monthly cash statements. He added that it was advisable that a copy should be kept, as only then could the WDL Accounting Department offer convincing proof to us that our accounting technique was rife with arithmetic errors.

Whatever these errors were, most of them, both the inadvertent and the not so inadvertent, were all eventually ironed out. When we were visiting a town, a bag of WDL cash in the hand was worth two such bags in the bush and was often regarded as a free-for-all resource for the exclusive use of whoever's possession it was in at the time.

The underlying philosophy was that there would always be a Peter who would pay Paul when WDL's cries became too strident for us to disregard. As long as we muddled through, that was good enough.

*

My three weeks of induction at Mwadui gave me a basic appreciation of what would be expected of me when I went out into the bush to confront camp life, undertake traverses, work with the *watu*, observe and report, and I was glad of it.

The next step was to put what I had learned into practice, to continue with my personal development and to attempt to live up to the expectations of others to the best extent that I could.

Rungwa Game Reserve perspective

The little Arab's *duka* at Iseke

The baboon's fortress *koppies* at Iseke

Corduroyed bridge across the Makasumbe River

The wet season arrives at the Kisigo River crossing

Iwambala village

The dry, elephant-dropping littered Njombe River in the Rungwa Game Reserve

Sampling team in the Kisigo River

8
Tayare, thabiti, Ugogo
Ready, steady, Ugogo

On my return to Mwadui from the Nimmo-sponsored visit to Bruno's camp I found that a South African Field Officer had taken up temporary residence at the Pink House. His name was Dick du Toit. He was stout of belly and florid of feature, an ebullient gung-ho type who looked as if he would have been completely at home in the bush.

His surname was pronounced "doo toy", reflecting the absorption of what was originally a nineteenth-century French Huguenot immigrant name into an Afrikaans-speaking vernacular. The most interesting treatment of such French surnames by Afrikaners was given to Labuschagne, which was pronounced as "labbuscackny".

Dick affected a large pointed moustache on his upper lip. It (the moustache, not the lip, although one never knew) appeared to be stiffly waxed. It was the kind of moustache that the American humorist Mr H. Allen Smith once described as looking like "the formal gardens at the House of Usher".

Dick's manner had a brittle edge, laced with overtones of a conscious superiority and a hint of military service lurking somewhere in his background. His *watu* trod on figurative eggshells when they were in his presence.

I met Dick for the first time that night in the bar of the Mwadui

Club. We didn't become instant friends, but I was moved to defer to his obvious experience, and as a result our relationship was always cordial. Dick enquired about my imminent field assignment. He asked me where the first camp I was to join would be located. I could only tell him that all I knew about it at the time was that the camp was being set up somewhere down to the south of Manyoni in what I understood was uncharted bush.

"You don't know much!" he said with great perception, and then went on to sound me out as to whom I would be working for. When he heard that my camp boss would be Tom Molyneux, Dick raised his eyebrows and pursed his lips, almost (but not quite) emitting a low-pitched whistle. He gave the impression not only that he possessed far more inside information than me (which he did) but also that he had no intention of enlightening me with any of its key aspects (which he didn't).

"Whatever you do," said Dick, "don't agree to work anywhere in Ugogo!"

"Why not?" I asked him.

Dick then recounted a story of a tragic incident that took place some months previously. It involved a reconnaissance exploration camp located in Ugogo, the homeland of the Wagogo tribe. Some unenlightened local tribesmen, observing teams on traverses out of the camp taking samples of both river sediments and residual soil, developed an idea that their tribal land was being systematically bagged up and stolen by *watu* of other tribes under *wazungu* direction.

Security of land tenure was the key priority governing the tribesmen's lives. Other issues of vital concern to them were the ownership and wellbeing of cattle, the timely arrival of the wet season and the detestation of any tribe other than their own.

It needed only a short leap of imagination, no doubt egged on by an advantage-seeking witch doctor or two, to link the size and shape of full sample bags with the heads of fellow tribesmen cut off by *wazungu*.

A group of suitably agitated Wagogo tribesmen armed with *pangas* then confronted a sampling team during a traverse on which it was being led by a young South African geologist.

The geologist was new to Tanganyika and was unable to rationalise the situation in which he found himself by using either a local or a South African-styled approach. As such, he was a man who was very much in the wrong place at the wrong time. One of the Wagogo tribesmen allegedly shouted, *"Chinja mzungu!"* (Kill the white man!). At which the tribesmen fell upon the geologist and hacked him to death with their *pangas*.

The outrage caused shock waves through the whole of WDL and De Beers, which resonated all the way up to Mr Harry Oppenheimer himself at the very peak of the parent Anglo American Corporation of South Africa. The perpetrators of the attack were hunted down by the Tanganyikan police to be arrested and subsequently charged with murder, given a fair trial, found guilty and sentenced. A number of them, as many as seven according to Dick, were hanged in the prison at Dodoma, the regional town at the heart of Ugogo.

Dick told me that he was a participant in the manhunt. He said that he had been armed with a pick handle and I learned later that he had swung it at running targets with a fair degree of success and lack of discrimination. I was led to believe that it was open to debate as to whether or not all of those who were eventually executed were men who were genuinely guilty. In the context of the time and given the nature of the crime it was presumably decided that an example of a few had to be made to "encourage the others".

I was unsure of what to think about what Dick told me, apart from reckoning that Ugogo and its tribal residents sounded to be the kind of cultural minefield that I would not have wanted to step into.

The critical lesson that WDL took from the geologist's murder was that sampling teams moving willy-nilly into tribal regions couldn't expect to have the local tribesmen welcome them with open arms and exhibit an instant acceptance of the conduct and purpose of all that was involved in exploration and sampling activities.

As was mandated in the pages of the *GFM*, we had to prepare the ground in advance of undertaking any work by means of providing comprehensive information to local chiefs and headmen who, in their turn, would deliver the information onwards to the rank and file of their subjects. The underlying assumption was that the chiefs and headmen would be amenable to listen and understand and that their people would take it all in when the word was passed down the line. The resolve of the chiefs was greatly aided in practice with gifts of various kinds, among which tobacco and alcohol ranked pre-eminently in their appreciation.

Some months later I experienced the procedure at a place named Mungaa in the Singida district. The tribe in question was the Wanyaturu. It all began with the Singida DC calling for a formal meeting of tribal elders at Mungaa on a specified date. The meeting was referred to as a *baraza*. It was a sort of high-level tribal council. I was assigned to attend the *baraza* on WDL's behalf in my capacity as the *mzungu* in nominal charge of pending sampling activities.

The DC was far too grand a personage to show his face at the *baraza*, which therefore took place under the chairmanship of one of his emissaries, a District Officer (DO). He was a callow youth, rigidly clad in starched khaki, and highly adept at mangling Kiswahili under the unfortunate influence of an execrable English public school accent.

On the specified date the *baraza* commenced when it started. Time was never of the essence on such occasions. Following a ritual half an hour or so of customary pleasantries requiring everyone in attendance to ask everyone else in attendance how they were, how they had been, how were their many days, how were their wives, their families, their livestock, their crops, their oxen, their asses and the strangers within their gates, the business of the *baraza* got under way.

In flat tones the DO delivered to the gathering the information that we had given him for that purpose. He paused with great frequency to allow his assistant, an *mtu* from HQ, to write verbatim minutes (which were made to seem like hours) of the proceedings in longhand with a scratchy pen that flicked from page to inkwell and back like a metronome. For his part, the assistant did his best to maintain the snail's pace of the occasion by asking for clarification of something or other at least once every couple of minutes.

From what I could gather, the DO's grasp of the technical aspects of our work offered a fine example of a little knowledge being a dangerous thing. I took it on trust that what he told those assembled at the *baraza* was what he was supposed to tell them and that what they heard from him made sense to them.

Once in a while during the DO's harangue, a chief, or a headman, or an elder of one rank or another ventured a word or two from the hard-packed dirt floor, but for the most part the whole assembly sat mute and seemed to let the entire thing go over its cumulative head.

The proceedings drew to a close when the assembly appeared to decide that sufficient unto the day was the evil thereof. The DO's final actions consisted of reviewing and appending his personal signature to the tortuously taken minutes and then calling on a couple of senior chiefs to endorse the document by appending their thumbprints to it as well.

I wouldn't have bet a single shilling on the senior chiefs knowing what they were agreeing to.

As a measure of whether or not this information-imparting procedure as a WDL standard did what it was supposed to do, there were certainly no further reported massacres of either geologists or for that matter of *watu* in the course of sampling work anywhere in the bush. A few violent incidents between camp *watu* and local tribesmen were another matter, but those were mainly of a minor nature and were managed when they took place. Veiled hostility directed at camps from local sources was something that no one could do anything about other than ignore.

The best means of maintaining the local peace came from our showing a friendly face to all and sundry, as well as ensuring that we were never short of having something to hand out in the way of an acceptable gift. The more ideal of relationships also incorporated a measure of good luck all round.

A *baraza* was as necessary an evil as, in my opinion, was the average character of the District official who was brought in to conduct it.

*

With Dick du Toit's salutary words in mind, it was not a little disconcerting to me to learn, on the day following the evening I had in his company at the Mwadui club, that the area I was destined to work in under Tom was located in the far southwest sector of Ugogo.

The key geographical features of the area were defined by approximately parallel stretches of the Great Ruaha and Njombe Rivers, both of which entered Ugogo from the south on courses trending from southwest to northeast. The two rivers were the twin arteries of the Rungwa Game Reserve, the Great Ruaha River forming the reserve's eastern boundary, and the Njombe River running through the centre of the reserve as a more or less *de facto* short-axis bisector. Where it exited from the Rungwa Game Reserve in the north, the Njombe River turned east and was renamed the Kisigo River for the fifty or so downstream miles that took it to its mighty confluence with the Great Ruaha River.

Below its confluence with the Kisigo, the Great Ruaha River flowed on through central Tanganyika to ultimately spend itself in the great multiple-channelled, reed-choked Rufiji delta, which bled into the Indian Ocean. The German warship *Königsberg* used the Rufiji delta as a hiding place during the first year or so of the Great War, emerging to strike at enemy shipping and then slip back to the cover of reeds in the true manner of a needle in a haystack. The *Königsberg's* security in the Rufiji delta lasted only until 1915, when the ship was located at anchor by its enemies and sunk.

Along its overall course to the ocean the Great Ruaha River, which originated and flowed east from ramparts of the Southern Highlands adjacent to the southeast flank of Lake Tanganyika, was given a host of names. The names reflected the respective penchants of the many tribes that the river met along the way—Wakimbu, Wagogo, Wahehe, Wasagara, Wavidunda, Wakutu, Wambunga, Wangindo and Warufiji—each tribe accepting the right to call the river what it would as the price of passage through its lands.

I considered myself lucky to have to cope only with the riverine names of Great Ruaha and Njombe directly and take a passing association with Kisigo on the side. As long as I knew where I was located on a map traced off an air-photo mosaic, I imagined that I would manage all right.

Tom's camp was set up adjacent to a river course of minor significance named Makasumbe, not far distant from a small village named Iwambala. The Makasumbe was a tributary of the Njombe River, coming in to join up with the latter from the north. To provide the camp with an identity, it was named Iwambala after the village. From the camp the main thrust of reconnaissance sampling would be focused on the Rungwa Game Reserve, in which it would also encroach on Wahehe and Wakimbu tribal lands.

Be all of that as it might, and since the game reserve was part of a tsetse fly paradise lacking any driveable access tracks and containing no formal settlements, the only people likely to move around in the game reserve, apart from us, would be the secretive and seldom seen Wandorobo.

Iwambala was perched on the edge of this vast tract of primeval bush that had been set aside for the preservation of game. It would have taken substantial wrangling and negotiating skills on the part of WDL to obtain the formal permission for us to work in the game reserve. It seemed possible that in the absence of any vehicle access track in the game reserve a requirement for us to construct one had prompted a positive decision to let us go ahead. One thing was for sure at the outset: a pot licence in the game reserve wouldn't be worth the paper it was printed on.

All of our activities were in any case subject to the scrutiny of the Game Department, for which purpose visits from a Game Ranger based in either Manyoni or Iringa (respectively dependent on whether we were working to the east or to the west of the Njombe River) were certain to take place when we least expected them to.

The 7,200 square mile area covered by the Rungwa Game Reserve was roughly box-like in shape when viewed on a map. It was about one hundred and twenty miles long on a northeast to southwest axis and sixty miles broad from southwest to northeast. There was little significant topographical relief. The river courses were mature.

As noted, the southeast boundary of the Rungwa Game Reserve was formed by the Great Ruaha River. It lay within the Iringa district. The northwest boundary was defined by a section of the national road between the villages of Rungwa (south) and Muwale (north) that linked Itigi up to the north with Chunya and Mbeya down to the south.

Tom spoke no more than the truth when he said that we were privileged to work in such an area of wild Africa. He had made no mention to me of his feelings regarding the attitude of the Wagogo to our presence among them, but then, to paraphrase the classic observation for all seasons that Miss Mandy Rice-Davies immortalised, he wouldn't, would he?

While in Mwadui I was issued with my standard field equipment and accessories and put in possession of far more official instructions than I knew what to do with. Furthermore, and somewhat miraculously, I was provided with a Tanganyikan driving licence and a battered grey Land Rover (licence number MZ 6172) to drive.

Nothing then stood between Mwadui and Iwambala beyond a solo journey for me at the wheel of the said vehicle.

*

Attired in brand new bush gear I felt quite as self-conscious as the circumstances demanded that I should, although my feeling was to some extent one of drowning in nervous anticipation as I drove through the open gates of Mwadui early one morning just as the sun was rising and headed off into the MMBA.

A canvas bag closed with a cork and bulging tight with a full charge of water hung outside the Land Rover's door on the driver's side from a stout rope attached to the door handle. The volume of water contained in the bag was, at a guess, at least five pints. The weave of the bag permitted water to ooze through the canvas fabric and to bead on the exterior. Exposure to the sun and the swish of air across the surface of the water bag as the Land Rover sped on its merry way caused the seepage to evaporate and consequently to lower the temperature of the liquid contents. A good cool drink of water was available for as long as the water in the bag held out.

A water bag left suspended on the side of a stationary Land Rover in the bush was likely to attract either a myriad of tsetse flies or a host of sipping butterflies onto its exterior. Once in a while a swarm of bees might need to be beaten away from the water bag, but carrying out that tricky manoeuvre depended on just how anxious we were to slake our thirst.

In the back of my Land Rover on the long road to Iwambala my personal effects and my standard issue of field equipment and incidental camp supplies were securely packed beneath a protective sheet of green tarpaulin. My arsenal, consisting of the Brno 9-mm rifle and Greener single-bore shotgun, was situated in behind the seats in the front cab, wrapped up in gunny sacking under a confident expectation that that was the way it would always remain.

A cashbox that I was taking to Tom sat on the floor on the passenger side of the Land Rover cab. Although it was empty it was chained to the hand-brake lever purely for the sake of appearances.

On the front passenger seat alongside me was a new Agfa 35-mm camera, loaded with slide film and contained within a still handsomely shiny leather case. I bought the camera at Jack's behest. Following a few initial misgivings I quickly came to realise that Jack's insistence on that particular purchase did me a good turn.

The route that I had to take to get to Iwambala was as follows: first, drive south from Mwadui, pass Shinyanga and continue to Tabora on the hundred-mile long road I knew already from my safari with Nimmo to Bruno's camp; next, turn east of Tabora and follow what was a road of lesser quality adjacent to the Central railway line for a hundred and fifty miles needed to reach Itigi and then Manyoni; after that, head south of Manyoni for fifty miles along a bush track to reach a village named Iseke; and finally, continue for a further twenty miles into the bush along a narrow track beyond Iseke. Thereafter, assuming that I had managed to avoid hitting anything animate or inanimate along the way and had located the correct roads and tracks, Iwambala ought to reveal itself to me.

The principal attribute of Iseke was, I was told, a small *duka* (shop) run by an Arab. The right-hand turnoff for the final section of track leading to Iwambala was, advised Tom in Mwadui in a tone of confidence that I couldn't reciprocate, located just beyond the Arab's *duka*.

It all sounded fair enough in principle.

The road to Tabora from Mwadui had lost none of its surface characteristics since my previous encounter with it. The PWD's tree-dragging technique in the interim had prevented the development of any serious corrugations. That was all to the good, since as a fledgling driver I drove with great caution; it meant that I had no cause to practice any overtaking. I was fortunate to have no head on meetings with either domestic or game animals, and I equally met very little oncoming traffic. It took me two and a half hours of driving to get to Tabora.

I then took the road leading east to Manyoni. The road adopted a close but casual association with the Central railway line. Sometimes the road and the railway line were comparatively near one another and sometimes they were not. It was difficult to see the railway line in any case, as thick bush pressed in on the road from both sides.

The road from Tabora to Manyoni could have easily been described as a glorified track without fear of contradiction. It offered me a challenge to drive along, since it seemed not to have seen much recent maintenance. The PWD gang that would offer me warm hospitality inclusive of a dinner of *posho* and catfish on that road at a later date were not then on station.

The road's surface looked to be extensively potholed and corrugated. I drove along it with impressive timidity and great respect for some time, although as the hours passed and the miles rolled away in my dust-shrouded wake I felt a slight growth of confidence in my ability to drive and began to think for the first time that I might after all get to Iwambala in one piece.

Along the road, a huddle of mud-walled huts here and there directed my attention to the likelihood of railway halts in their vicinity. There was otherwise not a lot to seize my attention, which in any case was primarily focused on spotting and avoiding road hazards.

I didn't stop the Land Rover between Tabora and Itigi at all, and in fact I was unwilling to halt under any circumstances. Something or anything could emerge from the wall of bush along the road at any time and it might not have friendly intentions towards me when it did. As long as the Land Rover kept going, it was Itigi or bust for me.

The worry was that the road gave every impression of being interminable. Its hemmed-in brown line, along and across which little or nothing other than tiny dust devils appeared to be moving, dwindled to a constant point in the unfathomable distance.

The still pattern was broken only once when something that was small, lithe and sinuous flicked across the road ahead of the Land Rover. At a later date when I found out what a mongoose was I decided that that was what the creature must have been. It was just as well that I didn't see two of the same together, as I thereby avoided having to refer to the creatures in the plural. Would they have been two mongooses or a pair of mongeese?

Finally, after about five hours of driving, there came some light at the end of the tunnel and I rolled into Itigi, a sombre little settlement located where a great road of national significance (the very same road that ran along the western boundary of the Rungwa Game Reserve) came up from Chunya and crossed the Central railway line on its way north to Singida.

I reached Itigi with gratitude. Manyoni was only twenty miles ahead. However, a feeling that all was well was tempered with concern, as by then it was already early afternoon and the day was starting to wane. I still had a long way to go beyond Manyoni into unknown territory and was extremely anxious to get to Iwambala before dark.

I didn't know what the exact time was as, by personal preference, I didn't own or want to own a watch. In Tanganyika's low latitudes sunset and sunrise worked on a regular twelve-hour cycle of separation, and apart from once in a while during the wet season when clouds and rain were in the ascendancy, it was easy to hazard a guess at the time of day with reasonable accuracy by looking at the length of shadows.

Although time was measured in Tanganyika by a twelve-hour clock, by local convention the numbering of the hours commenced at sunrise. What was regarded as six o'clock a.m. in *wazungu* circles became twelve o'clock a.m. (*saa kumi na mbili asubuhi*) as far as the *watu* were concerned. The Kiswahili hour count then took seven o'clock a.m. as *saa moja asubuhi* (literally "hour one morning") and continued through to *saa kumi na mbili usiku* ("hour twelve evening") when darkness fell.

The local system of time was simple to adapt to, not least because it made so much sense when set in its geographical context.

Thanks to Itigi's role at a major crossroads a large PWD road camp and depot facility was much in evidence there. It fact apart from a one-pump petrol vending station the presence of the PWD seemed to be Itigi's key asset. I stopped at the petrol station to refuel the Land Rover for the balance of my journey.

Itigi gave (or perhaps took) its name from a distinctive area of densely interwoven bush known as the Itigi thicket, which spread out to the north of the settlement. The Itigi thicket was not very tall as bush went, but was to all intents and purposes impenetrable to anything other than small game. An *mtu* armed with a sharp panga could expect to get short shrift (and shorter penetration) from the Itigi thicket.

The town of Manyoni was larger, busier and relatively neater than Itigi was or might ever aspire to be. Situated at an elevation above sea level of four thousand one hundred feet, Manyoni, depending on the point of view taken, was either blessed or cursed by a population of about a thousand, the vast majority of which comprised local tribesmen. The rest of Manyoni's residents consisted of a few Indian and Arab commercial traders and shopkeepers plus a handful of *wazungu* officers and administrators who occupied a well-appointed government HQ estate where they were presided over by a DC. The departments of government represented at Manyoni included those of Game, Veterinary, Agriculture and Labour.

The railway station at Manyoni was perhaps the most important feature of the town—to the east the road and the Central railway line carried on to link with Dodoma, the biggest town of the district, some sixty miles away. To the north, a road skirting the western edge of the Itigi thicket went to link up with the Itigi to Singida road at Suna, where Tony Knowles' "Drop Inn" camp was eventually instituted.

Manyoni also possessed both a hospital and a medical dispensary of sorts, a couple of churches, a government rest house in lieu of a hotel (no food provided), and what was ominously described as a "Grade III" landing strip for light aircraft.

By virtue of making meaningful gestures and by repeatedly and all too plaintively requesting of various Manyoni residents in my bad Kiswahili, "*Barra barra Iseke iko wapi?*" (Where is the road to Iseke?), a helpful tribesman directed me to what he seemed to think was the track that I should take. I thanked him profusely, trusting that his advice was, if not accurate at least well intended.

It took two more hours for me to drive along the fifty miles of narrow track separating Manyoni from Iseke. My informant had not lied.

Not far to the south of Manyoni the bush thinned out into a kind of open savannah that gave me a greater sense of perspective on the country that I was driving through. Apart from a small group of donkeys, however, one of which I was subsequently informed had mated with a zebra and produced a quagga-like offspring with stripes on its back legs, I saw nothing on four feet that looked remotely even half-wild.

Time was running in the direction of sunset so rapidly that the miles I covered felt as if they were increasing rather than reducing. The Land Rover had done me well and had so far exhibited no mechanical problems—or none that I could detect, which from the little I knew about Land Rovers was neither here nor there. The radiator didn't boil, the supply of water in the canvas bag held out, and the fuel taken on at Itigi was more than enough to take me all the way to Iwambala.

The thought of a night in the bush on my own didn't fill me with cheer. In particular, a night in the bush in Ugogo was not a prospect to be contemplated in any way lightly.

From the humped tops of rises in the track, of which there weren't many, the bush could be seen to spread away on all sides into a blue-hazed distance where faint outlines of hills and ridges looked like battleships sailing under sealed orders. The bush was characterised by widely dispersed umbrella-like acacia trees, standing tall and spreading feathery leaves over the dry and brittle thorn brush below them. Here and there, groves of broader-leaved, straighter standing trees seemed to be seeking solidarity in numbers. Wriggles of greenery marked the presence of river channels out in the middle distance.

Clearings within the array of bush were yellow-grassed and waiting for rain to fall. Some of the clearings were big and broad and others were long and trailing. Together they formed a virtual archipelago of open passage for game to move through the vast landscape.

The most unusual trees that I saw were baobabs. They were hugely dominant over all the others. Their great trunks, some of which were many yards in diameter, were clad with smooth-skinned pithy bark. They bulged outwards as they rose up, and at their heads they threw out a fountain-like multitude of stubby branches carrying thin leaves and a dangling host of seasonal fruit pods known to be a favourite with baboons. The combined leaves of a baobab tree provided precious little shade for the benefit of neither man nor beast.

These giants of the bush were sometimes referred to as "upside down trees" insofar as the arrangement of their branches resembled a configuration of roots. Ancient baobabs tended to rot from the core outwards and so develop huge hollow cavities that could absorb and store large quantities of rainwater and retain the same until well after the wet season had finished. Tales were told of human skeletons found at the bottom of deep baobab hollows—the fate of one-time seekers of water who fell in and were unable to get out.

It was curious that baobab saplings didn't seem to exist. I often looked for them, always unsuccessfully. The great baobabs must have exploded from the ground in a nascent condition of massive maturity.

The baobab fruit pods were brown, oval shaped, hard-husked, slightly furry to the touch and a few inches long when ripe. Inside each husk was a plethora of seeds contained in a white and fluffy edible pith, the texture of which was chewy and the taste of which for me was mildly astringent and not particularly pleasant. The pith was sometimes harvested by tribesmen as natural cream of tartar unless baboons got to it first.

*

As I neared Iseke, bizarrely formed naked granitic rocks, often of huge dimensions, stuck up through the bush in seemingly random jumbles. They were like grey-white monsters poking and thrusting above the trees, often reaching heights of a hundred feet or so. Some of the rocks exhibited great cracked bluffs, streaked here and there with greenery where vegetation had managed to gain a hold.

These dramatic assemblages of rocks, which the South Africans perceptively referred to as *koppies* (little heads), were known in Kiswahili as *malima*. Iseke was set all about with such *malima*, as if they were a race of giants laying siege to the Arab's *duka*.

High up on one especially impressive soaring bluff of granite, a mile of so out of Iseke, a large troop of baboons lived in elevated invincibility. They left their eyrie to target local *shambas* and take away seasonal crops, boldly and seemingly at will. They were equally adept, as I would learn later, at raiding bush camps and removing anything they could get hold of that was not either nailed or tied down.

The *shambas* of Iseke tended to be preferentially located quite close to the rock formations, indicating that the soil in such locations was relatively more fertile and more retentive of moisture than it was elsewhere. No doubt the baboons took the presence of the *shambas* as a gift. Dominant among the crops grown in the *shambas* was maize, the staple grain used for preparing both *posho* and *pombe*. Other crops were millet, chillies, spinach, beans, cassava, and (importantly) groundnuts and watermelons.

The *malima* in general were home to large groups of hyraxes, or rock rabbits, which were small social creatures that sunned themselves on high ledges in great gatherings. If the prolific accumulations of their droppings weren't an immediate guide to their presence, the pungent odour they gave off was a dead give-away.

Those who hunted either baboons or hyraxes did it in a spirit of pure vindictiveness, sure and certain in themselves as examples of Oscar Wilde's "unspeakable in full pursuit of the uneatable".

*

The village of Iseke was a collection of attractively constructed mud-walled and grass thatch-roofed huts set among shady trees. The roofing thatch was cut shortly after the end of the wet season when the grass was ripe and standing as much as six to eight feet high. The basic framework for the walls was a close-set assembly of wooden poles cut from the bush and held rigid by cross supports tied in place with tough and flexible strips of bark. Mud, preferably of the black cotton or *mbuga* type, was plastered over the framework to close all gaps. When dry, the mud was coated and smoothed over with a slurry of cow dung to create a completely rainproof finish. Applied to floors, the cow dung veneer formed an excellent and odourless surface capable of taking on a high polish.

No doubt the inhabitants of these huts couldn't have cared less if cow dung as a building material smelled or didn't smell. They were, one and all, living and breathing exponents of the fact that the odour of sweat mingled with wood smoke was, when there was a lot of it, much more than a match for any competition.

The huts at Iseke surrounded a large open communal square floored by hard-tamped dirt. All entries to the huts faced the square. Doors to close off the entries consisted of stiff mats of woven reeds, easily pulled into place. There appeared to be no window openings in any of the walls. A spider's web of well-trodden pathways radiated outwards from the square in the direction of the *shambas*.

Immediately adjacent to certain of the huts were rustic platforms a few feet high, constructed from rafts of cut poles laid down and tied with bark onto the forked heads of vertical uprights. The great baskets made of intricately woven reeds that stood on the platforms constituted the village granary. The baskets were charged full with maize cobs and kernels at harvest time. From the baskets the daily quota of grain was drawn for delivery to the women of the village for pounding into flour on a pestle and mortar principle using a narrow hollowed out log for the mortar and a heavy blunt-ended log as the pestle.

The Arab trader's *duka* stood off to the side next to where the track coming down from Manyoni entered Iseke. Its walls were built from durable brick imported for the purpose, and its business was conducted within under a covering roof of corrugated metal sheets.

Apart from the Arab trader and his family, I assumed that all the residents of Iseke belonged to the Wagogo tribe. To the extent that no single one of them appeared to display anything other than mild curiosity at my arrival, I sensed (or rather hoped that I sensed) no ill will directed at me. I thought that they were sizing me up, however, even if it might have seemed that their attention was directed elsewhere. They would certainly have seen Tom and other Iwambala camp traffic pass to and fro a few times already, so that the appearance of just another *mzungu* was already unremarkable.

The men of Iseke gave me a strong impression of being afflicted with an advanced degree of indolence; a characteristic in which they did not stand alone, as rural village life all over Tanganyika was dependent on much the same thing. The men sat or stretched out in various attitudes of repose beneath the trees as if their *raison d'être* was to prop the trees up and hold the ground down. Work was something to be avoided by them at all costs. Mundane tasks such as minding children, grinding maize, preparing meals, sweeping and tidying the huts and the communal area, hoeing, planting and harvesting the *shambas* and so on and so forth were incompatible with the dignity of men and were therefore delegated to the women. So closely were *shambas* and women linked that it was by no mere coincidence that the Kiswahili for "game reserve" was *shamba ya bibi* (the wife's field).

The men simply hung around and waited for something to happen, no doubt willing it not to. Small boys were appointed to look after any livestock and did so with great skill, knowing that they too were destined to grow into men and assume their rightful places of repose under the trees.

It was not easy to imagine how any of the Wagogo tribesmen that I saw at Iseke might get worked up enough to take any issue of any kind over either the practice of sample-taking or the *wazungu* associated with it. The men had long faces and narrow skulls. I suspected that they were morose by nature rather than by choice. All in all they appeared to be a pretty placid bunch clad in a fairly uniform assortment of dark togas, sarong-like wraps and well-perforated singlets.

Footwear, for those of them who had it, consisted of pieces cut to size from sections of worn out tyres and held in place on the feet (the soles of which were no less durable than the tyres themselves) by rubber straps that had much in common with the remnants of inner tubes.

Tribal custom favoured the men inducing their earlobes to assume perforated dimensions that nature never intended. The practice followed was to slit through the centre of the earlobes of baby boys and proceed to gradually open up the orifices by virtue of inserting the first of an eventual succession of graduated circular wooden templates. With the passage of time leading to the achievement of adulthood the template, surrounded by a rim of earlobe flesh, might reach dinner plate size.

When a template was taken out the earlobe hung down like a flaccid stick of liquorice. There was enough length in the greatest of stretched earlobes for their owners to thrust an outstretched arm through, or alternatively to use for strangling a cow if the mood so took them.

The Arab who owned the *duka* at Iseke was a diminutive gentleman. He emerged from his establishment to greet me as I arrived, having picked up the approach of my Land Rover with ears well attuned to the engine sounds of distant vehicles on the move. It was his stock in trade to come out and tout for custom. Regrettably I wasn't able to oblige him there and then owing to a pressing lack of time and my very limited facility with Kiswahili.

He was dressed in a long white *kanzu* with a round white woven cap perched on his head. Both items of apparel seemed designed to set off his milky coffee coloured skin and a tight black beard that showed every sign of having been recently trimmed by an expert.

Alongside his *duka* a great mango tree made a splash of rustling shade. I imagined that the Arab enjoyed a good relationship with the local people, even if his superior status in the community set him apart. He was of course one and they were many. Feudal attitudes were best expressed from the vantage point of relying on safety in numbers—a lesson not lost on the Arab and Indian traders who lived in most of Tanganyika's towns.

In all my dealings with the Wagogo people I would come to find them both friendly and hospitable. They invariably showed good humour in the face of adversity. Dick du Toit's negative view of them was based on a single appalling incident that resulted in all probability from a shortfall in communications and a failure to bridge cultural differences.

The area of Ugogo lying immediately north of the Njombe/Kisigo River in which Iwambala was located was remote enough to ensure the likelihood of the existence of isolated villages where, prior to the arrival of WDL in the vicinity, *wazungu* might never before have been previously seen. Most people, no matter who they were or where they came from, simply wanted to get on with their lives and do what they could do best in the security of their own lands. However, the potential for unpleasant shocks was high on both sides.

An encounter with serious overtones that I had with men of the Wagogo tribe at a later date involved my travelling up from Iseke to Iwambala in order to inform a local headman that one of his locally born *watu*, who formerly worked in my traverse team, had died of snakebite. From the description afforded by the two companions of the deceased at the time of his death it seemed that the snake that delivered the fatal bite was most probably a black mamba. The three were a long way away from camp when the incident took place, journeying out on their own time.

The story pieced together was that the two companions squatted down beside the snakebite victim and watched him for the forty minutes that it took him to expire. It was just one of those things, *shauri ya Mungu* as far as they were concerned, they said. My mission to Iwambala was to explain what had happened, return the dead man's personal effects, the body having already been interred (I knew not where), and agree a sum of compensation to be paid to the next of kin.

I entered the presence of the headman with great trepidation. The circumstances of the *mtu*'s death had to be brought to bear on someone, and the feeling of responsibility sat heavily on me. To my surprise, the headman met me on good terms and parted with me on better ones, no doubt aided by thoughts of the compensation to come.

Perhaps the *mtu*, more valuable dead than alive, was not greatly missed by those who knew him. The headman attributed the snakebite to *bahati mbaya* (bad luck). The reliable catch-all of *shauri ya Mungu* didn't enter the equation as far as the headman was concerned. It was bad luck, so that was that. There was no glory attached to the manner of the *mtu*'s passing to his way of thinking.

*

From Iseke I set out to the south in the imminence of sunset to drive the remaining miles to Iwambala. At first the terrain around me was open and grassed over, with only a scattering of trees set around the feet of a few encroaching *malima*. The ground looked as if it would get rather swampy in the wet season. Several cattle, a lot more goats and two lonely looking donkeys foraged for what little there was in the way of grazing. The cattle were small and thin, each one characterised by a floppy hump on its shoulder.

Not far off the track several geese stood around a circular depression that must have once contained water but which had become a desiccated bull's-eye of fading green in a yellowed wasteland of drought. The sun cast long shadows, softened the air and created a quietly contemplative mood that seemed almost but not quite to turn the scene into a pastoral idyll.

I learned at Iwambala that the geese I saw were of the spur-winged variety. Tom had managed to obtain four examples of the species from Mr Bill Moore-Gilbert, the Game Ranger based at Manyoni, and kept the geese, whose wings were clipped and whose destiny was the pot, in an enclosure at the camp. In the light of Tom's erstwhile shooting exploits, the gift of the spur-winged geese from a Game Ranger was a magnanimous gesture with a welcome back-to-the-fold flavour about it.

Linking the Manyoni Game Ranger's double-barrelled surname with the declared ambitions of the equally double-barrelled Bill Campbell-Whalley to join the Game Department caused me to wonder if a hyphenated surname was a prerequisite for the job. On the other hand, a WDL Field Officer named Stewart Pringle went on to disprove that surmise completely. Several years after I left Tanganyika I saw a television documentary filmed in a game reserve in what was then Rhodesia in which Stewart put in an appearance as a professional Game Ranger. In Tanganyika Stewart had a reputation for allegedly being ready, willing and able to shoot anything of any size that moved through the bush on four legs. His conversion was a classic example of the proverbial poacher turned gamekeeper and I wished Stewart well in his new role.

*

South of the Iseke grazing land, the track to Iwambala wriggled for a number of miles along a sinuously low-lying *mbuga* underlain by hard baked black cotton soil and flanked on either side by thin bush. I was excited to spot a group of zebra standing near the edge of the *mbuga*. They were Burchell's zebra, of the kind with broad stripes (as distinct from Grevy's zebra that had distinctively narrow stripes). They raised their heads to watch me carefully as I passed by and swished their tails constantly.

The cracked and concrete-like black cotton soil rattled the Land Rover mercilessly, to the extent that I was glad to get to the end of it. I was familiar with the great region of *mbuga* between Mwadui and Mwanza on Lake Victoria, and so the dry season characteristics of the black cotton soil that I drove over towards Iwambala provided me with no surprises. I did wonder, however, how driveable the track along the *mbuga* was going to be when the rains came.

Crossing an *mbuga* in the wet season required a sufficiently thick mat of "corduroy" to be laid on the black cotton soil surface to support the weight of loaded vehicles. Waterlogged black cotton soil was otherwise an impassable morass. Corduroy consisted of long, stout poles cut from the bush and sequentially laid down one after the other in opposition to the direction of the desired track. The best-laid schemes of corduroy required constant maintenance and augmentation in order that they should not "gang aft a-gley". There seemed to be no end to the capacity of corduroy to sink and disappear into black cotton slough under the testing weight of a Land Rover.

The *mbuga* that the track followed to the south of Iseke took a barely perceptible downhill gradient towards the Muhesi River, a tributary of the Njombe/Kisigo River. The Muhesi River entered the latter near the small village of Ilangali, twenty miles or so to the east of Iwambala. It formed a shallow-banked sandy swathe where it crossed the track to Iwambala—more of a pronounced dip than a hazard to be negotiated.

Both banks of the Muhesi River were cut and graded by what must have been substantial manual labour for a gang of *watu*. The result was a couple of gently sloping cuttings conducting the track from one side of the river to the other. The riverbed, perhaps ten yards wide, was fully laid with thick corduroy formed of a base of poles overlain by dry reeds. The corduroy was held secure by a neatly spaced set of vertical uprights, so that the arrangement took on the characteristics of a bridge. It would do its job well until the first flash flood of the wet season swept downstream and bore it all away.

I took the Muhesi River crossing slowly, but the Land Rover was up to it, and I didn't even have to engage four-wheel drive. Setting the four-wheel drive would have required me to stop the Land Rover; disengage the four-wheel drive lever alongside the gear lever in the front cab; get out to lock the front wheels in place by means of rotating the respective wheel hubs to a specified position; and finally re-engage the four-wheel drive lever in the cab again. According to GFM regulations it was an offence for anyone to drive with four-wheel drive engaged when it wasn't necessary. Travelling in four-wheel drive on paved roads (of which there were so few in the country that a chance would have been a fine thing) was singled out for special attention in this context.

South of the Muhesi River the track was smooth and sandy floored, hemmed in by walls of ever-thickening bush. It continued like that all the way on to Iwambala. A couple of tsetse flies, unaware that their time of day was about to run out with sunset, entered the cab of the Land Rover. I swatted one of them, and the other escaped.

Four guinea fowl emerged from the bush, nipped across the track in single file and vanished on the other side. Known as kanga, their speckled feathers were a lot more attractive than their vacant-looking blue and scaly heads, each one capped by a small horn-like protrusion. Kanga were quite large birds. They made excellent eating, providing about the same amount of meat as would a small chicken. They existed in the bush in great abundance and were correspondingly easy to hunt.

In the event that a Land Rover proceeding along a road or track met up with a flock of kanga, the practice of driving directly at them at the highest safe speed consistent with the local conditions had developed in camp circles. The kanga were relatively fast on the ground but were heavy and uncertain on the wing immediately following lift-off. It was always possible that one or two might either fly into or be struck from behind by the Land Rover—a case of wheels providing meals. Timing was all-important for the achievement of an optimum result.

Tom told me that he once drove a Land Rover at speed (accidentally he said, although I wasn't sure if I believed him) into a small flock of kanga on the road from Manyoni to Dodoma. There was a cannonade of bumps and a flurry of feathers, after which eight dead kanga were found lying in the back of the Land Rover. The tale might have gained a kanga or two in the telling, but it did no harm to the fair game credentials of the highly edible birds.

The bush thinned a little once more, and much to my delight, with light fading fast as if a celestial dimming switch had been thrown, the green canvassed facilities of the Iwambala camp appeared in view.

9

Iwambala

Tom's Iwambala camp was set up a short stroll away from the right bank of the Makasumbe River. Its location was no more than a hundred yards or so upstream from where the Makasumbe met the Njombe River as the latter emerged from its passage through the Rungwa Game Reserve.

The village of Iwambala was situated approximately half a mile to the west of the camp. To all intents and purposes this village represented an extreme outpost of southern Ugogo. It offered a pleasant-looking arrangement of huts that relied on the use of mud, sticks and thatch in much the same way as their counterparts did back at Iseke. Tall acacia trees shaded both the village precincts and some of the surrounding *shambas* in which the men of the village once again set foot purely by accident.

The proximity of the village to the camp worked in our favour. The village was far enough away not to intrude on camp life (and vice versa), yet was close enough to be easily reached when we needed to purchase key staples such as eggs, an occasional chicken (*kuku*), chillies and watermelons, or to hire casual labour for the sampling teams.

As I had already discovered, Iwambala was located well within tsetse country. As a consequence, apart from a collection of scrawny goats, the husbandry of any other four-footed domestic livestock by the villagers was impossible. Goats were consummate survivors. The lack of domestic animals probably didn't worry the villagers very much since the proximity of the Rungwa Game Reserve tended to ensure that there was plenty of small game available for legal hunting (dik-dik, duiker, impala and kanga) to place a steady supply of meat in their cooking pots.

On the other hand there were far too many dogs residing in the village. They were archetypal African "pie dogs", typified by curled tails, furrowed brows and a doleful sort of look that went a long way toward explaining the origin of the couplet "hangdog expression". It was possible that the dogs provided the villagers with a source of meat, although whether or not they did was something that I preferred not to know.

The local name given to this breed of dog was *shenzi*, which was a Kiswahili word meaning "uncivilised". *Shenzi* was also a term used by prejudiced urban types to express the conviction that their rural brethren were not characterised by qualities that smacked of sophistication. Any form of accusation that an *mtu* was *shenzi* was considered to be gravely insulting. The advantage of calling a dog *shenzi* was that the dog couldn't retaliate.

The *wazungu* sector of Tom's camp was erected, with all tents and associated facilities facing inwards, around the rim of a sandy-floored clearing canopied by spreading acacia trees.

A recently dug *choo* surrounded by a thorn *boma* lurked a suitable distance back under the trees at the rear of the tents, ever ready to accept depositions that were either liquid (*mkojo*) or solid (*mavi*) or both at the same time.

The word *mavi*, which translated as "shit", provided a stimulus to after-dinner conversation in camp in motivating us to translate some good English stock phrases into Kiswahili. A similar pastime had occupied the minds of Second World War POWs, who made the transition in their case from English to German and, in having done so ,gave us an assurance that we were in good company.

By changing *mavi* to *mavini* we came up with a local expression for "in the shit". It was a condition that we were not unfamiliar with. When applied to a noun, the suffix *ini* conferred upon the noun the quality of "being within". An example in general use was *porini* (in the bush), derived from *pori* (bush). The principle fell down a bit where words that actually ended in *ini* were concerned, as with *lakini* (but) and numerical multiples of ten such as *ishirini* (twenty). However, all languages were known to have the power to confuse beginners.

A selection of the vernacular gems that we came up with follows:

Changamfu mzuri onyesha	Jolly good show
Changamfu mzuri onyesha, nini!	Jolly good show, what!
Kwa Mungu!	By Jove!
Mzuri Mungu!	Good Lord!
Herufi kubwa, mtoto a kale!	Capital, old boy!
Hapana mbaya!	Not bad!
Mzuri na tosha	Good enough
Nyeupe na tosha	Fair enough
Usijui!	Don'tcha know!
Wewe choini	You're in the shithouse
Sisi mavini	We're in the shit
Sisi mavini kabisa	We're totally in the shit
Sikalikiti	It's not cricket
Mavi ya doumi	Bullshit
Weka juu kundu yako	Shove it up your ass
Huyu tundu ya kundu	He is an asshole
And last, but by no means least –	
Utakwenda kutomba!	Fuck off!

Thus did the time pass profitably on some evenings. As the exercise was reckoned by us to be *kilele kundu* (top hole) it was a mystery as to why the *watu* appeared to be so mystified by our scholarly prowess when they heard the results.

They probably sat in their sector of the Iwambala camp, the regulation few hundred yards away from where we performed our philological feats, neither understanding nor appreciating what was being done by us to further the greater development of Kiswahili, as they pounded on home-made drums, scoffed *posho al fresco*, and adopted the nearby riverbed as a *choo* sent from heaven.

The *wazungu* area of camp was blessed with not only a mess hut but also a kitchen and a bathroom complete with a fitted bath and hot and cold running water. All of these facilities were constructed on the tried and true standards of pole-framed walls and tarpaulin roofs. Mud had no involvement at all in the walls, but it was used in the guise of bricks to contain the fires for both cooking food and heating water.

The walls of the mess hut and bathroom were clad in cut thatch. The use of thatching was avoided only in the case of the kitchen in which the camp cook Simon kept alive a roaring, spark-whirling fire that was known to extinguish only by accident. Simon and his assistant Paolo Odhiambo prepared all meals destined for *wazungu* delectation on top of a heavy, cast-iron grille laid on an open-fronted box-like arrangement of mud bricks in which the fire was contained.

Simon, of the Wanamwezi tribe, was fat and jolly by nature in the great tradition of good cooks. He knew a score of ways to cook a kanga and all of them were memorable. He was regarded as an aristocrat among the complement of camp *watu* owing to his role as custodian of the *wazungu* camp and the impressive zeal with which he protected this position. Simon had already worked with Tom for a year and was accustomed to tailoring his skills to suit Tom's preferences. The culinary delights that Simon was able to produce from the most basic of ingredients made him worth his weight (which was considerable) in gold.

Paolo, who joined me as my camp cook when Tom graduated to a detailed work assignment and took Simon with him, was from Kenya and fortunate to be a member of a "good" tribe. His tribe was the Luo (or Jaluo), which hailed from lands in the Kisumu district on the east flank of Lake Victoria. The Luo were distinguished by jet-black skin and a thick-lipped cast to their mouths. Nilotic in origin, the tribe had come down from the north back in the far mists of time to settle by the lake. They tended to look as if they were sizing up anyone and everyone that they met and were not too happy with what they were seeing.

From my association with Paolo I came to think, perhaps unfairly, that Luo people might not necessarily be generally trustworthy. In fairness to the tribe, however, it at least held an advantage in its Kenyan nationality that it wasn't Kikuyu. A Luo luminary, Mr Tom Mboya was a prominent political focus for his tribe at the time in the Kikuyu-dominated struggle in Kenya towards *uhuru*. I bought Mr Mboya's book entitled *Freedom and After* at a Catholic mission-run bookshop in Dodoma and took very little time to decide that I needed something a lot less turgid than that to read in camp. Perhaps in writing the book Mr Mboya thought that he could bore people into supporting his cause as a counterpoint to the more coercive methods employed by the men of Mr Kenyatta's tribe.

The plan dimensions of our mess hut at Iwambala were approximately twenty feet by twenty feet. Reed thatch provided an impression of security to the walls. A Tilley lamp hung centrally from a roof strut, suspended like a sword of Damocles over a rudimentary communal table made from rough boards laid on a pair of trestles. The table, on which meals were served, was set around with our canvas-backed chairs.

The hissing Tilley lamp inevitably attracted the high-speed impact of innumerable nocturnal insects. The remains of insects that failed to survive the collision either crashed onto the table or made softer landings on top of our meals.

Alongside the back wall of the mess Tom's battery-operated record player and a short-wave transistor radio stood on a specially constructed supporting shelf. The radio allowed us to listen to the BBC World Service and its news bulletins, which were introduced to the stirring strains of "Lillibullero", with which we became very familiar.

We were also able to pick up the English service of the TBC (Tanganyika Broadcasting Corporation) from Dar es Salaam, and sometimes in the early mornings when reception was at its best we also received the KBC (Kenya Broadcasting Corporation) from Nairobi. For *wazungu* tastes, the KBC, which provided an accomplished imitation of the popular style of Europe's Radio Luxembourg (two-o-eight metres on the Medium Wave), offered a considerably preferable style of broadcasting to that which was provided by the TBC.

The TBC, which we believed must have stood for "Total Bloody Crap", was as dull to listen to as it was dreary to contemplate. To some extent its output reflected the weakness of professional production talent in Dar. What was most likely was that the process of what was unenthusiastically referred to as "Africanisation" of the TBC production staff was already taking hold.

A question current in bars where *wazungu* gathered in Tanganyika was, "Why is a banana like the government of an African country?" Well, went the answer, neither of the two are quite straight; both are slick on the surface and soft at the core; they each start off being green, go through a yellow phase and then always turn black.

Tom's record player was accompanied by one long-playing gramophone record, designed to be played at a rotating speed of 33⅓ rpm. The LP featured a collection of vocal performances by Mr Tom Lehrer. I had never heard of Mr Lehrer previously, but I liked all of his renditions the first time around. On its second playing the LP was even more acceptable, and after its third spin I felt that I was very much coming to appreciate Mr Lehrer's comic talent. Thereafter, however, my appreciation began to slip. By the tenth circuit of listening to him I would cheerfully have broken the LP had I thought I could get away with it. After a multiplicity of plays of the LP that Tom never seemed to tire of listening to, my thoughts began to turn to how nice it would be if I could just once get my hands around Mr Lehrer's throat.

Had I been able to sing I had no doubt that with all the lyrical repetition that I had absorbed I would have been able to reproduce each track of the LP, note for note, and nuance for nuance. "Be Prepared! That's the Boy Scouts' Marching Song" might have had some relevance to life in a bush camp where the range of facilities was nothing if not limited, but there were only so many times one could listen to it, or for that matter to "I Hold Your Hand in Mine" or to "Fight Fiercely, Harvard", and still retain an admiration for Mr Lehrer.

His most relevant number, I thought, was "The Hunting Song", in which the maximum that the game laws would allow—namely two game wardens, seven hunters and a cow—was shot by him. In the context of the WDL exploration programme the pertinence of "The Hunting Song" was lost on none of us.

When he moved to his detailed work assignment, Tom ditched Mr Lehrer's disc and replaced it with two newly purchased LPs, each one replete with classical music tracks. He deemed the classics to offer a more appropriate accompaniment to the Holy Grail cachet of social class that was known to accompany detailed work.

The camp bathroom was an altogether ingenious assembly. Tom had got hold of a sheet metal tank to serve as a bathtub. Its dimensions were about three feet deep, and four feet by four feet on both sides. The tank *cum* bath was set up in the centre of a square platform-like floor of tightly corduroyed logs surrounded for privacy by a tall thatch clad wall of poles.

Two metal pipes, each one-inch in diameter, entered the bathroom on a slight downgrade through what was thought of as the back wall of the establishment. The open ends of the pipes projected a few inches over one edge of the tank. A pair of neatly whittled wooden bungs were used to close off the open pipes in the manner of taps. At their far ends, a couple of yards outside the bathroom's back wall, the pipes were connected to the bases of a respective pair of flat-lying forty-four gallon drums. One of these drums was filled with cold water and mounted on a stand made from cut poles tied together with strips of bark. The second drum, also water-filled, lay on an open arrangement of mud bricks within which a roaring fire was encouraged to heat the water in the drum to near boiling point when bath time drew nigh.

It was Paolo's duty both to ensure that the two drums were full of water and that the fire was up and going in time to supply hot water to the bath in the early evening. Removal of the wooden bungs from the ends of the pipes resulted in hot and cold water flowing freely to the tank, where the two streams could be judiciously mixed either to provide the preferred depth and temperature of water or otherwise for as long as the water supply held out.

Replacing the hot water pipe bung was a hazardous procedure given the elevated temperature of the flowing water. The problem was solved by redesigning the bung using a forked branch from a tree. The new bung was then equipped with a handle and could be taken out and replaced safely once the volume of hot water in the tank was judged to be sufficient.

As far as I knew, this bath facility was unique in the existing world of WDL bush camps. Tom's metal tank bath beat the standard-issue canvas bag shower suspended from a tree into a cocked hat, if not into a pith helmet.

The great benefit of taking a bath in the tank, which could never be overstated, was the opportunity that it gave us to luxuriate in hot water at the end of a working day while the inviting fragrance of Simon's latest culinary triumph simmering fragrantly on the grille wafted over us. Even the strains of Tom Lehrer creeping out of the mess hut couldn't dent a feeling that all was well.

The leader of our *watu* workforce in camp was Tom's headman Vincent. As with Simon, Vincent was another of Tom's long-term associates. Vincent was perhaps forty years old, sternly protective of his status as headman, and always able to give the appearance of being on top of things. Tom gave his instructions for the *watu* to Vincent and Vincent ensured that the *watu* carried the instructions out. He drew attention to his appearance through wearing a colonial-styled sola topee or pith helmet that looked as if it had been salvaged from a DO's rubbish bin following the promotion of the DO to the appropriate level of incompetence that would permit him to wear a pith helmet with some plumes on top of it.

I never saw Vincent at work without the pith helmet set firmly on his head. It was such an attribute of his character that, had he appeared without it, I would probably not have recognised him. I imagined that he wore the pith helmet even when he was asleep.

One of Vincent's jobs was to appoint specific *watu* to the sampling teams and assign the same to the *wazungu* who evidently had no choice in the matter of whom they worked with. When I came to the camp at Iwambala the *wazungu* in residence were Tom and myself. The complement of *watu* was then twenty-five, inclusive of Simon and Paolo in the kitchen, an excellent driver named Idi Ramadhani, and a somewhat less adept assistant driver named Mwita Ntikira. Excluding Vincent, the twenty remaining *watu* were divided into two gangs of ten, one assigned to Tom and one to me.

The iron-willed would-be game ranger Bill Campbell-Whalley was also connected to the Iwambala camp, but, as mentioned previously, he worked on a roving commission in distant parts of the area assigned to us. We normally met him for briefing and coordination purposes during periodic supply replenishment and service visits to Dodoma.

Tom and I once went out of Dodoma with Campbell to visit a locality where Campbell was at that time currently working—I travelled with Campbell in one Land Rover and Tom followed us in another. The road that we followed ran straight and wide for mile after mile. Campbell told me that it was constructed during German colonial days. The road appeared to approach hills as features to be cut through rather than diverted around.

For the duration of the journey Campbell lectured me about the careful driving of Land Rovers. With so many WDL Land Rovers being written off all over the country, his instructions to me were not untimely, even if an element of holier-than-thou content made some of his tips grate on my nerves after a while. He paid particular attention to the technique of changing gears, applying a near venomous condemnation to anyone guilty of gear clashing, and went on to express his displeasure with drivers he knew of who habitually tapped the gear lever in and out when changing either up or down.

"The gear lever is supposed to be held in the hand for putting into place!" Campbell told me repetitively. Another regrettably widespread practice connected with a gear lever that Campbell deplored was directed at those who chose to envelop the knob on top with wet rawhide in the form of the scrotum of a species of game, impala preferred. The rawhide shrank as it dried and fused itself onto the knob. Constant manipulation (tapping or putting) wore away the hairs and placed a smooth gloss on the hide that was pleasant to the touch. Campbell was not keen, or so it seemed, to fondle any gear lever knob cover that had once contained a pair of balls.

Early in the new year following my arrival at Iwambala, when I had been based at the camp for almost three months, a third geologist was sent to join us, clean and fresh from his Mwadui induction. His name was Eddie McGinnis. He was Scottish by birth. His arrival meant that I was no longer the camp junior. I liked to think that I was by then progressing towards achieving "old hand" status, even if in thinking that I was only fooling myself.

Eddie, a year or so older than me, seemed to be a lot greener than I had been at the outset, to the extent that that was possible. He was an egghead both physically and intellectually, possessing a serious, almost introspective nature. Not unnaturally, he went on in future years to establish a successful career in the greater stable of the Anglo American Corporation of South Africa, in which he was highly regarded by his peers.

Eddie's first solo sortie out of camp saw him heading down into the heart of the Rungwa Game Reserve in a Land Rover on the cut track that we had put in along the course of the Njombe River. He was accompanied by a mandatory armed game scout, a team of *watu* and a load of essential gear. His task was to fly camp in a specified location and to sample the surrounding area for a period of three days before returning to Iwambala.

Not long after Eddie and his associates reached the location of the fly camp, three lions strolled by them in single file. If three lions were enough to dampen the enthusiasm of the *watu*, they were more than sufficient to deter Eddie and the game scout. Their desire to pass three days and nights in a locality frequented by *simba*, even with the supposed protection afforded by the game scout's rifle, evaporated in an instant. Undertaking sampling traverses shaped up to be much less of a priority for their attention than reloading the gear and hastening back to Iwambala in record time.

I wasn't sure how I would have reacted under similar circumstances, although in all probability I also wouldn't have hung around for long enough to find out. There but for the grace of God went I.

It was interesting that Eddie had actually seen lions in the Rungwa Game Reserve, as that was an experience denied to me. It was no secret that lions were there of course, as their nocturnal roaring was such a fundamental element of bush life that it was normally made conspicuous only by its absence.

*

The team of *watu* with whom I worked, with thanks due to Vincent for their assignment to me, were drawn from a range of tribal affiliations. A core group of four were members of the Waguni tribe from the Songea district in southern Tanganyika. The others comprised one Mnamwezi (Tabora), two Wasukuma (Mwanza) and three Wagogo (hired locally).

I preferred to work with *watu* from the Waguni tribe above all others. In my view they were imbued with a quality of character unmatched elsewhere in Tanganyika. With one exception, all the Waguni that I was privileged to know had great personal presence and were proud, strong (irrespective of stature), reliable, intelligent and inventive. The Waguni tribe was related to the Zulu nation, a northern offshoot of the great Zulu diaspora out of South Africa that had taken place a century previously. Their character was shaped by their heritage. The blood of Chaka flowed in their veins (as also did the blood of Lobengula, so the news wasn't entirely good).

The four Waguni who were in my team of *watu* were named Efrem Kassiani, Taji Mohammedi, Yusufu Mohammedi (Taji's brother), and Saidi Mohammedi. Other than through tribal bonds, Saidi was unrelated to either Taji or Yusufu and lived, for reasons best known to him alone, in Unamwezi.

The Waguni was an Islamic tribe, although as far as the religious aspects of their life was concerned they tended to practise the same unobtrusively. The most important consideration for such followers of Islam in the bush was that the meat they ate had to have been correctly *halalled*. Throat cutting of both game and domestic animals and fowl came to them very much as second nature. Taji, who was qualified with formal credentials authorising him as a *halal* slaughterer, was a noted expert with a sharp knife.

I appointed Efrem to be my personal headman. It was a decision that I never afterwards had cause to regret for as much as an instant.

Efrem, Taji and Yusufu all accompanied me when I eventually left Iwambala on assignments to work elsewhere in the country, and I considered myself very fortunate to have the driver Idi, another Mguni, come with me as well.

Saidi disappeared shortly after we left Iwambala, but I hadn't seen the last of him as he turned up a few months later at a camp I had up in the Singida district. The consequences of his return demonstrated that there was a joker somewhere in every pack, if not a piece of bad fruit in most sound looking mango trees. Saidi gave such an impression of reliability when he was in my Iwambala team that it was very disappointing when he deserted us without notice. One evening he was in camp, and by morning he was gone. He was small, thin and sharp looking. A moustache that Ronald Colman would have recognised with delight was his prime distinguishing characteristic.

I was worried by his disappearance, but I needn't have been. Efrem told me that Saidi had hitched a ride on the back of a truck and was on his way back to where he lived near Tabora. He was owed no money, although he would hardly have departed if he had had money to collect. He didn't appear to have stolen anything prior to leaving. The mystery was why he chose to go. I assumed that his decision was made on a purely personal and possibly irrational whim.

On his reappearance at the Singida district camp I hailed him as a near-prodigal son, yet verily did it come to pass that the camp had taken a viper into its midst. What happened next will be recounted in a later chapter.

The Mnamwezi in my team was named Hamisi Mrisho. He was a young man with strikingly good looks who was much addicted to anointing his skin with Lifebuoy soap. He liked to carefully rub a cake of Lifebuoy soap over the glissade of sweat on his skin to generate a fragrance that only he could have thought pleasing.

Through frequent combing and very infrequent trimming, Hamisi maintained his hair in a stiff-standing pile, the shape of which looked like a cross between a wedge and a pompadour. His hair evoked such an image of Elvis Presley's coiffure that Hamisi became an Elvis-type in my mind. I mentioned Elvis to him, at which Hamisi gave me a look so blank that I realised that the fame of the former had yet to arrive at the edge of the Rungwa Game Reserve. In terms of local style, Hamisi was clearly ahead of his time.

The pair of Wasukuma in my team were both named John. One was John Simon, and the other was John Mwita. In order to maintain what was a standard first-name basis of address they were first of all respectively known as John *moja* (John one), and John *mbili* (John *two*). No sense of status was supposed to accompany the numeration as it was made purely on considerations of seniority, yet the two Johns acted as they believed that *moja* counted for more than *mbili*. To prevent conflict it was necessary to backtrack and revert to calling them by their complete names instead.

John Simon was, for a Msukuma, a reasonable and thereby atypical member of the tribe. John Mwita fitted the norm of a Msukuma with a capacity to cause trouble for us, which was just what he eventually did when we were camped together up in the Singida district. That camp was by no means "lucky", as will be made clear later on. A camp and the people in it would normally be expected to make their own luck, and the fact that we didn't succeed too well in doing so in that place was both my responsibility and my fault.

I regarded the Wasukuma as the least pleasant and most untrustworthy of all of the tribes with which I came into close contact. The final camp of my time in Tanganyika, located in the Mwanza district of Usukuma to the north of Mwadui, gave me an opportunity to associate with far more of the indigenous tribe than I wanted to. I always sensed that I was very much a *mzungu* whom the Wasukuma "saw coming".

In Kiswahili the word *kuma* was used to specify a celebrated feature of the female anatomy. It didn't surprise me that that word formed the suffix of the Wasukuma tribal name, as it was just what they were a bunch of.

John Mwita was an average kind of worker who was neither good nor bad. He did no more than what was required of him. There seemed to be no one among the camp *watu* who appeared to like him, but I put the unpopularity down to his being Msukuma and possessing the sort of unattractive personality that was usually part and parcel of members of the same tribe.

The curious thing was that John Mwita was hired on the strength of a glowing personal testimonial, written in English and carrying a declaration that the bearer was the next best thing to sliced *ugali*. The author of the testimonial was a WDL prospector named Michael Annesley for whom John Mwita had worked. Michael was a true gentleman of the old school. I had the greatest of respect for him. If he thought that John Mwita was all right, then Amen to that.

Some time after I had parted company with John Mwita following a number of unfortunate incidents, I met Michael in Shinyanga and asked him about his former employee. Michael remembered him well. "What a trouble maker!" he said.

Then why, I enquired of Michael, did he provide John Mwita with such a splendid letter of recommendation?

"I had to do it!" Michael told me. "It was the only way that I could get rid of him!"

Since Michael's document of adulation concerning John Mwita was written in a language that the latter couldn't have understood even if he had been able to read, I wondered how John Mwita would have known what sort of information the testimonial offered unsuspecting future employers. However, I didn't think it worth pressing the point any further.

The other three *watu* in my team were Wagogo tribesmen. They were placid, easy-going rural characters who were not equipped with a shred of worldliness. I heard them referred to by members of other tribes in camp as *washenzi*. It was an opinion that I couldn't share, and I took steps to quash it at once. There was something utterly innocent in the Wagogo outlook on life. The most daring thing they might have done in their lives was to have their earlobes stretched.

One of the Wagogo whom I particularly took to was named Mwendambio Ngihimba. The prefix *mwend* bore reference to movement of a speedy nature and, that being the case, Mwendambio was singularly misnamed. Yet he possessed the physical attributes of a champion. He was tall, well built, muscular, strong, amiable and great of heart. It was a mere side issue that he was also as ugly as sin. His was not a face that one would like to meet up with in a dark back street in Dodoma. He epitomised the average village male at his peak of his sitting-beneath-the-trees indolence. It was impossible not to both like and admire him.

Mwendambio's approach to life was simple, his thought processes were snail-like and his intellect was slow. He was *mshenzi* in the pure sense of the word, no insult intended. I could not help thinking of him cast in the role of Lenny from John Steinbeck's *Of Mice and Men*.

*

In the company of my team of stalwarts I felt reassured that, to a greater or a lesser extent, I would weather whatever being *porini* (in the bush) could throw at me and hopefully along the way stop short of becoming too deeply *mavini*. Some members of the team were not an awful lot more familiar with the exigencies of working in the remote bush than I was, and they were not loath to demonstrate a state of fearfulness as to what was out there ready to either trample on them or eat them up. This meant that I was forced to demonstrate considerably more confidence in being in charge than I actually felt, as I was not confident at all.

When it came to encounters with the bigger game, as a team we performed in way that was much less equal than the sum of our parts.

*

From our Iwambala camp a well-trodden footpath led to the north bank of the Njombe River. The riverbank in that location was about ten feet high and sheer and crumbling at its lip. It dropped to the edge of a fifty-foot wide bed of dry sand and gravel through which sporadic ribs of black rock thrust up like strips of abandoned buffalo hide. On the far bank of the Njombe River the bush of the Rungwa Game Reserve kept its own counsel and protected its immediate secrets.

Walking along the footpath from the camp to the river with bare feet was a practice not recommended for *wazungu*. The retained heat of the sun in the coarse dust and the hard underlying soil was not to be trifled with. The soles of *wazungu* feet took a while to wake up, but when they did the sensation of treading on a pit of red-hot coals came in an instant. It was all too easy to be caught barefoot on such burning ground a hundred yards from sanctuary. The only course of action feasible under the circumstances was to sit on the ground with the feet in the air and hope that someone would come along soon carrying a set of footwear.

Clever *wazungu* didn't get themselves into such situations, but unfortunately it took time for us to learn cleverness in the bush, and for some of us there would never be enough of that sort of time available.

When I first arrived at Iwambala, a track crossing the Njombe River to access the Rungwa Game Reserve was already almost complete. The riverbank cuttings for the track were neatly graded, and only a final section of corduroy remained to be laid. A continuation of the track which would follow the Njombe River upstream into the game reserve was imminently pending. Under the terms of our permit to carry out work in the game reserve the pending track construction was required to make minimal impact on the bush. Although both the general direction and eventual destination of the track were planned on paper, how the track would be established in practice was a matter decided on the spot from day to day. As a result, the track wriggled like a snake in motion, threading around trees, detouring to avoid clumps of bush, and taking maximum advantage of the incidence of clearings. Gullies were avoided as a matter of principle.

It was fortunate that there was a lot of bush in the game reserve, as the raw materials for corduroying had to be obtained from somewhere. The ideal situation arose when an established elephant path coincided more or less with the direction of the track. Elephant paths, the fruit of what in many cases could have been centuries of elephantine traffic, were normally wide enough to accommodate a Land Rover, being both hard-surfaced and perfectly graded, however rough the surrounding terrain was.

The bush on the game reserve side of the Njombe River was what Tom described as "grey bush" in recognition of the fact that the dry season was then at its peak. Most of the grass was more or less crisped away by the sun, leaving only reedy clumps to survive here and there against the odds.

Viewed from a vantage point on top of a koppie, the Rungwa Game Reserve drifted off into blue distance splotched all over with the slow moving shadows of clouds. The distant bush and its associated jumble of huge granite boulders resembled moss spotted with pebbles. Closer by, a more clearly defined scattering of green-topped acacia tree umbrellas stood out within an array of grey, pillar-like tree trunks and tightly extensive underbrush. The bush overall gave an impression of being impenetrable, but once it was entered there was an ample feeling of space in which to move all around.

Our track along the Njombe River advanced at a rate of a few miles per day, without any call for bush cutting of significance.

The Rungwa Game Reserve was famed for its big game, prominent among which were black rhinoceros, elephant, buffalo and kudu. In addition the list included reticulated giraffe, Burchell's zebra, impala, hartebeest, roan antelope, sable antelope, ringed waterbuck, hippopotamus (wet season only), duiker, dik-dik, bush pig and warthog. Also present were untold numbers of our feathered friends the kanga, and a considerable population of a small ground-running partridge named francolin.

A hundred yards downstream from the Njombe River crossing near Iwambala, the riverbed made a sudden meander, on the inner edge of which a broad rib of black rock jutted out from the base of the bank. A hollow in the sand beneath the rock contained a shallow pool of water a few feet across. Water could usually be located by digging deep into riverbeds during the dry season—the little pool in the Njombe River was a naturally occurring water hole.

The water in the water hole was greenish in colour and was bordered with scum where it impinged on the rock. At almost any time during the hours of daylight, yellow butterflies lined up on the sandy outer rim of the water hole in a flittering fringe.

On one occasion I saw a vast flock of quelea finches drinking at the water hole. Individually tiny, the birds moved as one in tremendous numbers, almost in the manner of a solid block. The flock could have contained tens of thousands of the little birds, crowding the water hole in ranks a hundred deep, and wheeling over the surface of the water in such profusion that it was a miracle that none of them were drowned.

The water hole, which might also be utilised by an occasional small antelope like a dik-dik, was most notably attended every day at sunrise and sunset by very large numbers of kanga.

Since the water hole was located at the foot of the bank on the game reserve side of the Njombe River it created a burning question for us as to whether or not a kanga drinking at it should be defined as an inviolate protected species or as a fair game target. We decided that we would accept the mid-point of the riverbed as the effective boundary between what was in and what was out of the game reserve. A kanga scuttling into the wrong sector of the riverbed stood a good chance of being shot without fear or favour. The assumed boundary was reckoned, however, to incorporate a certain amount of flexibility. A yard or two on either side of it was, we reasoned, neither here nor there.

We built a hide of thorn bush and reeds on the Iwambala side of the river, and sat within it to observe, customarily in the evenings, incoming kanga assuaging their thirst at the water hole. They invariably came by the score and sometimes even in hundreds.

Tom was not slow to point out that so many kanga gathered together in one place presented us with a pot shooting opportunity that was second to none. Ever inventive, he used what he alleged was his Irish ingenuity to rig up a few snares on the fair game side of the assumed boundary. The kanga, knowing nothing of such *wazungu* techniques, managed to avoid Tom's snares so successfully that we believed they were exercising an altogether impressive aptitude.

Following on the heels of the classic example set by Wile E. Coyote in his endlessly abortive pursuit of the Road Runner (*beep, beep*), Tom's reaction to his failure to snare kanga was to rack the level of his offensive up a notch or two. He got one of the camp *watu* to prepare a wooden frame about a yard square, over which a piece of fine sacking that had originally contained *posho* was stretched and nailed tight.

A couple of *watu* carried this arrangement to the water hole and, under Tom's supervision, erected it a short distance back from the water hole's outer rim in a position leaning at a steep angle in the direction of the water and supported in place by a thin pole. One end of a length of stout cord was tied to the base of the pole, while the other end of the cord dangled back in the hide, ready to hand. In between its two ends the cord was hidden under a shallow cover of river sand.

Strictly speaking, the sacking-clad wooden frame was set up within the game reserve's half of the riverbed. It was a moot point as to whether or not our using the frame as a tool to trap live kanga was, naturally *sensu stricto*, to be considered as hunting or as poaching. The dilemma was resolved by assigning to the project scientific experimentation criteria involving no immediate intention to kill.

For anyone taking up a position of concealment in the hide the main requirement was patience. The kanga at the water hole had to be given the time to become so accustomed to the poised presence of the frame at their drinking place that they would confidently venture beneath its overhang in numbers. Once that state of affairs came about, a tug on the end of the cord within the hide would, according to Tom's master plan, dislodge the supporting pole and cause the frame to fall on and trap some unlucky birds beneath the sacking.

As a plan it was ingenious. The fact that it didn't work couldn't detract from the inventiveness that went into dreaming it up. No matter how precipitately the frame fell, the kanga moved with greater despatch. They must have had eyes in the backs of their horny heads. They were as elusive as the Scarlet Pimpernel, and noisy with it as they flapped and cackled in communal concern. Inside the hide the atmosphere was characterised by frustration.

On one particular evening, not long after Tom had gone to the hide to conduct yet another potentially fruitless experiment to catch a few kanga, I heard the sound of an explosion coming from the river. Accompanied by Vincent and two of Tom's *watu* I raced down the track in the direction of the hide with a feeling of great alarm. We arrived to find Tom on his feet in the middle of the riverbed brandishing my Greener single-bore shotgun.

The covered wooden frame lay mute on the sand beside the water hole, one edge of it almost in the water. Beneath the sacking there was sand and only sand. Behind the frame in a location which with a leap of imagination could just about be construed as being in the fair game half of the river were two dead kanga and a scattering of feathers.

Tom had obviously thrown in the towel as far as the science of the exercise was concerned. His right not to bear arms appeared to have been surrendered in the same way. Unbeknown to me he had taken my shotgun, having decided that he was going to succeed in getting his hands on a kanga by hook or by crook. When the trap failed yet again he had discharged the shotgun into the midst of the flock of kanga fleeing from the impotent frame. A brace of kanga was a result of sorts for what was the first time the Greener shotgun was fired in anger under my ownership.

At the time of Tom's discharge of the shotgun I had still to acquire a general game hunting licence for the pot and was therefore unable to use the Greener for anything other than target practice. As I had no wish to fire it, the lack of a pot licence didn't really worry me. I wasn't sure whether I should be more shocked by Tom firing a gun or by Tom firing my gun.

At a later date my attitude to hunting went through a radical change. I became familiar with the Greener and entertained no qualms in using it to shoot game for the pot. There were to be many evenings on which, armed with the Greener, I tramped through the bush around Iwambala (on the fair game side of the Njombe River of course) in search of kanga. It was rare that I did not bag one or two, and once in a while I managed to knock over a francolin as well.

In standard poultry terms kanga meat was predominantly "dark", whereas francolin meat was mostly "white". Both game birds were conjured into succulent meals when grilled, stewed, roasted or (my favourite) casseroled by Simon. The single complaint that I might (but didn't dare) have made to Simon was that his practice of dismembering the birds using a *panga* suffered from a certain lack of aiming skills and resulted in rather too many invasive splinters of bone in the meals. However, that was a small price to pay for good food.

I found that I was not at all adept at shooting kanga on the wing, and after a while I gave up trying in favour of adopting a practice of shooting them on the ground. I found that I could then get to any shot kanga quickly and deliver them a *coup de grâce* by breaking their necks. Tom told me that a true sportsman always gave game birds a fighting chance and shot at them only when they were on the wing. From this I took to heart that I was not a sportsman, taking comfort from the principle that in shooting for the pot it was results that counted. Shooting kanga on the ground helped to limit the number of shotgun pellets that turned up with the bone splinters as regular features in the dish of the day.

The question of my lack of sporting credentials took on an extra nuance shortly before my first Christmas in Tanganyika when the forcible arrival of the wet season made it prudent for us to undertake a temporary retreat to Iwambala from the fly camp in the Rungwa Game Reserve that we were working out of at the time. The alternative to retreat was that we would be trapped in the game reserve by the burgeoning inundation. Since Tom planned that we were to go to Dar es Salaam over the Christmas period it was essential to get out while we still could.

The exodus was an overnight trip made difficult by deteriorating ground conditions, although (as will be described in a later chapter) we got through eventually. Once we were out of the game reserve and in the vicinity of Iwambala we chanced upon a large pond of rain-delivered water, around which a fresh growth of reeds was already demonstrating an intention to turn rampant. On the pond were floating half a dozen waterfowl that from their appearance I assumed to be ducks.

During our previous week down in the game reserve based in the fly camp with Paolo as cook, food had been in such short supply that even the thought of catfish and *ugali* seemed appealing.

The opportunity to shoot a couple of ducks and have them prepared by Simon back in the kitchen at the main camp was too good to miss. Accordingly, we drew up our two Land Rover cavalcade near the pond. The Greener was with us, locked away together with the 9-mm Brno rifle in my tin trunk on the back of one of the Land Rovers. It was the work of a short while to access the tin trunk, open it up, get the Greener out and slip a bird shot cartridge into its single chamber.

*

I kept the weapons with me in the game reserve for both my and their security. The last thing I wanted was to have either one or the other or both of them stolen with all the serious consequences to follow that that implied. To that particular extent the weapons could be seen as representing a liability. However, I liked to have them near at hand for what I thought of as "self protection", notwithstanding that they were only suitable for stopping game that was either too small or too timid to do me any harm.

Although it was locked fast in my tin trunk during the hours of daylight in our game reserve fly camps, I always took the shotgun out at night and kept it close at hand alongside my bed. At such times I loaded it with a solid-head cartridge that Tom gave me as a souvenir of his authorised shooting days. As an alternative I could have loaded the shotgun with a cartridge containing the heaviest buckshot; of the two, it was the solid-head cartridge that gave me the greater sense of false security.

I did my best to entertain a self-conviction that a chunk of cast lead fired from a shotgun would either be able to drop any big game that came by in its tracks or else frighten it into flight when I pulled the trigger. The solid-head cartridge never came to be fired, although there were a couple of occasions, both of them at night, when shooting it off shaped up as a near possibility. The main advantage to me was that as long as I possessed it I could feel able to defend myself if I had to. To all intents and purposes the solid-head shotgun cartridge performed the rôle of a security blanket.

As it was, we had the formal companionship of Samuel, a game scout armed with a .404 bolt-action rifle, to rely on for protection when we were in the game reserve. He carried his rifle slung from a worn leather strap on his right shoulder. Appointed to our fellowship by Mr Bill Moore-Gilbert, Samuel was just one, whereas we were many. His attention to us on an individual basis was consequently spread thin.

We accepted Mr Moore-Gilbert's assurances that Samuel was proficient at his job, even though we had no choice in the matter other than to do so. The fact that more often than not when out with a traverse party Samuel chose to bring up the rear was probably a strategic ploy.

Samuel's appearance didn't inspire a lot of confidence, as he was as thin as a reed and clad in a khaki-coloured uniform that was in no way made to measure. His shorts were baggy and his safari jacket hung on him like an old discarded blanket. On his feet he wore a tattered pair of ankle-length plimsolls that may originally have been coloured white. The flip-flops cut from old car tyres that constituted the footwear of the common *mtu* were not for Samuel. His stamp of office was vested in a dark red beret mounted on the brow with a Game Department badge—he wore the beret pushed so far back on his head that the badge faced the sun head on and was probably visible only to vultures.

Samuel integrated so well with us that after a while he seemed to merge seamlessly into our team, making the uniqueness of his game scout status less recognisable. Any nocturnal patrols that he undertook around the fly camp perimeter didn't always encompass the *wazungu* tents, but then, there was always the Greener loaded with a solid-head cartridge for me to fall back on, just in case.

He went where we went, a genuinely pleasant character but with a presence that was strangely lacking in reassurance. I was never sure whether what worried me the most was the ever-present likelihood of a too-close encounter with big game or the thought of our having to leave it up to Samuel to deal with such a situation.

As it was, I never saw Samuel either raise up or hold his .404-calibre rifle in an attitude that contained any suggestion of a threat to man or beast. He was a firm believer in allowing game to make its own way on its own terms. From his example, which I thought was in the best traditions of the Game Department, it dawned on me that that was exactly what the game believed as well. In the game reserve we lived with game all around us in a spirit of uneasy truce. It was much better for Simon to wave a white flag than it was for me to flaunt a solid-head cartridge.

*

To return to the location of that seasonal pond that we found near Iwambala, I kept a tight grip on the bird shot-loaded gun as I shuffled along on my haunches towards the edge of the pond close to where the unsuspecting ducks sat on the water. The cooling engines of our two Land Rovers pinged gently behind me. After a lengthy wriggling manoeuvre I achieved a position in which I had a clear view of the ducks over the top of the young reeds. I raised the Greener, aimed it at the ducks and was at the point of squeezing the trigger when from behind came a raucous hullabaloo of shouting, accompanied by someone drumming on a Land Rover door.

Whereupon the entire complement of ducks (or complement of duck according to Tom who told me that a true hunter, which I was not, should always refer to game in the singular) took to the air with a splashing of water and a glittering of feathers and were last seen winging above some trees on the far side of the pond.

The author of the disturbance was none other than Tom, the very man who had once fired the Greener at a flock of kanga in the act of drinking at a water hole. It seemed only reasonable to ask him why he had scared off the ducks (or duck). He said that he had no choice in the matter since shooting sitting ducks (or duck) was not regarded as cricket by the hunting fraternity. No, he went on, birds could only be taken "on the wing". He described for me the niceties of shooting duck (or ducks) with a double-barrelled shotgun—he called the technique "left and right".

I took his word for it, but I was less than happy with the result. What did it matter, I suggested, how ducks (or duck) were shot if the overriding intention was to eat them?

*

One day in the camp at Iwambala we received a visit from a young white hunter and his entourage. The white hunter's name was Jack and his mission was to scout around for hunting safari opportunities in the area surrounding the Rungwa Game Reserve. Jack was very personable: an aristocratic type with an air of grandeur and professional competence. He did, however, exhibit more than enough of the inherited propensity for bullshit that his background provided and his work demanded. White hunting was a profession already living on borrowed time; although it was still important up in Kenya, it was rarely encountered in Tanganyika, and it was that which made Jack's visit such a rare pleasure for us.

In the arsenal that he carried with him, Jack possessed a high powered .22 rifle fitted with a telescopic sight. As a demonstration of his shooting skills he used the rifle to clip the heads off kanga over what seemed to be an impossible range. He never missed his target. His demonstration of marksmanship made a huge impression on me and became one of the subliminal stimuli that led me to take up hunting for the pot.

Jack's most prized firearm was a double barrelled .577 rifle. It was a massive affair taking bullets the size of the big pepper pots that graced tables in the dining room of the Dodoma Hotel. It was a quintessential elephant gun. Nothing hit by one of its bullets was likely to travel very far afterwards.

Jack, selecting the trunk of a tree as a target, invited both Tom and me to try a shot with his .577 rifle. I declined, as even the look of the weapon was enough to deter me. Tom, ever ready for a challenge, took the rifle up at once. His shot, a thunderous detonation, missed the target altogether. The rifle's recoil dumped Tom flat on his backside (a result that I imagined Jack had always intended) and left a blue bruise on his shoulder that took more than a week to fade away.

Jack stayed for a couple of days in the general area surrounding Iwambala and then moved on. He told us he would return, although we never saw him again. He was one of those memorable people that once met always remain in the mind. Some years later, when his name came up in conversation I learned that he was killed not long after we had seen him shoot the heads from kanga with the .22 rifle that he handled with so much panache.

10
Maji a kunywa
Water to drink

The initial few of the sampling traverses that I undertook out of the camp at Iwambala were located in the broad sector of bush drained by the Makasumbe and upper Muhesi rivers that lay just to the north of the Rungwa Game Reserve. The traverses were planned to terminate against an eastern boundary that was unmarked anywhere apart from on WDL's maps. The boundary separated the overall working area assigned to us at Iwambala from a similarly sized area assigned to other parties based in another camp. This other camp was set up close to a village named Ilangali, situated twenty miles to the east of Iwambala in the vicinity of where the Muhesi River joined the Njombe/Kisigo River.

A bush track linked Iwambala with Ilangali. It was suitable for foot traffic but impracticable for wheeled transport. This was something of a pity, since it placed an access barrier between us and the two *wazungu* who were based in the camp at Ilangali. The area that they were assigned to sample spread north of the Kisigo River and stretched onwards in the direction of Dodoma.

This pair of *wazungu*, both Italian by nationality, were our nearest neighbours. Their command of the English language was equally as good as their facility with Kiswahili, neither of which mattered to them as in their camp they conversed exclusively in Italian.

They presented an interesting study in social contrasts. The senior of the two was a geologist named Danilo Pedrelli. Tall and imperious of bearing, Danilo was born in the shadow of the Alps of northern Italy and exhibited not a single Mediterranean-styled physical characteristic. His fair hair curled naturally and was kept cropped close to his head in a fashion that could have been copied from a marble bust of Julius Caesar. Although Julius would almost certainly have approved of the look of Danilo's hair, he might have been less happy with the stubby beard that adorned the lower part of Danilo's sardonic face. Julius might have observed that that kind of thing was more common in Greek than in Roman statuary. Danilo, like Julius, was a man accustomed to issuing orders that were to be obeyed at once and carried out with the utmost deference to him.

His companion in camp was a Field Officer named Mario Zopetti. Mario, who hailed from the extreme nether sole and heel regions of the Italian boot, was small, dark and intense. His slightness of stature, darkness of hair, swarthiness of features and mysteriousness of disposition, coupled with an advanced tendency to use much gesticulation as an aide to conversation, were among a few of the definitive characteristics that Mario presented to the world.

Danilo and Mario might have been united in nationality yet they were divided by geographically related social conventions. Their relationship epitomised the aristocratic north of Italy versus the peasant south—master and servant, lord and serf. Danilo's attitude towards Mario, who for his part appeared to accept his place in the scheme of things, left me amazed that Danilo managed to avoid waking up one morning to discover a well placed stiletto sitting in between his shoulder blades.

Mario was always good fun when I met him on a social level. I saw him frequently in Dodoma as well as at Manyoni when a big WDL camp servicing depot was set up in that fair town. I could relate to who and what Mario was in a way that I never could manage with Danilo.

However, an attribute that Danilo did have that evoked my great admiration was a deep appreciation of the bush and its game. In that context Danilo always appeared to radiate the kind of competence that could take control of and manage any situation that came along.

Danilo owned an impressive arsenal of weaponry. He had a matched pair of Holland and Holland double-barrelled shotguns resting in a velvet-lined mahogany case; a collection of small-calibre rifles; and (his pride and joy) one twin-bored .404 rifle suitable for hunting the largest game. He cared for his guns with passion and was both an excellent shot and an accomplished hunter.

He was ever eager to receive verbal reports from either his *watu* or the local villagers and tribesmen on the presence and movement of big game anywhere within half a day's drive of his camp, and tended to respond to hearing such reports by exclaiming, "Fuck! I must shoot!" (Or as he pronounced it, "Fahkamusshoota!") As often as not thereafter he would proceed to be as good as his word.

Danilo's formal acquisition of hunting licences went well beyond the requirements of merely shooting for the pot. He took out hunting licences for both buffalo and elephant and was anxious to shoot to the limit of his quotas.

*

To help me get my bearings as well as to ensure that I would absorb as much as possible of what there was to know about sampling techniques, Tom accompanied me on the first three traverses that I undertook. The traversing distance to be covered, out and back in each case, was no more than eight miles. Led by Tom's redoubtable pith-helmeted headman Vincent, with Vincent's diminutive second-in command Omari taking up the rearguard, we proceeded on our way. We strolled along streambeds in which we identified likely gravel traps and excavated samples forthwith; we walked the length of cut traverse lines between baselines and took soil samples in prescribed locations; we returned the samples to camp for reduction by panning; and we completed all essential records and reporting requirements.

Omari cultivated a thin moustache that sat on top of a sardonic grin. It gave him the devil-may-care look of Douglas Fairbanks Jr and Errol Flynn rolled together, set off by a brightly coloured skullcap tilted at an appropriately jaunty angle.

The traverses undertaken with Tom taught me a key lesson that the bush was equipped with more species of thorns than it was reasonable to think about. The most virulent of these thorns was a densely configured and evilly hooked variety named *ngoja kidogo* (wait a bit). It always lived up to its name, seeming to reckon that it had a divine right to impede our traverses and inflict painful consequences on anyone among us who showed it disrespect.

I also found out that game animals both big and small were far more interested in avoiding us than we were in avoiding them. Signs of elephants (*tembo*) were everywhere, in their piled-up football-sized droppings, some of which were ominously warm and steaming when found; in trees from which thick branches and great strips of bark had been torn away wholesale; in trees brought down with a single headstrong push that had cracked them off at ground level as if they were matchwood; and in the graded roads and polished rocks against which generations of elephant feet had trod and countless elephant sides had respectively brushed.

Our practice on coming across recently dropped elephant dung was to break a turd or two open to make an assessment of internal temperature as a guide to how far away the author of the droppings might be. The contents of an elephant turd consisted of indigestible vegetable matter, clean and coarsely fibrous to the touch.

Occasionally we might chance upon an array of great bones scattered over a wide area centred on a boulder-like honeycomb-textured elephant skull set with eerily sunken eye sockets and round gaping holes where the tusks had once fitted. Legend had it that the bones of a dead elephant were dispersed thus by members of its former herd. Its companions were also believed to carry the tusks away to be placed in a secret elephant graveyard, the search for the location of which by *wazungu* and *watu* alike was never ending.

Out on traverse I soon discovered that my rifle, when carried slung on my shoulder over a distance of several miles, became an unpleasantly weighty encumbrance. When borne in combination with a full sample bag on my other shoulder the weight of the rifle brought out my limitations as a porter in no uncertain terms.

A photograph that I took of a group of seven *watu* that I was out on traverse with one day encapsulated the human condition of the process in which we were engaged. The seven were captured together by the camera, each in a personally adopted pose of one kind or another. Whenever a camera was pointed at an *mtu* and he was aware of it, he at once assumed a posture of dramatic content, a belligerent or otherwise pugilistic attitude being the most popular. If he was in possession of a *panga* or a knife he would brandish the same in a manner suggesting that a battle was imminent. Each *mtu* clamoured for permission to hold any available firearm when a photo was about to be taken and he who was allowed to take the gun made no secret of the fact, in the way he posed with it, that he had achieved the height of his ambitions.

In the photograph the seven *watu* stood in front of a grove of tall and coarsely barked acacia trees, one or two of which were clear victims of itinerant elephants. The dress code on display favoured bare chests, off-white singlets that resembled holes surrounded by ragged threads, and tattered shorts in shades dominated by khaki and olive green. The shorts were, relatively speaking, in slightly better shape than the singlets. John Simon occupied the far left-hand position of the line of *watu* facing towards the camera. He leant to one side, supporting a young Mgogo lad on his right hip.

Mwendambio, with his torso exposed to the world, was on the far right of the group. His face was stern yet typically untroubled. A full sample bag sat on his head, perfectly balanced.

The pair who stood to Mwendambio's immediate right were Wagogo hirelings from Iwambala, for whom our stock notice *hakuna nafasi ya kazi* had failed to apply. They both stood to attention. One of them was lurking almost shyly behind Mwendambio's right arm with a screen clutched in one hand; the other bore a shovel on his shoulder in a pose indicative of the fact that an order to present arms had been not only given but understood.

At the centre of the group of seven was Hamisi, offering a forthright stance with his arms akimbo. His eyes were fixed on the camera as if daring the photographer behind it to pass an adverse comment on his Elvis Presley credentials. Alongside Hamisi was Yusufu, his shoulder towards the camera. In his hands Yusufu held our unfolded traverse map. He appeared to be studying the map with a kind of intensity that suggested he had no idea where we were.

Next to Yusufu was his brother Taji, the seventh and final member of the team. Taji was holding my rifle and provided an impression that he was about to raise it to his shoulder to take a snap shot at the camera to reciprocate what the camera was doing to him.

*

I eventually reached a position on the learning curve at which Tom directed me to proceed on a solo traverse. In the company of my team of *watu* I was instructed to undertake a lengthy traverse going up the Makusumbe River and along one of its tributaries, there to put into practice the relevant sampling techniques that I was supposed by then to be familiar with. The traverse was intended to be a sort of baptism by fire that would exorcise any of my remaining demons of inexperience. I imagined that it would also highlight numerous facets of my incompetence.

We set off on the traverse in the cool and clear dawn of a day that promised not to remain very cool for very long. The early start was made in order to take the maximum advantage of the climate at its most equable. We were expecting to have the task completed so as to be back in camp by around two o'clock p.m. (or *saa nane* in the local convention), when any samples that were not panned down to manageable size during the traverse would be duly reduced; records and reports would be formalised, and Tom Lehrer would provide us with musical accompaniment.

Idi Ramadhani drove us all out in my Land Rover over the fifteen miles or so to our point of departure on the Makasumbe River. Idi's concessions to his profession of driver were vested in a pair of long khaki trousers in remarkably good shape and a black glossy peaked cap that looked as if it might have been lifted from the drunken mate of a small cargo ship berthed down in Dar for a few days. The cap sat well on Idi's head, and his thighs went forever unseared on the Land Rover's driving seat. Long trousers were essential garb for a driver, as any *mzungu* wearing shorts who sat on the front seat of a Land Rover that had been left overlong in the sun knew only too well.

We were dropped off and Idi took the Land Rover back to Iwambala. To allow ourselves enough time to complete the traverse we agreed to rendezvous with Idi at the place where he left us at three o'clock *(saa tisa)*. Our planned route called for us to follow the Makasumbe River upstream for a distance of approximately eight miles, at which point we would need to turn our backs on the river and head into the bush on a due south compass bearing. A couple of miles of walking would bring us to the specified tributary stream, which we would follow downstream to join the Makasumbe River once more and thereafter return to the agreed rendezvous. In principle it all seemed to be quite straightforward.

We strode out like heroes in the making, and that was just about that, as far as any element of glory in the day would be concerned.

I was wearing my safari jacket (with no shirt or vest underneath) and a pair of shorts in matching khaki. There were ankle length *velskoon* on my feet (no socks), and a light broad-brimmed hat on my head, the latter a gift from Tom. All in all, with the rifle hanging from its strap on my shoulder to set it all off, I was in general the very model of a modern major accident waiting to happen.

I was never sure, as no one ever told me, if I looked as ill at ease in that hat as I felt when I had it on my head. Although I did my best to get used to wearing the hat for protection against the sun, I simply couldn't bear it up there for long periods of time. Its sweatband lived up to its name through generating a copious quantity of salty trickles around my head that only just fell short of blinding me. I then decided that wearing a hat was not what it was cracked up to be, and packed it in from that moment on.

Our instructions were that we should sample the riverbed at intervals of no less than two and no more than three miles, taking into account the incidence of tributaries (both expected and unexpected in terms of what the map told us) requiring sampling. Locating suitable gravel traps and mapping and recording such basic geology as was exposed took much of our attention. Otherwise the traverse involved foot slogging to get to where we needed to go while avoiding chance hazards encountered along the way.

Unfortunately (or perhaps not) the incidence of outcropping rock in the riverbed was not very prolific. The rocks that we came across were all much of a muchness in appearance, indeterminate in character, and difficult to describe in terms of anything less generic than "gneiss" (pronounced "nice" although that was hardly the point).

To add a little colour to the geological monotone, we tagged Kiswahili words onto the petrological suffix "ite" to characterise a suite of rock types. These included *sijuite* (*sijui* = I don't know); *ninafikirite* (*ninafikiri* = I think); *hakunawazaite* (*hakuna waza* = no idea); *mungusaidiasisite* (*Mungu saidia sisi* = God help us); and *sikupamavite* (*sikupa mavi* = I don't give a shit—and perhaps not even a sh-ite).

No matter what rock type was identified in a given location, it was essential that the same name (supported by a rock specimen to be accurately identified by someone who knew more about those things than I did) should be applied to similar occurrences found elsewhere. Rock identification probably only really mattered when the locality of the rock was associated with a sample returning positive results for kimberlite indicator minerals. Otherwise, the true identity of many rocks that we came across was likely to remain forever pending.

There was so much to see, do, absorb and get excited about during traverses that recording the sameness of the geology seemed to be a rather mundane task, as a result of which it tended to be relegated to a position well down on the list of priorities.

We travelled along the elephant dropping-littered bed of the river, walking preferentially over the more durable surface offered by rough sand and drifts of coarse gravel. The riverbed offered us an open road to follow. While we were in it we knew that at least we couldn't get lost.On the other hand much of the sand that formed the bed of the river was soft and easily yielding to the feet. Advancing demanded a lot of effort, which forced our walking technique to become a laborious and strength-sapping trudge. Up on the riverbanks the ground was hard but the bush was thick and thorny. Progress was all a question of striking the right balance of factors. On our immediate approach to bends in the course of the river we moved with caution so as to be sure that if there was anything unpleasant on the hidden side of the bend, then we would see it before it saw us.

The burden on my shoulders consisted only of my rifle—the *watu* carried all the sampling gear and equipment apportioned between them in accordance with an unwritten law of precedence. The lower down an *mtu* was in the pecking order, the greater was likely to be his load. In addition two full water bags, which were destined to become ever lighter in weight as the traverse proceeded, were taken along with us. As far as imbibing water was concerned it appeared that none of the *watu* had yet learned much in the way of self-control. They all but emptied both of the water bags by late morning.

Not a single thought was given by any of us as to what would happen when the water contained in the two bags was all gone. In fairness to the *watu*, a water bag was usually offered to me as a precursor to any of them taking a swig from it, and I just as usually declined to drink in the mistaken belief that I was setting them a proper example. As a consequence the amount of water that I got before the water bags were emptied altogether was not much more than a few mouthfuls.

The sun rose in the sky like a flaming banner proclaiming that the dry season was still clutching us in its rapacious claws. The respite of shade was banished at a stroke. The sun's glare bounced off the hot sand as our team straggled along the riverbed. Although we were only just on the way out we were already looking like a rabble in retreat. The confluence with the tributary that we were to descend when making our way back appeared on the right-hand side of the river. It wasn't located exactly where the map suggested it would be, but it was real and that was good enough. Yet we seemed to have taken an inordinate amount of time to reach it, as if the distance along the river was expanding to spite us.

We climbed the bank of the river in the hope of making some more rapid progress on its top. It didn't help us at all, only serving to demonstrate that sand was a lesser evil than thorns, although neither was as great an evil as a pair of empty water bags.

Grains of sand worked their way inside my footwear, necessitating frequent stops to be made for me to take off the *velskoon* and tip the sand out. After a couple of hours the outer edges of my feet were abraded to a state of rawness from which localised blossoms of blood spread through the soft leather uppers of my shoes. The rifle was no less than a ponderous imposition pulling me down. I contemplated heaving it into the bush and resting content in the knowledge that I would never have to carry it again.

Half a mile upstream from where we met the cited tributary, we came upon a wide banked-up hollow in the riverbed. From all around the rim of the hollow, the sand sloped inwards to form a shallow cone about four feet deep at the centre. At the bottom was a small pool of cloudy-white water that was an inch deep at best.

The hollow was an ingenious example of elephantine industry. Although the excavation didn't appear to have been made very recently, evidence that sweeping tusks, flailing trunks and shovelling feet had once been in play at the site remained in an enduring tribute to an impressive job.

However, our first reaction was not so much to marvel at what had been done as to get at the water exposed in the pit of the hollow. We lay on our bellies around the water, sucked it dry, waited for seepage to replenish it, drank the water again, did what we could to get a little of it into our water bags and failed in the attempt.

The water was gritty on the teeth, but was cool to the lips and ambrosia-like to the soul. I felt more life return to me with each successive slurp, to the extent that I was reluctant to depart from the hollow to continue with the traverse and leave the water behind. There was still a good distance to cover on the traverse, and both time and a lack of water were not on our side.

It was all too easy for me to believe that I would never be able to even reach the point at which we had to make tracks through the bush towards intersecting and descending the specified tributary. My sole preoccupation was based on water and how to get it. The balance of the traverse seemed to have no point, but we went on because duty said we must. We moved slowly. I didn't know what the *watu* were thinking about, but the focus of my mind was directed towards the receding hollow behind us.

After an hour or so my condition was not much better than that of walking wounded. The sand, the heat, the absence of water to drink and the ubiquitous tsetse fly around us combined to create an enemy that I had no resources left in me to counter. I doubted that I could even climb the riverbank, let alone walk south to the tributary. The *watu* were in somewhat better shape than me, but all things were relative and none of them were doing very well either.

It all came down to water in the end.

I found that I could only walk for a short distance before I was overwhelmed by a need to stop and rest for a while. The heat seemed to be getting ever more intense. I had lost any ability to sweat. My periods of resting grew longer as achievable walking distances became shorter. I tried to cover a minimum of twenty paces between starting and stopping, but even that was impracticable when it became too much of a problem for me to count up to twenty.

I knew enough to appreciate that my first solo traverse was not only a battle lost to inexperience, it was also a personal debacle. I finally came to a point when I recognised that I could proceed no further upstream. The tributary was going to have to wait for another day. The lure of the water behind us was too intense to ignore. The only matter of importance was that we should all survive for long enough to get back to that wet-bottomed elephant-dug hollow.

The samples that we had taken thus far had been left in the riverbed to be collected during the return journey. We abandoned the traverse and began the retreat, myself bringing up the rear. As the sun crested its zenith and began to slip downhill towards an appointment with dusk I had to stop and rest with a steadily increasing frequency. The *watu* shuffled on ahead of me. They would pick up the samples and take them back to the rendezvous. They disappeared from sight as if an instruction that it was every man for himself had been issued and accepted.

The course that my feet wove in the sand was as erratic as if it were being backed by twenty-four IPAs, which most unfortunately it wasn't. A few yards, a collapse and a reprise of the pattern over and over again defined my progress. The will to go on was painful to sustain.

Following an age of stopping and starting, the talismanic hollow that formed my one objective in life at the time appeared in front of me. I fell into it. Getting there was all that had kept me going. The elephants that had made it were my saviours. I sucked up the thin skin of water in the bottom of the water hole that was left from the recent slaking of *watu* thirst, and licked impatiently at the slow seep of returning water.

When I finally summoned up enough strength of mind to crawl out of the hollow, the shadows were long and lengthening. I was alone with a vague realisation that I needed to go downstream to where the Land Rover was coming to meet us, although the time for the rendezvous was long past.

I set off and managed to advance no more than a couple of hundred yards before the magnetic drag of the water in the hollow caused me to turn and return to it so that I could drink again. Again I tried to go downstream and yet again I went back to the hollow. And so it went on until at last, with the sun close to setting, I was able to go neither forward nor back.

I lay down against the riverbank. I didn't know where I was. I was resigned to giving up and I felt both calm and relieved about it. All through the day's trial by sun and water, of which there had been too much of one and too little of the other, I had only myself to blame.

Surprisingly, my rifle was still on my shoulder. Its strap seemed to be welded to my safari jacket by crystallised sweat. I contemplated firing a shot into the air but dismissed the thought, as doing such a thing felt like too much bother.

I looked upstream in the direction of the hollow, and then downstream towards the rendezvous to behold a lone figure drifting over the sand towards me. It was an angel of mercy in the shape of Tom. He bore in his hands life-sustaining sustenance in the shape of a full water bag. At that moment the water bag was worth far more to me than all the diamonds of Mwadui.

With the aid of the water bag's contents, Tom, and a couple of *watu* who came along behind him, I reached the rendezvous and waiting Land Rover just as night was closing in. I was too much the victim of dehydration to recognise how lucky I had been to get away with it, and didn't reach that understanding until three more days had elapsed, during most of which time I lay on the Hounsfield bed in my tent at camp in a near state of suspended animation.

It was a fact beyond doubt that the Makasumbe River had got the better of me. My first solo safari had ended in abject failure. I had been tested, weighed in the balances, and found wanting. On the other hand I had been given the opportunity to learn a salutary lesson on how not to prepare for a traverse, as a result of which I would never again go out on traverse without an adequate supply of water and an appropriate contingency plan that would hopefully cover any unexpected eventualities.

A little more informed advice from a voice of experience (no name, no pack drill) at the outset of my abortive Makasumbe River traverse might have been beneficial to me, but on the whole I looked back on the episode and reckoned that I had been done a favour by being permitted to make my own mistakes.

It subsequently appeared that providing a rude awakening to newcomers was something of a general camp tradition that had come to be accepted by various Senior Geologists as their *droit de seigneur*. Eddie (three *simbas*) McGinnis was sent out from the camp at Iwambala on a similarly arduous solo traverse to mine, and lo and behold Eddie also didn't make it back to camp on his own two feet.

At the dénouement of Eddie's traverse Tom appeared out of the gloaming once more. On that occasion he brought along a bottle of Coca-Cola, and with that well-known beverage was Eddie revived. It was suggested during a camp discussion that the Coca-Cola company should be contacted about the incident, in the anticipation that the company could use it to publicise the restorative powers of its product. It was a good idea, but like so many of our good ideas it didn't go anywhere.

Water was preferable.

*

Tom's subsequent attempt to measure the level of experience that I didn't have came along a week or two after I had recovered from the Makasumbe River fiasco. I was by then carrying out successful traverses on the basis of good preparation and enthusiastic intentions. My second trial was by Land Rover—the fount of so many ups and downs in the bush annals of WDL.

We were to go on a scouting expedition into the Rungwa Game Reserve, taking two Land Rovers through raw bush beyond the current end of the track cut adjacent to the Njombe River. The objective of the exercise was to identify a suitable site for fly camping.

Tom drove the lead Land Rover and I followed him driving the other, the very same vehicle in which I had come down to Iwambala from Mwadui. We rolled out of camp early one morning and, in my case at least, edged gingerly across the neatly laid and still virtually pristine mat of corduroy spanning the Njombe River. With the crossing behind us we headed into territory that was familiar only to the game that inhabited it.

To begin with, the two-vehicle convoy and an accompanying swarm of voracious tsetse proceeded without incident to the end of the cut track. From there we drove onwards, threading the Land Rovers between trees and around bushes while maintaining visual contact as far as was possible with the great river on the right.

Tom, for personal reasons that probably included a desire either to leave the tsetse behind or to test my mettle, suddenly speeded up and pulled away from me. He whipped his vehicle around obstacles as if he were participating in the Monte Carlo rally. What for me had up to then been a simple matter of driving my Land Rover in slow comfort along the route set by Tom suddenly took on the unwelcome demand of an energetic manipulation of both the accelerator and the steering wheel in order to keep up with him.

Tree trunks were immediately transformed into objects of menace. They seemed to close in on one another. I did my best to avoid them, and actually managed to do so for a while as I struggled to stay as close as I could to the rear of Tom's Land Rover. It was of course inevitable that a big tree would jump sideways to make a glancing contact with the left front wing of my Land Rover. The trunk tore the Land Rover's wing panel away as if it had no more substance than mango peel. The mess of crumpled metal was spread across the passenger's side door, buckling the door inwards and jamming its lock. The wheel beneath the wing must have missed the tree trunk by the breadth of an elephant's tail hair, although the headlamp in front of it didn't fare very well at all.

The tree's impact on the Land Rover was as nothing compared to the shock it gave to me. Yet another personal test was shot down in ignominy. My confidence in driving, which had been improving by the minute until Tom put his foot down, evaporated like the first penny-sized raindrops of the wet season falling on a sun-soaked rock. Feelings of both guilt and shame at my causing so much damage to a WDL Land Rover loaded more weight on me than carrying three full sample bags would ever have done.

Knowledge of the fact that accidents of a similar kind were in no way unique in WDL's world of exploration brought me neither solace nor the opportunity to make any excuse.

As a consequence I was unable to drive any more on that day and for very many days afterwards. In fact, there was never to be a day during all of my time in Tanganyika when I came to feel entirely at ease behind the wheel of a Land Rover. The wing panel was a write-off. A protracted session of tugging and heaving was applied to remove it from the Land Rover altogether. It was tossed into the back of its vehicle of origin without ceremony.

The fly camp-seeking expedition continued with Idi driving my Land Rover and me sitting in as his passenger. We both got in through the driver's door. With the damage done, Tom led us with circumspection. I assumed that he had had enough fun to last him for a day or two.

The trip took us about twenty miles deep into the Rungwa Game Reserve. If the trip served to prove anything, apart from the fact that in terms of diamond quality I was a bush driver of negligible water, it was that access would give us no cause for concern. The terrain adjacent to the river was relatively flat and the bush appeared able to be negotiated without much need for cutting it. Trees, even the one that got in the way of my Land Rover, were inviolate of course.

Near a site that we selected as being ideal for our first fly camp, the Njombe River made a striking yet gentle curve that was at least one hundred yards wide. The banks of the river were approximately fifteen feet high, fringed by a host of tall, flat-topped trees that provided ample shade in which to set up the planned facilities.

The fly camp, possessing no permanent structures, would be a satellite of our base camp at Iwambala. It was designed to be either installed or dismantled in the space of no more than half a day. The site was selected for its strategic aspect, backing as it did on to the steep river bank and with sufficient dead bush in the vicinity to build a defensive *boma* behind which perimeter we could cower if we had to.

A good *boma* around the perimeter of the fly camp was considered to be essential. It was much better for us that the game, which enjoyed priority over us as far as right of way was concerned, should be deflected around a *boma* rather than being allowed to walk unimpeded through the camp. We had to direct our best attention to seeing the game before it saw us so that we could take evasive action when the game was of the big kind.

Although the riverbed was exceedingly littered with droppings denoting the frequent movement of elephants, we were not at all concerned as the riverbanks were too sheer for elephants to climb up. The clinching feature for the fly camp site's selection was the existence nearby of a modest water hole on one side of the river. I had good reason to know only too well how important that was.

Assuming that elephants stayed in the riverbed, they wouldn't bother us. Elephants were plentiful in the Rungwa Game Reserve, and we were fortunate that during the main body of our working day they were restful creatures whose chief ambition was to seek out shade and stand in it, flapping their ears gently while they counted off the hours to sundown and a cool visit to a convenient water hole.

We reckoned to enlarge the water hole near the fly camp site for our benefit and theirs as well, and we would make sure that we collected our water when the big game were elsewhere. Share and share alike ruled the distribution of water.

I developed a high level of respect for elephants that incorporated a certain amount of fear. The closest encounter that I had with the species involved three large cows and took place when I was out with my team on a sampling traverse. The three elephants came towards us along a track that we were following. They were coupled together in single file like a train, with trunks linked to tails. Their pace was rapid. The bush was thick, and all we could do was press ourselves into it as they went by, close enough to be touched, without giving us as much as a glance.

I was sure that nowhere in the game reserve were there any big game animals that were as scared of me as I was of them. They had no inherited concerns about being hunted and they almost certainly saw *wazungu* and *watu* alike as creatures presenting them with no great threat. As a rule they took umbrage only when we inadvertently blocked their path or came too close to their young. Apart from that, the principal danger to life and limb that faced us was most likely to come from chance involvements with venomous snakes when no snake-bite kit was near to hand.

All through the trip to select a fly camp site we didn't see any elephants, about which I wasn't too unhappy. Having a tree run into my Land Rover was incident enough for the day. We were, however, lucky enough to see a big male kudu at close hand. It gazed at us with liquid eyes in which I detected an imperious glint. Its horns were immensely-rising dark and glossy spirals. The kudu made no attempt to flee. It merely flapped its big rounded ears and stepped aside to be swallowed up by the bush in an instant.

Elsewhere on the trip a waterbuck, reddish brown in colour, white ringed at the rear, stocky in stature and characterised by a set of ribbed horns resembling the frame of a lyre, was rather less inclined to tolerate us. At its first sight of us it took off at a clumsy gallop and leapt into the river in its urgent haste to escape. It was fortunate that at the place selected by the waterbuck for its jump the riverbank was not very high.

As we entered an extensive clearing in the bush, four Masai giraffe and a dozen thick-striped (Burchell's) zebra respectively loped and trotted away to what they must have reckoned to be a safe distance. They pulled up and came to a halt against some trees on the far side of the clearing. Masai giraffe were characterised by a jaggedly irregular jigsaw-like skin pattern, as distinct from the quasi-geometric pattern on the skin of the much rarer "reticulated" giraffe species.

The zebra looked to be identical to one another in their uniform of alternating black and white stripes, but on further inspection their individual arrangement of stripes was seen to be as unique as human fingerprints.

They trotted on stiff legs and whistled at us in alarm as the great hooves of the running giraffe, which seemed to float over the ground in slow motion, thumped out an accompanying drum roll. As they all stood and looked back across the clearing at us, the zebra seemed like tiny toys placed beneath the towering protection of long-legged, long-necked associates. Zebra and giraffe often went around together, and appeared to like to congregate around the fringes of such clearings where a combination of trees and grass provided food for both.

The giraffe (*twiga*) was the national animal of Tanganyika, right up there as royal game in the society of the crowned crane. The hunting of giraffe was prohibited by government statute. Whether or not they were inside or outside of game reserves, giraffe gave an impression of being aware that they were safe and demonstrated this by treating all two-legged creatures with disdain. Perhaps that was why zebra, which weren't off limits for hunting, liked to hang around with giraffes for both the feeling of security it gave them and the deterrent effect it placed on their enemies.

Tom and Danilo (who much to his chagrin was unable to link fahka-musshoota with giraffe), told me that there had been one incident they knew of in which a Field Officer deliberately shot a giraffe. The single question the action begged was, why? What anyone would do with a dead giraffe baffled the imagination. It couldn't be eaten; it certainly couldn't be skinned to create a disposable "trophy", and it would have been so easy to kill that blasting duck on the water with my shotgun would have been the epitome of sportsmanship by comparison.

On the day on which we eventually took occupancy of the selected fly camp site I took a walk out of camp and up along the bank of the river with the intention of looking over the surrounding area. After I had covered a couple of hundred yards I saw, out on my left where it was darkly shaded by a patch of bush, what I took to be a large boulder or an outcrop of rock. I walked towards it to investigate, in the belief that I might have made an interesting discovery.

As I drew near to what I was assuming was rock, something flickered on its surface and went on to flicker again. Whatever type of rock it was that I had found, proximity to it led me to realise that it possessed an active tail and stood on at least two stumpy pillar-like legs. I was struck by a sudden revelation that I was standing far too close to something that was not only alive but also very big.

It looked so huge that my first panicked thought was that here was an elephant. I turned on a figurative coin of the denomination that I once gave to a Kikuyu porter at Nairobi airport and fled, desperately anxious to spot a suitable tree that I could climb high up into. A rhythmic snuffling and snorting sound came from behind me. There was a tramp of over-heavy feet, and any previous sentiments of elephant vanished as a rhinoceros trotted past me. Evidently we both shared a desire to put a lot of distance between our positions of first encounter.

This rhino (*kifaru*) was of the "black" variety. A black rhino was characterised by having a prehensile upper lip designed to strip tasty leaves from overhanging branches. By contrast, its South African cousin the "white" rhino was square lipped. The black rhino that I saw on that day near the fly camp was equipped with a squat nasal horn that was solid rather than long. Although it forged its way ahead of me with the single-minded full-ahead impetus of a tank, it gave an impression of delicacy in the way it moved its feet. I could hear it crashing through the bush for quite a long while after it was gone from sight.

There were many black rhino living in the Rungwa Game Reserve. When out on traverses we often met up with them both as individuals and in pairs. On one occasion I saw a party of three. They were always highly suspicious of us, and while they were quite ready to put on a threatening display I always reckoned that they didn't really mean it as not one of them in my experience ever became overtly aggressive.

It was possible that my rhino sightings took in some individuals several times, although I liked to believe that was not so and that there was a healthy population of them observing us working among them in the game reserve. However, I didn't set out to meet any of the rhinos by choice. They were a bit too big and unpredictable for us to trifle with. It was no more than par for the course that once in a while a rhino feinted a sideways lunge at one of our Land Rovers moving within its personally marked out territory, not least if it had a young rhino to protect. Reports of rhinos making head-on charges at vehicles were the fruits of over-active imaginations, I thought. Rhinos might not have been particularly clever, but they weren't stupid enough to injure themselves by doing that.

Tom came back to the fly camp from a traverse one day and told me how he and his team of *watu* had stepped out of thick bush into a small clearing and come face to face with a browsing rhino. He looked at the rhino and the rhino looked at him for a moment, both of them sizing up options on what to do next. Tom said that on an impulse he pulled off his Panama hat and ran towards the still thinking rhino, flapping the hat up and down and screaming, "Fuck off!" in the loudest tones he could muster. The rhino not only heard him but also understood the meaning of that universal invitation to make an immediate exit, as that was exactly what it did. Fortified by his matador-like experience, Tom declared an intention to take a similar action from that day on if ever he chanced on a rhino in the bush again.

One thing we shared in common with rhinos, and all other four-footed game in the game reserve for that matter, was an abhorrence of safari ants, known as *siafu*. Where right of way was concerned, *siafu* were always given precedence. They moved on safari in numbers so immense that they could never be counted. Their hordes flowed across the ground like black and glossy rivers. The greatest procession of *siafu* that I saw was around fifty yards wide and took an hour to pass me. Relentless and implacable, *siafu* poured over every obstacle in their way and devoured whatever they swamped that was edible. Any creature that was unable to get out of their way by reason of its small size or sluggish habits was doomed to be picked clean by *siafu* right down to the bones.

As Mr Micawber might have put it, an inch outside the edge of a flow of *siafu* stood safety; an inch inside lay doom. The edge was lined by so called *askari*, or soldier ants, which were not only larger than the *siafu* that made up the body of the flow but also highly zealous in the pursuit of their duty as guardian protectors of the safari.

It was not uncommon for *siafu* to pass through a camp. They could not be avoided as they moved entirely without discrimination. During the day we would not know that they were coming until the vanguard of the safari entered the precincts of the camp like the tongue of a flash flood. At night we could hear them arriving. So very many *siafu* moving *en masse* created a surf-like hissing sound that preceded them.

There was no escape from *siafu*. They were not a tide that could be turned. They could even extinguish fires through the sheer weight of their numbers. *Siafu* bit at anything and everything that they could sink their jaws into, and when flesh was involved they caused pain and drew blood.

It did no good to wave a Panama hat and tell *siafu* to fuck off. When the cry of "*Siafu!*" went up, we scrambled out to the edge of the seething safari, beat off the *siafu* that clung to us and stayed clear until the river of ants moved on. Then we could return to find the camp just as we had left it, apart from the disappearance of any food that was left uncovered when we fled.

Where *siafu* came from and where they were going to was anyone's guess. I never followed a safari to try to find out. Once they were gone from our vicinity they became someone else's problem.

"Someone else" might well be a colony of termites. Given the merest chink of an opening on the rock-hard carapace of a termite mound rising in columnar splendour to heights of many feet above ground level, a flood of *siafu* could gain entry and clean out every termite in the colony in short order. This was, in microcosm, as vicious a war as any other war fought between adversaries in the bush.

The South African writer Eugene Marais described a termite mound as a living entity in which termites flowed like blood through a complicated vein-like lacing of internal tunnels. The colony's brain was vested in the regality of the queen termite, and the mound took its breath from the lung-like fungus gardens that the termites cultivated in the shaft-accessed damp depths of their construction. Eugene Marais wrote that he fully expected termite mounds to evolve into developing the power of lateral movement.

From what I had seen, both during and following the fly camp scouting trip into the Rungwa Game Reserve, I was quite ready to believe that virtually anything was possible, although my becoming a good bush driver remained open to continuing doubt.

11
Dodoma

The job that we were intended to do was, as Gus had made clear in his *GFM* instruction to field staff, "not a holiday nor a wide scale hunting expedition". Moreover it was, in Gus's own words, "advisable that everyone realises this". After I had spent a month or so working out of the camp at Iwambala, I realised that Gus's message, although issued from the heart, must have fallen on quite a lot of deaf ears.

His words additionally contained a strong admonition against the tendencies of some of us to exhibit symptoms of either boorish or drunken behaviour (or both since the two generally went together) during visits to towns. He urged on us a need for cleanliness and comparative neatness in the matter of our personal appearances in public places.

With my first month of work in the bush completed, a visit to town for the purpose of replenishing camp supplies was necessary. Tom decided that we were to go to town for a weekend, during which we could kill a couple of birds with one stone in also seizing the opportunity to have the wrecked wing of my Land Rover repaired.

I was pretty sure that I could comply with Gus's criteria regarding my personal cleanliness and neatness, and boorishness had always been such anathema to me that it wasn't even worth considering. However, drunkenness was something else, and as an option to reckon with I kept it filed away in the corner of my mind where the spirit was willing but the flesh was weak.

Our nearest supply town was Dodoma, the capital of Ugogo. Dodoma was a key trading and transport centre where the Great North Road, which linked Mbeya and Iringa down in the south of Tanganyika with Arusha, Moshi and Kilimanjaro in the north of the country, crossed the Central railway line coming down from Manyoni (or alternatively up from Dar es Salaam). Dodoma, just like Tabora, had also been an important German colonial staging post.

As a town, Dodoma bustled. It had a lot going for it. It boasted, in addition to the usual provincial government departments over which the DC presided in all his grandeur, the head office of the Tanganyika Geological Survey; a hospital; an excellent hotel with bar adjacent to the railway station; a basic range of shops; a service garage and vehicle repair shop; bulk trading establishments galore under both Indian and Arab proprietorship; a bank (the manager of which had to be avoided by the likes of me to the maximum extent that it was possible); religious establishments to suit all tastes, not least those of the expatriate community; a *wazungu* club with an important bar and less important sporting facilities including a golf course and ample space for rugby and cricket; two cinemas; and an airstrip.

The population of Dodoma at the time of my first visit in late 1960 was approximately fifteen thousand, of which around three thousand were classified as being of Asian (Indian and Arabian) origin; three hundred were *wazungu* of one nationality or another, and the rest were Africans. It seemed to offer a good and positive ethnic mix.

We travelled to Dodoma in a convoy of two Land Rovers. Tom drove the one in the lead with me as his front-seat passenger and five *watu* as additional passengers sitting in the back. The *watu* were all willing volunteers to come along, assist us in the handling and loading of bulk supplies, and seek out some of the fleshpots of Dodoma while they were off duty. I was not yet up to driving a Land Rover anywhere, let alone into a big town. Idi, with four more *watu* on board, followed behind at the wheel of my wing-damaged vehicle. His (and their) main priority was to hold on to a position well clear of the dust cloud created by the lead vehicle.

On a direct compass bearing Dodoma was located only eighty miles to the northeast of Iwambala. On a map the distance appeared to represent a mere formality for us to cover, although I knew that that on the ground the journey would be much less simple than that. The tortuous nature of the tracks and roads on the way implied slow progress. Apart from the stretches of roads engineered by the Germans, the shortest distance between two points in Tanganyika was never a straight line.

The route took us back down the same track to Iseke that marked the last leg of my outward journey to Iwambala from Mwadui. From Iseke we headed along a stone-littered track leading east to a village named Ikasi that was situated at the top of an escarpment related to the Great Rift Valley structure. This track then zigzagged down to the foot of the escarpment from Ikasi to bring us to the edge of an extensive flat wetland area known as the Bahi swamp. We crossed the Bahi swamp on a track, that might not have been good but was at least an improvement on its counterparts left behind us, to reach the main road leading into Dodoma at the village of Kigwe. Beyond Kigwe the road to Dodoma was a foot-down breeze to drive along.

Tom's Land Rover was diesel-powered whereas mine was fuelled by petrol. This vital difference meant that we had to be sure that the correct type of fuel entered the fuel tank that was designed to receive it. This was simple enough to achieve when refuelling was carried out in camp using a supply from clearly marked forty-four gallon drums, but it was sometimes prone to error when we were out of camp and fuel (not forgetting water) contained in jerry cans entered the equation.

Each Land Rover carried at least two jerry cans in the back whenever it left camp. One held fuel and one held water for topping up the radiator. Given the heavy-duty work that the Land Rovers had to do, the engines heated and the radiators boiled regularly. The two great problems we had with jerry cans were: first, they all looked alike, and second, they weren't individually dedicated by appropriate marking to containing specific liquids—what was needed usually went into the first empty jerry can that came to hand, so that a jerry can that contained water yesterday might be filled with diesel today and then petrol tomorrow. None of the incremental contamination that this implied acted in the long-term interests of smoothly running engines.

It was up to the user to verify the nature of the contents of a jerry can before pouring any of the contents into an open fuel tank or radiator. Unfortunately, the sole guarantee that the user's acumen provided was that Murphy's Law was applicable. What could go wrong inevitably did go wrong.

There were many instances in the WDL bush annals of petrol going into a fuel tank in which diesel was required, and naturally enough vice versa. Similarly, water was now and then poured from a jerry can into both petrol and diesel tanks. A petrol-driven engine system was difficult enough to clean out under such circumstances, but its diesel-powered counterpart was a nightmare to bleed free of water by comparison.

Where a diesel engine was concerned it seemed that there would always be a stubborn residuum of the wrong stuff that refused outright to be flushed away, bled off, or shifted out of the system no matter what we tried to do to get rid of it. A diesel engine in a Land Rover gave us far less trouble than its petrol-driven equivalent ever did until something exotic found its way into the engine and turned field maintenance into an endless cycle of frustrations.

*

When we reached Iseke on the way to Dodoma we called in at the *duka* to greet its little Arab proprietor and do our duty to foster public relations. Local residents, all of the male persuasion, lounged around the entry to the *duka*, looking as if they hadn't moved since I passed by a few weeks back.

The little Arab was the personification of obsequiousness. He presented an image of Uriah Heep made flesh in Ugogo. He gave an impression of being a man whom it was best not to lose sight of when he was close by. At the risk of doing them an injustice, a similar consideration could be applied to most of the Arabs that I met in Tanganyika. They formed an essentially closed community. I assumed that they were well aware that they were living in a kind of limbo. Their wellbeing was entirely dependent on the overwhelming majority of black Africans, through their innate good nature, not running out of generosity.

We bought some bottles of cold drink from the little Arab. He extracted the bottles from a large and severely scarred paraffin-powered fridge in the manner of one who had just opened Ali Baba's cave with a well timed "Open sesame!"

The rocky track from Iseke to Ikasi wound through a landscape featuring tall trees, light bush and a scattering of characteristic granite *koppies*, bluffs and boulders. Then came the thrill of descending the escarpment from Ikasi at the top to the huge stretch of Bahi swamp at the bottom.

To put the escarpment in perspective, it was by no means the mightiest of its kind that the Great Rift Valley threw up along its monumental trajectory running down from the Red Sea and the dizzy mountain heights of Ethiopia in the north through Lake Rudolf, Kilimanjaro and sinuous Lake Nyasa to expire in the Portuguese territory of Mozambique to the south. From the head of Lake Nyasa, an arm of the Great Rift Valley thrust out to the west and north to incorporate Lakes Rukwa, Tanganyika, Kivu, Edward and Albert and to touch on the Ruwenzori mountains (the fabled "mountains of the moon") in Uganda. The two arms of the Great Rift Valley encompassed Lake Victoria as if that lake were the pupil of an immense eye shedding tears at the fount of the Nile.

The section of escarpment that we descended below Ikasi was no more than a couple of hundred feet high, yet its steep and rocky face and the peerless panoramic view that it provided us with over such a vast stretch of blue-hazed MMBA made its height sufficient to give a sense of being breathtakingly perilous.

The rough-surfaced track dropped down the escarpment at a shallow grade kept constant by a succession of hairpin bends. Wet-season runoff was presumably controlled with the help of a number of culverts, the condition of which suggested that they had been installed by the PWD a long time ago. It must also have been a PWD gang that had thrown up rudimentary banks of rocky soil on the outer edge of some of the more vertiginous portions of the track to provide descending vehicles like ours with a deceptive sense of security.

Out beyond the far rim of the Bahi swamp in the extreme distance a sloping column of thin smoke, making not much more than a light smudge against the haze, suggested that a train was proceeding towards Dodoma along the Central railway line. To a large extent the haze was due to dispersed smoke consequent on the widespread practice of "burning off" the land. Burning off involved tribesmen (or more likely tribeswomen) setting fire to dead grass and bone dry maize stalks at the end of the dry season with the objective of creating soil-enriching ash and clearing the ground prior to tilling it and planting seed before the rains came.

*

As a rule, burning off was managed with an expertise developed from countless generations of practice. Sometimes, however, a front of fire could get out of hand, race into places where it wasn't wanted and declare itself unstoppable.

At an unguarded early morning moment a cooking fire at one of our fly camps in the Rungwa Game Reserve jumped into the encroaching bush. We toiled for the best part of the rest of the day in an unsuccessful attempt to contain it. It was fortunate for us that the fire burned itself out, but that was only after it had consumed a few acres of grassland. In the normal course of events the imminent wet season would have rectified the situation by rejuvenating the grass, and the ground would no doubt have fared all the better for the burning. Unfortunately the scorched earth was spotted by the eagle eye of Mr Bill Moore-Gilbert, the Manyoni Game Ranger. He arrived at our fly camp in an equally fiery state of mind and took us to task in no uncertain terms over this inadvertently executed exercise in burning off.

Be that as it may, most bush fires were natural occurrences from which the bush recovered rapidly. As often as not lightning, at its peak of intensity during the run-in to the wet season, was the culprit to blame for bush fires.

We could sense the wet season closing in on us through days of oppressive liquid heat that became increasingly difficult to tolerate. The bush then took on the colour of the starkly pale sky above, bleaching out like elephant bones. The sun burned white and cast no shadows. The desire of *watu* and *wazungu* alike for the rain to come and bring relief to the land was urgent enough to taste and fertile enough to sow and grow seeds of discord in, as day after day rain failed to come to pass.

During the nights, displays of distant lightning blooming inside great accumulations of anvil-headed clouds made sharp silhouettes of hill profiles. It was as if *Mungu* were fiddling with a celestial switch in an abortive attempt to get the rain up and running. Alternatively of course, a battle might have been raging somewhere out there, letting us see the flash of big guns that were too far away for us to hear them booming.

These nocturnal pyrotechnic displays seemed to last for weeks. They went on out in the far distance for an inordinately long time without ever appearing to get any closer to where we were waiting. Now and then we sensed tremors in the air that the more optimistic among us declared were the resonant vestiges of remote thunder.

Then, finally, real thunder was heard and the sceptics fell silent. A light breeze ruffled loose flaps on the tents and was followed by wind full of the smell of baked and dusty ground slaked by rain. The wind offered us both a promise and a threat in conjunction; none of us was quite sure which would dominate.

In only a matter of hours continuous thunder rolled and shuddered directly overhead. Lightning flashed constantly and was so interwoven with thunder that it would have be easier to use chickens and eggs to work out an answer as to which of the two came first.

When it fell the rain lacked subtlety. There was nothing incremental about it. Where the first fall of rain was concerned, it was nothing ventured nothing gained. A deluge in an instant dropped on us in such volume and with such force that it was clearly making up for lost time. Its battering pulped the ground and shook the trees. It pounded on our huts and tents, coursed along gullies, and brought life back to the rivers with ultimately torrential flash floods.

Within a day of the first onset of rain the bush showed a flush of emerald green. Within three days the bush was transformed into lush green parkland, fresh, cool and sparkling with droplets. It was only unfortunate that the lawn-like carpet of grass covering the ground was short-lived. The grass grew longer even as we looked at it, and it went on all too soon to attain heights of six feet and more and to harbour within it all sorts of creatures, both pleasant and unpleasant (chiefly the latter, the bush being what it was).

Everyone and everything was delighted with the arrival of rain. It was appreciated as a blessing for a while, then tolerated as a necessity, thought of thereafter as a necessary evil, and then fervently wished away when it seemed to have lasted long enough and was still showing no sign of packing up.

*

The greening of the bush was still to come, however, as we descended the escarpment below Nkasi. In the ground that we saw being burned off we knew that rain would soon be instrumental in generating fine crops and good harvests. Goats and cattle would grow fat to the extent that fat on such animals was possible. It was always taken for granted that the rains would not fail, there being no worthwhile alternative.

From the bottom of the escarpment, the track that we took to cross the Bahi swamp was both hard-surfaced and built to stand slightly proud of the flat terrain that extended out on both sides. I assumed that it was an all-weather track, elevated sufficiently to avoid wet-season flooding, although that was something I would only know for sure if we had to use it during the wet season.

The Bahi swamp, although it was an area of perennial damp, was characterised by grassed-over ground that was slightly yielding to the foot rather than being boggy and cloying in the more conventional sense of what a swamp ought to be. It featured a number of scattered island-like areas of light bush. Wild duck, geese and other waterfowl congregated around a few of the damper areas during the dry season and gathered in profusion all over the swamp during the wet.

Near a village named Isanza, located in the heart of the Bahi swamp, stood a Catholic mission station. It consisted of a large complex of solid buildings including a church, a clinic, an accommodation block for priests, a school, and a range of workshops and outbuildings. Although the provision of creature comforts might not have been an objective of its construction, my overall impression of Isanza mission was that it had been built to endure.

The mission was run by an order of Italian priests known as the Pallotine Fathers who were in their turn associated with the Pallotine Prefecture Apostolic (whatever that was) based in Dodoma. The priests, in the noble tradition of the church universal, lived under rather better conditions than did the tribal flock they administered to.

With a vote of thanks of debateable sincerity accorded to Danilo, whose route of access to Dodoma from his camp at Ilangali went like ours via Isanza, Tom had developed a cordial relationship with the Pallotine Fathers at the mission. Since the priests spoke no English and Tom and I were non-conversant with Italian, Kiswahili came to the fore to demonstrate its merit as a lingua franca for breaking the barriers to communication.

On every occasion when we crossed the Bahi swamp, either going to or coming from Dodoma, we called at the mission to present our compliments to the priests. Most of them were simply glimpsed either in corridors or around the outer grounds when they were in the act of hurrying somewhere or other that did not involve their paying attention to us. We were invariably received at the mission door by one particular priest with whom the time of day could be discussed and from whom a routine half an hour or so of hospitality could be accepted.

I welcomed the fact that, in spite of the plethora of iconic trappings and tools of the priestly trade surrounding us when we were visiting the mission, religious considerations were maintained at a low profile in the conversations we had with the priest. He always made us feel welcome and ensured that we could each count on getting a cup of weak tea (no milk), a sympathetic ear, and half a paw-paw sliced longitudinally, deseeded and sprinkled far too liberally with lemon juice for my taste.

Against one wall of the room in which we normally sat to consume our halves of paw-paw a small table backed by a crucifix fashioned of plain wood was set up. On the table a pocket-sized young grey bush duiker (*nsya*) was lying and sipping a liquid that looked like milk from a yellow saucer. The little antelope looked at us each time it raised its head as if to rub it in that it had milk to drink and we didn't.

The main thing that the priest's hospitality at Isanza mission did for me was to make me averse ever after to eating paw-paw in any shape or guise. One rule of bush etiquette demanded that I must consume and appear to enjoy any food offered to me anywhere by anyone, and by following the rule to the letter I completely failed to acquire a taste for that over-bland fruit.

One Sunday afternoon a Land Rover in which Tom and I were travelling back to Iwambala from Dodoma broke down on the Bahi swamp track, fortuitously within reasonable walking distance of Isanza mission. A customary mob of local tribesmen sprang up as if from the soil around us and gathered around the Land Rover to offer sage comments on the situation. One tribesman offered the dray services of two donkeys that he owned for pulling the Land Rover onwards—we hired the donkeys and made our way to the mission grounds under two-ass power. The only thing missing, I thought, was that we should hammer on the door of the mission church when we arrived while yelling, "Sanctuary, sanctuary!" or its equivalent in Italian or Kiswahili. Perhaps a priest would have appeared in order to inform us that there was no room at the inn; who knew?

Sunday (*juma pili*) was a day of rest at the mission. That would have been fair enough under normal circumstances, but in the light of our situation it was not very helpful since the workshop facilities and their people were closed to us for as long as the Sabbath lasted. Our destiny was to wait for help to arrive at one second past midnight on Monday (*juma tatu*) morning when the strictures of the fifth commandment could be set aside.

The priests were not entirely immune to our situation, however, as they provided us with accommodation for the night in cell-like rooms that probably differed from their prison counterparts only insofar as the doors were not locked. The sleeping pallet in my cell brought an image of Lazarus being raised from the dead to my mind. Suspended on the wall above the head of the pallet was another wooden crucifix, this one large enough to be taken down and used as a battering ram against the door if the occasion ever called for such action.

*

The main road that took us to Dodoma from the point at which we came off the Bahi swamp track at Kigwe provided us with the only genuine opportunity for speedy driving in the whole trip. Before Kigwe the driving was slow by necessity; after Kigwe the driver's foot could go down hard.

It was when I was driving a Land Rover on that section of road later on during the wet season that I had my second vehicle-related accident. Recent rain had made the road surface slick and greasy, a condition demanding all due care and attention. On rounding a right-handed bend at a faster than prudent speed, the tyres of my Land Rover lost their grip on the road surface and commenced sliding to the left. I attempted to counter the slide and managed instead to convert lateral movement into at least two circular spins and probably even three.

The spinning came to an end when the Land Rover flipped over, falling on the driver's side. Preceded by a momentum-generated wave of mud and gravel, it slid to an eventual halt on the outer edge of the bend. Throughout this sorry episode I was conscious that the Land Rover was out of my control and acting with a mind of its own.

The slide, the gyrations, the inversion and the crash all appeared to me to take place in slow motion to the accompaniment of a continuous sound of breaking glass. When the Land Rover turned on its side, Efrem, who had been in the front passenger seat, broke his fall by dropping on top of me. The cashbox, chained to the gear lever, plummeted past my head like a stone, fortunately striking nothing breakable, me included.

The half-dozen *watu* travelling in the back of the Land Rover were instantaneously ejected as the Land Rover flipped over. They all landed on the muddy road and lay there like a collection of flotsam on the high seas.

My immediate concern was for what might have happened to them. The shock of the crash only affected me later on. Efrem and I extricated ourselves by climbing up and out through the door on the passenger side of the Land Rover. Miraculously under the circumstances, the injuries incurred consisted only of slight scratches, minor bruises, the attachment of a lot of mud to our persons, and another big dent in my self-confidence.

We assembled to confirm that lives and limbs were intact before turning our attention to the Land Rover. Oil was by then seeping over the mud from the direction of its engine. There was, much to my surprise, no sign of broken glass.

Showing impeccable timing, a five-ton truck came down the road behind us. Its driver pulled up, gave our situation a once over inspection and offered the services of his truck to pull the Land Rover back onto its four wheels again. He produced a length of worn steel cable, which, when attached to appropriate places on both the truck and the Land Rover and pulled at by the truck, did the job in a matter of seconds. Looking over the Land Rover, we could find no obvious mechanical damage, and following a check on fuel, water, brake fluid, battery fluid and engine oil levels, we established that there were losses to the latter only. The dipstick demonstrated that sufficient oil remained in the engine to get us as far as Dodoma, provided that the engine would start. In fact we were all amazed when the engine started up at the first turn of the key.

I drove the remaining distance to Dodoma at a slow pace. Although I felt severely chastened by the accident, I also believed that what had happened was surely accompanied by *bahati mzuri sana* (very good luck).

*

On arrival in Dodoma the first port of call was the Dodoma Hotel. It was a long, single-storey building that stood in its own grounds on a modestly rising terrace set perhaps thirty to fifty yards off the road. The railway station was located on the far side of this road, with the entry to its booking hall facing towards the hotel. A convex curve of paved driveway, one end of which was designated for the entry of vehicles and the other for their exit—although no one bothered much as to which was which—fitted neatly and symmetrically between the tangential frontage of the hotel and the road. Parking space for hotel patrons and a well tended array of flowering shrubs fought one another for precedence on both sides of the driveway.

On any given day of the week, and especially at weekends, paying guests in residence at the hotel were likely to include a good leavening of WDL men fresh out of the bush and all ready to ensure not only that anything could happen but also that it probably would.

The hotel provided us with clean and comfortable rooms. Each room accommodated two persons. The beds were allocated on a first come first served basis so that it was always something of a lottery as to who would occupy the other bed in the room that you were assigned to. The rooms were all lined up right next to one another in one of the hotel's two wings. The other wing incorporated an all-important bar and a rather less essential dining-room for the nominal use of both guests and members of the general public, as long as they were all white. Within the facilities a squad of black waiters, each one of them clad in a pure white *kanzu* tied at the waist with a red cummerbund and wearing a fez on his head and a brilliant grin on his face, glided around to satisfy the needs of the drinking and dining set.

It would have taken an ultra-brave *mtu* to enter that palace of burgeoning siege mentality in search of strong drink or a meal involving the use of knives and forks, even if he possessed the money to pay his way. Suffice it to pronounce that the Dodoma Hotel was *wazungu* territory pure and yet not altogether simple.

The trump card held by *wazungu* who were intent on excluding from their watering holes undesirables (such as anyone who wasn't white skinned) was vested in the application of dress code. This ploy formed the core of a creeping resistance to political and social change. For the opening shot, the wearing of a clean pair of long trousers and a long-sleeved white shirt was mandatory if entry to the dining-room was to be permitted. If an undesirable had the effrontery to comply with this requirement, the dress code list could then be extended with a demand for a tie, and escalated even further by citing a jacket, thereby paving the way towards setting the standard at the level of a lounge suit. For all I knew, there could be places frequented exclusively by *wazungu* somewhere in the country accepting entry by people only if they were clad in full evening dress. The dress code passed me by as soon as long-sleeved shirts became no longer enough for the good fight against black encroachment to be fought.

I enjoyed the contents of many bottles of beer in the bar of the Dodoma Hotel, and appreciated a lot of good meals in the adjoining dining-room, not the least of which were curry lunches topping a mammoth Sunday morning and early afternoon intake of booze by those of us who had survived the Saturday night session and were up for more of the same on the Sabbath.

In his mighty-girthed appearance, his cut-class English accent and his commanding tone of voice the manager of the Dodoma Hotel displayed a combination of various essences of colonial glory, both past and present. He seemed to have been born with an ability to reduce to trembling all lesser ranks than captain and to venerate all ranks superior to the same. With his backside overflowing the bar stool on which he sat with a glass of amber liquid clutched in one hand, a cigarette held languidly in the other, and a palpable intent to suffer fools badly, he was all that mine host catering for *wazungu* tastes ought to be. Had he run the only watering hole in town, those among us whom he banned for conduct unbecoming would have been in serious trouble. However, he didn't have such a monopoly, which fortunately left us with the freedom of choice to slake our thirsts elsewhere in Dodoma when his attention to our behaviour seemed be getting too intense for comfort. He provided ample grounds for us to suspect that he could be one of Gus's alleged network of informers.

The manager was ever a purveyor of well-modulated, if not necessarily well-intentioned, advice to travellers passing through Dodoma. On one occasion one of the recipients of his advice was me. It so happened that my being in Dodoma, for once in possession of a reliably functioning Land Rover, gave Bruno Brown cause to volunteer me to drive my Land Rover a hundred and sixty miles south from Dodoma down the Great North Road to Iringa in order to transport and deliver a reconditioned Land Rover engine and a stock of spare parts to the Senior Geologist in charge of a camp in the Iringa district.

I could have refused the assignment, but I didn't as refusal wasn't an option if I were to avoid being severely frowned upon by the WDL hierarchy. However, I was at the time still a very reluctant driver and inclined to be extremely nervous of taking a Land Rover anywhere that I hadn't been before.

The town of Iringa, a strategically located hill station sitting in rolling terrain at an elevation of 5,300 feet above sea level, was an important centre of the Southern Highlands. Its climate was equable and its appearance was made seasonally glorious by bright flowering flame trees. To the east of Iringa the highlands were flanked by another escarpment of the Great Rift Valley—to the west they fell steeply down to the flood plain of the Great Ruaha River, the very same river that defined the eastern boundary of the Rungwa Game Reserve.

I spent part of the evening prior to my journey to Iringa in the bar of the Dodoma Hotel, where I attempted in vain to imbibe some courage for driving. My Land Rover was parked at the front of the hotel, fully loaded, tied down and ready for an early departure on the morrow.

The hotel manager was seated on his customary stool at the bar in the company of another confirmed bar stool *habitué* whose absence would have been so unusual that it would cause concern over whether or not he was dead. I understood that he worked for a government department at the district HQ, where I didn't doubt that he would fit in as if to the manner born. I saw him often and talked to him regularly but never got to know his name, and he didn't seem capable of taking in my name either, even though I gave it to him repeatedly. He insisted on addressing me as "*Bwana*".

"No, *Bwana* is not my name," I told him.

"Yes *Bwana*," he replied.

Then, looking up from his beer he would say to me, "Who are you, Bwana?"

Our discourse was not replete with stimulation yet was not atypical of the intellectual level of conversation that consistently graced the bar of the Dodoma Hotel. The common interest shared by patrons was the consumption of alcoholic beverages, outside of which there was nothing much to say that was worth remembering, even assuming that anything could be remembered after a skin-full was taken aboard.

On hearing the news of my impending trip to Iringa, he and the manager looked at one another with what I thought could be best described as a wild surmise. They were, for a moment or two, silent on the twin peaks of their bar stools.

The manager pursed his lips and gave me the benefit of his superior wisdom. We-ell, he told me, the road to Iringa was mostly all right, however he didn't envy me having to drive up the escarpment on the final approach to the town sitting up on the top. He led me to believe that the escarpment road would provide a rigorous test for my nerves, offering me an impression of my heavily laden Land Rover on an ultra-narrow track, scraping against a ragged rock wall on the inside while the outer wheels were teetering on the edge of a great precipice. The perils of meeting with and struggling to either pass or give precedence to a vehicle coming down while I was going up were described by him in particularly loving detail.

The evident prospect facing me made me think that I was about to replay scenes from the Yves Montand film *The Wages of Fear*. The manager's commentary convinced me that I wouldn't make it to Iringa.

"What are you, *Bwana*?" asked his companion.

The manager waved a set of nicotine-stained fingers at me in disdain. "All you have to do if you don't feel happy on the road," he said, "is to stop, smoke a cigarette, and then carry on!" I didn't tell him that I didn't smoke, although I assumed that, as a keen observer of the passing parade in his bar, he knew that already.

Following a night during which I got little sleep, I set off for Iringa in the cool light of dawn in the firm belief that the escarpment of the shadow of death was awaiting me. The first fifty miles of road that took me down to a village named Funi were, however, driven over without incident. The surrounding land was rather featureless, being weakly bushed and only sporadically cultivated. After Funi the direction of the road ran parallel to the foot of the escarpment, the cloud-dappled face of which rippled with darkly shaded valleys as it soared a thousand feet up to its bushy heights.

I crossed my old friend the Kisigo River on a good bridge, at which point I was only seventy-five miles downstream from Iwambala. This river went on to slice through the highlands in a deep gorge before joining up with the Great Ruaha River. It was twenty-five miles on from the Kisigo River bridge that the road turned towards the escarpment to commence its forty-mile long ascent to Iringa.

Whatever the escarpment road held for me in terms of causing nervousness was eclipsed by the natural spectacle that it opened up. It was expertly constructed, banked up and cut out with a precision that could only suggest German engineering skills. The road was so well graded as it held to rising ridges and followed contours that it could have had an elephant track as its basis. The slopes above and below the road as it began its steady climb were studded with light bush and decked over with yellow grass.

The road was also a lot broader in reality than my informants had led me to believe it would be. Although I drove the Land Rover close to the inner wall of the road, I didn't really need to. In my slow progress to the summit I encountered nothing coming down. As I neared the top and the road began to level out, hazy slopes dropped off to the right looking like a crumpled blanket. Out in the flat blue distance the Rungwa Game Reserve was shimmering under the sun, its residents entirely oblivious to me looking towards them.

I thought of the manager of the Dodoma Hotel and his *bwana*-insistent associate and wished them good luck and as much soft bullshit as they desired to wallow in at the bar. Most terrors that had to be faced weren't nearly as bad as the imagination defined them, and little if anything ever lived up to the hyperbole of bar talk.

*

In Dodoma, although in the strict sense there was no identifiable "wrong side" of the railway track's bisection of the town, the track formed an effective "between stairs" divide separating a domain of social pretentiousness on its south side, where the Dodoma Hotel was located, from the down-to-earth "tradesmen's entrance" on the north side, where streets teemed with life and the bonds of commerce held it all together.

To access the north side of the railway track from a starting point at the Dodoma Hotel you turned left at the hotel driveway exit to follow the road for a hundred dusty yards or so to reach the crossing point. You turned sharp right at the railway crossing, having presumably paused beforehand to ascertain whether or not a train was approaching, paused again to get over the surprise if a moving train was actually spotted, and *Robeti alikuwa mjomba yako* (Bob was your uncle), your goal was attained.

If you chose to continue past the level crossing on the road to the south of the railway track, another couple of hundred yards would bring you to a garage and vehicle repair shop owned and managed by Mr George Kypris. George was a genial gentleman of Greek nationality, both middle aged and handsome with it in his prime of life. His business establishment was, with admirable unoriginality, known as

George's Garage and was famous throughout the Dodoma district and in parts beyond for the quality of the services it provided to motors and motorists alike.

It was George who saw to repairing the damage that a tree in the wrong place inflicted on my Land Rover. Whenever I called by his garage, then and subsequently, it seemed that George's mechanics were always engaged in knocking out bodywork dents and tidying up scrapes on one or more WDL Land Rovers while others waited on the forecourt for similar attention. George was good for us, and vice versa.

Outside of mere business considerations, George was a gregariously social animal who was rarely averse to tilting a glass with the best (and the worst) of us, either in a back room at his garage, where what appeared to be an unlimited supply of IPA was available, or in any beer-vending outlet where we might chance to meet. George's wife, a dark-haired lady of substantial elegance, was not so inclined and appeared to have restricted her socially oriented outings to putting in appearances at functions of the local *wazungu* club.

Mrs George gave expression to not a single vestige of approval regarding our back-room party association with George. She made her feelings known to us in such colourful terms on more than one occasion that even a hint of her imposing presence in the vicinity could clear the back room in no time flat. Mrs George berated us in a language that might have been all Greek to us but which carried a message that was unmistakeable in its tone.

To drive to the *wazungu* club you had to turn right on departing from the Dodoma Hotel, travel a short distance ahead and then turn right to take a narrow track leading uphill. The *wazungu* club was located at the top. Its stone-built clubhouse was quite as impressive as it was attractive, standing at the back of a swathe of loose-gravelled forecourt that looked extensive enough to park all the vehicles in town on and still have some space left over. Behind the clubhouse were green and pleasant rolling grounds containing facilities for playing golf, cricket, rugby, tennis and what have you. The quality of maintenance of the grounds suggested the constant attention of what must have been a mighty host of grounds *watu*.

Life as it was lived by the *wazungu* of Dodoma found its pride of place, naturally enough, to the south of the railway track. It was focused on the club, which was clearly seen by its members as a monument to the way things ought to be in an ideal world governed by those proper standards that my fellow passenger on the BOAC Viscount flight out to Nairobi had considered to be so important.

Most of the WDL bush types who were in town for the weekend normally put in an appearance at the *wazungu* club on Saturday evening. The club was regarded as a place we could go to in order to kick off a session prior to moving elsewhere in search of an atmosphere that was less restrictive and in which jollity was a more spontaneous quantity. An early attendance at the club ensured that when our much-vaunted symptoms of drunkenness and boorishness came to the fore they would be on display somewhere else. Most of us found it not difficult to wear out our welcome at the *wazungu* club. Established members could be observed quailing when we appeared at the club bar, even though we observed the correct dress code.

The Dodoma club, and all other clubs like it, was a shaky bastion of colonial entrenchment in which, if you were black you were there either to serve the *wazungu* members or to stand on the side and wait to be called to serve. Out on the loose-gravelled forecourt during the hours of daylight a number of *watoto* hung around, each among them hoping to be hired as a golf caddy so that he could thereafter be weighed down by a bag of golf clubs that was both bigger and heavier than himself and be permitted to carry it around the golf course, staggering in the wake of a strapping *mzungu*.

The club featured Saturday night dancing to the recorded music of virtuoso orchestras typified by that of Mr Victor Sylvester, whose strict tempo approach must have been both familiar and reassuring to members as their regular review of the merits of "home" and the shortcomings of locally hired domestic servants gained invective in direct proportion to the quantity of booze they had consumed.

My final visit to the club took place on one Saturday evening not long before I was assigned to leave the Dodoma district to set up a camp and carry out work in the Singida district. The relocation was therefore timely as I have no doubt that what took place on that particular evening would have been more than enough to have had me declared *persona non grata* by the club committee if I had shown my face at its doors afterwards.

A group of us were at the club to celebrate what was a kind of Iwambala old boys' reunion. The by-then cravat-sporting Tom was in town taking time out from his detailed work commitments, and I was in from my then current camp located near Iseke. In addition, the usual gang of WDL weekenders lent its thirst-quenching skills to a joint pursuit of raucous gaiety. *Bona fide* club members prowled around the perimeter of our festivities like prune-mouthed jackals circling a kill they hadn't made, watching us as we swore oaths of undying loyalty to one another. Other than the commencement of this get-together, I remembered little or nothing of what transpired afterwards, but I was conscious of feeling that, whatever it was, it was good while it lasted.

I woke to a state of awareness on what I assumed was Sunday morning, although I wouldn't have bet on it. An intense brightness was piercing through the skin of my eyelids. I had a sensation of being repeatedly prodded in the ribs by a blunt object. My eyes opened into a searing whiteness that made me wish I had kept them closed. Vague shapes that drifted in and out of the light resolved themselves into human form, and I realised that I was lying flat on the gravel forecourt in front of the club, surrounded by a caucus of would-be caddies, one of whom was kneading my side with one of his big toes. He was so proficient at it that I imagined he wasn't doing it for the first time. I assumed that his intention was to determine whether or not I was in the land of the living. I supposed that I was, but from the way in which my head was thumping in sympathy with the pulsing of my heart I wasn't absolutely certain. Nor could I recall what I had eaten during the recent festivities, even though if I had wanted to work it out the menu in question was exposed in all its crusted glory over the front of my shirt and cementing the gravel immediately adjacent to my head. I retched, but there was evidently no more internally contained material for me to get rid of. All that I managed to produce was a few thin threads of green bile.

I attempted to stand up and failed. My legs wouldn't hold me. With signs of my resurrection fresh in their minds, the caddies fled from the scene. A solitary WDL Land Rover was parked not far away from me, and so I crawled over to it and reached up as best I could to grip a door handle with the intention of using it as a purchase to pull me to my feet. The door handle yielded immediately to my touch. The door flew open so suddenly that explosive forces seemed to have played a role. It whacked against my left shoulder, knocking me sideways to measure my length once again on the gravel and to leave me feeling even more dazed than before. It at once became clear that the precipitate movement of the door could be credited to Tom's body leaning against it from within. He tumbled out and crashed in a heap across my legs. His overall physical condition at the time was not dissimilar to mine. Quite how either of us had come to be where we were was a mystery to be solved, however, it was beyond doubt that the route we had taken to get there must have been constructed on a drinking session of ultra-valiant proportions.

The Land Rover was Tom's. By dint of great perseverance we both managed to drag ourselves into its cab. Tom drove us in an uncharacteristically delicate manner down to the Dodoma Hotel where cleaning ourselves up and changing our clothes would be the first order of the day.

As we entered the hotel we met Bill Campbell-Whalley. He put on a stylishly acerbic performance, stamping around us and making various observations on our past behaviour and current appearance. His contumacious commentary was larded with words such as "disgraceful", "intolerable", "letting the team down", and last (but by no means least) "shameful". I had to accede that most of the bollicking that Campbell gave us was entirely justified. Had I felt up to it I might only have queried his use of the word "team".

Team? What team?

"Damaging the reputation of the club" was another allegation levelled at us by Campbell that might have been worth questioning, as I didn't know that the club's reputation was weak enough to be actually damaged by the likes of us.

It emerged from what Campbell had to say that, among others of our ilk, Tom and I were unlikely to be made welcome up at the club again. It seemed rather unfair that we should be candidates for blacklisting on the grounds of doing things that we couldn't remember doing.

We learned that one of the more reverberating issues of our fog-shrouded night at the club involved Tom cornering an *mzungu* of means and accusing him of being a fucking elephant poacher. This was about as serious an accusation as could be levelled at anyone. I didn't know the gentleman (assuming that that was what he was) in question so I had no observation to make on the legality of his hunting practices. However, Tom knew quite a bit about the technique of poaching, and his opinion on the subject always counted with me.

A consequence of the incident was to create the spectre of a scandal. Tom was invited to seek out the supposedly aggrieved *mzungu* in order to offer up an apology for an inadvertent accusation, which he did right away and had the apology just as rapidly accepted.

The single measure of comfort to be drawn from the whole sorry business was that, other than the clearly abstemious Campbell on the WDL side and a few equally sober members on the club's side, no one present at the club on that night in question was in a position to place a hand on a Bible (even one like mine that was partly chewed by termites) and swear a reliable oath as to what was said to whom or by whom, allegations of elephant poaching notwithstanding. All the same, we expected that, back in Mwadui, Gus would sooner rather than later be the recipient of a verbatim report of what had taken place.

*

On the subject of elephant poaching I might as well set out here and now how my experience with this nefarious practice came about, together with how it worked out in the end. It occurred when I was working with Tom out of a fly camp in the Rungwa Game Reserve.

In one way, many of us who shot game under the strictures of a pot licence might easily have described ourselves as "small-time" poachers, although for obvious reasons none of us chose to do so. We were not averse to substituting one game animal for another in filling the pot licence quotas that we were permitted to shoot. It was a question of going for what was available to us, given both the time and the place where we were able to hunt.

I was out with my traverse team in a dry tributary of the Njombe River one day when we came upon the carcass of an elephant lying in the riverbed. The unfortunate animal must have been dead for many days. We smelt it well before we came near it and were additionally made aware of the presence of death ahead of us by the jarringly discordant sounds of vultures squabbling over carrion.

The vultures surrounded the dead elephant in their hundreds. They were like a rapacious army in the act of looting a castle. They flapped and flopped all over the corpse, burrowing into its belly and tearing at its legs. A tight spiral of vultures wound in effortless circles in the sky overhead. A host of others squatted in the manner of spectators in trees lining the immediately adjacent riverbank.

We approached the scene with caution, anxious to make sure that four-footed predators were neither dining on the dead elephant nor hanging around anywhere in its vicinity. It was probable that we were on a fairly safe approach, as vultures were at the near bottom of the order of precedence for feeding, their assigned role being to consume what was left by the lions, wild dogs and jackals that had come before them. The final scavenge, once the vultures had run out of options, would fall to the attention of hyenas.

With a mighty beating of non-angelic wings, many of the erstwhile feeding vultures rose into the air as we came into their view. They dropped back to settle on the riverbed like a lynch mob, surrounding us in an open circle. Some vultures, gorged with putrid meat, took off with difficulty and wove ponderous courses in attempting to gain height. A fair few held their ground on the upper flank of the elephant as if they were daring us to get close at our own risk. As we moved towards them they simply hopped off the elephant and waddled away to the side.

What was left of the elephant's carcass was little more than tattered skin covering bone. The pickings that remained were slim indeed. However, and much to my surprise, the elephant's tusks were still in place. We braved the smell of decay and nipped in with the intention of recovering the ivory, which fortunately drew out easily with only a light tug being required. The tusks made a sucking sound as they separated from their rotten roots. The pair of tusks was long and slim and weighed about fifteen pounds a side.

We remained alongside what was left of the elephant for as long as it took to retrieve a number of the long thick hairs that fringed the elephant's tail. Such hairs, which were both flexible and glossy, were commonly woven by skilful artisans into adjustable bracelets to decorate the wrists of anyone pretentious enough to wear them.

The dead elephant was a cow. How or why she had died wasn't obvious, but old age had almost certainly played no part. She might have been mortally wounded by a hunter, perhaps one of the Wandorobo. I was genuinely pleased that we had managed to recover the ivory, which I envisaged holding on to as a souvenir.

We returned to the fly camp in mid-afternoon bearing the pair of elephant tusks together with our samples of the day. Once in camp I tidied up the tusks, paying particular attention to scouring out the root hollows, and with that done I installed the ivory in the bottom of my personal tin trunk. It didn't occur to me that this action could be construed as poaching, since I had had no hand in the death of the elephant. After all, finders were keepers, and holding on to the ivory made more sense than did abandoning it to its fate in the remoteness of the game reserve.

Lo and behold, two days later who should turn up at our fly camp once again but Bill Moore-Gilbert, the Manyoni Game Ranger. He was down on a regular tour of inspection, part of which included checking up on us. It appeared that he had spotted circling vultures homing in on the dead elephant and had gone along to investigate. His pointed remarks concerning the missing ivory filled me with misgivings.

Tom, undeniably keen to ingratiate himself with the Game Ranger, informed Bill that we were in possession of that very ivory. He said that we were holding on to the tusks for security with the intention of delivering them to an officer of the Game Department at the earliest opportunity. It all sounded quite plausible. The earliest opportunity was immediately deemed to be there and then.

I was less than happy with Tom's pronouncement, but I was faced with no option other than to go and retrieve the ivory from my tin trunk and hand it over. The Game Ranger accepted the tusks from me with a look of mild scepticism on his face, as well he might have done.

As I gave him the ivory I felt a sense of both tangible relief and of gratitude to Tom who had, whatever his intentions, done me a major favour in nipping my elephant poaching career in the bud. I didn't give up the elephant's tail hairs, however.

*

Somewhat to my regret I never discovered whether or not my name featured on the Dodoma club's black list, since I didn't go back to test the waters. It ought to have bothered me, but in truth it really didn't worry me much. I found consolation in recalling the popular song title, "I've been thrown out of better joints than this". The Dodoma club committee wasn't the first of its kind to consider that the functions that it presided over would be best run without my participation, and I reckoned that it probably wouldn't be the last.

The manager of the Dodoma Hotel had yet to ban any more than one or two WDL types from entering his domain, which was most likely due not so much to altruism as to an appreciation of the side on which his bread was buttered. For all that, the essence of his tolerance was a precious thing.

On the north side of the railway track a number of havens catered for a range of drinking habits, inclusive of bottles of IPA, *debes* of native beer and dishes of *skokiaan* tailored to taste. As another great song of the time put it, "Skokiaan! Man, oh man, oh man, you sing a-bing-a-bang-a-bingo!" These establishments were always ready to welcome anyone who was anxious to wet his own whistle in his own way. If (perish the thought) there had ever been a request for a *debe* of *pombe*, let alone *skokiaan*, at the bar of the Dodoma club, the very walls of the club would have come tumbling down.

There were two bars that we frequented regularly. One of the two, located in the commercial area of town, was associated with the less grand (all things being relative) of Dodoma's two cinemas, the exclusive specialisation of which was the screening of Indian films.

On the grounds that entertainment was a rare enough commodity to justify its being grasped wherever and whenever it was available I patronised the Indian cinema on two occasions, and that, as they say, was that as far as I was concerned. Once was enough, twice felt like a punishment. The films screened at the respective showings appeared to be indistinguishable from one another. Each featured a hero and heroine who were prone to burst into song far too often and invariably without warning. The heroes were over-moustached, overweight, greasy with it and possessing looks that were well able to induce anyone to flee from an encounter with them in a dark alley at night. The heroines, however, seemed unfazed by the appearance of their leading men. These beauties warbled away impromptu in high falsetto while all and sundry in the camera's field of influence downed tools and took part in an enthusiastic dance routine.

The second haunt to which we donated our custom was reached by turning down a sombre-looking side street on the left once we were over the level crossing. Its principal facilities consisted of rusting metal tables and creaking wooden chairs arrayed, with no particular attention paid to well-ordered symmetry, inside a quite large and high-walled courtyard. A string of naked light bulbs clung precariously to the top of the courtyard wall and provided a sufficient measure of illumination when it was most needed.

The courtyard was a very pleasant place in which to sit. The sole proviso governing seated *wazungu* was that safety in numbers was the best policy to adopt. The majority of the clientèle was local *watu*. From the conspiratorial way in which they put their heads together and looked at us with poorly disguised disparagement on their faces they appeared to make no secret of the fact that that they weren't exactly enamoured with the presence of *wazungu* in their midst.

And who could blame them?

Tanganyika was moving inexorably towards a well-publicised attainment of internal self-government, and although the call of *uhuru* was not yet being widely heard in Dodoma at least, it was in the process of being shouted from the rooftops up in Kenya. Someone's days were numbered and the *watu* in the courtyard evidently didn't believe that those days were going to be theirs.

Our drinking sessions in the courtyard bar were always accompanied by the broadcast output of a tinny-sounding radio cranked up to and maintained at maximum volume by the proprietor. The radio disgorged a steady diet of popular music recorded by African artistes of both East African and Congolese origin. Congolese music, together with the musicians who performed it, was of the highest quality. It shone a rare beam of light through the savage darkness of the Congo's legacy of the crimes of its former colonial power and the currently bitter fruits of a disastrous post-independence wave of violence.

Our outlook on life in the walled-in fastness of the courtyard was to all intents and purposes of such an apolitical nature for most of the time that it offered offence to no one. However, when radio broadcasting shut down for the night with a customary rendition of "God Save the Queen", all and sundry who were present received a timely reminder as to who was still in charge of the country and were motivated to react in accordance with their own dictates.

As "The Queen" was struck up the British contingent among the *wazungu* complement rose to its feet in unison. We stood to attention, rigid for the duration, in the full knowledge that back "home", there was probably not a man jack among us who, at the end of a public function, wouldn't have headed at speed for the nearest exit to escape at the first intimation of the anthem's opening drum roll.

Afrikaans-speaking South Africans, in a very rare example of commonality of interest with the *watu* present in the courtyard, remained in their seats. As well as our British attitude of attention would permit, we glared at them as ferociously as we could to signify our displeasure at their slight to "The Queen". We were surely indulging ourselves in the kind of patriotism that, according to Dr Johnson, was the last refuge of scoundrels.

The seated *watu* muttered among themselves as "The Queen" was sent not only victorious, but also happy and glorious into the bargain. They gave an impression of being not yet ready for action but fully cognizant that the time for them to take action was coming soon. They might have cast mildly disapproving glances at our antics, but there seemed to be little or no underlying aggression for us to worry about yet.

During one of my visits to the WDL service depot at Manyoni someone told me that on one occasion a small group of *wazungu* had attempted to forcibly induce a few of the more recalcitrant *watu* seated in the courtyard bar to get to their feet during a rendition of "The Queen". The reaction of the *watu* took an unexpected direction. The *wazungu* were compelled to make their exit from the courtyard by scaling the wall and hastening towards the level crossing in something of a hurry.

Please rise and lift your glasses to the Queen.

The Queen!

God bless her!

Gentlemen, you may smoke!

*

In the bright morning light of those days on which we had to turn our backs on the weekend festivities and return from Dodoma to camp we were required to collect and load up the supplies ordered from the traders that we dealt with regularly. The supplies generally included several sacks filled with the all-important *posho*, and other sacks containing *dagaa*, rice (occasionally), groundnuts, sugar and beans. There might, depending on seasonal availability, also be a sack of oranges for us to take along. The oranges were normally small, pithy and not all that sweet to the taste, but they played an important role in preventing the development of tropical ulcers in the *watu*. The traders additionally provided us with *debes* of both cooking and heating oil, and in some cases portions of formally halalled meat (presumably of bovine origin) that were individually wrapped in brown paper in accordance with ration weight specifications.

Of my five senses, the one on which Dodoma's commercial sector made the greatest impact was that of smell. The blend of wood smoke, dust and feral sweat laced with multiple layers of both well known and unfamiliar spices was sharp, pungent and evocative of the lightness and darkness of the spirit of Africa. I soon became so accustomed to it that I took it for granted.

The spices, heaped into great woven baskets for display, were yellow, red, brown and green and various shades thereof, of which I had only previously dreamed. There were cloves, turmeric, cardamom, chillies, cumin, gloriously anonymous curry powders, and a host of others breathing out the kind of potency that would gladden the heart of the cook Simon.

My ears resounded to a clamour of shouting voices, clanking metal, honking horns and the barking of both dogs and *watu*-directed orders. Some of the orders even seemed well meant.

My eyes took in ready smiles, occasional grimaces and an awe-inspiring array of ritual tribal scars.

The two trading firms that were favoured with our camp's custom were respectively owned by Mr Jaffer Ladak (an Arab) and the Patel Bros (Indians, two in number).

The front of the Patel brothers' store featured a kaleidoscopic array of spice-filled baskets set in between neatly stacked up sacks of posho. It was all there for the asking. Inside the store the route to an inner sanctum threaded between what seemed to be mountainous piles of sacked-up goods and vertical cliffs of assembled *debes* of oil that looked unstable enough overall to present the customer with a threat rather than an opportunity.

A number of *watu* scurried through the goods-lined gullies, performing missions for one or other or both of the Patels in a manner which suggested that their future depended on how fast they moved—which it probably did. As task masters, the Indians of Tanganyika were if anything tougher than the Arabs, which was saying something. Indians demanded much from their employees and in return gave them a bare minimum of wages and a solid maximum of abusive treatment. From what I saw of the relationships of both Indians and Arabs with their employees I was sure that if Mr Manji Dhanji ever did happen to stock his store at Singida with running shoes as he was advised to do by the WDL prospector, there would not be a single pair of the shoes that wouldn't attract either an Indian or an Arab customer.

Right at the back of the Patels' trading outlet was a small, secluded, windowless room. In it, favoured customers, not least among whom were WDL bush types like us, were the recipients of Patel hospitality. Orders were made outside the small room, but deals were sealed within, smoothly lubricated by a profusion of free beer. The pair of Patels, with reference to their religious convictions of course, touched not the cup that for us both cheered and inebriated. Since they also didn't wish to be seen to be plying beer to us, they generally left us to our own devices in the clandestine chamber.

To a greater or lesser degree we believed that the brothers' largesse was no more than a perk of the job. We bought supplies from them and took their beer unquestioningly, without any sense of awareness that great baobabs from diminutive cream of tartar seeds grew in the way that mighty oaks sprang from little acorns. This apparently unimpeachable quid pro quo didn't remain innocent for long. Certain traders dealing in WDL camp supplies raised the game by stocking creature comfort items such as cameras, radios, guns and ammunition, and followed up by dropping unsubtle hints in our ears that any of these could be ours without charge if sufficiently large orders for supplies were to be issued their way.

As the number of *watu*-intensive detailed work camps increased in the district, the competition among traders for supplying the camps knew few bounds. The enhanced spending power of many camp leaders was like a flag that could be waved on high in order to attract the highest bidder. Even George's Garage was not exempt from this feeding frenzy.

It was rumoured that some WDL types had entered into private arrangements with certain traders, whereby the former issued purchase orders quoting prices for supplies that were way over the odds and then split the traders' profits with them on settlement.

Some camps were believed to keep as many ghost *watu* on their payrolls as could be got away with—in a camp employing a hundred or more *watu* the inclusion of a number of ghost employees was neither here nor there. As long as all *kipandis* received at Mwadui were fingerprinted in the right place, the identity of the owner of the fingerprint was never a matter for debate.

These alleged irregularities may perhaps have been no more than bar talk, although I for one didn't doubt that what I heard was true. The most extreme example of mutual back scratching between a trader and a WDL man involved the latter being given a new Volkswagen Beetle car by an Indian trader new to Dodoma commerce. This Indian trader arrived to set himself up as a blatant opportunist. The light of his notoriety required no bushel beneath which to hide. Since references to his *modus operandi* must inevitably have filtered back to Mwadui, it was curious to note for how long he appeared to operate unscathed.

The beneficiary of the Beetle drove the vehicle from Tanganyika all the way down to South Africa when his contract with WDL ended. It was said that a load of other Indian trader-sponsored gifts went along with him on the back seat of the car. The driver of the Beetle was the man who, it was said, had once shot a giraffe. His motivation in hunting royal game baffled even those among his bush associates whose tastes leaned towards shooting first and asking questions afterwards. On the basis of his general conduct it was rationalised that he probably shot the giraffe to order, as a swap of towering proportions to be set against the gift of the Beetle.

The foundation of a WDL service depot under the management of Bruno Brown at Manyoni went some way towards reducing the role of traders in the camp supply chain. On the other hand, in its assumed role of primary supplier the Manyoni depot had to be supplied with supplies to supply, so that local traders continued to be part of the equation. I always assumed, however, that the Manyoni depot was operated with probity.

The practice of traders exchanging favours for orders appeared to be essentially an Indian trait. The wheels were to some extent greased as a result of Indians being generally more easily approachable than Arabs. On the other hand I didn't doubt that Arab traders were probably up to every trick in the book, and a few more besides, where maximising profit was concerned. An exception to the hard-sell philosophy of Indian traders was found in the Sikh community. Sikhs were admiringly referred to by the *watu* as the *wasinga singa*. One of the Patel brothers described Sikhs to me as the "Irish of India". Sikhs, he told me, were men who were good for fighting but not much else. The local Sikhs that I knew were blacksmiths and carpenters. They were handsome, turbaned men, muscular and upright. I never found them lacking in integrity in any respect. They all wore elephant hair bracelets, and it was a Sikh who made two such bracelets for me with the elephant tail hairs that I salvaged from that dead elephant in the Rungwa Game Reserve.

Every Indian trader shaped up as an example of the triumph of hope over adversity. All of them were hard working and optimistic to a fault. Whatever we required, an Indian trader would be ready to provide. Even when something that we wanted was not immediately available, we could count on being assured that it would be in our hands soon, if not sooner. "It's on order, *bwana!*" we were always told, "Coming next week!" This guarantee would be issued by the trader in tones of the utmost sincerity. He knew full well that he wouldn't see us in town again for at least a month, by which time we would probably have forgotten what it was we wanted anyway. If we hadn't forgotten about it, something would in all likelihood have turned up in the meantime to deflect our attention elsewhere. As a result everyone was happy.

I should have been aware that those of us who accepted free beer from the Patel brothers in the back room of their emporium were placing a foot on the bottom rung of the one-favour-deserves-another ladder. However, such a thought never occurred to me at the time. Any consideration that the practice might be corrupt didn't enter my mind. The positive gloss on those back-room activities was that those who partook of Patel hospitality were simply living for the moment.

Mr Jaffer Ladak, the Arab trader with whom we occasionally dealt, could also have issued favours to customers in return for customer favours to him, but if he did I neither saw nor experienced any indications of generosity from him. As an Arab and in accordance with the conventional wisdom of the day, Jaffer was what he was and he wasn't expected to be entirely honest.

Jaffer was a seriously fat man. He enveloped his corpulence in a tent-like, once-white kanzu, which could by no stretch of the imagination be considered to have been washed in the recent past. On his head he wore a dog-tooth patterned mantle.

He sat in a solid chair of state in his great dusty barn of a warehouse with the air of a Caliph in repose and barked a string of orders at hirelings who acted on his every word. I was intimidated by his domineering presence, and as a consequence I felt some reluctance to deal with him. It was impossible to look at Jaffer and his band of brethren and not have throat-slitting visions spring to mind.

*

A small bookshop, run by a Christian order of one kind or another, stood directly alongside the Patel brothers' store. Its shelves featured a proliferation of Bibles (in both English and Kiswahili), together with prayer books, a range of works couched in highly moralistic prose, and a side line in crucifixes, saintly effigies and-holier-than-thou tracts, all of which fell a little short of being enthralling.

However, there were also books of local interest in stock, and to someone like me these were a bit more like it. Among the books that I bought at the Dodoma bookshop were: a heavy, hard-covered tome bound in blue cloth entitled *Handbook of Tanganyika* (edited by J. P. Moffett); an *Upcountry Kiswahili* phrase book; *The White Nile* by Alan Moorehead; *Serengeti Shall Not Die* by Bernhard Grzimek; and that altogether invaluable guidebook *Animals of East Africa* by C. T. Astley-Maberly.

The lady who managed the bookshop was most likely a nun dressed in mufti. She was very accommodating and quite prepared to order titles of choice for us, provided that the said titles were appropriate to her tastes in reading.

The high profile accorded to the controversial publication by Penguin Books of D. H. Lawrence's *Lady Chatterley's Lover* in the UK at the time, preceded as it was by a highly entertaining court case, induced us to place an order for the book at the Dodoma bookshop. We assumed that the book's reputation might not yet be known in central Tanganyika.

However, it seemed that we were sadly mistaken in our assumption. Our order for the book received an immediate refusal delivered by the manageress with the backing of an impressive amount of indignation. It took a number of subsequent visits to the bookshop to pass before this vendor of Bibles was again prepared to acknowledge us without first putting a scowl on her face.

*

Our Land Rovers picked their way back to Iwambala from Dodoma with a certain amount of care, laden as they were in the back with sacks full of rations and a bunch of *watu* holding on to precarious perches on top of the same. The *watu* arranged themselves as securely as the situation allowed and then held on as best they could, either to one another or to the bulging sacks underneath them. The combined weight depressed the Land Rover shock absorbers to maximum compression and inverted the springs into downward pointing convex arcs.

We returned to camp retracing our outward route, inclusive of making two halts to respectively take a paw-paw break at Isanza mission and to offer a hail and farewell to the little Arab at his *duka* in Iseke. What he thought about us buying supplies from people like Jaffer Ladak he kept to himself.

We presumed that we had brought back with us all that was needed to sustain the *watu* over the next few weeks. To suit our own needs we had restocked with an adequate supply of tea, milk powder, flour, tinned butter (guaranteed to liquefy when exposed even inside the paraffin-driven fridge), cans of vegetables and enough eggs to be going on with.

The weekend was over, and such excesses as it had contained and the feathers that it had ruffled were already no more than fading memories edged with little regret.

I was always pleased to get back to camp after a weekend out of it. Camp was then a true haven of rest. No bed ever gave a more comfortable night of repose than my good old Hounsfield gave me.

Sampling team (*left to right*): John Simon, Taji Mohammedi, Yusufu Mohammedi, Hamisi Mrisho, Mgogo 1, Mgogo 2, Mwendambio Ngihimba

Efrem Kassiani and Hamiso Mrisho washing samples in the Rungwa Game Reserve

Game reserve sampling safari (*left to right*): Samuel (Game Ranger with rifle); John Simon; Hamisi; Efrem

Great white hunters on a dead buffalo (*left to right*): Tom Molyneux, Danilo Pedrelli, Jim Platt

Paulo Odhiambo and his cook's domain

Wazungu camp tent near Iseke

The hills and sisal plantations of Morogoro

Street scene in Dar es Salaam

12

Mwindaji

The hunter

Under Tom's inducement at one point during our first visit to Dodoma I applied for and was issued with a general game hunting licence, colloquially known as a "pot" licence, together with a bird-hunting licence. The documents were valid for a year. To all intents and purposes they stamped an official seal of approval on my ownership of a 9-mm Brno rifle and a single-bore Greener shotgun. Hanging over the possession of both guns and a pot licence like a dark cloud was the implication that sooner or later a creature that meant me no harm was going to have to be shot at for the purpose of being killed and eaten.

I accepted the shoot-to-eat intention governing a pot licence, but that was just about my limit of being positive about it. When it finally dawned on me that I was placed in the front rank of a thin khaki line to carry out a process of slaughter, I balked at the prospect.

The pot licence cost me a hundred shillings (*shilingi mia moja*), an amount equivalent to two and a half *kipandis* for one of our traverse team *watu*—or perhaps much as six *kipandis* in the case of an *mtu* working for an Arab. It was at least fortunate that I was classed for fee-paying purposes as a resident of Tanganyika, since had I been a visitor to the country the charge for my pot licence would have been one thousand shillings (*shilingi elfu moja*). Under the terms of my newly acquired pot licence I was entitled to shoot the following:

English	Kiswahili	Quota
Buffalo	*Nyati*	1
Bushbuck	*Pongo*	2
Dik-dik	*Dikidiki*	2
Blue duiker	*Paa*	2
Common duiker	*Nsya*	2
Red duiker	*Funo*	2
Patterson's eland	*Pofu*	1
Grant's gazelle	*Swala granti*	2
Thomson's gazelle	*Swala tomi*	3
Hare	*Sungura*	10
Coke's hartebeeste	*Kongoni*	2
Lichtenstein's hartebeeste	*Kongoni*	2
Hippopotamus	*Kiboko*	2
Impala	*Swala pala*	2
Oribi	*Taya*	1
Otter	*Fisi maji*	1
Suni antelope	*Paa*	2
Puku	*Puku (?)*	1
Bohor reedbuck	*Tohe*	1
Southern reedbuck	*Tohe*	1
Roan antelope	*Korongo*	1
Steenbuck	*Tondoro*	2
Topi	*Nyamera*	2
Warthog	*Nguruwe*	3
Ringed waterbuck	*Kuro*	2
Defassa waterbuck	*Kuro (?)*	1
Nyasa wildebeeste	*Nyumbu (?)*	1
White-bearded wildebeeste	*Nyumbu*	2
Zebra	*Punda milia*	3

The bird-hunting licence cost me a mere twenty shillings (*shilingi ishirini*). It permitted me to bag an unlimited number of specified birds, inclusive of ducks (or duck), geese, teal, quail, francolin, lesser bustard, snipe, sand grouse, pigeons and, last and absolutely by no means least, the ubiquitous kanga. All of which seemed a lot easier to peruse on paper than it would be to manage in practice.

As well as being required to possess appropriate firearms and ammunition, a would-be hunter needed to be something of an expert in game species identification, with a good knowledge of their individual distribution and habitat. The matter of identification was slightly complicated by a strictly "males only" pot licence shooting mandate where bushbuck, eland, Grant's gazelle, Thomson's gazelle, impala, puku, reedbuck and waterbuck were concerned. However, as males were normally adorned with distinctive sets of horns, identifying them at a distance was not as difficult as it might otherwise have been.

Antelopes were categorised in terms of their size: small, medium and large. I learned quite quickly to identify the characteristic shape, form and curvature of horns, taking to it as if it were the most natural and endlessly fascinating thing in the world. Pot licence hunters weren't after trophies, however. The taking of trophies was left to white hunters and their clients. A pot licence meant the acquisition of meat pure and simple.

It seemed completely incongruous that a buffalo and a couple of hippos could be shot on my pot licence. I assumed that this trio might have sneaked into the list of game quotas by mistake as my weapons were wholly inadequate for tackling game of that size. Similar considerations may also have applied to the eland and roan antelope that I evidently had additionally been granted the right to hunt.

The range of habitats favoured by species of game was a critical factor for a hunter to appreciate. On any hunt the likelihood of coming across more than just a few of the species listed on the pot licence was not high. The type of game to be encountered under thick bush conditions was quite different from what one could expect to find on the upland plains and in the open savannah.

If a full quota for a specific game animal was shot out during the validity of a pot licence, then, unless another such licence was taken out, any additional shooting of the species would constitute poaching. The pot licence documentation featured space on which the time, date and place of any species shot had to be recorded in association with any relevant remarks related to the circumstances of the shooting. It all seemed perfectly straightforward in principle, but when meat was needed the fine line drawn beneath a completed quota was occasionally erased as a matter of necessity.

There were very few camps in which at least one *mzungu* (and often more than one) didn't possess one or more firearms. A parallel consideration applied to pot licences. It created a situation that more or less guaranteed that regulations could be treated with a certain amount of elasticity. Substitutions within the quotas of game that was available for game that was not available tended to become standard practice over a period of time.

The authority for a hunter to shoot in excess of any of the quotas listed on a pot licence could be ensured by his taking out what was known as a "supplementary game licence". Supplementary licences were species-specific and came in two versions, one for so-called residents like me and one for visitors. The difference between the two lay in the fee, the latter costing roughly twice as much as the former. Even so, the fees were not onerous. Small game ran to ten shillings per supplementary kill for a resident. In the case of buffalo and hippo the resident's supplementary fee per animal was fifty shillings.

Supplementary licences were available for the hunting of practically anything that moved through the bush on two or four legs. Examples of the more exotic among these, together with what the cost of a licence to a resident would be, were: giant forest hog—fifty shillings; greater kudu (males only)—one hundred shillings; colobus monkey—a mere twenty shillings; oryx—one hundred shillings; ostrich—one hundred shillings; rock rabbit—five shillings and cheap at the price.

At the peak of the supplementary licence hierarchy came the elephant—six hundred shillings; rhino—three hundred shillings; lion (males only)—two hundred shillings; and leopard—two hundred and fifty shillings. With an eye to business, the respective fees charged to a visitor taking out supplementary licences for these big four were two thousand shillings, eight hundred shillings, five hundred shillings, and five hundred shillings. The critical stipulation placed on shooting elephants was that the ivory must weigh a minimum of twenty-two pounds for a pair of tusks, or at least eleven pounds when the number of tusks was only one.

Estimating the weight of ivory on a live elephant seemed to me to require a level of skill and experience that would always be denied me. As a consolation I told myself that it was the kind of skill that I didn't want to have. Whether ivory-bearing elephants were seen from a distance (the ideal view) or close up (which heaven forbid), when you were out on foot everything about them looked frighteningly big, not least their tusks. I formed a firm opinion that elephant were best observed when they were separated from me by a wide and deep-flowing river.

Hunting big game, as exemplified by the big four (or big five including the buffalo) was normally almost entirely within the remit of professional white hunters, although it did seem that anyone who could talk a plausible line and demonstrate that he had the requisite arsenal of firearms and friends in high places could take out a professional hunter's licence for a fee of five hundred shillings. A further option to obtain a trophy dealer's licence for two hundred shillings also existed. Nothing seemed to be ruled out for those who had the necessary shillings to place on the table.

*

To recapitulate my hunting credentials, I owned a rifle, a shotgun and a pot licence. The sum total of my experience was zero. Pressure was intensifying on me to redress the balance by shooting something, and nothing was more certain than that I would not be able to resist the pressure forever.

I wasn't entirely unhappy with my ownership of weapons as long as I didn't have to use them. I admired them, and I cleaned them regularly and enthusiastically. I revelled in the evocative smell of gun oil and the way in which it blued gunmetal and made rifled bores shine brightly from end to end.

It was not until I finally succumbed to being pushed into taking my rifle and shotgun out into the bush in search of prey that I realised that in buying them I had bitten off more than I could chew. The executioner's axe fell on me one day when the camp at Iwambala ran out of red meat. The few kanga that we were able to trap down at the waterhole were unable to fill the gap. Something more substantial was called for, and I was instructed by Tom to go out and bring it in.

The stock of my rifle was decorated by applying the tried and true principle typified by a scrotum sac on the knob of a Land Rover gear lever to a piece of dun skin originating from an unidentified antelope.

The skin was wrapped around the stock when wet and allowed to dry and shrink to assume an iron-hardness that mimicked every nuance of the wood that it covered. While the skin was drying its odour failed to please, but I got used to it in time.

I was reliably assured by a knowledgeable informant that a rawhide embellishment on a firearm was well in keeping with hunting etiquette for beginners, as indeed was the wearing of an elephant-hair bracelet, or a leopard-claw necklace or a buckskin vest. However, said my informant, the novice's choice of decoration that pressed the boundary of good hunting taste to its limit was a circlet of animal hide around the crown of his hat.

White hunters, all exempt from sartorial criticism, seemed to favour sporting "Stewart Granger"-styled hatbands made of either leopard skin or zebra skin. The WDL shooting fraternity, inclusive of fahkamusshoota types, almost always avoided the ostentation of hatbands, but irrespective of this concession to our disparate consciences, we always remained the unspeakable in pursuit of the eatable.

That peer among white hunters, Allan Quatermain (incidentally played on screen with the greatest of aplomb by Stewart Granger), would have seen us coming long before we saw him. In Rider Haggard's *King Solomon's Mines* Allan wrote, "There is no need to tell lies about hunting, for so many curious things happen within the knowledge of a man whose business it is to hunt".

*

And so was it with me when I set out from camp to hunt for the first time as the front seat passenger in a Land Rover driven by Tom. In the back were seated two *watu*, one of whom was armed with a knife, long, sharp, *halal* for the purpose of. The other *mtu* was there to ensure that there was at least one person on board who was capable of doing the heavy work. We entered the grey bush and it seemed ready to swallow us up. Tom Lehrer's hunting song, which was so much a feature of the background to our camp life, at once assumed an entirely new relevance.

The driving stopped after a few miles of fruitless bush bashing that produced no sightings of game, and we all got out to continue hunting on foot. I brought up the rear of our party of four, carrying my rifle in the manner of one who was on his way to face rather than participate in a firing squad. My fond hope was that we would come across nothing worth hunting. The tsetse flies were far less reticent about seeking prey and found us right away.

Tom carried a *panga*, and with it he demonstrated the art of blazing trees as an aid to our not getting lost. A quick sweep of his panga at a tree and a neat slice of bark fell away in an instant to expose stark white wood beneath. It was unfortunate that Tom blazed only on the side of the trees facing our direction of advance. Looking back in the direction from which we came there was not a blaze in sight.

I knew to my cost that in the bush one tree looked very much like another. It was not at all difficult to get lost. We were lucky that a sense of bush craft was second nature to the *watu* accompanying us, which was the best possible reason for bringing them along. At any given moment they knew where we were and where we had left the Land Rover, and they could walk a line between the two points with the homing skill of bees.

A point frequently and hotly debated in the bars where *wazungu* gathered was whether or not, in the light of such impressive native skills honed over countless generations, any *wazungu* explorers could genuinely claim to have "discovered" anything at all in Africa. The pieces of the Dark Continent's geographical jigsaw were all well known quantities to its people since long before the arrival of *wazungu* on the scene to pick the pieces up and attempt to reassemble them in even greater disorder.

For a while our little hunting party played a game of "follow-my-leader" through the bush. The leader in question was a black-throated honey guide, otherwise known as a "honey bird". The Latin name of this blunt-beaked, short-legged, long-tailed dun-coloured bird, whose sole claim to flamboyance was white flashes on its tail, was the singularly appropriate *indicator indicator*. Its stock in trade was to chatter at itinerant creatures to attract their attention and induce them to follow it as it flitted from tree to tree, keeping just ahead. Man or beast, all were treated alike by the honey bird.

The final destination of a honey bird was normally a specific tree that it knew of in which a colony of bees was flourishing in a hollow. The honey bird's understanding was that whoever or whatever it led to the tree would open up the hollow to gain access to the honey by employing a means most appropriate to the circumstances, would then take away only a reasonable proportion of the honey and would leave the rest for the honey bird to feed on. It was a highly cooperative arrangement in which all parties involved (other than the bees) were winners.

Following a honey bird created a diversion that deflected my thoughts away from the pressing fact that our primary interest in being out in the bush wasn't to look for honey. As it was, the honey bird was the first to call it a day. Perhaps it sensed a lack of interest on our part. It flew away in search of a more helpful set of benefactors. I had to take it on trust that we hadn't upset the honey bird too much.

There was no shortage of informed comment in the proximity of the bars to support the observation that a honey bird was apt to get quite annoyed when those that it selected to follow it to a source of honey failed to oblige, either by not following the bird at all or, if they did follow it to the end, by removing much more than their fair share of honey. Under these circumstances the honey bird would, it was said, lead its subsequent mark to where a black mamba was waiting in the grass or to where a lion (or two) was resting in the shade. It paid to stay on good terms with honey birds.

*

Tom suddenly raised his hand as a signal for us to halt. We did so and assembled in a cluster. He pointed towards a patch of thick bush perhaps thirty yards ahead of us. I could see nothing at first, but then I spotted a slight fluttering that resolved itself into the tips of a pair of rounded ears and below them the shadowy outlines of an indeterminate number of antelopes.

Tom made a stabbing gesture with an index finger. I took it as a signal that I was supposed to shoot at one of the antelopes in view. I slipped off the safety catch of my rifle and worked the bolt to introduce a bullet into the firing chamber from the magazine. I was hoping that the bolt action would make sufficient noise to alarm the antelopes into flight, but thanks to my ministrations the bolt was so clean and well oiled that its movement provided no more than a polite snicker.

On the recommendation of my peers the bullets that I was using were a "soft-nosed" variety. "Hard-nosed" ammunition was preferable for tidy killing, but using them required a degree of on-target precision that I didn't have. A soft-nosed bullet would be much more effective in bringing game down if a shot was a little off-target. Such bullets sometimes created dreadful exit wounds.

My rifle was loaded, yet I hesitated to take the next dreadful step.

My heart was racing so hard that I both hoped and feared that I was about to pass out. Tom's gestures became considerably more animated as I procrastinated further. From a sideways glance that I took at him I could see that there was a fair amount of heat being generated as well. It was do or die time for me. Faced with the inevitable, I sighted my rifle on the head of one of the antelopes standing in the shadows, and elevated the barrel by a few degrees before I pulled the trigger.

Before the explosive crack of the shot faded from my ears, three antelopes bounded out of the patch of thick bush and scattered to what might have been the four winds if there hadn't been only three of them and if it hadn't been a calm day at the time. They were a trio of female kudu, although I didn't know that until Tom informed me of their identity in quite forcible terms. As female kudu were strictly off limits for hunting it was just as well that I placed my shot over their heads. I was only too glad to see them disappear.

A blistering condemnation of my performance followed in short order. Tom must have recognised that I had pulled the shot and he wasn't at all happy about my aiming towards female kudu. He let me know that he hadn't even seen the kudu until they ran off. The prey that he was pointing at was a small duiker that he saw standing alongside a bush on one side. I was relieved to note that the duiker had also made itself scarce.

We moved on. As we had already come across three female kudu, one duiker and a honey bird, confidence grew in me that our fair share of game sightings for the day might have reached its quota. With a little more luck, I thought, the sounds that our feet were making, together with the steady chop of Tom's one-sided tree blazing and my recently fired elevated shot, would motivate any other game in our vicinity to seek out pastures new. However, such a thing was not to be.

We skirted along the edge of a rounded knoll, the shallow slopes of which were littered with boulders of granite. To the left the ground dropped down towards a winding gully floored with brown sand and patched here and there with rafts of yellow grass.

At the foot of the rising slope on the far side of the gully, perhaps a hundred yards from where we were, a lone impala buck stood in splendour, taking advantage of a rare blot of shade. Its only signs of movement were in a pendulum-like twitch in the tail and an occasional fly-swatting flick of an ear until it inclined its pair of finely curved lyre-shaped horns towards its back as it raised its head and quivered its nostrils as if sensing the possibility that danger was approaching. A shiver drifted across its flank on which a dark bar separated golden-brown upper hide from a white flash of underbelly.

Tom undertook what was by then becoming a familiar pattern of staccato gesturing directed at my attention to shooting. I shook my head and, acting on the assumption that if we got any closer to it the impala would have the sense to run off, I mumbled an excuse that it was much too far away from us for me to try a shot.

Tom's reaction to this was to order me to get closer by making my way down the slope under cover of some of the bigger boulders. It seemed that circumstances totally out of my control had caught up with me. I picked my way down the slope very slowly, partly stooping, mostly crawling, willing the impala to hear me and depart. With or without one of its characteristic whistles, all that mattered was that the impala should disappear. I didn't take a look in its direction until I got to the foot of the slope, at which point I was forty or fifty yards closer to where I had last glimpsed it standing. I was more than sorry to see that it was still there. A single glance back up to where Tom and the two *watu* were squatting behind a jumble of boulders gave me a strong impression that they were a trio tamping at the bit.

I readied the rifle, raised it to my shoulder, sighted it on the impala's shoulder for a while, and lowered it. My arms were trembling so much that I couldn't hold the sight on the target. I tried to sight the rifle on the impala for a second time and failed again. I might have made as many as five or six similar attempts, but couldn't recall how many afterwards as the pressure I felt myself under was so barely endurable that it eclipsed my memory. It did however take me to a point of no return—I sighted, closed my eyes and squeezed the trigger.

The concussion of the shot dulled my hearing. The recoil of the rifle's stock on my shoulder knocked me over to one side. I must have been holding the rifle too loosely. Opening my eyes I looked towards where I last saw the impala and was delighted to recognise that it was gone. A feeling that was almost euphoric swept over me, rooted in a belief that I had done my best, and although I hadn't exactly covered myself with glory I also hadn't disgraced myself. And in any case, missing the target was what I had wanted to do.

Then I was aware of Tom and the two *watu* bounding down the slope behind me. They dashed past and raced across the gully towards what I suddenly realised was the impala buck thrashing around on its side on the ground, a big bloom of blood on its left shoulder. My feelings switched to sudden panic. I leapt up and ran after them.

My bullet had struck the impala just behind its left shoulder. It wasn't a clean killing shot. The impala's legs were jerking and kicking rhythmically. Its eyes were both liquid and accusing and they burned an indelible image into my mind. I worked the bolt of the rifle and shot the impala through the head to still its pain. Its eyes glazed over and faded to black, unblinking as dust motes settled on them.

As I shot, the *halal* knife was in the process of being unlimbered by the *mtu* who carried it. He stooped and with no more than a flick of his wrist drew the knife across the impala's throat. A gush of blood stained the sand and splashed onto the lowest twigs of a small bush. Whether or not the *halal* process was effected in time to satisfy religious convictions was immaterial to me as I had more than enough other thoughts to occupy my mind. I staggered a few yards over to one side and vomited. Tom expressed some indignation concerning my second shot fired into the impala's head. He complained that I was "wasting ammunition" and said the *halal* knife should have been used as the tool for the final despatch.

I was sure that shooting the impala was the worst experience of my life to date. I slumped beside a boulder with my head in my hands while the unfortunate animal was being skinned. The *halal* knife played a major role in the skinning, which was carried out both efficiently and rapidly. If I had watched the skinning being done I would probably have appreciated the skill involved, but although I saw skinning take place at many subsequent kills I chose to miss it on this occasion.

The knife was used to make a neat circular cut through the skin around the neck and then down along the underbelly from neck to tail without disturbing the integrity of the sac of entrails. Slits were then made along the line of the four inner legs and extended into circles just above the hooves, all of which permitted the skin to be pulled off the carcass in one piece. The skin came away with a gentle sound of combined ripping and sucking. Its removal was assisted by the flat of the skinner's hand pushing between the hide and the underlying flesh. The head and horns were lifted away as a "trophy" of the hunt, assuming that such a term had any relevance.

The impala's horns were offered to me. I did not hesitate to decline to accept them.

The two *watu* carefully spread the skin on the ground with its wet side uppermost to make a "clean" carpet on which the impala's carcass could be butchered. They first of all opened up the sac of entrails and separated and removed the constituent organs consisting of the stomach (tripe), the lungs, the liver, the kidneys, the heart and various lengths of intestine. This "offal" or so called *matumbo ya mnyama* was destined to be consumed by the *watu* in camp, most of whom preferred eating offal to eating actual meat.

The impala's carcass was cut into four quarters, divided up along the line of the spine and crossways below the ribs. As a rule far less subtlety was demonstrated by the *watu* in cutting up meat than in their skinning and offal removing technique. Anatomical knowledge played no part in the procedures employed. As far as the *watu* were concerned, a cut of meat meant what it said. They swung *pangas* and let the blades fall at will. Bones sundered in the assault. An *mtu* could, in seconds, turn a good-looking leg of meat into a mess of shattered flesh studded with bone splinters.

The impala that I shot had stood about a yard high at the shoulder. On the hoof it weighed perhaps sixty pounds. Each of the four quarters weighed in the order of from ten to twelve pounds. On the return to the Land Rover three of us carried a quarter each. The skin with the collection of entrails wrapped in it plus the lightest of the four quarters were all borne by the stronger of the two *watu*.

What was left of the impala at the site of the kill was barely enough for a vulture to bother about, let alone to attract the attention of a hyena.

I didn't have very much recollection of our return to camp as I was in a state of feeling almost overwhelmed by the enormity of what I had done. The *watu* led us unerringly back to the Land Rover along the trace of Tom's wrong-sided tree blazes.

Back in Iwambala the skin, with its hair side down, was stretched out and tightly pegged to the ground to be dried by the sun after being given a good scraping to remove adhering scraps of flesh. Ants took care of anything that was missed by the scraper. When it was fully dried out the skin would be ready for tanning, but as that painstaking process was too much like hard work for *watu*, and since we had no women available to take it up, the skin was most likely to be cut into thin strips suitable for plaiting into rawhide ropes (*kambas*) and strings.

I was so distraught when we reached camp that I at once took to my tent. It was as if my body was no longer my own. I looked at myself as if from a distance and didn't like what I saw. I sensed the impala's dying eyes still fixed on me, and all of a sudden my legs became too weak to hold me up. Flopped on my Hounsfield bed, I entered into what could have been a state of near catatonia. It held on to me all through the subsequent night and onwards during the following day until early evening arrived.

I was aware of movements outside my tent and I knew that people were looking in on me, but I wasn't able to respond to them. Looking back on it, it seemed that all I wanted to do was mourn the death of the impala and wallow in genuine remorse.

With evening, almost as if a switch were thrown in my head, I felt anxiety vanish in an instant. I rose from the Hounsfield with vigour restored, much in the manner of a person who was once famously instructed to "take up thy bed and walk" and stepped into the open from beneath the flysheet of my tent with a feeling that I was the recipient of a divine ordination allowing me to be anything that took my fancy. I was reincarnated, vested with immense power and walking in the footprints of giants. The reluctantly taken shot that linked my rifle to an unfortunate impala suddenly seemed to make a bridge leading to a promised land.

Over the bridge lay a land of plenty. Its religion might have been named fahkamusshoota. For the first time I felt ready, willing and absolutely eager to immediately head out into the bush and shoot at anything that moved. It mattered not if the target were to be big or small, edible or inedible. A pot licence appeared to be no more than a weak fetter constraining opportunities for broader action.

As I learned later, this state of mind was known as "game fever" or "buck fever". It was a condition common to hunters making a first kill and, not to put too fine a point on it, was inspired by a desire to kill again and fuelled by a lust to spill blood. My symptoms of game fever waxed and waned for several months before they subsided and then thankfully faded away altogether.

While I was working in the Rungwa Game Reserve I was, much to my frustration, prevented from exercising my newly found will to hunt. Outside of the restricted areas I hunted regularly while the urge was on me and I was to all intents and purposes blind to reason.

For the record, my complete bag of game in Tanganyika was as follows:

Date shot	English	Kiswahili
18 October 1960	Impala	*Swala pala*
30 October 1960	Buffalo*	*Nyati*
1 November 1960	Elephant*	*Tembo*
20 December 1960	Oribi	*Taya*
10 January 1961	Dik-dik	*Dikidiki*
7 February 1961	Warthog	*Nguruwe*
10 February 1961	Ringed waterbuck	*Kuro*
12 February 1961	Silver-backed jackal	*Bweha*
20 February 1961	Bat-eared fox	*Bweha Masigio*
15 March 1961	Vervet monkey	*Tumbili*
20 March 1961	Rock hyrax	*Pimbi*
21 March 1961	Dik-dik	*Dikidiki*
14 April 1961	Eland	*Pofu*
21 May 1961	Thomson's gazelle	*Tomi*
24 May 1961	African hare	*Sungwa*
4 June 1961	Kenya wildebeeste	*Nyumbu*
4 June 1961	Thomson's gazelle	*Tomi*
8 October 1961	Thomson's gazelle	*Tomi*
9 October 1961	Thomson's gazelle (2)	*Tomi*
5 November 1961	Thomson's gazelle	*Tomi*

In addition to this list of victims that fell to my rifle—a list that in retrospect was not even illuminated by the faintest glimmer of hunter's pride—I used my Greener shotgun to dispose of a fair inventory of feathered game. These birds, shot on various dates, consisted of a brace of sand grouse; a dozen francolin; a score of pigeons; one spur-winged goose; and perhaps as many as fifty kanga.

My shooting was in principle consistent with pot licence stipulations. I held two pot licences during my time in Tanganyika, the first of which was issued in Dodoma in October 1960, as previously referred to, and the second of which was obtained in Mwanza about a year later. The type of game that I shot reflected, of necessity, the characteristic habitats that were accessible within a reasonable distance of camps that I worked from.

Between September 1960 and early January 1961 when I was assigned to Tom's camp at Iwambala, the paucity of the game that I shot was in direct proportion to the duration of the time of working in the Rungwa Game Reserve, where, although there was plenty of game to see, there was none at all to shoot at.

*

I must confess that the buffalo and elephant marked with asterisks in my bag of game were not personal kills as such. Although I was involved in a hunt during which Danilo shot them, their presence on the list may be construed as presenting the reader with a certain amount of false pretence on my part. Some qualification is necessary.

Hard on the heels of my triumph-through-tragedy despatch of the impala, as if endorsing my thereby obtaining membership of an exclusive hunter's club, Tom and I were invited by our Ilangali neighbour Danilo to accompany him and his underling Mario on a fahkamusshoota elephant hunt.

Danilo possessed a supplementary hunting licence for elephant together with a double barrelled .450-calibre rifle that gave him the adequate means to bring down an elephant. My 9-mm rifle would serve purely as back-up, if required, to Danilo's superior firepower. Out in the bush anything could happen. You knew it would, but you just didn't know when.

A legendary (if not notorious) elephant hunter named W.D.M. ("Karamoja") Bell was reputed to be able to kill elephants with a single shot using a rifle with a calibre as small as .275 or .303. It was claimed that Karamoja's knowledge of an elephant's anatomy was so detailed that, by approaching the elephants he selected as his targets almost within touching distance, he could place killing shots in the brain or heart with clinical precision.

It was reported that game scouts were sometimes sent out to conduct official culls of elephant herds using the exceedingly high power of .577-calibre firearms. Their practice was to fell an elephant with a leg shot and then move in close to make a second and final shot to the heart or head.

The story of Danilo's fahkamusshoota elephant hunt will be told in the next chapter. Suffice it to mention here that, with respect to incorporating both an elephant and a buffalo on my hunting list, both were killed during that hunt. The kills were credited to Danilo. My part involved shooting at both animals in what might have been a state of total panic.

As far as could be judged afterwards I missed the buffalo and hit the elephant in its trunk. The episode ought to have taught me that, whether or not I was afflicted by game fever, a rifle and its ownership by someone like me were in no way compatible entities. Sad to relate, I learned nothing and my illusions lived on for a while.

*

Between early January and late March 1961 I was in a camp located close to Iseke, following the conclusion of the Iwambala sampling programme and Tom's concurrent promotion to the heady world of detailed work. Around and about Iseke the game pickings were poor. The list shows that I took shots at a few creatures that deserved more respect from me. A vervet monkey was shot in error in a case of mistaken identity. It was unfortunately in the wrong place at the wrong time when the wrong person came by carrying a rifle.

The waterbuck, however, was fair game, even though waterbuck meat was reckoned by connoisseurs of game to be rather wormy. I shot it in the shoulder with what turned out to be my last bullet (a grave error of judgement)—it dropped and lay kicking on the ground. Taji, our *halal* expert for the day, came running in but was unable to get into a suitable position for cutting the waterbuck's throat for fear of being caught by one of its appreciably large hooves. With no more ammunition available to me, my taking an ultimate headshot was out of the question.

The delay was costly, as the wounded waterbuck heaved itself up onto its feet, staggered a bit, then turned and ran into the bush. We tracked it for several hours, following a trail of blood spots and splashes, but we never caught up with it. I had to conclude that either I didn't hit it vitally or else it was a very durable animal. The waterbuck shooting incident was regrettable. It taught me that while the *halal* procedure had to be treated with respect, the greater priority was to make a cleanly shot kill in the first place.

I left Iseke to go and set up a camp in the Wanyaturu tribal lands of the Singida district between late March and the end of June in 1961. This camp was established adjacent to a small lake named Mianje. The setting was idyllic and would have been appreciated even more if the social interaction between our camp *watu* and various residents of the nearby village of Mungaa had been less conflictive.

The forging of good local relations was not aided by the tribal Chief, who went by the name of Omari Mpahi and who possessed more faces than a rose-cut diamond. Nor were we helped much by the DO from Singida who came to a *baraza* to prepare the way for us in the manner of John the Baptist but did it a lot less well than John; regrettably for us, however, the DO did not have his head end up on a plate.

From the camp at Lake Mianje we were able to drive out to the east of Singida to go hunting on the great grass plains that surrounded a spectacularly isolated extinct volcanic cone named Mount Hanang. Substantial numbers of wildebeest and zebra wandered over the plains, keeping company with what appeared to be multitudes of tail-twitching Thomson's gazelles together with a scattering among them of the slightly taller Grant's gazelles. Small groups of hyenas and solitary jackals roamed the fringes of the *tomi* herds seeking to take advantage of any that were either slow or infirm or both at the same time.

The grass plains, flanked by the Eyasi and Manyara salt lakes to the west and east respectively, stretched all the way north to reach the mighty Ngorongoro crater and merge into the world-famous Serengeti National Park. Within the boundary of the Serengeti untold numbers of wildebeest lived, bred and plodded ever onwards in an endlessly circling pattern of migration. The area of the plains around Mount Hanang, which the *watu* told me were a *shamba wabibi* (game reserve) but weren't quite that yet when I was there, more or less marked the southern limit of wildebeest territory.

The eland featured on my hunting list was shot during the time when I was camped near Lake Mianje. The kill was erroneously credited to an English-speaking South African Field Officer named Bob McLeod rather than to me, but since I knew differently that didn't really matter and Bob could think what he liked.

The *wazungu* participants in the eland hunt were me, Bob, and Tony Knowles and Joker Mackenzie from the "Drop Inn". Bob was camped out to the west of Singida and used Singida as his supply base. It was logical that we would all come together to hunt something or other at some time.

Bob was tall, rangy and loose-limbed, given to wearing the style of shorts reaching barely half way down the thigh that were so favoured by South Africans. His most distinctive characteristic was a pronounced stammer, a very disconcerting trait to anyone who was unused to it. However, once Bob had imbibed the contents of a few bottles of beer—the more the better—his stammer evaporated like water dripped on sun-heated granite and he became as garrulously articulate in his speech as a troop of baboons.

The shot eland was a young bull, weighing well in excess of one thousand pounds. Both Bob and I shot at it, but only one bullet hit. I was as sure that the fatal shot was mine as Bob was that it was his. As I didn't really want to go through the tortuous process of arguing with the stammering Bob, he was allowed to "win" the kill by default.

Using fresh-cut poles from the bush as levers we manipulated the dead eland onto the back of Tony's Land Rover with what could best be described as extreme difficulty. We had to excavate a hollow to back the Land Rover into in order to reduce the lifting distance. The eland's hooves stuck out on one side of the back of the Land Rover and its head hung over the flap of the open tailgate.

Driving Tony's Land Rover, laden as it was with a cargo of eland and passengers, out of the bush towards the open road put a substantial strain on the vehicle's motor. The radiator boiled dry, the water bags were emptied to replenish the losses, the radiator boiled again and we were still some distance from easier going.

To nurse the radiator through the last long mile or two of bush and so avoid the likelihood of the engine seizing up we were left with no alternative but to line up in front of the open engine and, one by one, to climb onto the front bumper and urinate into the dry radiator. Piss did the job at the time, but what it was going to do to the longer-term future of the Land Rover's engine was something Tony would find out about in due course. What was certain was that the piss was never taken from any of us in a more meaningful way.

*

I closed the camp at Lake Mianje at the end of June in 1961 and left the Singida district on a work transfer to a camp in the *mbuga* country of the Mwanza district. The latter camp, although new to me, had already been established for some time. It was located about half a mile to the east of a village named Ilula that straddled the main road to Mwanza approximately forty miles north of Mwadui.

Ilula was a rather unpleasant little settlement. It was quite as dusty as its roadside situation suggested that it ought to be. What made it worse was that the local tribe was the Wasukuma. I did my best to try to like the Wasukuma, but I never succeeded.

Relatively speaking, the working area assigned to the camp near Ilula was, if not significantly populated, at least well trodden by Wasukuma tribesmen. Voracious goats consumed all the natural foliage that they were able to reach by either standing on their hind legs or climbing into the lower branches of trees. The goats looked almost as skinny as the cattle that fed by foraging for whatever the goats left for them. The only four-footed game available to me to shoot in the area was a scattering of Thomson's gazelles, which I supposed had strayed along by accident.

I remained in that general area, making only one further camp move to a rock-girt plain located twenty miles to the south of Ilula, until my tenure in Tanganyika came to a wet season-induced end in November 1961. The intensity and continuity of the rain that fell on us at that time was unprecedented. The *mbuga* soil became so cloyingly glutinous that all reasonable movement of men, animals and machines was rendered impossible. We were forced to strike the camp and retreat as best we could. The pull-out was not entirely to my regret as the choice was to either do it or sink out of sight into the surrounding morass.

That final camp was set up in the vicinity of a primitive village named Bubiki, around which there was what appeared to be a glut of small pigeons. Each pigeon carried only a little meat, but they were nonetheless game birds and were well matched to the wiles of hunters. Efrem shot a large number of them. I let him take the shotgun and a number of twelve-bore bird shot cartridges with him, and out he went and knocked the pigeons down. On his return to camp he handed the shotgun and the unused cartridges as well as the empty cartridge cases back to me, all of which were precisely matched to his bag of the day.

My allowing Efrem to use the shotgun probably meant that I was contravening the laws of Tanganyika, but I didn't worry about that as I trusted him implicitly. He never once let me down, and any thoughts of his shooting being anything more than reasonable practice never entered my mind.

I was never quite able to work out why the *wazungu* were so concerned about firearms getting into the hands of the *watu*. The latter weren't noted for their shooting skills, and in any case they had a whole host of ways and means of their own to eliminate *wazungu* at will if they chose to do so. The innate good nature of the vast majority of *watu* was a saving grace for the rest of us to appreciate.

As it was, when we ran out of dry weather in November 1961, I was still in full possession of my two firearms. A consequence of my assigned area being too wet to be worked was that I was offered an opportunity, which I considered and then accepted, to be seconded at very short notice to fill a De Beers opening in reconnaissance exploration for diamonds down in the Bechuanaland Protectorate, familiarly known as the "BP".

Owing to the time constraints governing this very long-distance relocation it did not prove possible for me to obtain near-future police permits to export my firearms to the BP. I was required to deposit both the rifle and the shotgun with the Shinyanga police pending the eventual release of the guns to follow me in the course of time as a secure export package.

The senior officer at the Shinyanga police station held the rank of inspector. He was a rare bird, being an early product of the process known as "Africanisation" that always set the *wazungu* trembling when it was mentioned. I knew the inspector quite well from numerous encounters in the bar of the Shinyanga Diamond Fields Hotel. We were drinking buddies at that convivial venue, and our social relationship began and ended in the hotel bar. I bought him far more beer than he bought me—not that that meant much as I couldn't remember him ever stumping up for a round. He was dapper and jovial, a large man whose company was there to be enjoyed.

When I had been working in the BP for some months and had still not received any communication from the Shinyanga police over the status of an export licence for my firearms, I wrote to the inspector to make an enquiry as to how things were coming along.

About two months after my letter was posted a response to it arrived. The response was a copy of a formal letter that the inspector had written to his Mwanza-based superintendent on the subject of me and my guns.

The letter declared that under no circumstances should I be granted an export licence for the two weapons. The grounds for the inspector's categorical assertion were (a) that I was not a person to be trusted, (b) that I was known to consort with undesirables, and (c) that he had frequently observed me to be drunk in charge of firearms at the Diamond Fields Hotel. Besides maligning my character he also appeared to cast doubts on the legitimacy of my birth.

I didn't know what to make of it. Although I found his lies hurtful, I thought his betrayal of what I had believed to be our friendship to be a much bitterer pill to swallow. However, much stronger allegiances than the one we had were blown away like dust by the winds of change preceding the gales of *uhuru*.

The inspector's letter was set out beneath the coat of arms of Tanganyika at its head. It probably took on a life of its own in official circles. His remarks would have been deemed accurate and not opened to question. I was too far away from him in any case to be able to conduct any form of direct protest to attempt to redress the balance in my favour.

I wrote a reply to my turncoat friend to set straight the record as I saw it, but I heard no more from his end.

My rifle and shotgun had to be abandoned to their fate, which went some way towards creating a happy ending as I was by then only too glad to be shot of them.

13

Tembo!

Elephant!

When Tom and I were invited to accompany Danilo and Mario on an elephant hunt I had not yet had the pleasure of making the acquaintance of the Shinyanga inspector of police. That worthy gentleman was probably even then honing his twin talents for writing fiction and cadging beer at the Diamond Fields Hotel.

I couldn't complain: I enjoyed full ownership of my firearms; one impala kill was notched up on the stock of my rifle; and I was ready for action.

Fahkamusshoota!

Danilo organised the elephant hunt after receiving reliable intelligence concerning the movement of an elephant herd through a sector of bush in which hunting elephant was not subject to any restrictions other than those imposed by the relevant supplementary game licence. The sighting of the alleged herd was made some twenty miles to the west of Iwambala.

Danilo's policy was to guarantee a reward to any *mtu* who provided him with a positive report on confirmed sightings of game within what he considered to be reasonable hunting range of his camp.

It was not always possible to take all such reports at face value, no matter how effusively they were dressed up. The *watu* generally tended to tell the *wazungu* what they thought the *wazungu* wanted to know, even when there was no reward in the offing. With a reward thrown in, the sky was the limit on *watu* capacity to generate information.

If an *mzungu* was interested in knowing where elephant could be found and was also willing to pay for the privilege, well, an *mtu* informant wouldn't consider disappointing him. The reason why the *mzungu* drew a blank when he followed the given directions and went into the bush to have a look could always be attributed to the fact that by the time he got there the game had moved on.

Danilo was anxious to shoot an elephant, and lo, it came to pass that a certain *mtu* informed him where he had seen an elephant herd lined up and waiting to be shot at.

The number of our hunting-party participants who set out to confirm the alleged sighting was fourteen. These were Danilo, Mario, Tom and me plus ten *watu*. The *watu* consisted of a driver, a cook, a tracker, and seven others who were loosely designated as labourers. We all travelled in three Land Rovers, plunging deeply into crisp and crackling bush to reach a location deemed suitable for setting up a base camp from which we could gather our resources for the hunting to come.

The positioning of the base camp was chosen to benefit from a group of shady trees standing at the edge of a relatively elongated open *mbuga*. The three Land Rovers were parked around the camp periphery in a *laager*-like arrangement that owed much to tried and true *voortrekker* practice.

The *wazungu* section of camp was demarcated in an area within the vehicular *laager* that fell well within the immediate radius of light and warmth cast by the cook's fire. The *watu* set themselves up in a diametrically opposite position to us in a space centred on a second fire that seemed big enough to keep marauding game at bay and to deter any *mzungu* from getting too close.

With the arrival of darkness, the bright flames and sparks rising from the fires to greet the overhead canopy of stars was a great comfort to us. We gazed into the flames and talked about nothing of material value before we turned in for the night. There was no shortage of wood to keep the fires banked high, and more than enough dry elephant dung in the vicinity to pick up and throw on the fire should the supply of wood collected be consumed too quickly.

A small coal of glowing charcoal encased in the core of a ball of elephant dung would hold on to its spark all through the day. This provided a highly effective means for generating a fire at any given moment. You opened up the ball of dung to expose the piece of charcoal; you blew on the charcoal a couple of times; and a flame was guaranteed.

Elephant dung was so common in the bush that it was only by its absence that it was made remarkable. A pile of elephant dung attracted nervous attention only when it was seen to be wet and steaming or otherwise felt warm to the touch when broken open for testing.

The *watu* constructed the base camp fires using that traditional technique involving three specially selected logs of dead wood associated with three strategically placed rounded boulders which I first saw when I was given dinner at a PWD camp on the road from Itigi to Tabora. In elephant country there was so much dead wood lying around that thoughts of certain civil service departments were difficult to suppress. In their treatment of trees elephants took no prisoners. I gained a strong impression from what I saw that if a tree stood in an elephant's path then the elephant would much sooner knock the tree over than walk around it.

A rather well trodden elephant track skirted the fringe of the *mbuga* beside our base camp. The track was both smooth-surfaced and beautifully graded. Elephants never walked uphill if they could avoid it, and the tracks they constructed tended to reflect a consistent preference to hold things on the level.

All things being considered, Danilo declared himself satisfied that the base camp was in an ideal location for elephant hunting and that we were sure to conclude a successful mission on the morrow. Little did Danilo know how soon he was to be proved correct with respect to location and how far off the mark he would be regarding success.

We had no tents at the base camp as bringing them along would have placed too much unnecessary burden on the Land Rovers, given the quantity of essential paraphernalia that we needed to bring in, and not forgetting the meat and trophies that Danilo was expecting to be carrying out. Danilo and Mario and Tom, all of whom were self-confessed bush-seasoned types, had the cook lay out their individual bedding beneath the trees, contained within suspended covers of billowing mosquito nets. Each of them was quick to inform me that they would be quite as safe as houses since no known species of game that roamed the bush would be prepared to molest a mosquito net. I wasn't so much worried about a mosquito net being molested as I was about the molestation of whoever was lying inside it.

As I didn't regard myself as possessing anything more than a sprinkling of bush-seasoning—the game fever feelings of over-confidence that came as a consequence of my shooting an impala notwithstanding—I was by no means inclined to test out the mosquito net theory. I elected to follow what seemed to me to be an infinitely more secure practice by dossing down on the front seat of one of the Land Rovers.

The moon made a sharp-edged, coldly-bright near-circle directly above the base camp. Although not yet quite full, the moon provided more than enough light to expose the camp, the bush, the trees and the adjacent *mbuga* in stark-shadowed clarity.

Sleep eluded me. The front seat of a Land Rover made such an uncomfortable bed that I contemplated giving it up in favour of stretching out in the open. A cacophonous chorus featuring linked elements of shrieking, whistling and whooping came in from points far and near to enhance the ghostly touch of moonlight. It took a sequentially tapering-off grumbling roar of a lion out in the distance to convince me that I should remain in the front of the Land Rover after all.

I was just on the point of dozing off when my reverie was severely interrupted by a frantic manipulation of the handle of the Land Rover's cab close to where my head was resting. As I had locked the door from the inside the handle failed to yield to the attentions of whatever it was that was not only out there but also evidently anxious to get inside.

I looked up and first of all registered Tom's face peering in at me through the window. In the background was what appeared to be a vast number of elephants (eventually agreed by a consensus of eye-witnesses to amount to about twenty—unless it was thirty or forty) ambling slowly through and around the camp and heading towards their track following the *mbuga*. Bulls, cows and calves were all together, moving slowly and surely as both they and their predecessors would have done in the same way and in the same place since time immemorial.

It was at once obvious that Danilo had located his elephant herd in a rather spectacular fashion. He then appeared outside the Land Rover at Tom's side with his .450-calibre rifle held at the ready. Danilo's left shoulder was hunched forward in an attitude suggesting that he was contemplating action. He gave me an impression that standing in the midst of a procession of elephants in the middle of the night was no more than a routine happening as far as he was concerned.

I released the lock on the Land Rover door. Tom heaved the door open and commenced, albeit in suppressed tones, to tear verbal strips off me. I accepted this as justified, knowing that he was only releasing the pent-up steam of distress as best he could under the circumstances. Danilo hissed orders at Tom and me to keep quiet. "Shattafahkupa!" sounded to be what he wanted us to do.

I heard Danilo's instruction clearly enough to comply with it, but I sensed that Tom must have interpreted it differently, as he at once commenced hammering on the open door of the Land Rover with the flat of his hand, while repeatedly screaming "Fuck off!" at the top of his voice. I imagined his reasoning was that since the same gambit had worked on rhinos it would be equally effective in inducing elephants to make themselves scarce.

We were all of us, including the passing elephants, left in no doubt of what Tom intended. The hitherto plodding herd hit top gear in the blink of an eye, making manifest the concept of departing "madly off in all directions". One elephant grazed against the passenger side of the Land Rover in which I was sheltering; another took out the *watu's* fire with a single thump of a mightily flat foot.

Of the *watu* themselves there was no sign. If they weren't trampled flat they must have melted away to secrete themselves in the bush as effectively as only they knew how. It was every *mtu* for himself where only the fate of number one counted for anything at all.

The elephants screamed, bellowed, trumpeted and blared while they ran. The bush fell before them. A moment, and they were all gone. Dust motes floated in the moonlight *in memoriam* of their thundering stampede.

I was very impressed to note, even in the panic of the moment, that the three mosquito nets were still hanging intact, untouched and undamaged. From then on I accepted that the game repellent credentials of such devices need never be questioned.

Danilo was quite beside himself with rage. His reaction was entirely predictable. As I interpreted his words he was, he told us, in the company of imbeciles who should never have been allowed to set foot in the Tanganyika bush. Our ignominy reigned supreme under his tongue lashing. What appeared to distress him the most was that he reckoned the elephant herd would be unlikely to stop running until it had gone too far for us to ever find it again.

If Tom had scared the elephants, I thought, they had done the very same thing to me, although I was starting to believe that elephants weren't half as frightening as the well-nigh apoplectic Danilo was. If the elephant herd was going to go a long way before it slowed down I was wishing that I could do the same thing by heading in the opposite direction.

We were lucky not to have been overrun by the elephantine rush. The moral of the incident was that, in the bush, the right of way of game (especially of big game) took precedence over any rights that we thought we had.

*

The crack of dawn placed a slightly better complexion on our chastened party. The *watu* drifted back from the bush in ones and twos when they determined that the coast was clear. We assessed the camp's inventory of gear and found, oddly enough, little amiss.

Led by a slightly more tranquil Danilo with his .450-calibre rifle broken open and carried across the crook of his left arm with true white hunter panache, our hunting party set out on foot at sunrise, following the elephant track. We assumed that the track was taken by the herd during its night-time flight. It was possible that we would meet either loose stragglers from the vanished herd or inbound newcomers that had yet to learn that we were around. My hope for the day was that we would come across neither one nor the other.

Mid-morning came and went. We moved on. The heat was severe. We were plagued by tsetse flies. All the same, I was happy enough to go through the motions and stay clear of anything that looked like an elephant. I was no longer sure if elephants were game for us or if we were game for them. There was dust and dry white bush with brittle twigs on the ground that snapped like fire crackers at the touch of a foot. Any game in our vicinity would have been extremely well aware of our advance.

Danilo did his best to mitigate the noises we were making by slowing down the pace of our column and casting a regular succession of dirty looks back at the rest of us from over his shoulder.

As we worked our way down a modest slope through a scattering of thorny trees, Danilo held up his hand to signify a halt. Ahead of us I heard the muffled clumping of many hooves overlain by snuffling and snorting together with a mysterious sandpapery swishing and castanet-like clicking. These strange sounds, as I soon learned, were respectively due to the abrasive contacts of coarse hides and bulky horns.

Half a dozen buffalo came into view a few hundred yards down to the right along the curving foot of the slope that we were descending. It soon became clear that these buffalo were the vanguard of a substantial herd of many scores of the animals. They came into view with heads inclined down, plodding heavily and for all the world looking like a "lowing herd winding slowly o'er the lea".

We stood in silence, in my case with admiration for the advancing spectacle muted by genuine fear that the herd was about to get too close for my comfort. The fear won out, as it always did. Danilo broke the silence with a single exclamation hissed through gritted teeth. "Fahkamusshoota!" It sounded so inevitable when I heard it that it would only have been surprising if he hadn't said it.

In the absence of mud to wallow in during the dry season, the buffalo maintained their natural grey-black colour. On their shoulders and at their hips the hides had assumed the burnish of oil-rubbed gun metal. The buffalo herd moved as a single multiple-backed unit looking like a surreal rippling landscape on a distant planet. Tails swished, flanks rubbed, horns clicked, saliva drooled in viscous strings from front extremities, and shit spattered on the ground from the rear.

The lead animal was a huge bull, weighing a ton or more on the hoof. It held its head at a slight upward angle and moved its muzzle from side to side in a broad arc as if it were using a built-in radar mechanism to pinpoint sources of potential danger. A few yellow-billed oxpeckers, better known as tickbirds, scrambled for pickings on its swaying back and around its twitching ears. The bull suddenly dropped a great splatter of shit in mid stride, and for some reason, the thought of conversations at the bar at the Dodoma hotel flashed in and out of my mind.

Danilo signalled his strategy to us. He indicated that the lead bull would be his target. I felt sure that, left to their own devices, neither the bull nor the herd that it led intended us any harm at all, even if they knew we were near at hand. The bull's motivation was to lead the herd on to pastures new.

Following the increasingly eager Danilo, we crept down to the foot of the slope where, with the rest of the party huddled behind him in the manner of a safety-in-numbers rabble, Danilo took up a position squarely in the path of the oncoming buffalo herd, his rifle at the ready,. He was either brave or foolhardy. I couldn't work out which was which so decided he was both brave and foolhardy at the same time.

I edged over to one side to get as close to what looked like a climbable tree as was possible, reckoning that it presented the best option for the rapid retreat that I was quite certain I would be making. There was a yarn I heard in a bar concerning an escapee from an angry buffalo who leapt into a thorn tree but wasn't able to climb to a sufficiently safe height before he became entangled. He hung in the thorns like a piece of strange fruit and bled to death as the buffalo licked the flesh away from his legs with its powerfully rasping tongue.

With the buffalo herd coming ever closer, the tree I had selected looked more and more like a lifeline. Danilo raised his .450 rifle, and I got my puny 9-mm firearm ready as well so as at least to offer him a willing impression. I was ready to drop my gun and go for the tree in an instant, however. With no more than thirty feet separating Danilo from the nose of the lead bull, Danilo took aim and discharged both barrels of his rifle one after the other, intending a pair of heart shots. I saw the dust of the impact of the shots puff from low on the buffalo bull's left shoulder. To avoid any accusations of not shooting and also to ensure that I did no harm, I placed my shot over the top of the herd.

The lead bull was stopped in its tracks. It staggered, then span about on the figurative denomination of the coin that I had given to a disdainful porter at Nairobi Airport a lifetime ago, and sped off like a grey-black tank in the direction from which it had come. It ploughed through the herd, which scattered in disarray, milled for a while, and then followed suit by stampeding in short order in emulation of the performance of the elephant herd that Tom had told to fuck off during the previous night. The buffalo were cattle-like no longer. All was dust, pounding hooves and bellowing panic.

Then they too were gone. It would have been all well and good for us if it hadn't been for the presence of a wounded buffalo bull somewhere out in the bush for us to locate and finish off. We knew that the bull was wounded, but no one, not even Danilo (who wouldn't have admitted anything anyway), was sure quite how severe its wounds were.

Our required course of action was prescribed. The wounded bull had to be tracked down and killed. There was no way around it. The bull was our joint responsibility from the instant Danilo's shots hit it. Tracking it was simple enough—we followed a trail marked by spots and splashes of blood—but was made seriously nerve-wracking by the legendary unpredictability and cunning tactics that wounded buffalo were known to use in their instinctive desire for taking revenge on hunters.

None of game's so-called "big five" were naturally aggressive animals in my experience. Some of them made kills when they needed to eat, and that was fair enough. They had an undeniable right to exercise their own style of pot licence. The big five were territorially defensive, highly protective of their young, and strikingly reactive to being unpleasantly surprised, all of which was both manageable and acceptable by third parties who understood this.

A wounded animal was quite another matter, however. When wounded, the big five were at their most dangerous, and of them all the most feared, the one that was *kali kabisa*, was the buffalo.

Tales of the strategies adopted by wounded buffalo were legion at the watering holes where *wazungu* gathered. Some of the personal experiences that I heard recounted may even have had threads of truth in them on the first telling. From gathering such rare threads together, a string of likely probabilities could easily be braided.

A buffalo bull possessed an impressive combination of qualities characterised by weight, size, manoeuvrability, strength, determination and intelligence. Its head was equipped with a pair of absolutely formidable horns spreading from a battering ram-like boss of gnarled carapace on its forehead. The horns, shiny with use, were like great hooks. They were as thick as they were vicious, curving outwards, upwards and then inwards again, tapering to needle-sharp points. These were perfect tools for ripping up roots, tearing bark from trees, fighting other bulls for herd supremacy, or goring the life out of a hunter.

A heart shot was normally chosen to kill a buffalo. The killing target for a heart shot was located just behind the buffalo's shoulder. If the heart should happen to be missed by such a shot it was likely that the shot would deliver a mortal strike to another vital organ. A brain shot, usually made via an eye or an ear, needed more precision since the target area was so small and the chance of the bullet being deflected by striking the virtually bullet-proof head boss was so great.

Danilo declared that his heart shot to the runaway buffalo had been bang on target. I wouldn't have expected him to say anything else; nevertheless, it didn't alter the fact that, irrespective of where it was or wasn't hit, the buffalo was gone.

Wounded buffalo were reputed to stalk their persecutors. They sometimes backtracked and ran hunters down from unexpected directions, and they were also known to lie in thick cover to spring an ambush. Whatever its purpose, a wounded buffalo guaranteed that the first human it came upon would be in deep trouble. It was an inviolate rule of the bush that a hunter must find and finish off game he had wounded, or else perish in the attempt.

With such thoughts in mind, we set off to find the buffalo bull shot by Danilo, who led the way, accompanied by the tracker. It was a toss up as to which of the two gave the better impression of reluctance. Tom, Mario and the group of *watu* followed, and I took up my accustomed place at the rear of the procession, trusting to fate that the wounded bull hadn't circled back.

We proceeded with caution. The blood splashes on both ground and bushes were too prolific to be missed. To that extent, tracking was simple. It seemed clear that Danilo's two shots had hit the buffalo hard enough not to let it survive for long.

We found the buffalo after only a few hundred yards of following the trail of blood. It was lying flat on its right side in behind an isolated thicket. The blood-coursed entry points of Danilo's two shots on the buffalo's shoulder were separated by no more than a couple of inches. That was impressive shooting, and Danilo was by no means reticent in demonstrating his satisfaction. The buffalo must have made its final run when it was already dead on its feet, powered by fighting spirit and raw instinct.

On the grounds that there were known incidences of such an apparently deceased big game animal getting up and killing the person who thought he had killed it, Danilo shot the bull once more through the ear. I made a mental note of the fact that Tom offered no criticism regarding Danilo wasting ammo.

The buffalo bull was huge. The spread of its horns was too broad to be taken in by my outstretched arms. Tom and I and Danilo, the latter at pains to ensure that an array of .450-calibre cartridges was prominently displayed in a line of receptive loops sewn onto the right breast of his safari jacket, sat on the buffalo in a row while Mario took a photo of us.

The *watu* set to work at once, using the combined cutting power of their knives and *pangas* to skin and butcher the dead buffalo. Although the time for the *halal* process was long gone, I felt it unlikely that that consideration would deter our followers of Islam too much when the moment came for the buffalo flesh to be consumed. There was an awful lot of meat to go around. The butchering took the line of least resistance in hewing the buffalo's carcass in as short a time as possible into the minimum number of pieces that would be of an appropriate size and weight for loading onto the back of a Land Rover.

While the butchering took place I remained on the killing ground with Danilo. Tom and Mario walked back to the base camp to get a Land Rover and drive it back through the bush to where the great mountain of buffalo meat, hide and entrails was building up beneath an ever-burgeoning cloud-like cover of flies.

Where so many flies that weren't tsetse-related came from was a mystery to me, but wherever they originated, their ability to seek, find and home in on blood and raw meat was as unerring as that of the vultures that were gathering in circles high above. The vultures wound their flight spirals ever lower as they sensed we were about to depart, ready to scavenge any remnants of the buffalo that the usual bunch of hyenas and jackals wouldn't able to chase them away from. A couple of vultures were already sitting in anticipation in a nearby tree.

The underbelly of the dead buffalo blossomed with clusters of great purple-bloated ticks that looked like evil grapes. The animal's immense weight meant that raising its legs to provide access to the belly so that an initial longitudinal slit could be made to start the skinning process was achieved only with great effort. Stout rope lines were plaited from lengths of bark taken from the appropriate trees in the vicinity. The lines were circled around the upper pair of the buffalo's hooves, and with four of us standing on the buffalo's side and hauling hard on the lines, the belly was exposed for as long as it took to make the first cut.

It was late in the day by the time the upper half of the hide was peeled back and the butchering was in full swing. The pile of meat was quite substantial when the first sounds were heard of a Land Rover thumping and bashing towards us over rocks and low bush.

The buffalo's head went to Danilo as his trophy of the hunt. It, together with four haunches, two sides of ribs and a selection of entrails, made a full load for a Land Rover. The rest of the carcass, including the hide and the balance of the entrails, was left for the scavengers. They weren't going to believe their luck. We made a slow return to the base camp, arriving there only just before darkness took over from sunset.

*

I hoped that that should have been the end of the hunt, but it appeared that Danilo had allocated one more day to the chase, as he was utterly determined to bag an elephant. Wiser counsel might have prevailed had wiser counsel not been inconsistent with a fahkamusshoota philosophy.

So it was that we had to spend a second night at the base camp. The single small mercy to be thankful for was that there were no nocturnal disturbances, although my anxious expectation that there would be didn't help me to sleep a lot.

The buffalo meat resided on the back of the Land Rover into which it had been loaded for all of that night and onwards through the following day. The querulous whoops of a few close by hyenas in the night served to demonstrate that the existence of raw meat was not a secret kept easily in the bush.

As to the ultimate fate of the buffalo meat, by the time we reached Iseke on our return to Iwambala and Ilangali late in the afternoon of that second day the odour arising from the meat made it obvious that the meat was on the verge of developing new life. The little Arab who owned the *duka* at Iseke was as pleased to receive the whole cargo of buffalo meat from us as we were to have him receive it. The gangrenous smell of the meat seemed to be gaining in strength by the minute. We might even have paid the little Arab to take the meat off our hands if he had shown any reluctance to do so.

*

The second day's hunting followed a similar pattern to that of the first day. We went out, we wandered around, the tsetse pestered us, and fate played a key role by bringing us in the late morning to a location where a lone elephant stood in the midst of a clump of thin yet tall trees backing on to a jumble of granite boulders.

The elephant was spotted by one of the *watu*, who was keener eyed than me by far. Its form, broken up by the trees, was shadowy and indistinct. The immediate giveaway was a gentle flapping of ears and the sight of a trunk sporadically extended to rip away twigs and small branches from the trees that were closest to hand.

Danilo, who was by then trembling with excitement, led us towards the elephant from a direction that he euphemistically described as being "down wind". There was not as much as a hint of a breeze in the air, but that didn't stop Danilo carrying out some ritual tests for wind direction. He first of all shoved his right index finger in his mouth to wet it, then pulled it out and held it on high to ascertain which side of the finger felt cooler. He bent down, picked up a handful of dust, stood up, held out his hand and allowed the dust to trickle away in the manner of an hour glass while observing the direction of drift as the dust sifted downwards.

Faced with such subtlety, I could only assume that his subsequent conclusions regarding wind direction were valid.

Danilo ordered us to keep under cover while he appraised the elephant for the weight of ivory it was carrying. The elephant remained oblivious to both our presence and Danilo's intentions.

The basic consequences of elephant hunting seemed to call for an elephant to yield up a couple of tusks to its hunter and provide a mountain of flesh and bones for the benefit of the scavengers.

I wouldn't have known how big the elephant looked as seen through Danilo's eyes, but from where I stood it appeared to be rather immense. Judging the likely weight of ivory was less straightforward for me as the pair of tusks was difficult to make out clearly in behind the partial cover of trees.

Danilo shook his head in a manner suggesting to me that he was doubtful that the elephant offered him much of a trophy in terms of ivory and that he was ready to pass it by. That would have been all right with me of course. However, it appeared that either we were not placed as advantageously downwind of the elephant as Danilo had calculated or we were simply too close to where it was, as the elephant suddenly raised its trunk vertically and swivelled the tip to and fro as if it was a submarine periscope looking for enemy battleships.

The tip of the trunk pointed directly at us. It flexed once or twice and stopped moving for the duration of no more than a couple of heart beats. Then in an instant the elephant flipped its trunk back over its head and, uttering a blood-curdling scream, reared up on its hind legs.

If the elephant had appeared big to me beforehand it now became positively gigantic.

It could have felt no more panic than I did. I was extremely keen to flee from the scene but my legs wouldn't move me. I heard two explosions go off in quick succession as Danilo discharged both barrels of his rifle. A strong suspicion that the elephant might be preparing to charge at us must have made its credentials as a trophy animal irrelevant to Danilo.

The elephant presented its left flank to us and two more rapidly reloaded shots from Danilo rang out. I raised my rifle and aimed at the hollow of the elephant's head just behind the eye where I had read that the skull bone was at its thinnest. I took a shot, but the head was jerking about so violently that I knew I had missed the target even as I pulled the trigger.

The elephant toppled over onto its right side with a mighty thump and a crackle of broken bush. It lay in a monstrous grey heap, kicking and screaming with its trunk thrashing about like a desperately out-of-control flail. We could not get in close to it. Danilo took up a position outside the range of these five deadly appendages, and fired three more heart shots into the elephant before the poor animal was silent in death.

The situation lacked even the smallest shred of satisfaction and felt to be totally without honour. All of us, probably even including Danilo, felt it. The final nail in the coffin of decency was derived from the ivory, which was puny at best. The pair of tusks had a combined weight of only thirteen pounds and they were devoid of any sense of pleasing form.

Two of the *watu* cut the tusks away from the elephant's head using *pangas*. The tusks had to be chopped clear of bone and cartilage before they could be withdrawn. They were not of the stature that an elephant supplementary game licence was established to promote. The dead elephant was a young bull. In death it didn't appear big at all.

The recording of such small ivory on a supplementary game licence log would very likely provide cause for the hunter to be censured by the Game Department. Danilo was very unhappy about it, and to cap his anger and provide him with a welcome opportunity to take some of it out on me, he deemed that my shot had hit the elephant in its trunk.

Carrying a pathetic weight of ivory and a collection of hairs gleaned from the elephant's tail, we left the spoils of the hunt behind us and quit the scene.

The hunting expedition was over and done with.

I resolved never again to hunt elephant, and never again to hunt anything in the company of Danilo. Fortunately I didn't have to worry about either option, as Danilo made it very clear that I would be unwelcome in any future hunting party that he chose to organise. Which was all to the good in my book.

Tom stood on the outside looking in, which was much to his credit.

Mario most assuredly took secret glee in his *de facto* master's discomfiture, on the strength of which I concluded that Mario was the hunt's principal beneficiary.

14

Kalismasi

Christmas

The wet season arrived at our fly camp in the Rungwa Game Reserve in mid-December 1960. For what seemed to be weeks in advance of its moving in on us the wet season had posed threats from afar, made promises that it didn't keep to end the heavy closeness of end-of-dry-season heat with a watery deluge, and teased our expectations to breaking point. When the first rain finally did fall on our fly camp it did so with what appeared to be over-excessive zeal.

During the period of waiting, rumours of rain were in regular and occasionally spectacular display at night. Lightning was seen to be dancing all around in the dark distance that surrounded us yet was so far off that it muted the sound of accompanying thunder. The lightning flares turned the hills into sharp silhouettes against our eyes and caused the hanging clouds to glow in their depths with luminous pulses of light. Any associated rain appeared to be falling everywhere except where we were. The fly camp existed like a mote in the eye of a great, all-encompassing, eerily silent exhibition of heavenly pyrotechnics.

Then came the night on which we sensed what was either a muffled drumming or merely the resonance of faint thunder in the densely and barely endurable oppressive air. We felt a hint of relief coming our way, but the storm harbingers of the wet season were like a tide that flowed towards us only to turn and ebb away again. As each day passed, however, the likelihood of rain came just that tantalising bit closer.

One night a strong wind pushed into the fly camp. It came up so suddenly that even though it was half expected its arrival was almost shocking. The wind was richly endowed with a spirit-lifting scent of damp earth. Rain followed close on its heels, falling out of a sky that looked like a single angry thunder-crashing bruise slashed by constant lightning. The first drops of rain were received by the land and we who dwelt therein as if they were manna falling from heaven. They were big drops that struck the ground with force, puffing up the dust on impact. The drops slapped against tent canvas and dappled desiccated tree bark in an ever-coalescing pattern of dark, penny-sized blots.

The frequency of the raindrops increased, and in less than a moment thick rods of rain began to strike all around and go on to form up into what felt like a solid wall of water that exceeded the capacity of the ground to absorb it. The rain water gathered in pools that swelled into ponds that overflowed first in trickles, then in gouts, and beyond into wave-like surges and mud-charged flash-flood torrents.

The flow of water took the line of least resistance towards the nearby river, exploiting gullies and depressions great and small, filling every channel with an irresistible force that moved all before it.

Our initial reaction to the coming of rain was one of extreme gratitude. The intolerably close heat that characterised the end of the dry season was no more. This feeling of wellbeing lasted for at least a few minutes before we realised that too much rain might be more of a nuisance than a blessing. The consideration seemed especially relevant since we were camped out in the rain and required to cope with its consequences when undertaking foot traverses or driving (well, some of us anyway) on tracks that rain was able to destroy in far less time than the tracks took to be made.

The relief that the first rain brought us soon gave way to days of the incredible dampness of being. Be that as it may, the miracle of rain took little more than a day to generate the greening of the bush. Buds leapt out of the branches of trees and the hitherto barren ground put forth a carpet of emerald grass spotted with delicate flowers. The monotonous bush surrounding the fly camp was transformed into clean-smelling parkland that was soft underfoot and boggy only in the low-lying areas where water lay. For a short while it was all a wonder to behold.

With so much fresh growth and water available to attract the attention of the game reserve's grazers and browsers, the hours of darkness were alive with the passage of game in the vicinity of the fly camp. Leopards were heard to cough and lions to roar. The game scout Samuel told me that a couple of hippos passed by on one night. I respected Samuel's powers of observation, but I had my doubts about the local existence of hippos.

After a week of the wet season the park-like condition of the bush altered dramatically as the grass thickened and shot up to knee level on its way to achieving ultimate head height and counting. The grass would eventually throw out large feathery seed heads shedding a host of barbed seeds that had the unerring capability of attaching themselves to our clothing and working their way into our skin. Grass seeds were particularly problematic for anyone wearing socks (thereby demonstrating a preference for *wazungu*) and were apt to get into the lower legs and ankles and initiate what could become deeply fearsome tropical ulcers.

Almost anything could hide itself in the tall grass—we often heard game crashing away from us as we cut our way through. Snakes in the grass were fortunately experienced in making themselves scarce before we reached them. One of the more unpleasant aspects of long grass was the presence of ticks, which dwelt there in legions. Ticks started off as brown flecks that attached themselves to exposed skin where, if undetected, they blossomed into purple grape-like protuberances bulging with blood. Sometimes a blood-full tick on the skin was detected only when it burst. A tick, in either of its small brown or big purple versions, needed to be removed from the skin with care to make sure that its head and jaws didn't remain embedded in the flesh as its body was pulled away. Many ticks attached themselves to me. Failure to get rid of the entire tick could (so it was said) provoke the unpleasant symptoms of tick fever. I took it on trust that tick fever was a tropical disease to be avoided, even though the *GFM* didn't refer to it.

One of the most pressing dangers of the first rains was flash flooding. We needed to be on constant guard against an unexpected flash flood caused by distant rain when we were working in dry riverbeds. The leading tongue of a flash flood hissed and grumbled as it seethed downstream. Anyone whose ears were attuned to the sound as a result of past experience got out of the riverbed at once on hearing it, moving as if his life depended on it, which in fact it did. Either bank of the river was a safe haven, but it was recommended to choose the bank on the side of the river on which the camp facilities were located. Selecting the far bank alternative meant that you might be separated from your camp by a raging torrent that could take anywhere from hours to days to subside.

The first visible manifestation of flash-flood water in a dry riverbed was a tongue of thick brown foam sliding over the sand. For a few moments this would be barely wet enough to bother the feet, although it brought with it a warning to be immediately heeded, since coming not far behind it was a forceful wave of water laden with sand, small boulders, brush, thorns, driftwood, elephant dung and more or less anything and everything that had failed to get out of its way in time and had not been big enough to avoid being overwhelmed.

Almost before there was time to gather breath the river was running in full spate between its banks in a roaring, blood-red torrent tumbling with great deadfalls of timber looking like the keels of wrecked ships, accompanied by still-living trees both big and small that were undercut at the roots and toppled into the river from the collapsed banks they once stood on.

When the level of flood water in the great river beside our fly camp dropped and its flow turned placid and even, the colour of the water became an opaque shade of drab olive. It was then safe for us to either swim or wade across the river in places where the water was shallow enough. Here and there rocks in the riverbed penned up substantial pools as the water level fell. The *mbugas* of the game reserve were glutinous morasses, able to be crossed only by foot-slogging giraffes on dinner-plate sized hooves.

The river water took on a great appeal to the *watu* for activities that included washing, bathing and swimming, not that any of them were particularly accomplished swimmers. They ran a rope across the river and, with each end of the rope secured to a stout tree trunk, they used it to drag themselves hand over hand between the banks through the deeper water. In addition they lashed a couple of empty forty-four gallon oil drums together with lengths of flexible bark and mounted a few logs on top of the assembly to make a raft that served as both a recreational facility and a serviceable ferry in conjunction with the rope. With river sport in mind they also obtained the use of a hugely inflated inner tube from a Land Rover tyre. Although a few bits and pieces of nondescript vegetation continued to float downstream once the force of the flood was over, these were of no significance as far as inconveniencing fun in the water was concerned.

A commotion arose from the *watu* late one afternoon when a pack of ten African hunting dogs (*mbwa mwitu*) appeared on the riverbank across from the fly camp side. The pack trotted along the edge of the river in single file, casting what was interpreted as a lean and hungry look in our direction. Their tongues lolled, their big rounded ears were up and alert, their white-tipped tails trailed and their spotted coats blended from one into another. It was a rare sighting. Hunting dogs were fearsome predators, but fortunately they showed no interest in entering the water, out of which a number of horrified bathers were already making a speedy exit with the fly camp as their intended destination.

On another occasion when Tom and I were together with the *watu* in the river taking advantage of the deeper water while it lasted, I watched a large monitor lizard—bullet-headed, flat-bellied and possibly as much as seven feet in length—scuttle along the far bank in the jerkily undulate gait typical of the species. As if acting on a sudden whim, the monitor lizard made a ninety-degree switch in its direction of advance to launch itself like a guided missile that soared out over the water and down into it, entering the water at a perfect angle and causing barely a ripple.

In spite of a feeling of horror, I could not help but admire the elegance of the monitor lizard's dive. On the other hand, it signified that a very big reptile was at that moment sharing the water with us in our immediate vicinity. Although we knew where it went into the water, we didn't know where it was going afterwards as clarity was not a quality that the water possessed. Every one of us who was in the river appeared at once to make an independent decision that the monitor lizard was coming directly for us.

The word "panic" was not strong enough to cover what then took place. I would not have wanted to swear on my termite-chewed Bible that one or two of the *watu* didn't rise from the water and flee along its surface in the best Christ-like tradition. There was a thrashing and a splashing as we all threw caution to the winds and entered an every man for himself scramble to get out of the river by fair means or foul.

There was no subsequent sighting of the monitor lizard, which must have been astute enough to remain underwater until it knew it was well clear of us. No one dared to go back into the river again on that day, and even on the following day those who were brave enough to enter the water didn't stray far from the bank or venture anywhere that was out of their depth. Thoughts of what might lie beneath the surface of the once inviting water, thanks to the monitor lizard, made faint hearts of us all.

Several of the *watu*, commenting from a vantage point of having their feet on dry land, expressed regrets that a concerted attempt hadn't been made to catch the monitor lizard. I wasn't sure how inviolate big reptiles were in a game reserve, but I was quite happy to give them the benefit of the doubt. It was claimed by the *watu* that monitor lizard flesh was a tasty delicacy, being especially succulent and incorporating all the favourable characteristics of high-quality chicken.

My policy regarding the eating of flesh was that I would try anything once. I consumed part of everything that I either shot or was implicated in the shooting of, and I found that in some cases trying anything once was more than enough. The least palatable meat that I was induced to try came from a zebra, although I had no trouble in believing that a portion of monitor lizard was likely to be just as bad.

A need to kill reptiles on sight was an essential facet of an *mtu's* instinct. Whether or not an encounter with a reptile took place in or out of a game reserve, an *mtu* saw the creature as a blight to be despatched under a "do unto it before it does unto me" principle. To an *mtu* a snake was a snake was a snake. A venomous species of snake merited identical treatment to a non-venomous species. Even if an *mtu* could spot the difference he didn't care. The only call worth bothering about was *chinja nyoka!* Kill the snake!

It was fortunate for the snake and lizard population in areas where I worked that we didn't come across very many of them. We did our job and they did theirs by getting out of our way. Being bitten by a snake was no more or no less than the purest of bad luck if it happened, as a headman at Iwambala once observed to me with great insight.

*

The arrival of the rains coincided with Christmas shaping up as an increasingly attractive prospect for us in the very near future. Tom weighed the situation up and decided that we should make a strategic exit from the game reserve in order to avoid the possibility of the wet season locking us in and preventing us from celebrating the festive season in a more congenial place. Christmas was coming, but no goose, spur-winged or otherwise, was going to be getting fat in our fly camp.

We therefore carried out a concerted campaign of sampling under increasingly wet ground conditions in an attempt to wind up the stream sampling programme before running rivers put a temporary end to it. The rivers were becoming virtually impassable, and our track following the Njombe River, where it wasn't rutted to bits by runoff, was sinking into a despondent ooze that would take far more corduroy logs than we could cut to allow us to continue driving regularly on it. There were some risks that weren't worth taking in such an isolated location, not least for fair weather professionals—like us—at the top of their game.

During the third week of December it became clear that we were reaching the point of diminishing returns as far as our ability to take any more samples was concerned. We needed to leave the game reserve while Tom believed we still could, although even he had to admit that our chances were perhaps a little shaky. We took comfort in the fact that we (or in the event Eddie—three *simbas*—McGinnis) would come back to complete (or in Eddie's case not to complete) the game reserve sampling campaign at the earliest opportunity in the New Year when improving weather conditions permitted.

As it all turned out, the work remaining to be done in the game reserve, which consisted of more or less tying up loose ends, was probably never completed. The analytical results that were returned for the samples we had already taken provided zero counts for kimberlite indicator minerals, which was sufficient to eliminate any thoughts of detailed work. For everyone and everything involved, albeit whether or not they were two-footed or four-footed or crawled on their bellies, it was the best possible outcome.

*

Shortly before our rain-inspired withdrawal from the game reserve, Tom suggested the opening line for a piece of poetry to commemorate our experiences. This trenchant line was, "There's a hoodoo on the kudu in the Rungwa Game Reserve".

There was an appealing lilt to it, and for some time thereafter, both in and out of the game reserve, much deliberation went on between us as to how such a promising start could be extended to produce a finished piece of verse.

Contributions to the piece such as "the buff don't give a stuff", and better yet, "the waterbuck don't give a fuck", were rejected in the same kind of spirit in which they were made as being inconsistent with the intent of the verse and, moreover, unfaithful to our feelings of celebration of one of Africa's great game reserves.

A final draft, of the poem, published here for the very first time, was as follows:

> There's a hoodoo on the kudu in the Rungwa Game Reserve,
> And the lion are all dyin' to know why.
> A giraffe was heard to laugh,
> Quoth an elephant, "Irrelevant!"
> And a jackal gave a cackle in reply.
>
> The roan just want to moan down in the Rungwa Game Reserve,
> A buffalo gave a gruff "Hallo!" from the thorns.
> "Haven't seen ya!" whooped a hyena,
> As a cheetah chased a bleater,
> And a rhino chanted, "I know! Let's lock horns!"
>
> O the *tembo* make us tremble in the Rungwa Game Reserve,
> Where the *twiga* stand much bigger than the trees.
> Since a *kongoni* is bony,
> And the *nyani* are too canny,
> On a tasty *nguruwe*, an ever-hopeful *chui* dines with ease.
>
> If a *nyati* threw a party in the Rungwa Game Reserve,
> Would a *simba* all be limber for the feast?
> Would a *fisi* find it greasy?
> Would the *swala pala* swallow?
> Would its hoodoo cause the kudu to desist?"

That was it. It was the greatest—and, moreover, in all likelihood the only—piece of verse ever to emerge from the Rungwa Game Reserve.

*

Getting out of that place of such hoodoo-inspired wonders proved to be no easy task. We dismantled the fly camp, cleaned up the site, loaded our gear into the Land Rovers, filled in all the incidental excavations and abandoned the location in the early afternoon of a day characterised by a persistent drizzle and grey skies.

The twenty-four hours that it took for us to reach Iwambala was a time of continuously hard graft as we slithered through more mud than any of us ever wanted to come across again. All of the slopes on the track, no matter how gentle the gradient, were major obstacles to negotiate. We were steadily cutting and laying corduroy, shovelling and digging around bogged-down tyres, levering, pushing, pulling and generally manhandling the Land Rovers set in permanent four-wheel drive. The tyres had to be deflated to almost pancake flatness to allow them to gain a minimum of traction. We walked over a lot more of the route than we rode.

We could easily have been forgiven for thinking that the wet season was out to get us. Afterwards it was apparent that we made our escape with little time to spare. At one point in the night when the lead Land Rover was badly bogged down near the top of a rise in the track with its engine roaring and headlights blazing, its front was inundated without warning by a multitude of squishy-bodied, long-winged flying ants. They came out the darkness in what must have been their millions to pile up and bury the front of the Land Rover from the saturated ground to the top of the radiator by sheer force of numbers.

The *watu* downed tools and fell on the mound of flying ants, grabbing the insects up by the handful and stuffing them, wings included, into their mouths. They gobbled down the ants with expressions of the utmost pleasure on their faces as if they were cats swallowing cream, while spitting out the residue with practised aplomb.

I ate one or two of the flying ants, and that was enough for me to decide that they lacked appeal. The taste was not exactly unpleasant, but nor was it memorable—perhaps it had to be acquired. On the other hand I learned that even if eating flying ants broke certain *wazungu* taboos it was not a health hazard. I took a lot of joy in the Dodoma club in occasionally picking up and chewing an intrusive flying ant so as to observe the horrified looks that some club members gave me while no doubt making a mental note against my name for later insertion in the club's book of candidates for the black list.

At a later date on the occasion of another light-attracted invasion of flying ants a couple of the *watu* showed me the way to make the insects more acceptable to squeamish tastes when they took a sampling pan, placed a little cooking oil in it, set it up over a fire and used it to fry a whole batch of the insects to golden crispness. I was given a handful of the delicacy and was pleased to pronounce it excellent.

As we struggled out of the game reserve towards Iwambala, we both heard and sensed that there were much larger creatures than flying ants out in the dripping bush around the track. All we could do was to try to ignore them as best we could. The only game animals that we saw caught in the beam of the Land Rover headlights were small, consisting of a couple of civet cats, a duiker and a warthog.

We were genuinely lucky to have only one significant river to cross in between the fly camp and Iwambala, which under the rain-ridden circumstances was just as well. The river crossing was the corduroyed and graded Njombe River ford, close to which many kanga had gathered in drier times to tantalise Tom at a small water hole.

When we reached the ford it was obvious that the carefully laid corduroy bridge was no more. The river ran red-brown and appreciably fast, although we could see that it had fallen well below its prior flood level. To judge from spate-borne debris caught up on the riverbanks and in the overhanging and dangling branches of bushes and trees, the river in flood must have been more than ten feet deep in the very recent past.

We stopped on the game reserve side of the ford and waded out into the river to test both the depth of water and the firmness of the bed with our feet and the assistance of probing sticks. In general, the depth of water was not much more than knee high, but we found some deeper hollows that it would be wise to have the Land Rovers avoid when they crossed the river.

We unloaded the Land Rovers to lessen their weight prior to attempting a crossing. The hazardous pitfalls in the flooded riverbed were clearly marked by virtue of some of us standing in them. The vehicles edged their way across, pushing slowly through the running water, and it was with a great feeling of relief that from my position in the river I watched them enter the cutting on the home side and, shedding copious amounts of water, grind their way up through it.

Mungu was smiling on us as it was only by guess and by him that we made it safely to Iwambala.

The Land Rovers might have got through, but the unloaded gear still remained near the top of the cutting on the game reserve side of the Njombe River. We portered it across, piece by piece, and loaded it on the Land Rovers again for its final transit to the camp at Iwambala.

The fact that Simon's cooking, a mug of tea, dry tents and a hot bath were all waiting for us in camp went some way towards compensating for those thwarted attempts I made at the time to bag a couple of ducks (or duck) on a pond.

*

It took the best part of two days of a genuine pre-Christmas rush for us to get our affairs in order with all the samples sorted and bagged, the camp cleaned and tidied, the reports written up to date and the *watu* monetarily compensated. In short, all was safely gathered in and the hatches were battened down in preparation for our festive season break.

The Land Rovers were then loaded (or more probably overloaded) with all of the *watu* who, irrespective of their religious tendencies, wished to celebrate Christmas in Dodoma. Only a skeleton crew of *watu*, each among them fortified by firm assurances regarding the handsome compensation they were about to receive for their sacrifice, remained behind as custodians of the Iwambala camp. We additionally took all the samples and reports into Dodoma with us for their onward despatch to Mwadui.

The long stretch of track through the *mbuga* between Iwambala and Iseke was both slick and slippery but was manageable by the Land Rovers with due care. As a consequence, Tom decided to avoid the Bahi swamp track, so that from Iseke we travelled instead up to Manyoni to take the all-weather main road following the railway into Dodoma. I was by no means as sorry as Tom expressed himself to be that we were unable to make a call at Isanza Mission to wish the Pallotine fathers the compliments of the season over paw-paw halves that were too liberally sprinkled with lemon juice.

Once we were in Dodoma, our Land Rovers were left at George's Garage for servicing. George, mindful of the time of year, came up trumps with his back-room beer supply. Then, with a post-Christmas rendezvous agreed, the *watu* who came into town with us dispersed to commence the pursuit of their own particular pleasures.

Tom decreed that he and I would take our Christmas break down in Dar es Salaam—it sounded a lot more attractive as an option than Dodoma did. In keeping with the words of the Writing on the Wall, I already understood that my broader social association with Dodoma had been weighed in the balances and found wanting. Spending

Christmas somewhere else would help prevent the balance tilting any further against me, not least up at the Dodoma club.

In the company of Mario Zopetti and an English field officer named Bill Hughes, Tom and I obtained second-class return tickets at the Dodoma railway station and boarded a train heading down the line to Dar es Salaam via Kilosa and Morogoro (where Tank had lived it up in jail at the governor's pleasure).

Mario told us that Danilo was off on a *fahkamusshoota* hunting expedition over Christmas, perhaps seeking an elephant that was more in keeping with his big ivory aspirations. As far as Mario was concerned, he wasn't exactly missing his camp partner and for that matter neither was I. Mario was full of life—a different person when he was out of Danilo's shadow.

Bill was a man in his late twenties. He was tall, languid and handsome. He impressed himself on me as being a true man of the world. I greatly enjoyed his company whenever we met and invariably wished that some of his panache would rub off on me. Wherever we met, a bar was normally not very far away. Bill was a keen sportsman and, as such, he was instrumental in opening up to me the morale-boosting benefits of organising team sports in bush camps.

As a consequence of Bill's influence, in my post-Iwambala camps football matches became an important and highly popular recreational activity for the *watu*. Our practice was to get hold of a small stock of match-quality leather footballs, select a patch of ground needing minimum clearing to prepare a pitch, post the corners with small cairns of rocks, mark the side, centre and penalty-area lines with white river sand and build the goalposts from straight-limbed cut saplings lashed together with bark.

Fifty miles out of Dodoma the railway line passed just south of Mpwapwa and the Kongwa district, which was notorious as the location of the ill-fated "groundnut scheme" of the early nineteen-fifties. The groundnut scheme was originally held to be a masterpiece of planning by colonial authorities that had little or no first-hand appreciation of what they were getting themselves into. To that extent, things still hadn't changed much.

Morogoro, which at that time was a town with a population of about twelve thousand, was one hundred and twenty-five miles from Dar es Salaam. The view from the train as it chuffed out of Morogoro station was spectacular. The railway track paralleled the northern flank of the Uluguru Mountains on the right, a great blue-hazed massif of serrated crests and crumpled ridges made to appear razor sharp through the intervention of black-velvet shadowed valleys. Between the railway and the foot of the Ulugurus extensive sisal plantations stretched in row upon row of precisely ordered stalwart plants that flicked by almost hypnotically as the train clacked past them. Workers, watching the moving train with the practised resignation of people who were trapped in an endless routine, stood among the lines of sisal plants as if they were acting as punctuation marks.

Finally, the train rolled into Dar es Salaam. We had yet to arrange any accommodation, and although that could have been problematic for us it wasn't. Bill knew of a suitable hotel situated not far from the railway station; we followed him to it and found that rooms were available for the two-day duration of our stay. We had arrived on Christmas Eve and were to return to Dodoma on Boxing Day. The hotel was adequate and comfortable, but not especially memorable.

My principal difficulty was related to struggling (and failing) to reconcile the prevailing tropical conditions with the spirit of Christmas while trying to set aside recurring pangs of homesickness.

Dar es Salaam, or "Dar" (as it was commonly referred to by its *wazungu* familiars), was both the capital and the principal seaport of Tanganyika. According to my *Handbook of Tanganyika* the population of Dar was in the order of one hundred and thirty thousand, of which four and a half thousand were *wazungu*, and ninety-five thousand were Africans. The balance of the population was Asian, most specifically Arab and Indian communities.

The reputation of the Arabs was undeniably linked to their leading role as masters of the historical slave trade, which took the island of Zanzibar, out in the Indian Ocean forty miles to the north of Dar, as its monument. Zanzibar was where the principal slave market had been located. The Arab population of the island remained substantial, but its long-term future was rumoured to rest on an extremely uncertain foundation.

My impression of the type of *wazungu* who lived in Dar was obtained from my listening in now and then to locally made radio programmes in the English service of the Tanganyika Broadcasting Corporation. They appeared to believe that Dar was a kind of Nairobi-on-sea, and were determined to present themselves as Nairobi-styled sophisticates. It took a bold person to mention both Dar and urban sophistication in the same breath. The TBC strove to garland itself with a cachet of topical relevance, but it never quite succeeded in making of itself anything more than a faint shadow of the KBC ex-Nairobi.

What shaped the *wazungu* of Dar (and for that matter of Tanganyika in general) was that, unlike their Kenyan counterparts, they were transients without either the intention of taking up permanent residence in the country or the backing of long-standing stake-in-the-land traditions. It was of course the practice of entrenched *wazungu* traditions that was countered by the growth of Mau Mau in Kenya. On the strength of that, Dar could rest very well on its laurels when compared with Nairobi.

When the reception was good we listened to the KBC on the radio by preference, and eked out its broadcasting content with the General Overseas Service of the BBC as a reliable source of news. Sometimes we were able to pick up Lourenço Marques (LM) commercial radio out of Mozambique, which was much to our pleasure as LM radio was solidly dedicated to broadcasting popular music. Its presenters were white South Africans, among whom the most famous were Mr David Davies (who pronounced his surname "Day-vees") and Miss Esme Everard, who struggled in vain to keep the lid on her strongly Afrikaans-accented English.

Dar boasted a number of attractively designed buildings featuring red-tiled roofs and neatly balconied frontages that offered a solidly colonial manifestation of what living beside the Indian Ocean was all about. These buildings clustered together like little islands of privilege set in a sea of sprawling squalor or something close to the same in which construction had relied on the prolific use of corrugated metal sheets, mud blocks and coconut palm fronds. There were no prizes for guessing where Dar's ninety thousand Africans resided. Lanes characterised by varying widths and depths of fetid gutters were available to conduct the traveller through the residential maze, always assuming that the traveller knew where he was going.

Uninviting though some of these thoroughfares appeared, my experiences in Dar (as elsewhere in the country) were that it was safe to wander in them at any hour of the day or night. The presence of an *mzungu* might be more welcome in some locations than in others, but he could nonetheless feel secure. If he got lost he could always find someone to point him, with consummate cheerfulness, in the right direction.

Once we were checked in at the hotel that Bill took us to, we all went to visit a beach on which yellow sand was lapped by clear ocean water that was lukewarm to the touch. It was the first time for me to set foot in a tropical sea. Offshore, a bulky dhow-rigged craft slid over the tranquil surface of the ocean on a north heading, perhaps bound for Zanzibar. I wouldn't have wanted to speculate on the nature of its cargo.

We then embarked on the somewhat greater priority of making a tour of the sights of Dar as seen from the interior of a succession of seedy bars located in the labyrinth of side streets. In such *watu*-catering hostelries dress code counted for nothing, which suited me down to the ground. I wore *velskoon* without socks on my feet, a well-used pair of khaki shorts and a tattered shirt of lighter hue, and the various managements didn't even bat an eyelid. If the beer wasn't as cold as it ought to have been when it reached us, it was cool enough when set against the heat and humidity outside the premises, and in any case it went down the throat at a sufficient rate of knots to stop it warming up any more.

With dusk creeping into Dar from the sea we retreated to our hotel to partake of a Christmas-styled dinner in the hotel's restaurant. The dress code for that event was unfortunately at odds with my preferences, but my familiarity with the regulation jungle of the Dodoma club had me well primed to cope. The hotel restaurant required the wearing of shoes that not only could be polished but were also presumably clean (but who was checking?), socks, long trousers (neatly pressed), a long-sleeved shirt of any colour (provided it was white) and a tie.

I was only grateful that the hotel's demands didn't include a jacket. I assumed that the management was still holding the jacket option as part of its rearguard strategy in defence of civilised standards (ho hum) once the anticipated wave of *watu* clad in white shirts with ties, long trousers and polished shoes broke at its gates.

There was madness in the methods that were used to continually raise barriers in an attempt to delay the inevitable. *Uhuru* was coming whether *wazungu* (and not forgetting Indians and Arabs) liked it or not. If the various factions didn't swim together then the minorities would have to settle for the best that they could get rather than what they really wanted. With every day that I spent in Tanganyika it was becoming more and more clear that rather than swimming together we were all likely to sink separately.

My appearance at the dinner table appeared to satisfy the dress code criteria of the hotel management almost to the letter. My *velskoon* provoked no comments, and as I had no tie the management loaned me one for the occasion, drawn from a stock of the same that they held in readiness in a drawer to cover such pressing contingencies. I wondered if a similar service would be extended to a tie-deficient *mtu* seeking a table and presumed that there were absolutely no circumstances under which it would. There evidently wasn't any Kiswahili word for "tie", which I found rather reassuring.

Our party of four entered the hotel restaurant in the manner of princes. We were ushered to our table by a waiter resplendent in a stark white *kanzu* topped off by a red fez. There were black faces aplenty on view, but their owners were all part of the waiting profession. The restaurant, set in an attractively verdant open-air courtyard leaned over by several coconut palm trees (minus coconuts for obvious reasons), was already crowded with seated *wazungu*.

We made our way into the courtyard from the street outside, where a relatively large crab that was just about as broad across its back as the flat of my hand, chanced to scuttle past my feet. I picked it up using a secure behind-the-claws grip learned from fishermen on the north coast of Cornwall. The crab's claws were long, active and eager to nip.

All four of us made an inspection the crab. One of us decided to christen it Henry, and on that jolly basis, operating under the influence of seasonal cheer enhanced all round by the recently imbibed contents of a sequence of IPA bottles, it was mutually agreed that Henry should partake of dinner together with us. Thus Henry was taken into the restaurant courtyard enveloped in a not especially clean handkerchief. Henry was of local origin and his dress code was non-existent, but he came into the restaurant representing a small victory against the system of discrimination.

We sat in our places at the restaurant table. I unwrapped Henry, who showed himself to be an opportunity-seeking creature of mettle by clicking his claws and leaping sideways in the instinctive manner of his species to land on the floor under our table and run off, at large in the restaurant. The last I saw of Henry was his disappearance beneath a table a few feet away from us at which were seated two middle-aged men and a pair of bejewelled ladies radiant with ostentation and sipping from fine-fluted glasses something that bubbled and was not beer.

Henry's escape should have been seen as a *fait accompli* and left at that. However, having brought him in as a member of our party, we felt it to be important that all five of us should stick together, dine together and depart together. A course of action to seek out and recover Henry commenced at once. Naturally enough, in the context of time and place, a surreptitious approach was called for.

I pushed my chair back, got to my feet and stepped to the side of the adjacent table where I last saw Henry. Angling my head slightly, I endeavoured to peer down between two of the seated foursome to get a glimpse of what if anything was on the floor beneath. The four immediately ceased sipping their sparkling beverages and looked at me expectantly.

The most appropriate thing that I could think of doing in order to rise to the occasion was to bow towards them, putting into the bow as much servility as I could muster, and ask them if everything was all right. My white shirt and borrowed tie carried the day, as in return I received four smiles characterised by a lot of exposed teeth and poorly disguised insincerity. They informed me, as one, that not only was everything all right, it was also excellent.

In what was a spreading ripple effect, diners at other tables turned their heads towards me, looking as if they too wished to be asked how things were with them. I was left with no choice other than to move as graciously as I could (all things being relative) from table to table with that key query on my lips. I adopted a smiling countenance that proved increasingly difficult to sustain as I made the round of tables.

From the ebullience of the responses received I judged that there was not a single malcontent in the courtyard, unless it was the gentleman (*mzungu* of course) representing the restaurant management who advanced towards me and, rather than asking me if everything was all right as far as I was concerned, demanded to know what the devil I thought I was doing.

Tom and Bill and Mario were also on their feet to conduct a search for Henry, and although they were behaving with a lot more discretion than I was, the management representative acted on the understanding that we bore a collective responsibility for what he saw as an affront to his authority.

He took us all to one side of the courtyard and there, backed up against the trunk of a palm tree, requested an explanation of what he referred to as our outrageous conduct. We found much beer-inspired humour in the situation; humour was, however, a sentiment not shared by our interrogator in any shape, size or form.

Of Henry there was no sign. He must have vacated the premises, just as we did thereafter, following a suggestion from the management representative that that would be the most fitting course of action we could take. He said that we were welcome to dine anywhere that night as long as it wasn't in his restaurant. The best that could be said of our exit was that, although it was an eviction in all but name, it was carried out with moderate dignity.

I hadn't expected my Christmas visit to Dar to be so successful in my getting slung out of somewhere so soon. I walked away with a song in my heart—I'd been thrown out of better joints than this, I'd been thrown out of better joints than this. I'd been thrown out of better joints by far better men, and it wouldn't hurt my feelings if they threw me out again.

We were compelled to dine that Christmas Eve on what was known as *njugu na mishkaka*, a rather unusual combination of groundnuts (*njugu*) and spiced meat kebabs of no great dimensions (*mishkaka*), which were both roasted at the roadside over a charcoal fire brazier made from half a forty-four gallon oil drum. This blend of disparate ingredients worked well and was popular throughout the country, particularly in urban centres where the tastes of *watu* were catered for.

The source of the meat on the kebabs was not disclosed. It was best not to query its identity and to permit the spices, which were made all the more significant through Dar's fame as one of the world's great spice ports, to preserve its anonymity.

We consoled ourselves with the thought that with *njugu na mishkaka* we probably fared better on Christmas Eve than we might have done in the courtyard restaurant, with or without the company of Henry. The street vendor who served us didn't ask if everything was all right as he didn't need to. There was no question that, whether or not we were in or out of the courtyard restaurant, the spirit of the festive season was being felt in Dar that night.

At only a couple of days, our time in Dar was a little too limited to make a properly relaxing break of it. I wasn't sorry to step off the returning train at the railway station in Dodoma on Boxing Day and set my feet back in the comfort of what was more familiar ground.

From Dodoma, Tom and I went back to Iwambala, Mario headed for Ilangali to once again take up his version of the white man's burden under Danilo, and Bill shoved off to I knew not where as I never saw him again, much to my regret as he was such a good-all-round man.

*

During a conversation at WDL's new service depot at Manyoni some months later I heard that Bill had left WDL and was rumoured to have gone over to the Congo, where at the time huge amounts of money were being paid to *wazungu* willing to contract their services as mercenaries for as long as either the contracts or the *wazungu* survived, whichever came first.

The independence of the Republic of the Congo was proclaimed on the thirtieth of June 1960, just over two months before my arrival at Mwadui. The proclamation was made in the city of Leopoldville by none other than the King of Belgium, following his signing a friendship treaty between Belgium and the Congo on the previous day. The first Prime Minister of the new republic was named Mr Patrice Lumumba. His Head of State was Mr Joseph Kasavubu.

The friendship treaty was short lived. National chaos followed hard on the heels of independence. That well known tradition of inter-tribal violence involving widespread slaughter of the innocent put in an immediate appearance as various protagonists jockeyed for power. A mutiny in the Congolese army resulted in the wholesale replacement of officers; ministers of state were selectively assassinated; and there was a random outburst of destructive and murderous retribution attacks on people and property perceived to have been associated with the former colonial regime.

In an attempt to regain some form of order, the United Nations (UN standing for Unhelpful Nincompoops) intervened by sending in an international peace-keeping force.

The province of Katanga, under its leader Mr Moise Tshombe, promptly seceded from the Congo, thereby adding much fuel to the fire and starting up a war aimed at returning Katanga to the fold. Mr Tshombe's star rose to great heights before its inevitable demise.

The national government of the Congo broke up into two factions respectively claimed by Mr Lumumba and a so-called "upstart" named Mr Joseph Mobutu. Mr Lumumba was captured by Mobutu's forces, and, in best Second World War tradition, he was killed while trying to escape.

It seemed that in those frantically negative months every action created an even more negative reaction until it seemed that there were no depths of depravity left unplumbed in the Congo. In his untimely death, Mr Lumumba was accorded worldwide a martyr's celebrity that he might not altogether have merited.

What should at the outset have been the best of times immediately became the worst of times. The Congo experience did little to dissuade other then-current colonial regimes from concluding that independence was far too precious a commodity to squander on the peoples of Africa. Could or would similar things happen in *baada ya uhuru* (post-*uhuru*) Tanganyika? This question was often asked, frequently discussed and never adequately answered.

It was fair to say that I was relatively ignorant of the implications of *uhuru*, since those of us who worked out in the remote bush coped with day-to-day priorities that left little time for thinking about much else. To that extent the unravelling disaster in the Congo was so out of sight and out of mind that it might have been taking place on another planet. We only really came face to face with the situation in the Congo when we saw forlorn groups of Belgian refugees on trains passing through places like Dodoma. The likely fragility of what lay in Tanganyika's future was as much on show in the appearance of the refugees as it was in Mr Manji Dhanji's prospective stock of running shoes up in Singida.

As the weak fabric of Congolese society fell apart, so the opportunities for the participation of white mercenaries burgeoned. The latter didn't have to worry about what was right or what was wrong in either a moral or political sense. As long as the money was good, mercenaries were happy to fight for anyone against anyone else.

I was aware that there was a recruitment drive for mercenaries and had heard that rival agents of both the Congolese national government and the breakaway province of Katanga had been searching for candidates in Dodoma, although not both at the same time. There were rumours that a few WDL Field Officers with previous military experience had actually signed up for the more popular cause of Katanga.

The independence-related rallying call to the masses in Tanganyika was "*Uhuru na kazi!*" (Independence and work!) It was normally coupled with that great but seldom realised ideal of "*Mtu moja, kura moja*" (One man, one vote).

The cynics (and there were more than a few of them) among the *watu* claimed that the slogan "*Mwanasiasa moja, gari moja*" (One politician, one motor car) was much more to the point.

Rumours were rife to the effect that the accoutrements and accessories of the observed lifestyle enjoyed by the *wazungu* would be assumed by the *watu* once *uhuru* dawned, although such rumours weren't being taken quite as seriously as they ought to have been.

15

Iseke

In the official WDL camp mail that we picked up in Dodoma on returning from our Christmas visit to Dar we found two formal notices. One was an instruction to Tom to wind up the sampling programme from the Iwambala camp in order that he might move as soon as possible to take up a detailed work assignment. The other was a directive that I should leave Iwambala and relocate to the vicinity of Iseke to set up a new camp and carry out a reconnaissance sampling programme in the surrounding area.

It seemed that visiting Dar had been something of a swansong for both of us. In practice such directives were orders to be obeyed without question. With hearts that were heavier that they ought to have been, there was no alternative open to us other than to be compliant.

Looking at my move on the bright side, the core team of *watu* that I had thus far been working with regularly were, with one or two local exceptions, happy to accompany me to Iseke. These characters, a welter of highly individual personalities, were my inspirational headman Efrem; my Luo cook Paolo Odhiambo; that great driver Idi Ramadhani (a stroke of luck for me in getting him); the *halal* expert Taji and his brother Yusufu; the Elvis look-alike Hamisi; the ever-solid Mwendambio; the naturally bland John Simon; the soon to disappear Saidi Mohamedi; a rudimentary administration clerk or *karani* named Atanasio Boniface; and last and by all means least, John Mwita, the incendiary Msukuma with the glowing testimonial.

I had to accept that Paulo's cooking skills were on a par with the quality of my driving. I was a little uneasy about this, although Paulo was for the most part adequate in the kitchen, and I assumed that he must have learned a few things along the way from Simon. The domestic services that Paulo provided for me at Iseke were best described as being "not bad" rather than "good". He fell somewhere short as a cook, but he ran the camp kitchen entirely to his own satisfaction.

Atanasio, my *karani*, performed all of his duties in camp and seldom ventured into the bush. He did as little in the way of sampling as he thought he could get away with. Atanasio read and wrote in Kiswahili, and these attributes led him in the grand tradition of his clerkly profession to believe himself to be a cut above all the other *watu* in camp, inclusive of Efrem. He was tall and elegant in appearance, which, coupled with an uncommon propensity to wear clean clothes for most of the time, did in fairness at least render him unique. As he was charged with keeping the stores inventory in order and issuing daily rations to the *watu*, he was able to revel in the implied power that this conferred on him.

Mwendambio brought two dog pups to Iseke with him. They were not very welcome at the outset, but we soon discovered that they were rather good at keeping watch at night and so were accepted into our team. No creature of any significant size could approach the camp on two or four legs without the two dogs alerting us. The two dogs were of the so-called *shenzi* breed, characterised by hunched shoulders, dun brown coats, rounded backs and hangdog faces. One of them possessed a great upward curl of a tail. The other dog's tail was unusually straight, presumably as a consequence of the tail having been broken at birth. I named him "Jack". His companion, for obvious reasons, was known as "Shen". The dogs hung around camp in the manner of Paulo and Atanasio. They barked when barking was required and made bold gendarmes of themselves by being never there when danger loomed. For their own good reasons they were particularly fearful of baboons, which as it turned out was a bit of a handicap for them at Iseke.

*

Aided by Tom and his Land Rover, all my gear, equipment and *watu* were transported down from Iwambala to Iseke over the span of a couple of days. The wet season held back from hindering us too much, which we took as a good augury for the Iseke project.

Our camp was set up in a location about half a mile to the north of the little Arab's *duka*. The *duka* was close enough to us to get to when we needed its services and any items out of its stock, but was far enough away from camp to be avoided otherwise. The location of Iseke placed it, when compared with Iwambala, closer to the trappings of civilisation. The *watu* felt this even if I didn't. All things were relative, and as far as I was concerned such sophistication as Iseke could lay claim to took modest pretensions to extreme limits.

I deeply regretted parting company with Tom, but at the same time I couldn't help but welcome the personal independence that running my own camp at Iseke brought me. Although I wasn't sure in my mind that I was genuinely ready to go off on my own, I was confident that with the help of the *watu* I could pick it all up as I went along.

I was discovering that I was not only enjoying the work but also feeling comfortable in the full-time pleasure of associating with the *watu* in the solitude of what I was increasingly coming to think of as "my" bush. This was a revelation. Whatever happened there would be up to me. I was becoming affected by a territorial imperative which caused me to resent any white visitor to my camp from the moment I heard the first distant sounds of the motor of an approaching vehicle. Such people were intruders and I didn't like it. In any case it was very rare that visitors coming down from Mwadui brought good news with them.

I was well on the way to developing classic symptoms of what was known as "bush fever", a condition not unrelated to the by then familiar buck fever. Anyone afflicted by bush fever was said to be "bushed". All of us who worked in the bush for WDL were bushed to a certain extent, which went some way to explain (although perhaps not to justify) some of the more outlandish aspects of our conduct during weekends in town. The ultimate symptom of being bushed was an unwillingness, manifested principally by the more die-hard of the WDL prospectors, that fell not far short of a personal inability to leave the perceived security of the assigned working area and go to town at all. My affliction never progressed quite that far, but it came close enough.

We set up the camp near Iseke beneath the spread of a grove of tall and wonderfully shady trees. The main misfortune for me to contemplate was that the steel tank bath at Iwambala was consigned to the fond mists of memory. For ablution purposes at Iseke I was reduced to using the standard shower bag arrangement suspended from a tree, which I knew would take a bit of getting used to.

Our new campsite backed on to a jumble of those variously sized grey-white granite boulders that were such typical features of the area. The boulders were smoothly rounded with barely a jag or a sharp edge to be seen or felt on any one of them. It was quite an attractive place. Around us was spread a great expanse of pleasant savannah, liberally studded with the characteristic boulders and the hugely isolated granite formations that the South Africans called *koppies*.

There were some *koppies* with precipitate pinnacles of naked granite rising to sudden heights of a hundred feet and more, looking as if they had been thrust into prominence by deep-seated primeval forces. Seamed by open joints and faults highlighted by green traceries of precariously clinging vegetation, the *koppies* made weird and dramatically blocky profiles against a background of sky.

Many of the *koppies* were home to colonies of rock hyraxes. These little creatures looked like large, grey-brown guinea pigs and were more familiarly known as rock rabbits (*pimbi*). In what was hopefully left of my termite-chewed Bible such rock hyraxes were referred to as "coneys". They were seriously inactive animals, dedicated to lying motionless on ledges for as long as the sun shone on them. Their colour combined with this immobility to provide excellent camouflage. However, if the power of an observer's sight failed to identify their actual presence, his sense of smell would work every time. Thanks to the significant accumulation of droppings strewn around their preferred resting places, rock rabbits were invariably smelt before they were seen.

Somewhat daunted by the smell, I assumed that rock rabbits probably wouldn't make good eating. This sentiment was confirmed by the *watu*, who made not a single move to hunt rock rabbits in spite of their proliferation on the *koppies* around the camp. As far as the hunting of rock rabbits went, the creatures were just about as safe as if they were designated royal game.

Half a mile or so to the west of the camp, two large *koppies* reared up in stark grandeur. They were separated one from the other by a distance of no more than a quarter of a mile. One of the pair of *koppies* dropped down to bush level from its summit in a sequence of sheer granite faces that from a distance gave an impression of a gigantic staircase. The second of the two *koppies* consisted of one mightily soaring block of granite that was rounded off at its crest and associated with an acicular pinnacle of a similar height across a separation gap of only a few yards.

These two *koppies* were, both individually and in combination, home to a large troop of baboons (*nyani*). The baboons occupied the heights for security and descended when the need took them to forage and feed in the surrounding district. They raided local *shambas*, and when chased away, as they always were by the irate *shamba* tenders (all women of course), they escaped back to their *koppie* fortresses with impunity. Centred on the *koppies* that the baboons called home, their troop's radius of interest included our camp. Considerable numbers of baboons, enough to scare me more than a little, came to reconnoitre the camp on a few occasions. They stalked towards us, slipping between the trees and through the bush with a characteristically deliberate and measured four-legged stride. They circled around the campsite, moving slightly closer in towards us with each circuit.

To face up to these bold marauders I took out my shotgun and fired off a couple of shots into the trees to rattle the leaves above them, whereupon the baboons ran away with the utmost despatch. They returned a few days later and were again provided with a shotgun performance. It was only following their third attempt to invade the camp and the expenditure of two more shots into the trees that the baboons took the sour grapes way out and decided that our camp was no longer worthy of their attention.

I hadn't seen the last of the troop of foraging baboons, however, as I came across them every now and then when I was out with the *watu* on sampling traverses. The number of individuals making up the troop was impossible to count accurately, but I was sure that there were at least a hundred, comprising adult males and females (the latter with and without clinging babies) and gambolling youngsters. When I saw them I merely had to make a motion with either my shotgun or my rifle for the baboons to distance themselves from us like a rapidly spreading olive-green ripple.

In his camp at Ilangali Danilo kept for a while as a pet a young baboon that he was said to have found abandoned in the bush. The little baboon was an engaging creature, but as it grew and got older it was reported to be developing an aggressive level of determination to be no-one's pet. I saw it only once when it had reached the stage at which its key purpose in life seemed to be directed at pulling or biting to pieces anything that came immediately to hand. In addition it chose to demonstrate a lack of discrimination as to where and when it urinated. I subsequently heard that the young baboon and Danilo had parted company under circumstances that were clouded in mystery.

During one traverse I came face to face with what must have been the leader, if not the king, of the Iseke-based troop of baboons. He was perched on a rotting tree stump about twenty yards away from me, a hulking beast of undoubted age, strength and wisdom. For once I didn't have a gun along with me to wave at him, and by his attitude he indicated that he knew that I didn't.

He showed no sign of fear as he raised his great head, leaned back, opened his mouth and gave us a few barks. At first his tones sounded derisive, but then they became both angry and accusing. He left me in no doubt that he was not happy with having had a shotgun fired over the heads of his troop back in the vicinity of our camp. What impressed me most was his exposing the most savage-looking set of canine teeth that I had yet seen or ever wished to see again. Those teeth must have been several inches long. The upper set was pointed towards me like a couple of deadly daggers.

The king baboon showed signs of being more than ready to pick a fight with anyone foolish enough to take him on. I chose discretion over valour and attempted to show that I was going to ignore him by moving on with the traverse. I hoped that he would get the message before I lost my ability to resist a growing impulse to take flight. He must have reckoned that he had sufficiently exercised his dominion over us, since he knew only too well that if push came to shove he could readily tear any one of us, Mwendambio included, limb from limb.

In the tradition of one of his regal predecessors, the king of the baboons made it plain that he was not amused. He dropped down from his tree-stump throne and strolled away in the manner of one who was born to be nonchalant. As he went, having won the round rather convincingly, he mooned us with an intricately bulbous red backside that Queen Victoria probably imagined seeing only in her dreams.

*

In the late afternoons I sometimes left camp carrying my rifle to walk over towards the two big *koppies* where the baboons lived in order to try to stalk them. The usual failure of this exercise made me wonder as to who it was that was playing games with whom. The sense of sight that was the heritage of every one of the strategically posted baboon security guards up on the heights was far too keen to allow my approach to their castle to go undetected.

They scampered along the cracks and clefts of the *koppies* on breathtakingly sure feet and gathered in groups on some of the more substantial ledges to yell a chorus of insults at me. Not to be outdone, I fired an occasional shot at the rocks up above or down below where they stood, putting my response to their taunts into the crack of the shot and (hopefully) a screaming ricochet to follow.

In spite of my elephant-trunk standard of marksmanship, I usually managed to hit the *koppies* with my shots. The echoes bounced back at me, and reverberated several times between the two *koppies* before they faded away. The baboons disappeared much more rapidly than the echoes did, however. In the blink of an eye it was as if the rocks had opened to swallow them up in a single gulp. I assumed that up on the heights there were numerous caves and hollows in which the baboons took refuge. If there was anything positive to come out of these games of bluff and counter bluff, it was in the provision of additional assurance that the baboons would continue to give our camp a fairly wide berth. The local *shambas*, where the pickings for the baboons were in any case better than anything our camp could provide, fared less well.

I discovered that when I stalked towards the *koppies* without a firearm the baboons treated me with total indifference. I concluded that they not only knew what a firearm was but were able to recognise one when they saw it. One day, to put the theory to the test, I approached the *koppies* porting a pick handle over my arm as if it were a rifle. The baboons reacted to the sight of it by simply going about their normal business without the appearance of having a care in the world. I then returned to camp, dropped off the pick handle, collected my rifle and walked back to the *koppies*. When the baboon sentries saw me coming again they at once proved me right by stopping whatever it was they were doing, sounding an alarm and marshalling their charges as they all ran for cover.

*

Even less welcome than baboons as visitors to the camp at Iseke were itinerant *watu* who not only knew with absolute certainty where diamonds were to be found lying on the ground out in the bush but were also willing (for a price, part-payable in advance) to guide me at once to that very spot.

These knowledgeable characters dropped by quite frequently. As I subsequently discovered, many WDL bush camps could count on similar visitors appearing from time to time. Some of the visitors may even have had genuinely sincere motives, although unfortunately no one like that ever approached a camp that I was in.

Common sense dictated that their entreaties should be rejected out of hand by issuing them with a politely delivered *unakwenda kutomba* request. However, the situation was less simple than that in practice. They presented us with a dilemma, as there was always a chance that one of them really might know something useful. If advice on the existence in the bush of diamonds was not followed up then a discovery of significance could possibly be missed, and none of us wanted that to happen.

The route from bushes to riches, as epitomised by WDL's great Tanganyika diamond hunt, was first and foremost a process of elimination of valueless options. Reconnaissance sampling was designed as much to determine where diamonds could not be as to where they might exist. Whether we liked it or not, wild goose chases were a definite element of the overall game.

On the other hand the number of time-consuming false leads that came along to be investigated built up an increasing feeling of frustration. It was debateable as to whether or not, throughout Tanganyika, any definite occurrence of diamonds on the ground did get overlooked thanks to there having been just too many preceding incidences of informants crying wolf.

The way in which it worked was typically as follows. An *mtu* with a strikingly *shenzi* appearance in which rags and sweat played key roles came to the camp during the middle or late part of the afternoon. He informed me that he was the bearer of tidings of great joy and could, as *Mungu* was his witness, lead me to a place where diamonds were strewn about on the surface of the ground to be picked up and where even more could be easily excavated with only a little digging. I asked him why he hadn't picked any of the diamonds up for himself, or for that matter why he hadn't brought along at least one or two of the stones to show me as proof of his good faith. He didn't answer, electing merely to incline his head as coyly as he could manage while assuming a conspiratorial expression. I half expected him to wink at me while tapping his nose with his right forefinger and was a little disappointed when he didn't. Well then, I asked him, where was this place of alleged riches? He declared, while pointing in a specific direction, that it was *kule*, over there, not very far away maybe. The problem was that as I knew from experience that *kule* was a word endowed with great versatility, depending on how its first vowel was drawn out. *Kuuule* signified "a bit further over there". *Kuuuuuuule* implied a place that might well be up on the far north side of Lake Victoria. However, the bearer of good news usually commenced with a *kule* pure and simple and only opened the extension up once a few shillings in advance payment had been dropped in his hand and when his ensuing guided tour was in progress.

A journey to a place where diamonds were supposed to be typically began with us all travelling in a Land Rover, pushing through the bush on the strength of the directions given by our guide. A honey bird might have been equally as certain of itself as our guide was of himself and would almost certainly have been a lot more direct. At length the bush put a stop to our Land Rover supported advance, either when the growth became too thick to penetrate or when the ground beneath was too rough to drive on. When that happened we were on foot for the rest of the trip, setting out on what shaped up to be a hike of unspecified duration, on which we were limited only by a need to be back at the Land Rover before sunset. We didn't want to find ourselves a long way out of camp with night threatening to fall on us like a curtain. The foot journey concluded when it became evident that the guide was making the route up as he went along, which came as no surprise at all. The guide expressed profound disappointment in our falling short of the target destination. He promised us that he would return at an earlier hour on another day to give it a second go, following which he faded into the gloaming a few shillings to the good, never to be seen again. I characterised such diamond hunting excursions as travelling hopefully in the sure knowledge that our intended destination was one we would never arrive at.

Guides like that, who I thought of as the *wanafasi*, were relatively harmless tricksters for whom I had a certain amount of sympathy. There were, however, other itinerant strangers associated with rumours of diamonds that it was less easy to think kindly about. The likes of these were sometimes reported to be afoot in the vicinity of the camp. I heard about them but never met any of them, although now and then an individual reputed to be of their number was pointed out to me, normally from a vantage point of considerable distance.

These men were said to carry with them small glass jars (presumably clean) containing raw diamonds. By repute they were bush couriers working for the criminal overlords who ran the "Illicit Diamond Buying" (IDB) business. They were by no means *wanafasi* and were moreover potentially dangerous men if some of the stories about the big-moneyed world of IDB were to be believed.

The diamonds carried by these alleged couriers were most likely to have either been stolen from the diamond mining operations of WDL at Mwadui or otherwise brought into Tanganyika from the Congo. The courier routes were supposed to slip through the bush in stages from *duka* to *duka* (trading post to trading post) and so on down to Dar and the coast for the onward shipment of accumulated diamonds to fuel more than enough of the greed-ridden ills of the world at large.

The couriers were simple *watu* for the most part. They were the small cogs that kept the big wheels of IDB turning. None of them were indispensable, and any one of them was only too easy to replace. Occasionally one of them might be arrested by the police as part of a formally contrived process to "encourage the others" and so impress the general public, but the more common reasons by which these small-time types dropped out of IDB were that they got themselves irretrievably lost in the bush; or they were the victims of predators *en route*; or they were liquidated either by third parties or their own bosses.

If arrested, a courier was a prize of no real value as he would know little or nothing of the business of IDB beyond the limits of the restricted bush tracks that he was paid to tramp over. To those in the know, the bush was riddled with such tracks. If one was discovered and closed off, another could be immediately opened as a replacement.

The *duka* and trading-outlet staging posts in the IDB chain were, assuming they were genuine, under either Indian or Arab management. If I had been asked to put my money down on who the prime movers for IDB were I would have placed it on the Indians. As far as guile and enterprise were concerned, the Indians had the Arabs beaten hands down.

It was only the truly big boys down at the end of the chain who knew how the whole intricate IDB jigsaw fitted together. I didn't know and nor did I want to know the who or why or where or what of such gentlemen, but with the social hierarchy of Tanganyika being what it was, I assumed that IDB was only able to exist as a viable organisation with some form of direct high-level involvement of *wazungu*. It was only *wazungu* who were able to count on the kind of broad-scale mobility and big-picture insight that were so essential in controlling the highly compartmentalised IDB structure.

Wazungu enjoyed an extra advantage in that, just like Caesar's wife, they were regarded (by a majority of the members of all other racial groups) as being above suspicion. They were seen as the custodians of ultimate integrity, which would have been quite laughable if it wasn't so seriously mistaken.

I entertained no illusions whatsoever about the capability of *wazungu* to play any kind of game that would suit their own advantage. I assumed that in both national and district government circles *wazungu* officials did their duties with probity—although I needed to admit that I did meet one or two DOs whom I wouldn't have wanted to buy a used car from. As time went by I learned the truth of what Bernie McBride once told me: that where diamonds were concerned, not only was any act of dishonesty possible but also far too many of those who came into contact with the gemstones had their price.

There were gifts that one or two of the WDL bush camp types were alleged to have received from certain Indian traders that were far too costly to justify on the strength of merely creaming a few shillings off the top of an inflated unit price for bags of *posho* or *debes* of *mafuta*. Not counting a giraffe allegedly shot to order, there must have been some other quid pro quo involved, IDB not being outside contention, to support a gift like a VW Beetle.

*

The blinds on the trading window of lucrative opportunity were partly drawn when the WDL service and supply depot (known simply as "the Depot") was established at Manyoni under the leadership of Bruno Brown. The Depot's area of influence took in the Singida and Kongwa districts up in the north, Iseke, Ilangali and the Rungwa Game Reserve down in the south and Dodoma to the east, and it extended west to a point half way to Tabora.

The supply side of the Depot carried a line in various key elements of *watu* rations, which was all to the good, and provided storage bunkers from which we could collect bulk supplies of petrol or diesel fuel. There was in addition a postal facility at which we could drop off samples and reports for despatch to Mwadui, post personal mail out, and pick up any incoming mail that was routed down to us from Mwadui.

Unless we chose to use a local *poste restante* address in one of the larger towns for our personal incoming international mail, the mail was delivered in the first instance to a WDL "private bag" postal address in Nairobi. A WDL geologist showed me a letter that he had received from "home" in which he was asked, "Who is this private bag that you have in Nairobi?" He once told me that his sister in the UK had informed their grandmother that she was going out with a South African boyfriend. "That's good," said the grandmother, "but what's wrong with a nice white boy?"

From that private bag newly arrived mail was carried to Mwadui, where it was sorted for distribution, on the regular Dakota flight schedule. I didn't get my mail sent to the Depot as I preferred to use the Dodoma post office for that purpose. Not the least reason for my preference was that it provided an extra excuse to go into town and perhaps continue with one or other of the social activities that the Depot's service capability was supposed to be deterring.

Whatever the good intentions behind the operation of the Depot might have been, its establishment never quite seemed to succeed in eliminating a need in the camps that it served for independent external trading arrangements, probably because the point was never pushed hard enough. The bigger picture was overwhelmed by Bruno's obsession with keeping records. At the Depot, paper ruled the day. As long as our camp records were made up on time and appeared to be in order we were home free.

The Depot was easily reached from Iseke. I went up the track to visit it about once every ten days on a routine basis, and in the interim I went up only when needs must. I made other visits when I passed by the Depot on the return (never on the way out) from any trip to Dodoma. A particular attraction for me in calling in was that the Land Rover maintenance workshop at the Depot was graced for a time by the presence of that always entertaining prince of bullshitters Gerry Wilson as chief mechanic.

The Depot also contained a good mess unit in which visitors were served with meals provided that the said visitors were there at the scheduled time for the meals and were able to pay (by signing a chit) for the same. For overnight visitors a bed could be provided with a beer or two beforehand, the required payment for which was strictly in advance and on cash terms only.

Bruno presided over the Depot as a relatively benign yet unpredictably bombastic dictator. I learned to tread carefully in his presence. It was a matter of keeping a low profile as then there was more that you could get away with. The best policy was to show your face to Bruno and make sure he recognised it before getting on with what you wanted to do.

One of my Depot experiences was not quite as low profile as I would have liked, however. Sitting at the mess table one evening, Bob Kotze, a South African Field Assistant, decided to take me to task for crimes that he suggested were committed by the British Army during the Boer War. That particular war, which had ended some sixty years prior to Bob's tirade, was a subject on which I was singularly unqualified to make any pronouncement of any kind. I didn't know much about Bob and he probably knew even less about me, but that didn't stop him heaping national guilt on my shoulders. For both of us a little knowledge was a dangerous thing, especially since Bob was several beers ahead of me. Bob's bugbear was vested in the establishment of concentration camps by the British to contain the wives and families of active Boer guerillas. He seemed keen to fight me over the issue there and then. I was incidental to his cause, as anyone else from the UK would have served Bob's purpose just as well. The fact that South Africa had recently left the British Commonwealth was used to add strength to his declarations that South Africa's white Afrikaans-speaking community (unkindly referred to by their English-speaking counterparts as Dutchmen) were God's chosen people. Anyone who disagreed with him was a candidate for a bashing.

Bob was big-bellied and beefy in the best tradition of his red meat and beer addicted breed. He was a well-balanced Dutchman, having a chip on both shoulders. The best I could do was to let him have his say and then get up and slowly walk away when he ran out of steam. I resolved both to read up a little on the history of the Boer War and to try to avoid Bob to the extent that it was possible from that day on.

*

If more congenial company than Bob and the accompaniment of a beer or two was needed, I had the option to drive the twenty-five miles north of Manyoni to the Suna crossing, where Tony Knowles and Joker Mackenzie had their "Drop Inn" camp. The atmosphere at the Drop Inn was always enjoyable. Tony and Joker bought in beer in bulk. Those who came along to drink it either paid cash for their consumption or made a donation of one kind or another to the wellbeing of the camp. The drawback at the "Drop Inn" was Tony and Joker's pet bush baby. It was a pretty little creature whose great vice was to sleep all day and wake up to dash around the camp all night. Its big liquid eyes caught and amplified every last vestige of light that came its way. It gave out a squalling cry in what seemed to me on an occasion when I stayed at the Drop Inn overnight to be all but incessant. I wasn't the only one to define that little animal as a prime irritant.

The bush baby disappeared one night, presumably a victim to a lucky predator. Its place as camp mascot was soon taken up by a very appealing genet cat, a lithe animal about a yard long from the tip of its nose to the end of its characteristically long stripe-ringed tail. Perhaps it was one of the genet's relatives that took the bush baby. The Drop Inn genet's coat was beautifully marked with spots. It was also a creature of nocturnal habits, although unlike the bush baby none of these were intrusive on would be sleepers. Its movement was like a flow of water, elegant and sure of itself.

*

All things, whether they were good or bad, came to an end eventually. There was only so much reconnaissance sampling work that we could undertake from the camp at Iseke, and once it was done the time came for us to move on.

I received orders, routed to me though Bruno up at the Depot, that I was to relocate to continue with reconnaissance sampling over a large regional area located to the east side of the road linking Suna with Singida. This area, newly defined and offering me something of a step forward in responsibility, was contiguous to the north boundary of the area assigned to the Drop Inn camp.

The camp for the new area would be of the two-*wazungu* variety. My companion in camp was to be a recently arrived geologist named John Clutterbuck who was more familiarly known as "Buck". As I was the "senior" geologist (in terms of time served at the working front rather than in age, as Buck was a year or so older than me) the job of camp leader was to be mine.

Buck was slight of stature, very clean cut, and cautious to the point of being obsessive in his approach to the bush and all that therein was. This feeling of personal insecurity lessened his ability to exercise authority over the *watu*, and it didn't help that he sported a rather ragged looking chin-fringing beard of the kind favoured by students who liked to be regarded as academics. In the bush the beard looked slightly silly. It was difficult to believe that Buck would easily adapt to the job and bush conditions, which was the way it turned out as he quit after a number of months to go on to do things that suited him better in more civilised surroundings.

I took it on trust that Buck and I would get on well together in camp, and that if not then we would at least co-exist in a state of placid truce for which there were numerous precedents. At the same time I worried about our potential relationship becoming conflictive as I was well aware of the pitfalls involved. I resolved to do my best to run a model camp while knowing that if such camps existed I hadn't yet come across anyone who had worked in one of them.

I had been very lucky at Iwambala in my relationship with Tom. Such inter-personal clashes as the two of us had were no more than the run-of-mill trivial. It helped that I was generally ready to defer to Tom's superior know-how on most issues that came up.

In my work at Iseke I developed a preference for me to be the only *mzungu* in camp, although I supposed I always knew that such a state of serendipity and independence was too good to last.

Two *wazungu* sharing a camp, whether they got on with one another or not, was normally a manageable arrangement. There was a desire on the part of both parties to avoid conflict, which evolved into a kind of mutually acceptable state of separate existences. The two took their meals apart under the respective flysheets of their individual tents and usually came together only around the fire in the late evening to talk the day's work through, plan for the morrow's and chat in a cordial atmosphere prior to retiring to their tents for the night.

More than two *wazungu* in a camp generally provided the classic ingredients of a recipe for discord. There was nothing like a few *wazungu* living together day after day in an isolated camp to bring out, emphasise and magnify the foibles, habits, mannerisms and attitudes of each of them as perceived by the others. The most modest of habits, such as the way an item of cutlery might be held, the quality of a certain tone of voice, the scratch of a nose, the incidence of verbal tics and so on, were able to generate the most deep-seated distaste in others forced to observe the same over and over again.

With three *wazungu* in camp, the balance all too often was set at two against one. It was a case of divide and rule in the raw. The life of the one was sure to be made miserable. The two gravitated together on the spurious basis of common interests and joined forces to leave the one out in the cold. Such situations did not occur intentionally, but nevertheless they occurred. We ignored our own social shortcomings while condemning out of hand similar shortcomings perceived in our camp companions.

An ultimate state of mutual loathing was inevitable—it was at its worst when it spilled over into the working environment. There were numerous *wazungu* in far too many camps who were working against one another to the extent that the negativity infected their respective teams of *watu* and sometimes even induced blood to flow in the *watu* camp. In the big camps that held more than three *wazungu* conflictive social divisions were enhanced rather than eased. With four *wazungu* involved, the division would be along the lines of either 2–1–1 or 3–1. It was never 2–2. The camp imperative called for feral dominance rather than equality. The pecking order established in camp was no different from that of the game that prowled the bush all around.

With this in mind, it was something of a miracle that in all the host of WDL camps, no *mzungu* was subjected to serious violent treatment at the hand of another. I would have been surprised, however, if there hadn't been many unreported incidents that fell under the category of "close run things".

In town of course, when the WDL *wazungu* came together to unite under a common flag of making the most of the weekend, all was invariably sweetness and light, assuming that discussions related to the conduct of the Boer War were shut down as and when they came up.

Lake Mianje, Singida District

Camp construction near Lake Mianje; Efrem standing on left;
John Mwita squatting second from left in front.

General view of camp near Lake Mianje

Author's tent at camp near Lake Mianje

The grassing of the Game Reserve after the first rains

Mount Hanang and its grass plains

Zebra and wildebeest on the plains around Mount Hanang

Wildebeeste kill: (*left to right*): Idi Ramadhani, Taji (with halal knife), Efrem (with rifle)

16

Mianje-Mungaa

Buck and I arranged to rendezvous one day in Manyoni at Bruno's Depot. From Manyoni we drove in a Land Rover together up the road through the Itigi thicket and on past the Drop Inn towards Singida. Our objective was to scout out a part of the area we were assigned to sample in order to locate a suitable first campsite.

It was a pleasant surprise that finding an excellent campsite took us very little time. The availability of a good supply of water was a key priority for us, and on the prior advice of a DO at the Singida district administration HQ we went to investigate the area surrounding what he told us was a small fresh water lake named Mianje situated in open upland savannah some twenty miles to the southeast of the town of Singida. Lake Mianje and its setting commended itself to us as soon as we saw it. It made an ideal location for a camp. Compared with Iseke and Iwambala, the setting was virtually idyllic.

The general area around the lake was known as Mianje-Mungaa. Mianje stood for the lake, and Mungaa stood for a tribal (Wanyaturu) village of quite large dimensions that relied on the lake as a source of water for its population and their domestic animals as well as for locally commercial fishing. The paramount tribal chief, whose full name with title was Chief Omari Mpahi, lived in Mungaa. His presence went some way towards explaining why the village was a big one. Great Chiefs were magnets for fawning sycophants living within easy reach.

The shape of Lake Mianje was roughly oval in plan view. The lake was a good half-mile across on its short axis—making the lake not quite as small as we had been led to believe by the Singida DO. To give the DO the benefit of the doubt, when he defined Lake Mianje as small he might have been comparing it in his mind with Lake Victoria.

The sparkling blue water of Lake Mianje lapped against a sandy shore only a few yards wide which backed into a more substantial fringe of thick standing reeds. All around the lake, crowding in on the outer edge of the reeds the ground was patched with *shambas* resplendent with high standing ranks and files of both maize (*mahindi*) and millet (*mtama*). Millet was a crop more widely grown in that particular locality than it was anywhere else I ever visited in Tanganyika.

A few ponderously unstable-looking dugout canoes trailing long fishing nets plied to and fro on the waters of the lake. A free end of each fishing net was attached to a pole at a given point on shore—the fisherman carried the remaining bulk of the net in his canoe and paddled the craft out into the lake and back to shore again on a course describing a great arc over which he shed the net continuously into the water. Once fully shed, the net was drawn in to shore, together with such fish as it managed to pick up on the way, by virtue of a pair of fisherman's assistants heaving hand over hand on it at each of its two onshore ends.

Once we had a camp set up near Lake Mianje we were able to buy some of the lake fish directly from the fishermen for our own consumption. The fishermen told me that the principal species of fish that they caught was named *t'lapi*, which I assumed meant tilapia. Although small, the tilapia were sweet and succulent and made a welcome addition to a bush diet in which fish, apart from the unfortunately ubiquitous catfish, was normally in short supply.

Lake Mianje occupied a natural depression in the terrain, as if it were a flooded amphitheatre. Outside the tonsure of beach, reeds and *shambas*, the lake was surrounded by shallowly sloping ground that rose to a height of no more than thirty or forty feet before levelling off. The site that we selected for our camp was at the top of this slope on the south side of the lake. From it we looked towards distant outlying huts of Mungaa over to the north and west. The site was covered with a fair amount of scrubby bush, although there were very few trees tall enough for us to count on for providing shade. However, given the unlimited water and the availability of an abundance of reeds down by the lake that we could use for thatching our mess, cook's quarters and store, the arrangement was not far short of being ideal. For creating the framework of buildings we cut and imported poles from the infinite growth of the same down in the Itigi thicket to the south of the Drop Inn.

The *watu* were not slow to get moving on marking out a football pitch on an open area of the lake flats and to utilise the pitch for everyday recreation in association with the actively competitive participation of football enthusiasts from Mungaa. Footballs were obtained through the good offices of Mr Manji Dhanji at his store in Singida.

On the opposite side of the lake to the campsite, a long pinkish-white stippled trail of flamingos numbered in their hundreds shimmered and shifted this way and that as they fed in the muddy shallows. The tall birds seemed to be strutting on clouds mirrored in the lake water around them.

The biggest flamingo colonies of Tanganyika were found in the huge salt lakes Eyasi and Manyara way up to the north of us in the vicinity of Ngorongoro, but for all that, the flamingo colony on Lake Mianje was good enough for us to be going on with.

A hard-surfaced all-weather track led from Mungaa to the small village of Puma, twenty miles to the west on the Suna to Singida road. Singida was only a short fifteen miles drive away from Puma.

A second track from Mungaa headed northeast towards mighty open plains that swept a sea of grass around the foot of an extinct volcanic cone named Mount Hanang. On its way up to Mount Hanang this track followed the crest of an escarpment and commanded a view of the kind that conjured up thoughts of being shown in a moment of time all the kingdoms of the world and the glory of them. This wondrous panorama spread itself across the Kondoa district and the endlessly eastwards rolling Masai lands out in the far distance. At the deep down foot of an escarpment, Lake Balangida Lelu caught the sun's glance and winked at travellers.

The kingdoms of the world that were there for me to behold included those of Masai-related tribes named Watatoc, Wagorowa and Wairaqw who were of Hamitic and Nilo-Hamitic origin. Also there were the lands of the Wasandawe, who were click-speakers with Bushman roots. It seemed exotic enough to make Unyaturu seem very insignificant.

*

Yet, first things had to come first, and as an essential preliminary designed to promote (as it would be asking too much to guarantee) the smooth arrival and peaceful establishment of our camp near Lake Mianje, a statutory information *baraza* for Chief Omari Mpahi and his cohorts was organised to take place at Mungaa through the good offices of the Singida DC.

The DC delegated the chairmanship of the proposed *baraza* to one of his DOs. The job of the chairman was to provide all those attending the *baraza* with a clear and comprehensive explanation of where camps were to be set up; what sort of work would be done; what was involved in sampling technique; how samples would be taken; and how the people at the camp were keen to conduct all manner of trade with local entrepreneurs.

The attendees would be chiefs, sub-chiefs, headmen, tribal elders and what have you. Figurative cards would, it was hoped, be placed on the table by all interests present. Any questions from the floor would be welcomed and answers to the same would be guaranteed to let the questioner know what he wanted to know. The anticipated outcome would (hopefully) be complete satisfaction and co-operative understanding across the board.

The critical issue on the agenda related to soil sampling, which involved a suspicious-looking ritual of digging into and removing portions of local land in canvas bags that were head-shaped when full. In tribal society the ownership of land was a communal right to be defended at all costs, even unto death if needs must. The kind of misunderstandings concerning the interpretation of sampling practice that took place down in Ugogo and led to the murder of a young South African geologist by tribesmen were not to be repeated.

At the Mungaa *baraza* we needed to convince the assembly that our sampling didn't equate with theft of land; that sample bags did not contain either blood-soaked sand or human heads; and that the results of the sampling could possibly bring benefits to the local community. When I met the DO who was sent to chair the proceedings I hoped that he would put on a convincing performance on stage, as the first impression he gave me made me think that with him on our side we could be in trouble.

The DO was as thin as one of those infamous hippo-hide whips that the slave drivers called a *kiboko*, and the South Africans named a *sjambok*. He was as stiff in his bearing as the liberally applied starch that made his dress-khaki safari jacket and knife-edged shorts so rigid that his body moved independently of them. The garments could easily have stood up and conducted the *baraza* on their own. His shorts did us all a service by being long enough to cover up a pair of knobbly knees capable of taking first prize in a relevant contest at a Butlin's holiday camp.

The DO was unfortunate enough to have a pinched, hawk-like face and, even more unfortunately in my book, to speak English in a cut-glass public school accent that at once failed to endear him to me. Not to put too fine a point on it, all that he did subsequently to our first meeting merely served to confirm my first impression of him as a snooty little bantam cock full of his own importance and representing a range of the less admirable aspects of colonial administrators.

The DO made arrangements for the *baraza* to take place in the Mungaa courthouse at an appointed date and at a specified time, and so did it come to pass. The glory of the courthouse was vested much more in its title than in its appearance. It was a long, low structure capped by a peaked roof clad with sheets of corrugated metal and otherwise open on all sides to the attention of the elements and the scrutiny of the public. The courthouse floor was furnished by an array of wooden backless benches of a kind that I was familiar with from attending a weekly cinema when I was growing up in north Cornwall. The benches in the courthouse had been extremely well polished by the action of what would have been generations of fidgeting backsides covered by garments that were less clean than they ought to have been. It was difficult to imagine anyone attending a *baraza* in anything other than a state of reluctance to endure the kind of lengthy proceedings that, like it or not, were full of menace.

At the front end of the courthouse there was a small stage consisting of several planks of wood laid side by side on a set of trestles. It was not a very elevated stage, but even so the dignitaries who mounted it were required to mind their heads owing to the proximity of the roof above. On the stage stood two small tables and half a dozen spindly-backed wooden chairs fitted with seats of stretched cowhide. Each chair was an individual work of art in its own precarious right.

As the DO mounted the stage with a set of documents in one of his hands he managed to convey an impression that Kenneth Williams had arrived to commence rehearsals for a new episode of "Hancock's Half Hour".

As soon as the proceedings of the *baraza* commenced it was obvious that the DO spoke Kiswahili with a similar accent to the one that he applied to his English. Its effect was to make me cringe inwardly. I dreaded to think what it might be doing to the cream of Unyaturu society assembled down on the benches.

Although I wasn't at that time able to write in Kiswahili, I had learned to speak the up-country version reasonably well. I absorbed the *lingua franca* from the *watu* whom I worked with in the way that a baby might pick up its mother's tongue. I hoped that I spoke Kiswahili much as the *watu* did, although one of the *watu* once told me that my accent sounded a bit like that of an Arab. Perhaps he was damning me with faint praise. The DO probably learned his Kiswahili at a Foreign Office course "back home". Accent aside, he didn't so much talk to his audience as down to it. As he droned on and on my opinion of his performance was that for us he was more of a liability than a benefit—an asshole rather than an asset.

The DO held the chair at centre stage. Chief Omari Mpahi was seated to the DO's right in the manner of a truly anointed son. Buck and I were given chairs placed at left stage rear. Completing the cast at the table alongside Chief Omari Mpahi sat Mungaa's version of Hansard, a *karani* with a pen, a bottle of ink in which to dip the pen and a record book in front of him.

I cast my eye over the courthouse assembly. There were about fifty in attendance, and as far as I could judge there was not one of them who looked as if he was there for any other reason than that Chief Omari Mpahi had ordered him to come. Some of the fifty showed the kind of dusty weariness of men who had walked in from far away. The vestments on view were chiefly robes and rubber-tyre sandals offset by a few hats. Arising from the audience was a pungent odour of long-established sweat blended with wood smoke that seemed to lose little time in spreading to assert its dominance over the protagonists on the stage.

It was fairly obvious why the courthouse was left open on all sides. A breeze straggled in from outside but was unequal to the challenge of diluting the atmosphere. Although I had briefed the DO in detail beforehand on the various aspects of our work, he must have understood little of what he was told, as he behaved as if he was a lawyer wrapping up a few facts in a slippery welter of words in order to provide onlookers with an impression that he knew far more than he did.

In other words he was a consummate bullshit artist.

The formal protocol for the *baraza* did not allow either Buck or myself—or for that matter anyone other than the DO—to speak unless he was called on to do so, and as the DO didn't see fit to defer to anyone, we remained at the back of the stage listening in silence to what was in effect a one-man harangue directed at a compliant mass.

The key to the success of the exercise as far the compliant ones were concerned, was the implication that by his presence on stage Chief Omari Mpahi was a supporter of our work. With the Chief on board it mattered not what the DO either said or didn't manage to say, as there would be no dissent coming from any of the Chief's followers. Any opposition to the Chief's will would be made, or so the rumour had it, entirely at the dissident's risk to his own life or limb.

Chief Omari Mpahi could only be described as roly-poly obese. He sported a colourful rounded cap on his not inconsiderably sized head. His mighty bulk was clad in a smartly voluminous safari suit of light blue. The jacket was short-sleeved and the trousers were long. He wore the safari suit as if it was a fashion statement for absolute power.

As if to confirm that he was no ordinary man, Chief Omari Mpahi's feet were shod with genuine leather sandals featuring hand-tooled designs and bright buckles. The only rubber tyres that the good Chief was going to cover ground on with were still on the wheels of his official car. In his right hand he carried an elegant-looking fly whisk made from the tail of a wildebeest, of which there were very many on the hoof roaming the grassy plains around Mount Hanang to the north. A fly whisk was considered to be an essential accessory, both for prominent African politicians and less prominent would-be African politicians. It was Mr Jomo Kenyatta, the well-known Kenyan prison graduate whose release was imminent, who set the fly whisk standard for others to emulate. Even in the absence of flies from his vicinity Chief Omari Mpahi flicked his fly whisk repeatedly, using a lazily economical, well-practised hand action. I knew nothing of any political ambitions that he might or might not have entertained, although with *uhuru* in the air it would have been surprising if Chief Omari Mpahi, a man who was clearly addicted to power, didn't see himself taking up political responsibilities at some future juncture. His sub-chiefs and headmen sat through the entire proceedings of the *baraza* in an attitude of mute submission. For them there was only one man of importance on the stage, and it wasn't the DO.

The DO's performance in what was essentially a bun fight held in the absence of buns was seen by the audience as no more than a sideshow held within the imposing shadow of their Chief. When, with the conclusion of the DO's monologue, the *baraza* was at long last over, Chief Omari Mpahi heaved himself up on his expensively sandaled feet, turned to Buck and me as if was recognising us for the first time, and shook each of us by the hand. His seal of approval was thereby conferred on us. His disciples on the courthouse floor then left the scene without comment. The only sound they made as they left was in the rustle of robes and the shuffling tread of rubber-tyre soles on the hard-packed dirt beneath their feet.

The DO took his leave of us in a not dissimilar manner. He faded away in the direction of Singida like a Cheshire cat. I barely had time to thank him for his services. If I had known at the time that I would never see him again I could have provided him with an advance version of the Cheshire cat's smile. In spite of the DO's best efforts, it seemed that we were home and dry to go ahead with our camp and exploration plans.

I found it curious that Chief Omari Mpahi did not interject his voice into the proceedings at the *baraza*. Presumably there must have been some clarification of what he heard that would have been useful, and he might also have been motivated to make an occasional observation on the DO's discourse. It was probable that he didn't speak because, being an autocrat, he didn't need to. At least his *karani*, whose long-hand written technique of recording the minutes of the *baraza* moved as slowly and as hesitantly as a chameleon stalking a fly, didn't have to be subjected to the considerable stress of having to write down the Chief's words verbatim.

Whatever the message was that went out from our *baraza* in the Mungaa courthouse to the scattered villages within Chief Omari Mpahi's demesne, not one of the local problems that we experienced later on were related in any way to our sampling practices.

Chief Omari Mpahi was a not infrequent visitor to our camp once it was set up. I always made him welcome even on the occasions when

I didn't feel particularly welcoming towards him. The truth of it was that a little of his company went a long way. His visits to the camp were of a social nature and involved him demonstrating a mastery of freeloading technique that could have been the envy of any politician with *uhuru* set squarely in his sights.

He always arrived for his visits in his own chauffeur-driven car, which in both instances—chauffeur and car—looked slightly the worse for wear. Chief Omari Mpahi, however, was always turned out immaculately in a trademark safari suit, with only the colour of the safari suit of the day providing any variation on the theme. Fly whisk at the ready, he plonked himself down in our mess hut, called for refreshments, and drank his way through an impressive volume of beer for as long as our stock of the same held out. He drank his beer in conjunction with salt, his practice being to place a fair quantity of salt on the back of his left hand and take a lick at it prior to downing each great swig.

When I got to know him better in the course of time I found Chief Omari Mpahi to be an avuncular type who regarded style and image as being far more important than substance. I quite liked him, although I didn't really respect him, and I didn't trust him at all. It was prudent to be wary of such men whose power in their own sphere of influence was absolute.

On most of the occasions when he settled himself in the camp mess we talked of nothing much in particular. All of my attempts to interest him in the work we were doing fell short of success. He asked few questions, and he volunteered few genuine answers to questions I asked of him. Political topics were strenuously avoided. Although I gathered from him that he liked the concept of *uhuru*, it seemed that one-man-one-vote didn't fit at all into his philosophy of how a government should be installed.

The most interesting talk that I had with him concerned a current serialisation in the London *Sunday Times* newspaper (which I received on subscription and which normally arrived through the post a few weeks after its UK publication date) of a new edition of the diaries of Mr Henry Morton Stanley. One instalment offered a strong indication that Stanley had passed through the Mungaa area on an expedition towards Lake Victoria in the mid-1870s. From what I read in the newspaper it appeared that Stanley had made contact in the Mungaa area with local chiefs. I mentioned it to Chief Omari Mpahi, who for once expressed considerable interest.

Chief Omari Mpahi, who was the incumbent in a long succession of Wanyturu paramount chiefs, told me about an encounter with an *mzungu* and his retinue at Mungaa that existed within the oral scope of the tribe's historical tradition. From what he told me, the encounter took place at a date which suggested that the *mzungu* in question could only have been Stanley. It was intensely exciting to know that I was talking to a man whose grandfather or great-grandfather might have actually met Stanley.

On the other hand, Chief Omari Mpahi, encouraged by salt and beer, might have been indulging in that great tribal tradition of telling an *mzungu* what he thought the *mzungu* wanted to know. Chief Omari Mpahi was powerful enough not to need to tinker with the truth, but he also had political leanings which brought with them a mandate to be economical with the truth on demand.

*

With the *baraza* out of the way and Chief Omari Mpahi allegedly on our side, we set up a camp overlooking Lake Mianje, and proceeded to get on with our sampling programme. On the whole everything went quite well. Washing samples and reducing them down on the lakeshore were straightforward activities that the fishermen didn't object to. We took our finished samples, together with the appropriate records and reports down to the Manyoni service depot for onward submission to Mwadui, not omitting to drop in at the Drop Inn, both on the way down and on the way back.

My personal team of *watu*, headed by Efrem, formed the initial core of the Lake Mianje camp workforce. Since Buck, being new, still had no established team of his own, we hired a head *mtu* and a few likely-looking *watu* for him in Singida and filled out the rest of the complement that he needed by hiring local labour from Mungaa, as was promised at the *baraza*. With that particular sop to Chief Omari Mpahi's patronage completed, a *"Hakuna nafasi ya kazi"* sign was prepared and posted in a prominent position at the camp entry point.

Meat for the *watu* was purchased from Chief Omari Mpahi in the form of live cattle on the hoof. He sold us the cattle at a grossly inflated price, but as we were faced with Hobson's choice in the matter no complaints were made. In order to ensure that *halal* requirements were followed to the letter, we took the responsibility for slaughtering the animals onto our own shoulders.

This was the way it worked. A cow destined to provide an imminent issue of meat rations was driven to the lake flats below the camp by a cowherd who looked as if he could be at least five years old. He carried a stick to control his charge and wielded it like an expert, even though the stick was twice as long as he was.

Immediately after receiving the doomed animal from the cowherd, four of our *watu* manhandled and wrestled it flat on to the ground. Three of the four sat on the downed cow to keep it still while the fourth grabbed its horns to draw the head back and expose the throat to the ministrations of Taji and his keen-edged *halal* knife. With one swift stroke of Taji's knife the job was done. The copiously gushing blood was collected in sample washing pans to be borne away to the *watu* camp for which purpose I neither knew nor wanted to know.

I didn't like this process of bloody slaughter at all and eventually insisted on making some changes to set up a practice that seemed rather less inhumane. This involved me first of all shooting the cow in the head with my rifle. The shot dropped the cow in an instant, and even as it fell Taji ran in to pull his knife across the cow's throat and spill blood before the heart ceased pumping. In that way the *halal* criteria were apparently satisfied since the butchered beef meat went on to make rations that were consumed by all of the *watu* in camp, irrespective of their religious convictions.

It was not unlikely that throat-cutting hard on the heels of shooting could have provided profound material for a scholarly debate in any fundamentalist Islamic forum on the pros and cons of this amendment to *halal* practice, but as far as the *watu* were concerned the practice met with general approval and became adopted as a standard.

According to regulations as set out in the GFM, all meat purchased for the provision of rations was intended to be consumed by the *watu* in its entirety. That was perfectly fair. Following the aforementioned slaughter of a cow however, Paulo generally managed to come up with a choice piece of the same for *wazungu* delectation, and for our part we turned a blind eye to its provenance.

If throat-cutting was an art, the practice of butchery was not. *Pangas* and axes played the major roles in dissembling a slaughtered beast as indiscriminately as could ever be imagined. A small team of *watu* needed very little time to render a cow's carcass into a multitude of mangled portions. The technique of hacking that they employed looked as if it had been learnt on the basis of participation in post-battle massacres of a defeated enemy.

In terms of local purchases, *wazungu* meat supply normally involved only chickens. Local alternatives to poultry were considered too dodgy in quality for us to reckon with. The customary sources of meat that we used in camp at Lake Mianje were first of all a capable butcher in Singida whose shop we patronised a couple of times each month, and in the second place game hunted and shot under the auspices of a pot licence up on the grasslands around Mount Hanang.

*

Of all the district centres serving the areas in which I camped and worked in Tanganyika, Singida was my favourite. Singida was a free and easy town with an anything-goes atmosphere that would not have been out of place in the Wild West. I very much enjoyed my visits to Singida, and as often as not I returned to camp afterwards with a feeling of regret.

Singida, thanks to there being only a small number of relatively anonymous *wazungu* in its population, was a town blessed with few toffee-nosed pretensions. It did not aspire to be anything other than what it was—a kind of sleepy outpost marking the north end of the road coming up along the western edge of the Rungwa Game Reserve and on through Itigi from Chunya and Mbeya in the south. All points north of Singida were served by tracks of systematically reducing quality that eventually petered out in the Serengeti plains.

My *Handbook of Tanganyika*, as bought at the bookshop in Dodoma, recorded that the population of the Singida district numbered approximately three hundred thousand. Its population was the largest of all of the Central province districts. According to the most recent census declaration, the *wazungu* population of the Singida district, almost entirely associated with either government departments or religious missions, was only one hundred. Indians and Arabs numbered around six hundred and five hundred respectively, consisting largely of shopkeepers, merchants, and traders plus dependants. The vast majority of the population of Singida district was African, most of whom were Wanyaturu tribespeople.

The town of Singida was situated at an enervating altitude of four thousand nine hundred feet above sea level. Its key features included a government HQ *boma*; a hotel; a few bars; several shops and other commercial outlets; a barber who (surprisingly) was well able to cut *wazungu* hair; a small hospital; a garage described in the *Handbook* as offering "poor" facilities (which I found to be far from the truth); and a single cinema exclusively dedicated to the showing of Indian films that suited tastes other than mine.

The town's name of Singida was, according to the *Handbook*, derived from a local name (*msingida*) for a species of tree from which circlets of wood were cut and carved for tribal traditionalists to use as decorative inserts in open loops that were cut in their earlobes. An alternative explanation given for the naming of the town was linked to a belligerent tribal chief named Singeida (translating apparently as "zebra") who had lived in the general area very many years ago. He allegedly had the misfortune to be born on the day on which a zebra was killed for the purpose of providing medicinal items for his mother. Singeida could have been a distant ancestor of my pal Chief Omari Mpahi, although I didn't want to stretch my imagination quite that far.

*

When I was in Singida overnight I always stayed at the town's only hotel, which went under the nondescript name of "Central Hotel". I became great friends with its owner (and mine host in its bar) Mr Mohammed Ali Wolji and his son (and able assistant) Ranjit.

The general layout of the town of Singida was uncomplicated. The arrangement of the streets was not unlike a grid scratched out for a game of noughts and crosses. The commercial heart of the town comprised two relatively long parallel streets that were set a wide block apart and which rose gently in a southerly direction, together with a couple of cross streets, on one of which was located the Central Hotel.

In Singida nothing was ever very far away from anything else. On the west side of town the government *boma* stood like a small oasis of whitewashed privilege, with an inevitably associated club not much further on. Surrounding the town centre was a blur of mud huts and tin-roofed shacks by means of which the African population that dwelt therein could, if it liked, place the commercial sector under virtual siege.

Mr Mohammed Ali Wolji was short and rotund in a way that suited the best traditions of one who held the proprietorship of such a unique watering hole. He had a full head of jet-black wavy hair, which in a certain light aped the style made famous by Mr Spencer Tracy. With that particular characteristic accounted for, any further resemblance that Mohammed Ali bore to Mr Tracy was at an end. Mohammed Ali wore a style of thick-lensed glasses that provided him with the look of either a studious arbiter of momentous events, or a master of ceremonies who wished he could preside over festivities of the kind that he knew he would never come across in Singida.

He put most of his energy into dispensing beer across the bar of the Central Hotel in a room of rudimentary attributes. The bar was run entirely without reference or deference to race, creed or colour. It was a veritable melting pot. There was invariably a good crowd in it. Music that was surely popular with some of the bar's clientele—although who they were was never clear to me—belted out from a loudspeaker mounted at the right-hand side of the bar. The tones of the music, which were so tinny that they might have been recently mined, fought their way through a thick fug of clamour, of smoke hanging in memory of very many kali cigarettes, and of an intensity of customer-generated body odour that was a near marvel in its own right.

It went without saying that Mohammed Ali's *wazungu* patrons had little in common with the *wazungu* from the government *boma*. The latter inevitably gravitated to their club for the purpose of slaking individual thirsts that were no doubt as substantial as mine. I was never invited to set foot in the club and took comfort in knowing that, as a result, it was an establishment that I wouldn't get thrown out of. Perhaps the Singida club shared a black list with its Dodoma counterpart and had been forearmed with the information that I was coming.

The few *wazungu* who patronised the bar of Singida's Central Hotel bar typically consisted of WDL bush types in from their camps for a night or two plus any itinerant characters who were there by chance and whose interests lay in either commerce or hunting. The Central Hotel was a friendly haven designed mainly to accommodate short-stay guests.

Ranjit did not look a lot like his father since he was dramatically thinner and had a much darker skin than Mohammed Ali. His key distinguishing feature was gleaming hair as straight as a die, held down in orderly comb-tracked lines by virtue of regular applications of what I assumed was coconut oil. Had he washed his hair more often the fresher applications of coconut oil to his hair might not have had to fight so hard to overcome the smell of their slightly to positively rancid predecessors. A line of black down marked Ranjit's upper lip and pretended to be a moustache that was visible only if and when he turned his profile into the light.

The Central Hotel in which Mohammed Ali and Ranjit presided was built in the form of a single-storeyed blockhouse. Its myopic frontage stood on one of Singida's two significant cross streets. The door through which the hotel was entered was an open grille of stout metal filled in with multiple panes of thick frosted glass reinforced with wire mesh. Immediately above the top of the door a light bulb protected by a murky glass globe attracted countless insects when it was illuminated after dark. The consequence of this was that every time the door was opened, which was often, insects zoomed into the hotel corridor behind it.

Other than by the door, the monotony of the front wall of the Central Hotel was relieved by two small windows that looked like a pair of weary eyes. The window on the left side of the door was associated with one of the hotel's guest rooms. The window on the right opened into the dining-room.

The hotel's layout was simple. On entering, the guest was faced with a long and narrow dim corridor receding into the near distance. Let into the left wall of the corridor were six doors in succession, individually marked with numbers and each providing access to a separate guest room. The guest rooms were clean and comfortable. Each contained two beds fitted with starched sheets and all-enveloping mosquito nets that had the virtue of being free of any holes large enough to admit a mosquito. In addition there were a couple of wooden chairs for guests to sit on and a single table for them to sit at. Mohammed Ali allocated the rooms to incoming guests on a first-come-first-served principle. I sometimes got a room to myself, but it was always a matter of chance as to who might be allocated the second bed as the Guest Book filled up.

On the right-hand side of the main corridor there were only two doors, one of which led into the bar, the other into the-dining room. The dining-room was big enough to be fit for purpose, although its dimensions were much smaller than those of the bar. The food served to guests in the dining-room was prepared by Mrs Mohammed Ali

Wolji in a kitchen located in the Wolji family living quarters out beyond the far end of the corridor. It was most excellent food, a perfect fusion of classical Indian spices with locally grown vegetables such as yams, okra, tomatoes and a mighty abundance of chillies. Mutton curry as the dish of one day tended to alternate with spicy chicken stew on the next. What the menu lacked in variety it made up for in quality.

*

When he visited Singida from his camp, a WDL prospector named Bill Hilditch, who enjoyed a fearsome reputation for not suffering fools gladly, habitually booked himself into the Central Hotel for a stay covering three or four nights. On his arrival he entered the room exclusively allocated to him and to him alone, and as far as I was aware he left it only to proceed to and from the hotel's communal lavatory in accordance with a not infrequent call of nature.

Ranjit, who served as Bill's sole contact and batman-like intermediary for the duration, was kept busy delivering a steady succession of full bottles of beer to Bill's room and then removing the empties. The beer flowed freely, and following a short time lapse so did Bill's bladder. I learned very quickly that if I chanced to meet Bill when he was on his way either to the lavatory or back to his room I should offer him no greetings. I greeted him once only and the biting vituperation of his response made me twice shy ever after. Bill was always sober when he came to the Central Hotel and always appeared to be sober when he left. As to Bill's condition in between his arrival and departure, only Ranjit knew about it for sure, and Ranjit didn't tell tales.

The integrity of the Central Hotel's front door was sorely tested late one night when Bob McLeod (the self-same Bob who once claimed as his own the eland that I shot and who stammered almost uncontrollably when he was sober and not at all when he wasn't) allegedly targeted the light above the door using a .38-calibre handgun. At the particular moment of the shooting Bob was not stammering at all.

A licence to carry a handgun was so difficult to obtain under all but absolutely extreme circumstances that to all intents and purposes acquiring one was a near impossibility. It could have been safely assumed that Bob's handgun was not licensed. At the wheel of his Land Rover, Bob made a couple of slow passes along the street at the front of the hotel, cracked off two shots at the light each time, and then sped off into the night. All of Bob's shots missed their intended target. Two of his bullets hit the hotel wall, and each of the other two blew holes in the door's frosted glass panes and sped along much of the length of the inner corridor where one buried itself in a wall and the other in a ceiling. The hour was late, the bar was closed and the entire hotel was at rest. By the grace of *Mungu* the corridor was unpopulated when the bullets came in.

I was staying in the hotel at the time of the shooting and, thanks to a prior surfeit of beer, some of it taken in Bob's company, I was oblivious to what took place. The broken panes in the door were initially attributed to an act of vandalism, with WDL men not unjustifiably placed high on the list of suspects. Following a subsequent report of shots being heard in the night in the vicinity of the Central Hotel, Mohammed Ali called on those bold yet wary public guardians who were the Singida police to conduct an investigation. It did not take the police long to discover the bullet marks and determine the true nature of the incident. I didn't know if the police ever made a related arrest, since they certainly never caught up with Bob. They did, however, look on all WDL types with ever more jaundiced eyes than usual for some time thereafter.

I came into contact with this increased police surveillance one night when I was patronising a bar located on Singida's main street. The bar was raided by a squad of police in what was allegedly a routine measure designed to round up the usual suspects.

The raid was carried out in a heavy-handed manner. There were about a score of people in the bar, among whom I was the only *mzungu* present when the police came in. The police appeared eager to meet the kind of resistance that could provide them with a *carte blanche* opportunity to break as many heads as they could. All of us were forcibly herded into the outer darkness where a police truck fitted with a cage at its back stood in readiness for our reception. We were goaded to enter the cage and then locked into it to be driven all of fifty yards down the street to reach the police station where, following disembarkation, we were ordered to form a queue prior to being individually questioned.

I felt much more nervous than scared, not knowing what to expect. At the same time I took some pride in a sense of solidarity with my erstwhile bar companions. We were presumably all guilty of one thing or another, but in the matter of our being together in the bar we were entirely innocent. I would have been upset if I had been excluded from the roundup on the basis of skin colour.

When my turn to be questioned came up I was asked what I had been doing in the bar. It was, my interrogator informed me, not a favourite haunt of *wazungu*. The police wanted to know exactly how I came to be acquainted with the people with whom I had been rounded up. In fact I didn't really know any of my companions particularly well, but for the sake of appearances I decided to tell the police that they were all *warafiki yangu* (my friends). With that declaration made I was surprisingly permitted to walk away from the police station without a stain on my character related to the raid. Only *Mungu* knew that my character was not stain free in more than a few other respects.

I was in the bar where the raid took place on a number of subsequent occasions and, as luck would have it, I experienced no more police raids. One incident did occur, however, when I left the bar one very dark night and failed to step onto a broad concrete slab that served to bridge a four feet deep storm drainage culvert intervening between the front of the bar and the street. The consequence was that I stepped unexpectedly into the open culvert and hit the bottom with a thump that jarred most of my bones and gave me a shock that left me wondering who I was, let alone where I was.

I lay on the floor of the culvert for a while, trying to decide if I was alive or dead, and went on to assume that the former condition applied when my companions hauled me out. I was badly shaken although fortunately not injured beyond having grazed my elbows and knees. On the other hand, down at the bottom of the culvert I came into intimate contact with a seep of what was euphemistically referred to as "night soil". It could truly be alleged that when I fell into the culvert I was *mavini*. As I was being pulled out I couldn't help thinking of the words of an old song, "you must know a man who boozes by the company he chooses—and the pig got up and slowly walked away".

The street on which the precipitous culvert, the bar of the late raid and the police station stood also contained the trading establishment of Mr Manji Dhanji and the workshop of an Indian *fundi* (craftsman) who befriended me, much to my gratification.

The *fundi* went by the name of Babu, It correctly resonated that he was a fatherly figure held in great affection by those who knew him. Babu was first and foremost a shoemaker by trade, but as if that was not enough he also ran a vehicle service and repair workshop. Through what he did he showed that the intricacies of shoemaking and the search for mechanical solutions had much in common.

The vehicle repair side of Babu's business, which was by no means as poor as the *Handbook of Tanganyika* had claimed, was managed by one of Babu's close relatives. It was known throughout the district as "Babu Garage" which I always took to offer much more of a tribute to Babu than "Babu's Garage" would have conferred. I met Babu on business related to his garage and got to know him better through his shoemaking.

Tony Knowles showed me a pair of knee-high leather boots made to measure for him by Babu. The boots were beautifully fashioned and finished, ultra comfortable on Tony's feet and legs from the first fitting. They were partly designed to minimise the risk of Tony being bitten by a snake anywhere below the knee, which was the sector of the body considered to be most vulnerable to snakebite.

After seeing Tony's boots I had no hesitation in commissioning from Babu not only a similar pair in brown leather but also a pair of heavy leather brogues. As it was, I only wore the boots a few times while traversing in the bush owing to their propensity to allow grains of sand, small pebbles, thorny twigs, dry leaves and grass seeds to fall into them at the top and cause not inconsiderable discomfort. The boots were works of art, but one couldn't have everything.

Babu made shoes to order on a veranda-like platform open to the street at the front of Babu Garage. A flight of wooden steps led up to the veranda from the street. To commence my footwear commission he required me to remove the *velskoon* I was wearing and to place my stocking-clad feet flat down on a large piece of brown paper, He ran a stubby pencil around the outside of my feet to prepare a basic sole outline, and with that as a form of guide he moved on to cutting appropriate pieces of leather from sheets of the same that were both supple and hard. The various pieces were brought together in the finished items of footwear using a range of traditional skills.

Babu sat cross-legged on the veranda as he shaped, carved, trimmed, moulded, sewed and united his pieces of leather. On one side of the veranda he kept a heavy-duty stitching machine, although mostly he seemed to prefer to do his sewing by hand.

I spent many good hours sitting on the wooden steps to chat with

Babu as he worked and never tired of delighting in observing his expertise. Babu's customers, including me, were required to visit him regularly while their shoes were in preparation for fitting and adjusting on, under and around the toes, heels, feet, ankles and (in the case of boots) the lower legs. Then, lo and behold, one day the customer would arrive to be presented with a pair of wonderful shoes that fit his feet as if they were made to measure, which come to think of it they actually were.

Babu, in keeping with his larger than life image as a *fundi*, was a most corpulent man. He contained the folds of his great belly under a sarong, worn purely for comfort. Although he exuded jollity and friendship, Babu was nevertheless a man of business. Insofar as he was Indian it would have been most odd if an eye to making a good deal hadn't been fundamental to his makeup.

I progressed from spending time with him at his place of work to being invited into his home to partake of whatever meal was on the floor at the time. Mrs Babu was an equally voluminous lady made to look even larger under the all-encompassing cover of a colourful sari. Babu and his wife had at least seven big-eyed children all below the age of twelve, each one of them appearing ultra-thin in contrast to their parents. The children looked at me with a mixture of interest, curiosity and not a little suspicion.

The Babu family meals that I shared were communal affairs. We squatted to eat in a circle on the cement floor around a centrally placed enamel basin of mammoth proportions and heaped high with steaming rice. The rice was accompanied on the side by a number of both vegetarian and non-vegetarian dishes and a tall stack of freshly made chapattis. We used our right hands to pick up the food—immersing a ball of rice or a torn off piece of chapatti in one or other of the accompanying dishes and transferring the same directly to the mouth and letting the drops fall where they might. Politeness ruled, but no one waited for anyone who moved slowly. The meals that I took with Babu and his family were among the most enjoyable that I had anywhere in Tanganyika. There was enough heat and spice in Mrs Babu's cooking to make hair curl even under a thick application of coconut oil.

Babu's kindness and consideration for me were heart-warming and never to be forgotten. I could only trust that Babu and his family would be deemed pre-eminent among those who didn't need a pair of running shoes when Mr Manji Dhanji got in a stock.

In my eyes, both Babu and Mohammed Ali Wolji were Singida's most virtuous sons.

*

The ever-bespectacled Mr Manji Dhanji was tall, dark, heavy and greasy in appearance. He was an utterly consummate man of business who considered that he would ultimately be far more right in the way he conducted trade than any of his customers would ever be. His business dealings were something of a well constructed maze—he lurked at the centre with the sole aim of luring customers into the labyrinth and placing on them an obligation to remain there until he came to get them and suck them dry.

If we bought our camp supplies from anyone other than Mr Manji Dhanji in Singida it needed to be done as a cloak-and-dagger-styled operation in order to keep Mr Manji Dhanji in the dark. We then had to make an exit from town by a circuitous route so as to avoid driving anywhere near Mr Manji Dhanji's store for fear that he or one of his agents would spot what our Land Rover was carrying.

I made a cardinal error one day in pulling up my Land Rover in front of Babu Garage with two sacks of groundnuts bought from someone other than Mr Manji Dhanji in the back of it. As Mr Manji Dhanji's store was located directly across the street from Babu Garage I realised too late that I had entered into a danger zone in which I could be easily spotted when in possession of contraband. Mr Manji Dhanji charged out of his store and across the road, demanding to know from where the two sacks of groundnuts had originated. He left me in no doubt that he considered me guilty of the worst kind of betrayal. He seemed close to tears.

Forced into a corner and required for once to think on my feet, I assured him that the groundnuts hadn't been bought from anyone, they were actually a gift. I could judge from his agitation that he didn't believe me for a moment, even if he wasn't prepared to accuse me of lying. To mollify him I told him that I was at that very moment on my way to purchase four sacks of *posho* from him. He at once retreated back across the road to his store to get ready for the said transaction that I had no choice but to follow up.

To his credit, Mr Manji Dhanji nominally fixed his charges for supplies at more or less the going rate and chose to deviate upwards only when he thought he could get away with it. Since he was a well practised shark, getting away with it was something he often did. Cold beer (sold to us at cost) was available in yet another small-room-out-at-the-back of his store in which a couple of chairs and a small splintery table were placed for the ease of customers.

The beer-taking pitch was to some extent queered by the fact that a toilet cubicle, devoid of a door, opened up off one corner of Mr Manji Dhanji's small back room. Apart from its capacity to attract flies, the presence of the toilet cubicle did little to maintain freshness in its immediate atmosphere. The toilet itself was of the "hole in the floor" variety. A couple of long tiles set in the floor in front of the hole signified the recommended location of the feet for those who wanted to use the facility. The feet were placed on the tiles from a position of either facing or backing onto the hole, and then all the user had to do was take aim and fire away.

There was ample evidence that many previous users of that toilet had not exactly been on target, whether or not they had been using it either in or out of paw paw season.

17

Matata mingi sana

Lots of trouble

Since there were twenty-five or more *watu* resident in our camp at Lake Mianje it was not possible for us to take more than a few of them at a time into Singida for recreational purposes because passenger numbers were limited on the available Land Rover transport. Numbers were further restricted thanks to the Land Rover normally being required to return to camp loaded with supplies. As a consequence, many of the *watu* decided to satisfy their after-working-hours cravings and recreational desires by attending to the fleshpots of Mungaa over on the far side of the lake.

Mungaa presented the *watu* with seemingly unlimited access to *pombe*, *moshi* (in all probability) and women, all of which combined to provide numerous opportunities for inter-personal or inter-tribal altercations, not omitting face to face confrontations and hand to hand combat. Tribal differences and *pombe* always made an explosive mixture. Although I knew that we were likely to have some difficulties with the local people, I had assumed these would all be of a relatively minor kind that would be reasonably easy to contain.

There were so many regular calls for me to get out the medicine chest in order to treat the *watu* who came along with bloody noses, bruised cheeks and skinned knuckles that it all became pretty much a routine with no questions worth asking of the afflicted beyond the standard one as to how the other parties had fared. There were, however, a few incidences of badly cut arms, one of which was additionally broken, which were beyond the treatment capability of our supply of medical materials and our inexpert medical know-how to treat. One of the *watu* turned up outside my tent one evening to show me a thin jet of blood jumping a full three inches horizontally out of a deep knife wound just below his knee.

For all injuries we provided immediate first-aid to the extent that we could, and then, depending on the severity of the situation, we sent the patients either to the nearest mission clinic or to the hospital in Singida. Referrals of patients to the hospital were frequent enough to permit the hospital's senior sister in charge, who was named Hanna and who came originally from Mbeya, to become a virtual member of our extended camp community. Sister Hanna occasionally carried her banner as well in the bar of the Central Hotel, where she made it plain that her motto was diametrically opposed to the one in which all work and no play made a dull girl of her. She was anything but a dull girl.

The most serious wound inflicted on one of our *watu* on a visit to Mungaa was a one-inch wide stab wound in his lower abdomen. Blood bubbled from the wound as if the knife used in the stabbing had tapped into a spring. The wound was treated and sewn up at the Singida hospital, and that was that. The fun at Mungaa could continue unabated. With this stabbing a point seemed to have been reached at which it was fairly clear that our *watu* as a whole were not being held in high regard by local residents. It was worrying to think that the camp was well on the way to becoming an isolated island set in a sea of resentment. Inter-tribal conflicts were almost impossible to resolve amicably—a fact of life that was confirmed when I consulted Chief Omari Mpahi and requested him to intercede by placing a diplomatic word here and there. He listened to me, nodded sagely, offered a few non-committal words in response and went on in the manner of an aspiring politician to do nothing further.

The situation turned critical when John Mwita (he of the glowing testimonial) was accused of raping a Mungaa woman. As there was no direct evidence accompanying the accusation the alleged crime was impossible to prove, although since John Mwita was involved any benefit of the doubt was difficult to apply. A small mob of angry local tribesmen gathered on the lake flats below the camp from where they bayed threats up at us for a while only to disperse when Chief Omari Mpahi turned up to assume command. The Chief came into the camp mess, drank beer, licked salt and expressed a feeling of extreme disquiet over the deterioration of our relationship with his tribal subjects. He went on to suggest that a second *baraza* of his sub-chiefs and headmen should be called in order to defuse the current situation. On that basis, said Chief Omari Mpahi, the slate could be wiped clean and a fresh start made.

With respect to John Mwita, that mutual thorn-in-our-feet, Chief Omari Mpahi demanded his dismissal. Since I had already decided to sack John Mwita, in his remarks to me the Chief was preaching to the converted. At the same time I wasn't quite as sympathetic to Chief Omari Mpahi's approach as he would have liked to think I was. I believed that in Mungaa the camp *watu* were more sinned against than they were sinners.

Chief Omari Mpahi concluded his discourse by dropping broad hints to the effect that a little monetary compensation wouldn't go amiss if it was placed within his easy reach, and moreover he undertook to be the conduit for the onward distribution of the compensation once it was received.

I accepted the chief's *baraza* suggestion with alacrity, and it was with alacrity that he reacted since the baraza was arranged and carried out all within the space of the two subsequent days. In contrast to the DO-chaired original *baraza* that presaged our arrival in the area, the second *baraza* was less formal in character and attracted far fewer participants. Once again, however, the Mungaa courthouse was the venue and the stage was furnished for the proceedings much as before. The same *karani* sat on the stage on the same chair with the same minutebook opened at a page in front of him that was as blank as was the expression on his face.

Chief Omari Mpahi took the chair. He delivered a lengthy harangue in which, in what were the most strident of tones, he denounced our camp and all that therein was and all who therein dwelt. His audience on the benches before him drank in his words and needed no salt to assist in the task of swallowing them entire. The Chief's bombast all went down on paper in the *karani's* longhand and long-winded record book as if it were being written in letters of blood.

As very little of what the chief said at the *baraza* was in accordance with what he had previously told me he would say, I should have felt betrayed by him, but I let that go as it seemed that the Chief was simply conducting the game according to his own rules. I was coming to realise that a man like Chief Omari Mpahi used his power over others to push his own agenda rather than to seek out justice. The Chief was a master of superficiality.

Since there was no reasonable alternative open to me, I chose to assume that Chief Omari Mpahi, in saying what he did, was "playing to the floor". I imagined that he was subliminally racking up the amount of monetary compensation that he would no doubt disburse to his own satisfaction at the conclusion of the *baraza*.

As it was, he ordered us to pay a sum in the way of a fine of five hundred shillings. The fine was levied on the basis of no hard evidence supported by a heap of carefully selected false witnesses. I made one interjection during the proceedings of the *baraza* to the effect that at our camp we had always shown ourselves open to build co-operative relationships with the local people. Had not Chief Omari Mpahi been an honoured guest at the camp on numerous occasions? Did I not consider him to be my friend?

Warming to this theme, while taking care to stop short of asking, "If you prick us do we not bleed?" as that might have been highly inappropriate under the circumstances, I alluded to the various occasions on which the chief and I had broken bread and imbibed libations together at the camp. Unfortunately my rendering of the drinking aspect of our social intercourse (*sisi me kunywa pamoja*), was understood by those present who spoke Kiswahili better than me (which didn't leave many out) to signify that Chief Omari Mpahi and I had got drunk in one another's company.

At this revelation, a sharp intake of collective breath from the floor indicated either a shared perception by his gathered subjects that Chief Omari Mpahi had just been maligned or otherwise that my remarks had correctly caught a key aspect of the true character of the man, notwithstanding that in the view of his people the Chief was infallible, no matter what antics he got up to. I sat down thinking that the best option was to let events move as they might and wondered if Stanley had faced similar problems on his way through the district. I concluded that he probably had.

In addition to the five hundred shillings fine, Chief Omari Mpahi placed a banning order on *watu* from the camp making visits to *pombe*-dispensing outlets at Mungaa until further notice. The ban lasted for all of a day before it collapsed under the weight of the unspoken consensus of those on both sides of the commercial divide. A day was as long as the purveyors of *pombe* were prepared to stick it out and tolerate the lost custom.

I was very relieved when the *baraza* concluded, and in my relief I felt that we had come through it with no genuinely hard feelings remaining. When Chief Omari Mpahi rose from his chair and strode across the stage flourishing his fly whisk and bearing a devious smirk on what I was increasingly coming to think of as his *nguruwe*-like face, however, I changed my mind.

Even though I knew full well that I couldn't stop the Chief from visiting our camp when he wanted to, I resolved that when he came he would be made to sense that he wasn't welcome. I hoped in my heart that he had enjoyed his last glass of beer and shake of salt at my expense because he wouldn't be getting another. Yet, what the hell, I expected that when push came to shove, goodwill would prevail. Bush hospitality wasn't a tap for anyone to turn on and off.

*

The final item of any other business on the agenda was the question of the immediate future of John Mwita. He simply had to be got rid of without delay. I had little experience of sackings and hated to think that I had to fire someone. It was not difficult to appreciate the motives that had driven Mike Annesley to give John Mwita an over-the-top letter of recommendation in order to ease the acrimony of John Mwita's departure. However, John Mwita was not going to get a testimonial from me this time.

On my return to our camp after the *baraza* the first thing I did was to ask Antanasio to gather together John Mwita's papers and his current *kipande* and to calculate the amount of pay due to the miscreant. With that task done I called for John Mwita to come to the mess hut where, with trepidation, I informed him that we no longer required his services, citing the grounds of unbecoming conduct which had jeopardised the security of all of the rest of us in camp. I presented him with his papers, told him how much he was going to be paid—inclusive of his allowance for immediate transport to Singida and onwards to his home in Usukuma—and as he couldn't write I invited him to accept it all by making his thumbprint in the required place in lieu of a signature.

John Mwita didn't receive the news of his dismissal very well, although he must have expected that it was coming. He began to remonstrate with me in a loud voice, holding and waving his hands on high in a symbolic refusal to set his thumbprint on any document at any time. I told him that whether or not he confirmed his agreement with a thumbprint was immaterial. The camp was finished with him. He had to take the money coming to him and leave camp at once; one of our Land Rovers was ready to drive him and his belongings to Singida. Once he got to Singida he would be on his own.

In hindsight I could almost certainly have handled the appreciably charged situation with more consideration, but at the time unfortunately John Mwita didn't shape up as an *mtu* meriting much consideration from anyone.

I stood up, intending to take hold of John Mwita's right hand and guide it to the place of signature. On one occasion at Iwambala I saw Tom carry out a similar action on a recalcitrant *mtu* who, like John Mwita, was also up for dismissal. That *mtu* was known as Majani (grass) on the basis of a grass green shirt that he wore constantly. Tom always referred to him as "that green bugger".

My success in obtaining a thumb print through coercion was far in arrears of that of the more practised Tom. John Mwita reacted to my approach by pushing both of his outstretched hands at my chest and shoving his lowered head forward in the attitude of a charging buffalo bull. I was sure that he was about to attack, and as an instinctive counter I swung my right fist towards him. My fist collided with the top of John Mwita's head. A jangling shock ran up the whole length of my right arm from fist to shoulder. The arm seemed to have been struck by a bolt of lightning.

John Mwita turned away from me on his rubber-tyre heels, leapt out of the mess hut and ran off towards Lake Mianje, screaming at the top of his voice as he made his way down slope. By the time I looked out he was sprinting across the lake flats in the direction of Mungaa (where I guessed he might not be received with open arms) while still maintaining a steady stream of shrill invective.

I asked Efrem to take a couple of the *watu* and go and find John

Mwita and tell him that he had one hour to return to camp in order to be taken to Singida in the Land Rover. Efrem took John Mwita's papers and pay to hand over to the latter. The incident had shaken me to the core, not least along the line of my right arm. Efrem and the two *watu* caught up with John Mwita, who took his documents and pay from them but still refused to append his thumbprint to anything. Nor did he come back to be taken to Singida and, as a consequence, he was left to his own devices as to where he went and how he would get there.

According to what Efrem told me, John Mwita intended to report me to both the police and a labour union in Singida on the alleged grounds of unfair dismissal and an assault on his person. All in all, the day was turning out not to have been the best one that I had spent to date in Tanganyika. John Mwita worried me a lot more than I was prepared to admit. Whatever the rights and wrongs of the situation that I found myself in might be, I realised again that in the march towards *uhuru* justice was unlikely to favour the party with the white face.

I was unable to sleep much during the night following the *baraza* at Mungaa and the subsequent sacking of John Mwita. Part of what kept me awake was the thought of John Mwita stealing back into camp in the dark with vengeance in mind. Jack and Shen, our two camp dogs, were good at alerting us to the proximity of wandering game (not that there was much of that around Lake Mianje for them to practise on), but they weren't quite so vigilant when it came to dealing with *watu*. The main thing preventing me from sleeping, however, was a constantly shooting pain in my right hand and forearm. The hand was severely swollen and I was unable to move the little finger which appeared to have sunk a couple of inches in the direction of my wrist. Whatever John Mwita's personal failings were—and they were many—I knew by then that softness of head was not numbered among them.

By the next morning my right hand was to all intents and purposes incapacitated. The discomfort it caused was so intense that it left me with no choice but to be driven into Singida in order to get it attended to at the hospital. Since I was going to Singida a further attempt was made before I left to locate John Mwita and take him with me. I learned that he returned to the camp in the night to collect and bundle up his belongings and had left camp afterwards, carrying the bundle. As to where he had gone no one knew for sure, but it was suggested by one of the *watu* that he had hitched a lift into Singida during the hours of darkness on the back of a truck out of Mungaa.

I was treated at the Singida hospital by a middle-aged *mzungu* doctor ably assisted by Sister Hanna. The doctor pronounced that my little finger was dislocated and chided me with some indignation over my delay in coming in for treatment. He told me that I had made his task of putting the digit back in place so much more difficult as a consequence, and he cited the increased swelling and accompanying tendency of the little finger joints to seize up as the result of the delay. He and Sister Hanna then proceeded to conduct a tug of war with my right hand, she heaving on the wrist and the doctor hauling on and manipulating the little finger.

The job was done without the benefit of local anaesthetic (which I suspected the doctor thought would serve me right) and the pain flooded over me in far more sick waves than I cared to remember before the little finger was pulled back into its rightful place to be properly strapped up and secured.

As a requirement for his report on my treatment the doctor asked me how the dislocation injury had occurred. I told him that I had stumbled over a rock and fallen on my hand. He looked long and hard at me, but made no observation, and so a false cause was recorded for posterity. As I departed, he gave me a second look, this one more searching than the former.

"You didn't really fall, did you?" he asked, placing a pronounced accent on "really".

It was a question and yet at the same time it was a statement. I didn't want to lie again so I answered by giving a slight shrug of the shoulders. As my eyes met his I knew that he knew more or less what I knew, and left it at that.

With the restoration of my right hand now complete (bar the healing process), it seemed fitting that prior to heading back to camp I should pay a visit to the Central Hotel to partake of the hospitality of my friend Mohammed Ali. He was as welcoming as ever.

While I was in the midst of the process of depleting the contents of a tall glass of beer, an *mtu* whom I was acquainted with from previous sessions in Mohammed Ali's establishment entered the bar, approached me, and presented me with a sealed envelope that he drew from one of his pockets. I liked his friendly company and quite admired him for the distinction of his having a relatively clean and essentially sweat-free normal appearance.

The *mtu* was a leading light in the Singida branch of the Tanganyika Transport and General Workers Union (the TTGWU), an organisation motivated by (thus far) great aspirations that were unfortunately supported by little political clout. He told me once that when the day of *uhuru* finally dawned the TTGWU was going to acquire every bit of the we-are-the-masters-now muscle that it so yearned for. His words conjured up a vision of Mr Robb Wilton commencing one of his famous monologues with, "The day *uhuru* broke out, my missis said to me…"

I took the sealed envelope from him with my left hand, opened it up as best I could, and withdrew from it a single sheet of paper bearing a typed invitation for me to attend a hearing at the offices of the TTGWU, located not far away from the Central Hotel in the direction of the government HQ, to consider the case of John Mwita's wrongful dismissal. It sounded as if the TTGWU had already chosen its side. The date set for the hearing was one week hence, which was fortunate for the TTGWU if not for me as I was due to return to Singida on that self-same day to have the condition of my right hand re-examined at the hospital. At the foot of the letter of invitation, handwritten in ink, were set in sequence the four letters "RVPZ". A little knowledge of the etiquette of invitation writing was clearly a dangerous thing in the remit of the TTGWU. John Mwita had let no grass grow under his feet in making contact with the organisation, and albeit grudgingly, I had to grant him a measure of approval for his enterprise.

In hindsight I should no doubt have taken informed advice on my best course of action regarding the TTGWU issue, but RVPZ spoke for itself and I told the bearer of the letter there and then that the TTGWU could count on me attending the scheduled hearing.

The TTGWU offices would have been more appropriately described as the TTGWU office as what there was consisted of a single room in a windowless mud-walled hut that was roofed over with the inevitable sheets of corrugated metal. To the lack of political clout of the TTGWU could be added a perceived lack of monetary resources. I arrived at the said office at the appointed date and at the precise time set for the hearing. There to meet me was the bearer of the previous week's RPVZ invitation, together with what I assumed were three of his TTGWU colleagues. John Mwita was, much to my relief, not present.

The office was furnished with an unsurprisingly ancient wooden table and an array of unmatched and equally antique wooden chairs. The floor was made of dusty cement. The filing system on display consisted of many jumbled documents piled up in corners and a few other documents, presumably representing current business, mounted on black-plastic-coated clipboards suspended from nails driven at various angles into the mud of the dingily whitewashed walls.

The hearing began, and it was immediately clear that current policy was one of giving a fair trial as the precursor to a hanging. There were four of them against one of me. Each of the four vied with the other three to find out who could adopt the most aggressive attitude. The one whom I already knew showed an unpleasant side to his character that hadn't ever been hinted at in our Central Hotel bar association. It was another wind-of-change sign of the times that I was starting to get used to.

I was increasingly saddened to realise that no matter how cordial I thought were the personal relationships that I enjoyed with all types and conditions of the people of Tanganyika, there was a lot of finely balanced superficiality about it. When the balance was tipped it was never going to favour the likes of me. I was sure that if the roles were reversed I would probably behave exactly as they did.

My four opponents appeared to want to all talk at the same time. Each one of them demonstrated an impressive lack of willingness to concede the floor to any of his fellows. The gist of their argument could be summed up in one question: namely, what was I going to do about John Mwita? The TTGWU quartet demanded that he should be reinstated immediately in his former job. When they saw that that was impossible for me to agree to, they deliberated at length and moved on to Plan B, which called for substantial compensation to be paid to John Mwita in recognition of the loss of future income following his "unfair" dismissal; and for what they implied was the trauma caused to John Mwita by my alleged assault on the top of his head.

As I had been at the hospital just prior to the start of the hearing to have the bandages removed from my right hand, there was no direct evidence of that hand in closed-fist format having come into contact with anything. If I extended the hand out flat with palm down, however, my little finger stuck out at an acute angle to the index finger; but I didn't show them that.

I gave them an account of John Mwita's employment record and the problems that he had caused for all of us who worked with him, but it all fell on four pairs of deaf ears. They simply weren't interested in any evidence supporting John Mwita's dismissal. I suspected that the TTGWU hearing had no legal standing and believed that I could have simply walked out and left them to argue among themselves— although that would have provided no resolution of the case. It was in the interest of all five of us present to settle the thing as amicably as possible and let the welter of talk work itself through.

Expressing a regret that I hadn't already done so, I suggested to them that the best I could do was to pay John Mwita for an extra full *kipande* in lieu of notice and add on an allowance to augment the travelling expenses for his return to Usukuma that he had already received. The suggestion was then tabled as a firm proposal.

With the scent of money in their nostrils, the TTGWU four put their heads together and showed an altogether keen sense of willingness to make a settlement. The deal was clinched when I offered to give the money directly to them so that they could hand it over to John Mwita. They agreed to the offer with almost unseemly haste, and declared that they would not only handle the transaction but would ensure that I got John Mwita's thumbprint for receipt of the same.

I left the agreed amount of money plus a little extra with my four erstwhile interrogators, and for a second occasion in Singida I was free to take up my stain-free character and walk away.

I was certain that I would never get to see John Mwita's thumbprint, and needless to say, I didn't. If any of the money that I left at the TTGWU office ever went into John Mwita's hand, I would have *mekula kofia yangu* (eaten my hat) in good heart.

*

That in effect concluded the saga of John Mwita, yet all was still not lost in terms of the potential for dastardly deeds connected with the camp at Lake Mianje. Not long afterwards the diminutive Saidi Mohammedi, that lost *mtu* of Iseke, unexpectedly turned up looking about as destitute and undernourished as a wandering *mtu* could—all things being relative of course.

Saidi's movements during the string of elapsed weeks separating his disappearance and resurrection remained a mystery, as did his motivation for returning. He looked diminished and had clearly walked a very long way. It was impossible not to feel sorry for him. I was very glad to see him again, and at once took him back on the camp payroll with a position in my traverse gang. It was as if a prodigal son had come home. All that the situation lacked was a fatted calf to shoot and *halal* in his honour. On the other hand there wasn't much fat on any of the cattle that trod the soil in the land held in thrall by Chief Omari Mpahi.

Approximately two weeks later, an hour or two after the fall of darkness when I was inside my tent getting ready to retire for the night on my Hounsfield bed, I heard someone outside the front of the tent seeking my attention by repeatedly calling out, "*Hodi bwana?*" I didn't issue the standard response of "*Karibu!*" (or for that matter, "*Ka-fuckin-ribu!*") but rather went out to meet the caller directly and find out what he wanted.

He was one of the *watu* from camp. He expressed an urgent need to be advanced a few shillings from the wages currently due to him. I asked him what he wanted the money for, to which he replied with the stock phrase that all *watu* used on such occasions to signify a state of some hardship, "*Ninashida*". I assumed that his hardship was to be alleviated by the consumption of a few pots of *pombe* at Mungaa.

I went back into the tent, released the camp cashbox from the secure chains that bound it to the central pole, unlocked the cashbox, and withdrew the small sum of money as requested.

The cashbox was normally referred to by the *watu* as *sanduku ya fedha*, the literal meaning of which was "box of money". The coastal Kiswahili pronunciation of *fedha* was "fetha", although up-country where we were, the *watu* pronounced *fedha* as "fezza". The older and greyer of the *watu* tended to call the cashbox *sanduku ya hela*, with *hela* being an archaic word for money derived from the German *heller* as used during those good old Teutonic colonial days of half a century back.

Leaving the loose and open cashbox behind me on the tent floor, I took the cash advance out to the presumably increasingly thirsty *mtu*, handed it over to him and got him to make a thumbprint to confirm receipt. The entire transaction from the initial *hodi* through the intervening pleasantries to the final thumbprint took no more than two or three minutes. Having pocketed his money the *mtu*, no longer in hardship, set off on his no doubt merry and soon to be merrier way.

I went back into the tent again with the immediate intention of closing and securing the cashbox. To my surprise the cashbox was not in the place where I had left it. In fact, I quickly discovered to my horror that it wasn't anywhere in the tent at all. A long slit at the base of the back flap of the tent indicated where the cashbox must have made a very recent exit in the hands of a person or persons unknown. It was another less than good moment for me.

I got hold of Buck and together we roused the camp by virtue of beating with a piece of tyre iron on a section of car spring suspended from a frame that we customarily used to call up the morning assemblies prior to work. A nighttime assembly was unprecedented. All that seemed to be missing for a properly dramatic effect was someone stamping around the *watu* camp shouting "Raus! Raus!" as the clangour of the beaten spring rang out.

The *watu* trickled along to the assembly point in front of the mess hut in a manner displaying a considerable amount of communal reluctance. Once it seemed that the assembly was complete, inclusive of the *mtu* whose request for a few shillings of advance had precipitated the drama, we took a roll call. With one exception, everyone on our payroll register was accounted for. The exception was Saidi Mohammedi. On the strength of that, Saidi took on the role of prime suspect in the affair of the presumably stolen cashbox.

Around the camp, black night reigned supreme. It was a safe bet that the purloiner of the cashbox was at that very moment escaping under the cover of darkness. It was frustrating. We couldn't move until the crack of dawn allowed us to see our hands in front of our faces and so we had to wait for that moment. Shortly after dawn finally did crack another assembly was called, another roll was called up yonder, and once again only Saidi remained conspicuous by not being there.

The *watu* were split up into a number of parties. Some were set to scout around the general vicinity of the camp in case the cashbox had not been moved far. Others were sent out into the surrounding district to question anyone they met as to whether Saidi or the cashbox or both of them had been seen and to try to pick up any incidental intelligence on where Saidi could be going.

I was fairly sure that all of this would come to nothing and the results were in keeping with my expectation. Saidi had disappeared once again. Finding him in a country in which it was so easy for an *mtu* to hide, and where his sympathisers would no doubt be legion, would be a matter of battling against huge odds at best. I was suspicious that the *mtu* who came to get an advance was an accessory to Saidi's caper, but it didn't take us long to establish his innocence. He was an incidental link in a chain of events that caused the cashbox to be unlocked and thereby vulnerable to the attentions of someone who must have been busy looking for the main chance. It seemed to me that Saidi probably turned up at Lake Mianje with such a definite plan in mind.

I couldn't forgive him for it as my main feeling was one of being badly let down by his abuse of my trust. However, if I had been in Saidi's position, I couldn't say that I wouldn't again have behaved similarly if presented with the mighty temptation of a loose cashbox available to be picked up.

The regulations demanding that the cashbox be secured in its lock and chains at all times when it was not attended by an *mzungu* were clear. I had left the *boma* gate open and allowed a predator to slink in and carry off a prized cow.

I went into Singida to report the theft of the cashbox to the police. They were familiar with me by then. A duty officer wrote down on a formal report sheet the details that I gave him concerning the incident. He wrote laboriously, moistening the tip of his pencil frequently. Then he placed the report in a tray of items that I assumed were to be left pending until they could be reliably forgotten.

The police made it plain that they had far too many other things to do (raiding bars for example) to permit them to spend much of their valuable time on my case. Locating Saidi, they implied, would be like trying to find a specific thorn in an acacia tree. They told me, however, that they would pass a copy of the incident report on to the police in Tabora, which was the administrative centre for Saidi's home village in Unyamwezi. I had no doubt that they wouldn't do any such thing.

A couple of months later Hamisi (the Elvis hair-styled tribal associate of Saidi who was one of my core team) told me that he had heard news of Saidi being spotted near his home village. The news must have come in by tribal drum telegraph. It was interesting news to know, but by then the time when I could do anything about it had passed.

The cashbox, unfortunately empty of its former contents, was recovered four days after it was stolen. It was carried into our camp on the head of one of Chief Omari Mpahi's finest. By his deportment he seemed to believe that he was in the vanguard of a triumphal procession. He said that he had come across the cashbox half-buried in a disused aardvark (*muhanga*) hole.

It crossed my mind that a leading role for Chief Omari Mpahi in the case of the stolen cashbox might be more than circumstantial, but I let that thought go as being unworthy of me. The bearer of the cashbox left me in no doubt that he was keen to be rewarded with a finder's fee. Much to his chagrin the payment of his fee had to be deferred owing to the fact that, for obvious reasons, there was no money available in camp when he brought the cashbox in. He was paid eventually, and that cheered him up no end.

When I informed the Chief Geologist Gus Edwards and his sidekick Trevor Rodger over in Mwadui about the theft of my cashbox, both their formal and their informal reactions were as caustic as I expected they would be. They didn't regard the actual theft to be as serious a matter as were the circumstances leading up to it. The bulk of their criticism was levelled at me for having allowed the cashbox to be of my sight when it was unsecured.

This placed yet another negative mark against me. Injury was added to insult when it was decreed that, in view of the unchained and unlocked state of the cashbox when it was expropriated, all applicable terms and conditions of insurance were voided. I was required to accept full liability for making good all of the incurred losses. I felt not a little hard done by, but I got over it. Rules were rules, and like it or not I accepted that I was just as much to blame as was the thief, assumed to be almost certainly Saidi.

The burning need was to determine exactly how much money was involved in the loss, as it was not only the camp cash and payroll float that were taken but also a number of receipts for goods, services and materials received from various suppliers.

The latter were all relatively easily to verify of course. A couple of other issues, however, were rather more difficult to deal with. The first of these was that, in common with informally accepted practice at many other camps, the cashbox was used as a kind of bank of convenience for the dispensation of petty cash for the personal use of the *wazungu* in camp as and when such cash was required. My personal money was thrown in with WDL's money in the cashbox. When my money was gone I used the WDL money as if it were mine and vice versa. Accounting as to who owed what and to whom was in principle brought up to date in accordance with regular month-end reporting. The accounting practice, however, was nothing if not slack, and so a cloud of uncertainty covered how much (if any) of the money was mine prior to the theft of the lot. The second of the problematic issues related to savings from wages that I was holding for safe-keeping in the cashbox for a few of the *watu*. Each *mtu* who saved in this way had his savings kept in an envelope marked with his name and placed in the bottom tier of the cashbox. The arrangement was based on trust. The *watu* trusted me and I trusted them. They gave me their money to put away, and that was what I did. I didn't count their money, issue receipts or maintain a record. The individually identified envelopes and contents were always available to be handed over to them on demand. As I never received a single query regarding saved money when it was handed back to its owners I assumed that the cashbox banking system was working to everyone's satisfaction.

I didn't know what was in the savings envelopes and I had to ask each of the savers to let me know exactly how much money was being held for them. I accepted that the figures they gave me were correct and assured them that their savings were safe. There was not a single *mtu* in the whole of Tanganyika, literate or not, who wouldn't be instantly on his toes if he thought that he was being short-changed.

When it was all worked out the final tally that I was liable for as debtor with respect to all creditors great and small was in the order of three thousand shillings (*shilingi elfu tatu*). In sterling terms this amounted to around one hundred and fifty pounds, which, when set against my then current gross salary, was seven weeks of pay. It came as a blow although not as a body blow. I bit the bullet.

The powers that were at Mwadui reacted with a surprising flush of kindness. They accommodated me by garnishing my salary to the tune of twenty-five pounds per month, thereby implying that it would take me six months of appropriately curbed social activities to settle my debt.

The loss of the cashbox taught me an enduring lesson. The new cashbox that was sent out to me from Mwadui to replace its stolen counterpart was allowed to serve neither as a personal bank for me nor as a savings bank for the *watu*. I paid out the lost savings and terminated my responsibility for ever holding anything similar again. If my record-keeping and accounting practice were not exactly of a professional standard thereafter, they were at least substantially sharper than prior to the robbery.

I left Tanganyika in November 1961, approximately six months after the theft of the cashbox. Gus and Trevor didn't let me forget the loss of money—which was unnecessary effort on their part since the incident was lying as indelibly in my mind as was "Calais" in the heart of Mary, Queen of Scots.

I occasionally had a flash of an odd idea concerning what I might do to Saidi if I ever caught up with him, yet as time slipped away so too did any vengeful feelings that I harboured. In fact I was never interested in revenge as a dish taken cold. If Saidi had appeared again and said he was sorry I would probably have greeted him and given him a job.

A postscript to the cashbox affair that took place two and a half years later is worth mentioning. I was then in Nyasaland, working on reconnaissance exploration for diamonds for De Beers. At that time I was suffering from severe bouts of malaria, for which I was again to blame for probably forgetting to take my regular anti-malarial tablets. The malaria manifested itself in alternating crippling fevers and chills accompanied by hallucinations of such vivid clarity that they seemed real when they occurred, although they were impossible to recall when they were gone. Saidi featured in one of my more severe malaria-induced hallucinations. It was in graphic detail that I observed him suffer a dreadful fate at the hands of others. I could recall only the sense of what I imagined immediately afterwards, and soon that also faded. Saidi's duplicity must have been buried deep in my subconscious like an evil genie in a bottle waiting to be let out. When an attack of malaria pulled the stopper from the bottle, the traumas surrounding my association with Saidi were released.

From that day on I was clear of him. I hoped that the money Saidi took from the cashbox brought him good luck, as he needed as much in the way of good luck as I did.

*

Once in a while when I was camped alongside Lake Mianje I looked at my general game (pot) licence and imagined how much more attractive it might look if species like Chief Omari Mpahi appeared on the list of game quotas. There wasn't anything at all on the lists that existed to be shot in the vicinity of camp. The shooting of cows to provide meat rations was neither here nor there. Cattle also didn't feature on any pot licence listing—unless the name of the licence applicant was Mr Tom Lehrer.

It was my ever-helpful friend Mohammed Ali Wolji who pointed me in the direction of appropriate hunting opportunities. In the grand tradition of Indian men of business Mohammed Ali was no hunter, but as the recipient of much general intelligence passed across the forum of his bar at the Central Hotel, there were very few subjects of local interest that he couldn't comment on and very few related queries on which he couldn't offer advice leading to a solution.

He told me that there was game aplenty to be found in the Mbulu district some fifty miles out to the northeast of Singida, where great plains surged like an inland sea of grass around Lake Balangida, Katesh and Mount Hanang. On a map, the boundary of the Mbulu district was shaped like a gigantic arrowhead tacked onto the Singida district. Lake Eyasi and the Ngorongoro crater flanked the western edge of the arrowhead. Lake Manyara was on the eastern flank with the Great North Road linking Dodoma with Arusha running through nearby.

Early one Sunday morning just as the sun was rising, when there was as usual no maiden singing on the flats below our camp, Efrem, Taji and I, in a Land Rover driven by Idi, set out to leave troublesome Mungaa to its own devices for a day by following the track northeast towards Mount Hanang to see what we could find. We took along my two firearms, rifle and shotgun, together with a good supply of ammunition for both.

Once we had reached and moved beyond Ilongero, the last vestiges of whatever had passed for civilisation in the northern part of the Singida district faded away and disappeared as surely as did the bush and trees. We came upon a vast plain on which two-feet high yellow-headed grass shimmered and rippled like an ocean without limit under the twin influences of sun and breeze. The plain rolled away to what it took little imagination to reckon as infinity in a progression of shallow dips, hollows, ridges and mounds. Fluffy white cumulus clouds drifted above in the deep blue sky, casting shadows that sailed in slow majesty across the endless sea of grass. We were in a "Big Sky" world.

A long way off to the east of us, the grand and blessedly extinct volcano named Mount Hanang thrust its truncated cone up above the plain in a single breathtaking surge. Mount Hanang's blue-hazed slopes were darkly blotted with cloud shadows. A line of clouds looking like the links of a chain streamed downwind towards us from the summit of the mountain as if they were declaring that there was life in the old volcano yet.

Not forgetting our Land Rover, we had an immediate impression of our being the only animate objects in that whole immensity. However, once we had our eyes in tune with the spectacle, stippled shadows on the undulating terrain began to resolve themselves into sizeable and widespread herds of grazing game.

A procession of game stood in sharply silhouetted profile on the crests of a rise against a background of sky as cloud blotches slid past them. We identified large numbers of wildebeest, zebra and *tomi*, some presenting their sides to us and others with heads turned towards us, not unnaturally sensing danger in the offing. The numbers of game that we saw might not have been enormous, although we were tempted to think in terms of there being a thousand or more as the game was soon all around us, here, there and everywhere. They were surely numbered in many hundreds and offered as many targets to shoot at as the owner of a pot licence could possibly wish to take advantage of.

We stopped the Land Rover to get out in order to take stock. Idi shook his head at the prospect of hunting and said that with so much game around he believed we must be in a *shamba wabibi* (game reserve). He could be forgiven for thinking thus. I had some doubts as well, but as I had previously checked to make sure that the plains around Mount Hanang were open for unrestricted hunting, I didn't entertain the doubts for long. *Uhuru* permitting, it was easy to imagine that one day the plains could be incorporated in a future game reserve, but such an eventuality was considered to be some way off yet. The Serengeti National Park and its associated reserved lands were located substantially to the north of Mount Hanang; it was curious to contemplate that the plain on which we stood was situated almost precisely midway between the Serengeti National Park and the Rungwa Game Reserve.

The immediate problem facing a hunting party like ours was an obvious one—on open grassland the game could see us at least as easily as we could see it. As a consequence the game was at pains to keep its distance from us by continually moving just outside of reasonable shooting range to go about its normal business with an air of nonchalance that was designed to frustrate us. As we walked towards the game so it moved away as if we were creating a consistently spreading ripple effect.

Groups of wildebeest drifted along in silvery columns, with zebra acting as their uniformed outriders. The *tomi* engaged in an habitual stiff-legged jumping exercise known as "stotting" before they trotted off in long and sinuous files, dun backs rising, white rumps flashing, and tails twitching as regularly as if they were in training to become Chief Omari Mpahi's future fly whisk.

I thought that I spotted a few Grant's gazelles (*granti*) in among the many *tomi* but couldn't get close enough to them for a positive confirmation. The chief identification characteristics for a *tomi* were the distinctively back-curved horns of males, a black blaze along each flank, and a black tufted tail that never ceased to swing to and fro like a metronome. It was said that the only time a *tomi's* tail stopped twitching was when the *tomi* was dead.

A full-grown *tomi* buck weighed about fifty pounds on the hoof, whereas a mature male wildebeest weighed ten times that much. There was little debate leading to a decision that it was in the best interests of the camp that we should hunt the latter.

We walked for a couple of miles. The Land Rover behind us looked to be a dreadfully forlorn piece of pale green flotsam in the boundless sea of the plain. The closest group of wildebeest to us was a quarter of a mile away on the far side of a rolling hollow that we stood on one edge of. They were hump-backed animals with metallic grey shoulders that were vertically marked with fine dark flashes. As we moved, so did they at the same pace. A quarter of a mile seemed to be as close as we would be able to get to the wildebeest as long as they were able to see us. The distance was too great for me to attempt a shot at any one of them.

A new tactic was required. The only feasible one that suggested itself was that the wildebeest needed to be stalked. I decided to lie down in the grass and under its cover to crawl to a more fitting position where I could take a closer shot and make it count. Efrem, Taji and Idi were to remain where they were in sight of the wildebeest. I took my rifle from Efrem who had been carrying it, dropped to the ground and commenced my stalk, wriggling on my stomach in the direction of the herd of wildebeest, and hidden from them by the grass. It seemed to me that I was acting like a snake in the grass in more ways than one. Then

I regretted drawing such a conclusion as it made me only too aware of the possibility of my coming face to face with one of these creatures as I slithered along.

Something moved the grass just ahead of me at one point. The rustling set my heart beating so hard that I was sure it was sending tremors through the ground all around me. It suddenly occurred to me that if the grass was providing cover for me as a hunter then it could do the same thing for any other predators, such as a lion, which was known to be rather partial to the taste of wildebeest.

A young *tomi* then appeared before my very eyes. It was picking its gentle, tail-flicking way through the grass. I could have reached out and touched it but didn't, and it merely moved on. I wasn't even sure that it looked at me. On the strength of that, my stalking was so far very successful and following a short pause for me to recoup my nerves I continued.

Every now and then I lifted my head a little to assess the distance remaining between me and the group of wildebeest. They weren't standing still but were moving very slowly as they grazed, apparently unaware that I was on my way towards them. On the last occasion I looked up it was to see the nearest wildebeest, who was a big male, not much more than fifty yards away. From the general behaviour of the wildebeest group it seemed that my presence might soon be no longer unknown. Their heads were up, their nostrils were agitated and there was a certain amount of milling around. I knew I couldn't get closer without spooking the whole herd into flight. I had to act there and then or not act at all.

I lifted the rifle, worked the bolt to chamber a bullet, sighted in a heart shot on the left shoulder of the big wildebeest and squeezed the trigger. At the sound of the shot, the entire group of wildebeest switched into immediate overdrive and set off for the far distance with a pounding of cloven hooves and a vision of flying tails and receding backsides (which brought Chief Omari Mpahi to mind once more). It seemed in an instant that all that remained was the settling dust of retreat.

Stiff in all joints I got up on to my feet and brushed myself down. Efrem, Idi and Taji came racing up from behind me. I was surprised to find out later that my stalk took the best part of an hour, and even more surprised to see the big wildebeest that I shot at was still there and down on its side. In the confusion of the stampede precipitated by my shot I hadn't seen the target fall and assumed that I had missed it. Perhaps the strangest thing of all was the sight of Idi actually running. As a rule, running was anathema to a driver.

The big wildebeest was not quite dead as its legs were thrumming and paddling to and fro. My shot had hit it a foot or so behind the spot at which I had aimed, but it was a mortal shot for all that. Taji was the first to reach the downed wildebeest. With his knife at the ready, he dodged the hooves with the grace of a ballet dancer and the aplomb of practice to open the animal's throat from ear to ear with a single neat flicker of steel. At that, the wildebeest expired in a proper state of *halalled* grace.

Idi, who was back to walking at his customary *pole pole* pace, set off to return to the Land Rover and drive it up to the kill. In the time that it took him the wildebeest was totally eviscerated and the unwanted portions of the entrails, which admittedly weren't many, were discarded to one side for the scavengers to clean up.

We manhandled the carcass of the wildebeest onto the back of the Land Rover. Skinning was a job to be carried out back at our camp. The four hooves stuck up in the air in an ungainly way that looked rather poignant. We were elated with the prize of so much meat taken from the plains.

We all boarded the Land Rover. Idi drove to the track that had brought us to the plains and we turned our backs to Mount Hanang to go back to camp, where the skinning, quartering and apportionment of meat to the *watu* took place that same evening. Buck and I got a portion of the wildebeest meat as well. I rated it as tasting better than beef, but best eaten when cold.

I was also offered the wildebeest's tail. Efrem said he would get it skinned and made into a fly whisk for me. It was an offer I had no hesitation in politely declining; a wildebeest tail fly whisk signified Mr Jomo Kenyatta and Chief Omari Mpahi. As for my joining company like that, it was thanks but no thanks.

I made two subsequent hunting trips up to the plains around Mount Hanang, and on each occasion the bag was a *tomi*. Both were clean kills, welcomed when made but regretted when thought about too much.

*

Reconnaissance camps were by nature temporary affairs. Once the area they were set up to deal with was fully sampled, the camps lost their reason for being and were struck to be moved on to pastures new.

So it was that the time came for the tents at Lake Mianje to be folded in order that we might steal away. Among those who were neither local residents nor members of the Wanyaturu tribe there were few who had much reason to regret the end of the camp. Since the John Mwita incident we had been living in a state of fragile truce with the local population, and no matter how bright a face we tried to place on the situation it was not good for camp morale. I felt that holding on to morale was much more difficult for the *watu* than it was for Buck and me.

The day arrived for the camp to be dismantled and its effects packed and loaded for transportation elsewhere on a couple of five-ton trucks (one truckload for Buck and one for me). The trucks were loaned to us courtesy of Bruno Brown at the Manyoni Depot. The *watu* who chose to go with us travelled on top of the gear on the backs of the trucks. The rest of the *watu* were paid what was due them in accordance with regulations and individual circumstances.

Buck was to be reassigned to carry out work in an area located down in the south of Tanganyika. I was transferred to work in the great *mbuga* country of the Mwanza district and to cover an area situated to the north of Mwadui, approximately half way between Mwadui and Mwanza.

My reassignment seemed at first sight to present me with a welcome opportunity to call into Mwadui on a regular if not frequent basis and have access to supplies of the fresh vegetables and dairy produce that were flown in several times a week from Nairobi. The pleasure of finally getting hold of fresh milk could not be overrated. As for the rest of Mwadui's alleged attractions, I had already been there, done them, weighed them in the balances and found them wanting, so I knew I could survive without them very well.

The parts of the camp alongside Lake Mianje that we couldn't take away with us were the thatched-over constructions such as the mess hut, the cook's kitchen area, the store hut, the shower and latrine containment and so on. None of these was very substantial, but they were all sturdily constructed. I was considering leaving them all standing after we left for the possible use of local residents. However, I soon found out that the departing *watu* were by no means like-minded. They were unwilling to release anything at all for the benefit of people who had not always enhanced their quality of life.

Rather than either leaving the thatched structures in place or razing them to the ground, we decided by consensus to burn them. They were put to the torch in the early hours of the morning scheduled for our exodus. The thatch was very dry, and the vehemence of the conflagration both amazed and frightened me. The mess hut exploded in a great billow of flame that Mount Hanang in its active heyday might have envied.

The fires lit up the ridge like daylight as they surged, crackled and boomed in a hellish inferno. Then they were gone. All that remained for us to do was to level off the debris, which consisted of a few smouldering stumps of uprights and a deep drift of ashes, and cover it up with soil at dawn.

I was never quite able to decide if the burning of the thatched constructions was a reasonable act or if it was a gesture of meanness. I tended towards the latter of the two options, but when we moved on it seemed to be a matter of no consequence either way.

The village of Ilula on the road to Mwanza

General view of the camp on the great *mbuga* near Ilula

Procession of domestic animals near Ilula

The author's hut at the camp near Bubiki

General view of the *watu* camp at Bubiki with rain threatening in the background

The Mchawi and his box of cobras

The Msaidizi and serpentine friend

The Mchawi (standing with cobras) and the Msaidizi (seated on the right)

18
Nchi ya Mbuga mkubwa
Big Mbuga country

I returned to Mwadui from Singida as a passenger in a Land Rover driven by Idi. We took a more or less easterly route out of Singida along what was a not particularly well defined track.

Under Efrem's command the *watu* and the accumulated camp materials and gear (together with the dogs Jack and Shen) were travelling the long way to Mwadui from Singida on a much slower five-ton truck. Their journey would take them first of all to Tabora via Itigi and thereafter north to Mwadui by way of Nzega and Shinyanga.

I expected to reach Mwadui at least one full day before the arrival of the five-ton truck, enough for what I hoped would give sufficient time to have all the arrangements made for an immediate move to our new campsite when we all eventually met up. The route we took in the Land Rover was something of an unknown quantity for me, and I suspected for Idi as well. As ridge succeeded ridge along the line of the track, and more and more of the same showed up ahead of us, I began at one point to feel that our beating the five-ton truck to Mwadui was by no means a dead certainty.

Sixty miles out of Singida we came to a village named Sekenke and shortly afterwards to the Wembere River, which was wide but dry and easily fordable on a hard laid base of rocks and corduroy. As an incidental point of local interest, gold was mined in the area around

Sekenke in the good old days when Tanganyika was a German colony. The gold bullion was taken from Sekenke to Tabora where it was minted into coins that, when the British assumed the role of colonial power, became familiarly known as "Tabora sovereigns".

There was no current evidence of mining activity around Sekenke when we passed by, however. I ceased looking for it once we were across the Wembere River, as the already poor quality of the track deteriorated further to become the prime focus of attention. The Land Rover was forced to rattle and bump over stony ground and rock-hard desiccated and cracked *mbuga* soil for a further sixty miles of slow going before we could feel the relief of nearing Nzega. After Nzega the going was much easier for the forty-mile run up to Shinyanga and the quick dash thereafter into Mwadui. The Land Rover's journey, which commenced not long after morning gilded the skies and our hearts awoke without cries, came to a grateful end at the knell of parting day.

I was keen to spend as little time within the fenced-in precincts of Mwadui as I could. As a consequence of the free and easy bush life that I had enjoyed for the greater part of a year, being in Mwadui for anything other than the collection of fresh groceries gave me a feeling of claustrophobia. The township felt cloying, and more than a few of its *wazungu* residents seemed to be forever putting on both the agony and the style at the same time. It didn't help that I had learned to my cost that a *wazungu* club-oriented society and I had little or nothing in common.

For the day or so that I spent in Mwadui I was once again accommodated at the Pink House. The fears that I had felt at the Pink House after my original arrival at Mwadui were long gone, even from memory. Staying at the Pink House for the second time was truly a *kipande ya mkate mtama*—a "piece of cake". The residential rats and lizards bothered me not at all—*hata kidogo!*

It was no less distinguished a personage than Mr Trevor Rodger who handed me the details for my next assignment. He said that he was expecting good things of me (which was fair enough) since he considered that I had done very well in the Singida district (which was news to me). For reasons that only Trevor must have been aware of he didn't then choose to take advantage of the opportunity to refer to the loss of my cashbox. It could have been that Trevor was exercising what was (for him) an abnormal level of benign diplomacy. Either that or thoughts of using the lost cashbox as a weapon with which to wound hadn't occurred to him yet. You never knew where you were as far as Trevor was concerned.

He told me that I would be taking over an already established camp located approximately forty miles to the north of Mwadui on the Mwanza road, just to the east of a small settlement which for some reason was officially named Runere but known locally as Ilula. The camp had originally been set up by Dick du Toit, whose views on the savagery of the Wagogo had so misinformed me before I went to work under Tom Molyneux at Iwambala. Dick was due to leave Tanganyika to return to his native South Africa with immediate effect. Indeed the effect was so immediate that it didn't allow Dick any time to spare for a proper handover to me.

During a short meeting that I had with him in the bar of the Mwadui club, Dick did explain where the camp could be found and how I could gain access to his records and reports. Beyond that, everything was *kwa heri* to Dick. He told me that he had left only a skeleton crew of *watu* at the camp, which was fortunate as I was coming in with my own team of stalwarts, and I would have hated to start at the camp by laying off any of Dick's *watu* who were surplus to requirements.

My task was to continue with the sampling programme started by Dick to the west of the Mwanza road in both Shinyanga and Kwimba districts. The southern limit of the area to be sampled was not far removed from the northern environs of Mwadui's outer security fence.

The far from comprehensive quality of Dick's handover notwithstanding, an attractive aspect of the work was that I would be doing it "on my own". In other words, I would be the only *mzungu* in camp, and I liked the thought of that. It made me recall a remark made by a South African Field Officer in Dodoma who, on seeing a PWD gang numbering about twenty strong (inclusive of two *wazungu*) in the act of digging a ditch to extend a storm drainage culvert (for someone like me to fall into) along the side of a street, said, "Shit a brick! So many to do one job! Give me half a dozen *watu* and I could do that job on my own!"

In the company of Idi and my Land Rover I met with my team and camp gear on the five-ton truck shortly after the whole kit and caboodle arrived at the gates of Mwadui. We drove up the Mwanza road to Ilula in a convoy of two, the truck following the Land Rover.

I was familiar with that road thanks to a former driving lesson. It was dim and dusty (the road, not the lesson) with an all-weather surface of gravel fixed by lateritic clay, which was both competently graded by the highly effective tractor-towing-a-tree method and modestly elevated in the manner of a causeway wherever it traversed any *mbuga*.

The village of Ilula was a road stop that was, if anything, dustier than the surface of the road that its few buildings lined. Its outpost on the south side was a tired-looking Mobilgas fuel (petrol and diesel) and vehicle service station. Through Ilula both sides of the road seemed to feature both *dukas* and other shabby trading establishments that fortunately incorporated a couple of bars. If you drove through Ilula at speed (which most vehicles on the way to Mwanza appeared to do, and hence the dust) you could easily miss the admittedly not much of what there was to be missed.

The walls of the roadside buildings were for the most part constructed of mud, of which in the wet season there were unlimited quantities to be dug out of the *mbugas* that surrounded Ilula. To judge from their appearance the walls had been whitewashed, although not recently. The roofs, all with shallow-angled peaks, were clad in the ubiquitous standard of corrugated metal sheets. Extra sheets of corrugated metal were appended to the front edge of some of the roofs to stick out horizontally and rest on vertical timber supports in the manner of rudimentary verandas. Additional shade was provided by a few bushy acacia trees that looked to be much older than the manmade constructions they favoured.

The traders and shopkeepers in Ilula were all Indians. There was not an Arab to be found. I came to learn that all of Ilula's commerce was owned and run along strictly feudal lines by a single extended Indian family. This family was an important local employer which ministered to the needs of its employees and hanger-on tribesmen (Wasukuma) with an entirely even-handed fund of invective, chastisement and disdain.

The Indians of Ilula were stamped from a die that was far different from the one which produced my Singida friends Mohammed Ali, Babu and, yes, even Mr Manji Dhanji. In Singida (not forgetting Dodoma as well) the Indians knew how to blend their cunning in ways of business with both warmth and charm. At Ilula I came across little or no cordiality of manner from the Indians. They ran a business monopoly and knew only too well that their customers' choices were to take it or leave it. There were no back rooms with cold beer at hand in Indian establishments in Ilula.

I assumed that constant exposure to the Wasukuma would have been enough to test the capacity for goodwill of even the most charitable of Indians sooner or later. I was not fond of the Wasukuma—they were as sly as they were treacherous in my experience, and associating with them gave me no delight. The bars of Ilula as a result did not fill me with personal pleasure on any of the occasions when they received my patronage. I preferred to use a pretext of having to call in at Mwadui as a means of getting down to the Diamond Fields hotel in Shinyanga when the need for me to frequent a bar proved irresistible. The atmosphere of the Diamond Fields hotel always made me feel at home.

The camp vacated by Dick was located a mile or so to the east of Ilula. It was reached by taking a right turn from the main road down a rough track just at the southern fringe of the village. The track, such as it was, was defined solely by the wear and tear of the tyres of Dick's Land Rover travelling to and from the camp over scantily vegetated hard *mbuga* soil.

When I arrived at the camp the black cotton soil was at the peak of its dry season rock-like consistency. Desiccation cracks up to a few inches wide slammed at tyres and made it only too obvious where my Land Rover's loose bolts and rivets were to be found. The lumpiness of the track seemed designed to shake both vehicle and passengers down into their constituent parts. The approved technique for minimising all the jolting and the rattling was the one employed on road corrugations, namely to shove the foot down and go fast. In that way the tyres were induced to skim the crests of the bumps and to glide over the gaping cracks. The optimum speed had to be finely judged, but Idi knew all about that, and once he was accustomed to the technique it became second nature and he could ensure that we got an acceptably smooth ride.

The area of the great *mbuga* that I was assigned to work on was in essence a flat and barren expanse underlain by black cotton soil, occasionally relieved by drainage channels, gullies, mature river courses and reef-like protrusions of smooth grey granite. Such grass as remained was yellow and brittle, crumbling at a touch. There were few trees, and such as they were they were far between. It was possible for me to look towards the sun-shivered horizon in any direction and count every tree in sight without taxing my powers of concentration. Wherever we wanted to go in that empty vista all that was necessary for us to do was to get in the Land Rover, point it towards the intended destination and simply go for it.

Here and there lonely lines and clusters of spiky sisal plants, looking like the advance units of an army of spear-carrying *askaris*, jumped up to relieve the monotony of the plain. Each sisal plant thrust up a great seed-headed wooden flagpole above its explosively spine-tipped, succulent-green, fibre-bearing heart.

I was to find out, fortuitously as it happened, that the sisal poles were of considerable importance in a tribal society inured to living in an environment bereft of an appropriate supply of timber and decent thatching material for hut construction. As was seen along the main drag of Ilula, mud bricks and corrugated metal sheets tended to rule the day as materials of choice for the erection of buildings.

The problem was that on the great *mbuga* any length of cut timber other than a sisal pole was targeted by particularly virulent little bugs. They were a species of woodworm or woodborer. Their purpose in life was to form up together in exceedingly large numbers to invade and consume wood in the shortest possible time.

However, for reasons of taste best known to themselves, these woodborers had no interest in sisal poles; hence the latter were grown for domestic support and regarded by the tribal residents of the great *mbuga* as a premium product.

At the heart of the camp near Ilula was an ample house-like building constructed under Dick's direction and for his personal use from mud bricks, of which it could be said that in the vicinity of Ilula there was no shortage of supply.

The preparation of mud bricks was a local industry of substantial importance. Each brick, measuring perhaps two feet by one foot by three or four inches, was manufactured from puddled black cotton soil that was thoroughly invested with *panga*-chopped dead grass stalks and compounded to shape in a wooden form prior to being turned out to dry in the sun. With so much raw material available a casual observer could be forgiven for thinking that making a mud brick was child's play, but, as in all things where artisans were concerned, some mud-brick fabricators were better than others. When mud bricks were needed it was false economy not to hire a manufacturer with a reputation for expertise. His mud bricks would be guaranteed works of art, made by employing instinctive skills passed down through countless generations.

The mud-brick walls of Dick's house were raised to a height of about eight feet to enclose an interior measuring roughly twenty feet by ten feet in plan. An internal wall, also made of mud bricks, separated a sleeping chamber at the back of the house from a general-purpose area (mess cum office) at the front. When I got there the roof consisted of a green tarpaulin supported by a framework of acacia struts cut and brought in from a more wooded locality somewhere down to the south of Shinyanga.

The woodborers must have welcomed the acacia struts as a gift. They were into the struts in a big way, to the extent that a modest but persistent sound of a myriad of them munching wood was always there in the background, day and night alike.

A steady, gentle rain of fine wood dust floated down from the acacia struts and formed a cumulating deposit on everything beneath. Had the dust been the only thing to worry about the situation wouldn't have been so bad; however, the dust sifting out of the wood was accompanied by not infrequent creaking interspersed by ominously sharp cracks. Taken as a whole, the sounds offered a definite impression that a collapse of the entire roof structure was not only inevitable but imminent.

By dint of much foraging around the district we managed to source and buy, at a price that was at least as inflated as Chief Omari Mpahi's ego, enough sisal poles to replace the partially consumed acacia struts and so render the roof secure from crashing down on me at night.

Quite a lot of goats and cattle plus a handful of donkeys moved listlessly across the bone dry ground in search of any scarce pickings of grass that still hung on within the desiccation cracks. The cattle brought with them an infestation of flies that appeared to be naturally attracted to settling on all food set in front of me. The one positive thing about those flies was that they were not tsetse.

The goats were adept at playing the survival game. They were capable of eating anything that either smacked of vegetation or could claim vegetable antecedents. At a pinch the goats were quite prepared to climb into trees and take up precarious poises on the slimmest of branches in order to consume any greenery that was out of their reach on the ground. Both the cattle and the donkeys were feeble-looking creatures, many of them seeming to consist of not much more than scarred hide stretched over jutting bones. They were all engaged in a race against time—either the wet season would arrive to save them or they would perish.

A few patches of manually loosened black cotton soil still supporting the withered remnants of last season's cotton bushes suggested that local tribesmen were anticipating the wet season as well. They were getting ready to plant their seeds and seedlings at the first intimations of incoming rain and live on in hope of realising a good crop thereafter. Black cotton soil was tilled with difficulty, but in Usukuma it was once again the women who wielded the *jembes* to hack the ground into shape.

A hundred yards behind the line of the *watu's* camp tents the outer curve of a broad and sandy-floored river channel meander lay up against a tall black cotton soil-faced cut bank. The channel wriggled away to the northwest in search of Lake Victoria. It was pretty exciting to contemplate that the wet season's floodwater that went down the channel would very probably go on to augment the flow of the White Nile.

Down in the elbow of the meander Dick's *watu* had evidently dug deep to excavate a water hole to supply the camp. Around the water hole they had set up a thorn-bush *boma* in an attempt to keep out only the less resourceful of the local goats. Most goats could eat their way through a *boma* in short order. Every morning at the water hole we baled out water sufficient unto the day for both our domestic and sample washing needs. The water was drinkable—just—when we boiled it, and we didn't complain about our good fortune in having water in such a handy location.

When I first saw the camp it was from the vantage point of being in a Land Rover driving towards it over the rutted track in from Ilula. I couldn't resist an impulse to laugh. I was used to camping in places where the presence of bush and trees was taken for granted, but no such conditions existed around Ilula. I counted four trees in the immediate field of view. The panorama ahead was *wazi* (open) to the extent that it was *waaaaaazi*.

The tarpaulin-roofed, mud-brick-walled house that Dick (or rather Dick's *watu*) had built stood close to one of the four trees. The capacity of the tree to supply shade was neutralised by the fact that the house was large and the tree not so large. A tent erected just to the right of the tree, fronted by a scattering of utensils and other kitchen paraphernalia, was clearly the domain of the cook.

The array of tents in the *watu* camp were pitched in two distinctive groupings, one to the left and the other to the right of Dick's mud-brick mansion, looking as if they were a pair of widely separated brackets. The entire camp was spread over a distance of at least a quarter of a mile, all of it subject to the unmitigated attention of the sun's rays and whatever other meteorological phenomenon could be thrown its way.

The camp looked like a last outpost of crumbling empire in a land where foes outnumbered friends by a big margin. Dust devils both great and small flitted across the blasted heath around the camp on which nothing, including the domestic animals, moved with any apparent sense of urgency.

Apart from the small skeleton crew remaining at the camp, there were no other employees for me to take over from Dick. *Watu* accustomed to coping with the peculiarities of one particular *mzungu* wouldn't necessarily adapt with ease to the vagaries of another. Dick's former team would have known that all too well. It was as normal for Dick's team to have left when he went as it was for my team to come with me. I knew I would need to engage a few more *watu* locally, the problem being not so much in finding labourers to hire as in finding labourers worthy of their hire.

I was less than willing to take any Wasukuma on to the payroll, but since we were actually in Usukuma where there were rather a lot of them I had little choice in the matter. All the same, Efrem and Idi did the hiring down in Shinyanga where the selection of suitable *watu* was wider and better. Their judgement on such things was always better than mine.

Once we had moved into the camp it was found to be a comfortable enough place to occupy. The fact that I was "on my own" put me at ease. My mud-brick-walled house was a welcome novelty and, in spite of the prevailing lack of shade, was much cooler to be inside than a tent would ever be. Possibly the thin lace of shade that was provided by the nearby tree provided a cosmetic advantage that helped.

Although we had to go out and forage around for firewood, the task was not overly difficult. Since we were undertaking daily sampling traverses it was a simple matter for us to gather up caches of firewood wherever we found it along the way. Then, when the Land Rover detail was sent out in late afternoon to collect up the heavily filled sample bags of the day it brought the firewood back to camp as well.

My rifle and shotgun accompanied us regularly on traverses. Both firearms were generally no more useful than dead weight, as game was extremely scarce in the area. Now and then we saw a few *tomis* but they were even warier than their counterparts in the Mount Hanang plains. They always maintained their distance and, with the absolute dearth of cover, were well-nigh impossible to get near. However, hunting was about persistence, and so on one traverse I did manage to shoot a *tomi* for the pot and on two other occasions when we went further afield to hunt in the late evening I got two more of the same to augment the *watu's* meat rations.

Sad to relate, we saw no kanga at all, which meant that there was very little call for my services with the shotgun. Efrem sometimes took the shotgun out and invariably bagged several small pigeons each time, enjoying a lot more success in hunting with it than I ever did in the Mwanza district. My allowing him to take and use the shotgun, with or without my supervision, would no doubt have been severely frowned on by the Tanganyika police had they known about it. Efrem had my complete trust and was meticulous in caring for the shotgun and accounting for every shot he fired.

*

The location of the camp gave me three options for "going to town", which were namely Mwanza to the north and Mwadui or Shinyanga to the south.

I tried Mwanza on for size twice, only to find that its *wazungu* society was a little too polished to absorb me easily. The attraction of visiting the shores of Lake Victoria, that vast and sparkling inland sea, was a powerful draw, although the lure of the lakeside connection was diminished by the inevitable presence beside the water of a yacht club that relied on the exclusive patronage of *wazungu*. I didn't own the sort of attire that would let me traverse unhindered through the yacht club's portals in the unlikely event that a member would invite me to do so, and as a consequence I never sampled the yacht club's delights.

For all that, Mwanza was an excellent supply centre. It was connected by rail to most of the important urban centres of Tanganyika and was a key hub for lake-based floating traffic, including ferries and cargo and fishing boats, and for commercial shipping bound for all lakeshore points north as well as into the catchment basin of the upper reaches of the White Nile. Furthermore, Mwanza could lay claim to having a self-styled "international" airport with regularly scheduled flights to Nairobi, Entebbe and Dar.

In many ways Mwanza offered its visitors the best of all worlds. Its name meant "the beginning", and Mwanza was all of that. It was only a century ago that the explorer John Hanning Speke had come to Lake Victoria in the vicinity of Mwanza on an expedition in search of the source of the White Nile. It was inferred that Speke "discovered" Lake Victoria, but under the caress of the famous "winds of change" that were ruffling a lot more than lake water in Africa, an increasing number of voices were ready to declare that no *mzungu* (presumably including *habitués* of the Mwanza yacht club) had ever actually discovered anything anywhere and at any time on the Dark Continent since local tribesmen had known all about what was there from time immemorial.

My visits to Mwadui from the camp were made in order to obtain fresh food produce prior to continuing on down to Shinyanga both to pick up sacks of basic *watu* rations from an Indian trader and to spend a little time in the bar of the Diamond Fields hotel. Shinyanga had a population of approximately three thousand, among which were enough Indian traders and their dependants to justify the existence of a cinema featuring films from the home sub-continent to entertain them.

Holding to a policy of "nothing ventured, nothing gained", I went once to the Indian cinema and was interested to note that the patrons appeared to show more curiosity in my presence among them than they did in what was being shown on the screen. The cinema was packed with patrons all doing their personal best to contribute a breath or two to an atmosphere redolent of rancid ghee and pungent spices. As I didn't want to be seen as a glutton for punishment, I didn't attempt a second visit to the cinema.

The Diamond Fields hotel was located alongside the Shinyanga railway station. The hotel bar was long and the walls around it were nicely wood-panelled. The guest rooms were small, clean and comfortable. The food was excellent, served in a well-appointed dining-room by a very genial waiter who knew precisely when to come to the bar and tell me, "*Chakula tayare!*" (literally "food is ready!" but in effect, "dinner is served!") One evening, when the pressure of participating in a session in full swing in the bar made me more lax than usual in heeding the waiter's repeated advice, he delivered a hand-written message in English to me that proclaimed, "Dinner is deadly". *Chakula tayare* would have suited me better.

What I particularly liked about the bar of the Diamond Fields hotel was that there was always a possibility of finding other WDL bush types calling in on their way to or from Mwadui. These impromptu get-togethers were always enjoyable and were conducted in a spirit that formed a perfect antidote to the "home thoughts from abroad" ambience of the Mwadui club up the road.

I had some very pleasant encounters in that Shinyanga watering hole with Mario Zopetti, who was jolliness personified now that Danilo's cry of fahkamusshoota no longer rang in his ears, and with Gerry Wilson (late of *Badu Kidogo* motors in Mwadui), whose line in bullshit was like vintage wine, travelling well and improving with time.

Sometimes one or other of the WDL prospectors who were presumably giving Mwadui a miss for personal reasons could also be met in the Diamond Fields hotel bar. One of these was Mr Albert Künzler, the *de facto* tribal chief and celebrated artist. Albert, with whom I enjoyed a few sessions, was barely able to squeeze his vast bulk in through the bar doorway. He always ensconced himself near the bar to hold court. His yarns of times past in Tanganyika were ever-entertaining. I delighted in his company and revelled in the warmth of the consideration he showed me when we met.

Since I was often in the bar of the Diamond Fields hotel at the same time as the Shinyanga inspector of police, I gravitated into becoming his drinking companion. That worthy, an African gentleman already promoted to a position that exceeded his level of competence (a quality that would be universally enshrined a few years later as the "Peter Principle"), regularly favoured the bar with his august presence. He was deferred to by all and sundry around him in an obsequious manner that I could never quite bring myself to emulate. I liked him for both his apparently down-to-earth attitude and his general sense of humour, although the zeal that he applied to leaving none of us in any doubt as to who and what he was seemed to be a much less admirable trait.

He didn't apply as much as a vestige of dedication to putting his hand in his pocket to pull out the price of a round of drinks, but I could easily live with that. From the conversations that I had with him it was fairly certain that his mind was set on a golden (or even diamond-studded) personal future in an independent Tanganyika.

On the seventh of July 1961, when I was still camped near Lake Mianje, Tanganyika had acquired a legislative council (known as the "LegCo") in Dar that was planned to be the precursor to a full measure of internal self-government on the way to the final goal of *uhuru*. The LegCo arrived in place almost unheralded and for a while it had all the hallmarks of a non-event of substantial proportions. I heard about it and promptly ignored what I heard. Since few if any of those who were in positions of political or administrative authority seemed prepared to place their personal hands on their personal hearts and declare their belief that *uhuru* was likely to occur at any time within the next decade, it wasn't my place to disagree with them.

The arrival of the LegCo was celebrated in a popular song entitled "*Saba saba*" ("Seven seven") which referred to its date of birth on the seventh of July. The words and music of the song were heard with over-repetitive frequency in the bar of the Diamond Fields hotel, initially on the radio, and then on a gramophone record acquired by the hotel management. "*Saba saba*", so the song told us, was Tanganyika's great day, the "*siku kuu ya Tanganyika!*"

As it was, with the LegCo in place, a definite momentum for *uhuru* commenced immediately, gathered pace and turned into a headlong rush. *Uhuru* was realised on the ninth of December 1961. "Nine twelve" (or *nane kumi na mbili*) didn't quite have the cachet of *saba saba*. As far as I knew, as I was not in Tanganyika at the time, "nine twelve" was not commemorated in song. *Uhuru* was a boulder rolling downhill, gathering no moss and taking no prisoners as it crushed whatever stood in its way.

Since he was who and what he was, the Shinyanga inspector of police must have been running on an inside track in the build-up to *uhuru*, and with hindsight I suppose I should have sensed that our friendship was in all probability rather superficial. Even as I spent time with him the inspector must have been marking out his territory and jockeying for the position of power that he expected to be awarded when the big day finally came.

I should also have been more aware of a tendency to changes in the acceptance of the *status quo* by a number of the *watu* with whom I worked and associated. I accepted them all on trust and thereby missed that pivotal moment after which the general feeling of "us" in camp altered to "us and the *mzungu*".

It was rumoured that local politicians, dominantly allied to the Tanganyika African National Union (TANU) party of Mr Julius Nyerere were out and about actively making promises concerning the post-*uhuru* largesse that they would be delivering in return for votes to the masses in rural areas all over the country.

TANU enjoyed what was virtually a free run for the simple reason that anyone who opposed the party's aims was forcibly induced by its agents to change their mind. It didn't matter that what was being promised neither could nor would be delivered—what counted was that the promises were widely believed. For people who had nothing, the possibility of anything coming to them was seen as a step forward.

My friend the inspector of police was equipped with the chameleon-like qualities that no doubt would ensure his post-*uhuru* future, at least for the short term. He put himself about as if he was all things to all people. He was a black Vicar of Bray in both body and spirit.

As was recounted in a previous chapter, I discovered the sting in the inspector's tail some months later when I was working in the Bechuanaland Protectorate and the export of my two firearms from where they were being held in safe keeping at the Shinyanga police station was turned down on the strength of his official view that I was untrustworthy (wrong); drunk in charge of a rifle (not altogether wrong although never in his presence); and one who consorted with undesirables (quite correct as I had spent much time in his company).

I concluded that *uhuru* placed a definite obligation on the shoulders of its enthusiasts to regard *wazungu* with disfavour, erstwhile friends included.

*

One morning, Trevor Rodger paid a surprise visit to the camp just as I was preparing to set out on the daily sampling traverse with my team. Had I known that he was coming I wouldn't have baked a cake but would have made sure I was out of camp before he arrived. To judge from the attitude he showed, he didn't like what he was seeing at the camp. Nor for that matter did I. It was the first time that I saw

Trevor in the field. He stepped from his Land Rover, the Mwadui freshwashed gleam of which was already tending to dull under a light pall of road dust, and strode manfully across a stretch of black cotton soil towards my mud-brick house.

Trevor was sartorially immaculate in a dazzling white shorts and shirt combination enhanced by long socks of a similar shade and a pair of highly polished brown leather brogues. He avoided either touching or brushing up against any object, animate or inanimate, as if he knew that his apparel was an attractive target for whatever the locality could throw at it.

He made it immediately clear that his interest was vested much more in finding fault than it was in handing out plaudits. I realised that it was my bad luck to be camped close enough to Mwadui for people like Trevor to be able to nip up and drive back home again in the course of a few hours so as to kill a working day very nicely. On the other hand Trevor might have been on his way to Mwanza to associate with the haves and the have yachts and chosen to use my camp as a means of justifying his trip and its eventual expenses.

It was a fact of life that the top-ranking people like Trevor normally only visited bush camps to look situations over with jaundiced eyes that saw half-empty glasses in whichever direction they peered. They were more adept at complaining about what was wrong than paying tribute to what was right.

Trevor made it clear that he didn't care at all for the mud-brick house. He said that he found the construction to be both ugly and substandard. He disapproved of the location of the camp, its layout and what he saw as an absence of good order. I was roundly blamed for all of it, even though the set-up was still exactly as it was when I inherited it from Dick. I thought of mentioning that to Trevor but decided against doing so in order to avoid any further censure for my failure to make changes.

Trevor then told me, as he had before in Mwadui when I came across from Singida, that in his opinion I had done good work in Chief Omari Mpahi's domain, and this, he went on to say, made what he was seeing at the camp all the more disappointing for him. I looked at Trevor, and *tundu ya kundu* sprang to mind.

Having done what he obviously came to do, Trevor voiced additional complaints about the presence in camp of the two dogs, Jack and Shen.

They appeared at his feet when he was on his way back to his Land Rover. It is possible that one or other of them smudged one of Trevor's shoes, truly a heinous crime. Trevor left the camp, having contributed not a single iota of anything constructive that I could recall and feel grateful for.

As it was, we were at the time engaged in winding up the part of the sampling programme based on that particular camp as we had more or less exhausted all of the traversing options within feasible reach. We would soon be getting ready to strike the camp and move to a new site further south towards Mwadui. Trevor's negativity could be therefore be safely ignored.

The climate was giving us much more cause to be concerned as the approaching wet season (my second of such in Tanganyika) was building great anvil-headed towers of clouds, as yet unfulfilled by rain, which dominated every horizon during the day and bloomed with bursts of silent lightning during the night. Any sound of thunder was still too faint to be heard, but its waves trembled in the dense air and brought with them a familiar sense of damp earth and rain-laid dust. I was only too well aware that if we wanted to avoid being engulfed by mud we would need to be camped elsewhere in a place that was not underlain by black cotton soil when the rains came.

Just prior to the rains the heat of day was unbearably oppressive, and even after dark there was insufficient cooling to bring relief. Tempers shortened and a patient attitude became ever more difficult to sustain under the burden of the enduring closeness of the air.

We moved the camp to a place near a little village named Bubiki located twenty-five miles to the south of Ilula. Bubiki was situated not far to the west of the main road to Mwanza. The camp facilities were set up on a south-trending shallow sandy slope that drifted away from a group of small, smoothly rounded granite–gneiss *koppies*, up against the side of one of which our store was erected. The slope was broken by a scattering of convex humps of the same rock that, when viewed from the *koppies*, looked like the rising backs of hippos. At that late end of the dry season the local soil was all but barren of any vestiges of vegetation. Apart from a few scrubby thorn trees that had managed to anchor themselves to cracks in the *koppies*, an absolute dearth of tree life around Bubiki made the Ilula area seem modestly wooded by comparison. Whenever I lifted up mine eyes from those hills to gaze unto the south, it was to look on nothing which marred a panorama of featureless terrain in any significant way.

As there was no suitable source of water for the camp in the immediate vicinity of Bubiki, I obtained a wheel-mounted 500-gallon tank from *Badu Kidogo* Motors that could be coupled up to and towed by the Land Rover. With it, we were able to make a run down to Mwadui to fill the tank with potable water whenever the supply ran low.

What made camping near Bubiki village interesting to me was the existence of a large and isolated hut walled with sticks and mud and roofed by an expertly assembled peak of thatch that I was told was currently vacant and possibly available for my use. The hut had the appearance of being ideal for living accommodation, apparently so well constructed and ample of proportions that following an inspection I took out an option to rent it from its owner right away.

Whether or not the *mtu* from Bubiki with whom I made the rental arrangement actually owned the hut was never confirmed. All I knew was that he said he owned the hut and no one else disputed the assertion. He wanted to be paid fifty shillings in rent per month for the duration of my occupancy. We shook hands on the deal and I moved in. The hut became my personal quarters. The *watu* pitched their tents across the way in a neat line close to Bubiki. As an overall set-up the camp had its imperfections, but for all that it was preferable to being camped near Ilula.

Bubiki, such as it was, sprawled its assembly of huts over the down-slope of a vague rise of ground situated approximately a quarter of a mile to the east of my hut, which was far enough away for the comfort of all concerned. The gentleman who, owing to his superior manner and the way in which everyone in the village deferred to him, I assumed to be Bubiki's headman, was most helpful to us as we settled into the locality. I consulted him in advance of our arrival. He was dressed entirely in black, in attire consisting of a short-sleeved shirt and a pair of long trousers. However, he appeared to have no fondness for footwear at all and chose to walk about on bare feet with soles that looked leathery enough to plonk on sun-baked sandy ground at noon with impunity.

He was a man much given to indulging in the lengthy pleasantries of greeting. Each time I saw him we enquired of each other as to how we were, how the various members of our families were, how our cattle were getting on (well, his cattle anyway), how life was treating us, and how had we come through the kind of recent past that was always referred to in terms of the strangely evocative "many days" (*siku mingi*).

It was this headman who pointed me in the correct direction for renting the vacant hut and who additionally found for me an alleged expert, or *fundi*, in both the preparation of mud bricks and their use in subsequent constructions. The *fundi*, the headman claimed, would carry out high-quality work at a competitive price.

Among the works that the *fundi* wrought for me out of mud bricks in close proximity to my hut were a shower cubicle, a containment around the latrine hole (a brick shithouse in absolutely literal terms), and an oven and utensil platform for the use of Paulo the cook.

I took to the black-clad Bubiki headman at once and went on to hold him in very high regard. His sable appearance caused me to recall a famous BBC radio programme entitled *The Man in Black*, which featured in the title role that well-known character actor Mr Valentine Dyall narrating tales of horror in a uniquely splendid atmospheric voice. Perhaps it was no coincidence that the Bubiki version of the "Man in Black" was, as I found out, a bit of a dabbler in the black arts in his own right. Subsequent events demonstrated that he would have been well able to give Mr Valentine Dyall a run for his money.

I was told to begin with that the name of the Bubiki headman was Mchawi, although it soon emerged that this was not so much his given name as a description of his profession. *Mchawi* in Kiswahili meant "sorcerer" or "witch doctor". Thereafter for reference purposes I always thought of the Bubiki headman as "the *Mchawi*". From his appearance the *Mchawi* was somewhere between thirty-five and forty-five years old; his age was not easy to estimate. He was more than six feet tall, and although he was heavy-featured his skin was clear. This combination of characteristics made him look passably handsome.

The *Mchawi* lived in a circular compound containing three huts, not unnaturally constructed from mud bricks and covered by thatch, that were placed around a clean-swept open communal area of about fifty feet in diameter. The entire compound was surrounded by a live *boma* of intensely interlaced succulent green plants about four feet high on the average. I went to his compound to talk to the *Mchawi* about the nature of the local sampling we were to carry out from the camp, only to find that he was reasonably well in the picture already. Bubiki was situated within the range of Mwadui's influence, and as a result there was very little mystery in the minds of most local tribesmen as to what was involved in the practice of exploring for diamonds.

The *Mchawi's* compound was graced by the presence of a few women, several children and one elderly man. I assumed that they were all members of the *Mchawi*'s family. The women were engaged in pursuits of great industry as they swept the ground, scoured pots, crushed maize kernels for *posho* and instinctively kicked scrawny chickens out of their way. Their endeavours were only partly impeded by the children's antics. The elderly man regarded the action from a sedentary position—some things never changed as life ambled on.

Against the sides of the huts were jumbled piles of variously sized clay vessels, a few three-legged cast-iron cooking cauldrons, and an impressive number of cowhide covered drums. The latter were brought into service each evening as soon as darkness fell. Throbbing and rolling rhythms that I couldn't even begin to work out the significance of and didn't want to think too much about in terms of the possible message they were belting out, were a feature of most nights for an extended number of hours. Once I got used to the drumming I found the pulse of it to be rather comforting, not least when it distracted my attention from the equally regular whooping of nocturnally wandering hyenas.

The elderly man who held station in the *Mchawi*'s compound was bent of back and furrowed of features. Lines that were etched sharply into his face seemed to be natural extensions of the longitudinal braids of hair that lay like windrows on his head. I assumed that he was the *Mchawi*'s assistant and as a result thought of him as the *Msaidizi*. As his sole upper garment he wore a sort of black jacket that had, like him, seen better days. Over one shoulder of the jacket and crossing his chest he sported a whitish (or light-coloured) sash that gave an impression that he might be a member of either a professional or a religious order. His lower regions were clad in a long wrap-around sarong decorated in a chain-like pattern of black ovals set against a once-white background. His sandals were made of conventional rubber tyre soles held on by cowhide straps.

Both the *Mchawi* and the *Msaidizi* were men of individually imposing presence. When they were together they formed a duo that was much greater than the sum of its two parts.

The *Msaidizi*'s most prized possession appeared to be a worn wooden box of the type that looked as if it might once have contained dynamite. Its lid, which was tied down by a length of thin rope, reflected a patina of age formed by the repetitive touch of hands that were far from being free of sweat and grease. Within the wooden box was a pair of lively cobras, each measuring a minimum of six feet long.

I heard about the two snakes a couple of weeks after we set up the new camp at Bubiki. At the time, the arrival of the wet season was still threatening but rain as such was maintaining an appreciable distance. Our sampling was going quite well. Even Trevor Rodger, in the unlikely event that he would have been so motivated, might have been induced to offer a little praise on the progress we were achieving. Efrem came along to my hut late one afternoon to tell me that the *Mchawi* had sent a message down to him at the *watu* camp to let me know that he had something he would like to show me. I stopped what I was doing and went over to the *Mchawi*'s compound at once.

I arrived to see the *Msaidizi*'s rope-tied wooden box sitting on the ground at the centre of the compound. The *Mchawi* led me over to the box, beside which he squatted on his haunches and proceeded to untie the knots in the rope. The knots looked to be as tight as they were complex. Pandora's box could not have been closed up in a more secure manner. I stood with the *Msaidizi* to one side, from where I could either watch the mystery unfold or take to my heels and run away in the opposite direction if necessary.

With the rope loosened, the lid of the box was lifted off. The *Mchawi* reached his two hands down into the box and with a flourish that was pure theatre he withdrew two great snakes, one gripped by each hand. As the *Mchawi* stood up, one snake hung head down like a pendulum to the level of his knees. Its head was thrust forward, pointing like a small flickering tongued wedge set at the top of a spreading hood. The second snake chose to twist around the *Mchawi*'s arm and run its head up to the back of his neck.

The *Mchawi* placed the two snakes gently on the ground, where they both immediately assumed a classic cobra aggressive-defensive posture with flared out hoods poised a couple of feet up above a gathered heap of coils. The hoods were curved-like springs ready to let the heads strike with speed, force and accuracy. Together with the three *watu* who came up to the *Mchawi*'s compound with me, I retreated with cautious despatch to the green *boma* fringing the compound. If either cobra elected to make a least move in my direction I was ready to crash through the *boma* and not stop running until I reached my hut.

The cobras were generally light grey in colour, although dappled or speckled on the dorsal side in a more brownish shade of grey. At a later date, using a photograph that I took at the time, I provisionally identified them as being a variant of the common Egyptian cobra (*naja haje*) that was normally rather darker in tone and with a banded pattern to its dorsal scales. All I was sure of when I first saw the cobras was that they were big snakes with a fearsome aspect that all my instincts recommended me to stay well clear of.

The *Mchawi* reached down again, picked up one of the cobras and handed it to the *Msaidizi*. The latter took the snake, which promptly slid up along his jacket by way of the sash, cast a couple of coils around his neck and pushed its head through the central furrows of his hair.

When he had taken back the snake, the *Mchawi* then brought both cobras in his hands to me and asked me if I would like to be the next one to take them. He assured me that they would do me no harm. It seemed that he was offering me a poisoned chalice both figuratively and literally. I didn't want to oblige him, yet the *Mchawi*'s powers of persuasion were compelling to the extent of being almost mesmerising and I was not proof against them. Against my better judgement I found myself taking the cobras from him.

Not to suspend my unwillingness completely, I grasped each snake firmly just behind its head, held them out at arm's length and let the long balance of the creatures dangle freely. The *Mchawi* came to retrieve them from me, which was a task not made easy for him as I was afraid to let the heads go for fear of triggering a random farewell bite.

Thus it was that the pair of cobras was returned by the *Mchawi* to the wooden box whence they came, and the show was over. The *Mchawi* was not too proud to accept a number of shillings in recompense for the exciting performance that he and the *Msaidizi* had put on.

Apart from the show I had felt the power of the *Mchawi*'s personality and began to accept that witch doctors were people of profound depths that could be appreciated but never fathomed out. In my dealings with him the *Mchawi* generally showed a benign face. Whether or not I understood what made him tick, I liked him and never felt ill at ease in his company.

I realised of course that the *Mchawi's* talents could be a force for ill as much as for good and assumed that there would be some aspects of his behavioural practice that were unlikely to be entirely edifying.

*

As briefly alluded to above, once night fell hyenas prowled all around the vicinity of Bubiki. The camp was not exempt from their attention. Occasionally one or more of these scavengers came up to the outer walls of my hut and whooped and cackled like the damned. Such close proximity to hyenas was at best disconcerting and at worst quite terrifying.

The *Mchawi* instructed me at an early stage of our acquaintance to make sure that the single entry portal to my hut was secured against the possibility of a hyena intruding, for which purpose I obtained a section of heavy board which could be wedged in place over the opening at night. And just in case, my shotgun stood ever-ready to hand with a cartridge chambered and the safety catch off.

It was alleged that the hyenas, known as *fisi* in Kiswahili, were summoned by the *Mchawi*. *Fisi* were said to be his familiars, and he was reputed to be theirs. He walked among them at night. I heard on good authority from some of the *watu* that the *Mchawi* was able to fly through the night to distant places on the back of a hyena. The same *watu* also told me that the *Mchawi* could transform himself into a hyena whenever he wished to. The *Mchawi*, in other words, was alleged to be a genuine "hyena man", an African version of a werewolf.

The dictates of good reason pointed out to me that this was no more than the stuff of legend and therefore not to be taken seriously—yet I knew that there were many African traditions that defied logic. I was certain that the *Mchawi* possessed powers that went well beyond my ken and felt that it was not my place to deny that he consorted with hyenas.

The *Mchawi* was able to tell me precisely how many hyenas would come around the camp on any given night and, moreover, let me know at what time I should expect to hear them. What he said would happen always came to pass. He warned me to stay in my hut and not under any circumstances to look outside while the hyenas were on the prowl. As I invariably followed his instructions I never saw him walking with hyenas, but I soon came to have no doubts that he did.

If where the hyenas summoned by the *Mchawi* came from in the night was a mystery, so also was where they went to during the day, as on all the traverses I undertook while I was camped near Bubiki I saw little sign of hyenas other than a cluster of their bone-white droppings once in a while. Since we had so many regularly visiting hyenas in the area there should have been an awful lot more such hyena shit on the ground. The hyenas of Bubiki were much more than mere scavengers on the make. I even got used to the noises they made once I established complete faith in the *Mchawi*'s assurances that as long as we followed the rules they intended us no harm.

Legends of men who were able to assume the form of lions or leopards were widespread in the tribal traditions of Tanganyika, not to mention in many of the country's popular bars. In stories that I heard the transformations were associated with membership of clandestine cults or secret societies, the motives of which were chiefly focused on exacting murderous revenge in order to sustain both inter-tribal conflicts and long-standing family feuds. Crimes committed in the realm of the supernatural were rarely punished. The seeds of the Mau Mau movement could well have been sown in such receptive ground.

In one popular tale a marauding leopard was shot and the body of a man bearing a bullet wound was found lying in the precise place where the leopard fell. I was assured by an informant in the bar of the Dodoma Hotel that the incident actually did happen and I would not have dared to disagree.

In the vicinity of Tsavo in Kenya during the construction of the Mombasa to Nairobi railway in the late 1890s, an organised group of man-eating lions preyed on the railway workforce with unprecedented intensity. Their story was told in a book by Colonel J. H. Corbett, whose assigned task it was to eliminate them. The lions, whose depredations significantly depleted the workforce, were so inventive in their hunting technique and so adaptive to countermeasures taken to thwart them by the railway company, that they must surely have been vested with lion-man qualities, including the power of logical thought.

Before I went to camp at Bubiki I thought that tales of lion men and leopard men were of a cautionary nature ending in dreadful morals designed by witch doctors to still the voices of the opposition. At Bubiki, with the *Mchawi* and his hyena pack drawing me to believe implicitly in hyena men, I found myself regarding the existence of lion men and leopard men with very little scepticism.

*

In the meantime, life at the camp went on. We progressed with our traversing schedule. I paid as small an amount of attention to Mwadui as I thought I could get away with and gave my bar-related patronage to the Diamond Fields hotel as often as I could.

My hut, once the interior was thoroughly swept out and the floor was treated with a smoothed, tamped down and dried off slurry of *mbuga* mud, made clean and comfortable living quarters. The Hounsfield bed was set up adjacent to the back wall to the far left of the entry. A table was strategically placed to catch as much as possible of the light entering the hut via the portal, and all the administrative paraphernalia and sampling accessories were all installed on the side at the right of the table.

The mud-brick-constructed ablution facilities (shower and latrine) seemed to be both sound and solid. All in all I had a home from home that beat living in a tent into a cocked sola topee that a DO would not have been averse to wearing. I thought myself lucky that I was in a hut and not in a tent owing to both the proliferation of nocturnal visits by hyenas and the way in which inside the hut the heat of day was mitigated more efficiently than it would have been in a tent. The heat was naturally oppressive as clouds gathered, thunder rumbled ever closer, lightning jumped and the smell of rain drawing nigh intensified.

During one afternoon of torpid heat the *Mchawi* appeared outside my hut. In one of his hands he was carrying a small sack, within the folds of which it was clear that something was moving. He was, the *Mchawi* told me, very pleased with the interest I had taken in his pair of cobras. As a gesture of his appreciation, he went on, he had brought me a present. With that, he undid the string that held the sack closed and poured its contents out on to the ground.

Those contents unravelled themselves of their own accord and proceeded to head north at an appreciable speed. The *Mchawi* was not having any of that, however, and with a hop and a jump, he plonked one of his feet on the would-be escapee to arrest its forward momentum. He reached down, picked it up and held it out to me.

What he had was a snake, mostly coloured black and about four feet long. As far as I could tell from the fact that it flared out a hood, even though the hood was one of modest proportions in comparison to those of the pair of cobras kept in the *Msaidizi*'s wooden box, the black snake was a venomous cobra of sorts. At the base of its neck, in the place where its chest would have commenced if a snake had a chest, the glossy black of the ventral scales was marked by two white bands which made a striking display in more ways than one.

The *Mchawi* declared that if I wanted it, the black snake was mine. If I had searched my mind to think of anything I wanted less at that particular moment, I would have drawn a blank. I sat on the horns of a serpentine dilemma, since I was not anxious to reject a gift from a man who went out at night and kept company with hyenas.

As if sensing my reticence, the *Mchawi* told me that the snake would do me no harm. All I had to do to be safe from it was not to show it any fear. In any case, he said, he had already removed its fangs. To confirm the veracity of this assurance he prised open the snake's mouth and invited me to take a look. I wouldn't have known if he was telling the truth or not; however, following a few moments of hesitation and a further pause to recall where the camp's supply of snakebite anti-venom kit was located, I took the snake from the *Mchawi* and let it slide over and through my hands. It flowed like the smoothest of silk and showed me not a shred of aggression.

The *Mchawi* beamed and said something like "Into your hands I commend my serpent", before turning on an unshod heel and departing to return to his compound.

I watched him go, and had the thought that there goes my friend the witch doctor. *My friend the witch doctor!*

The immortal lyrics of Mr David Seville's song of the same name were never more relevant:

> *He taught me what to do!*
> *Oo ee, oo ah ha, ting tang, walla walla bing bang;*
> *Oo ee, oo ah ha ting tang, walla walla, bing bang!*

I put the black snake back in the small sack that was also left for me by the *Mchawi*. Before he went he let me know that the snake had recently consumed a rat and therefore wouldn't need to be fed again for some time. For how much time he didn't say, but I knew I could ask him about it when next I saw him.

Over the next couple of days I handled the snake frequently. Familiarity with it led me to fear it not, and for its part it still appeared to bear me no ill will that was obvious.

As I then needed to make a trip to Mwadui I took the snake down with me in its sack. I was interested to show it to anyone I met up with in Mwadui who might be able to tell me what species of snake it was and give me some additional information on it. I supposed that in taking it to Mwadui with me I was treating the snake not only as a curiosity but also as a trophy.

The first stop I made in Mwadui was at *Badu Kidogo* Motors in order to have my Land Rover given an advantageous once over. Derek Visagie remained in charge of the facilities and was then being assisted by Mario Zopetti. Mario was clearly enjoying his hard-won *uhuru* from the Danilo regime. Derek's former assistant Gerry Wilson, that great purveyor of hyperbole, was somewhere out in the field in exile.

Derek took one look at the snake when I showed it to him and ran for the nearest exit screaming, "Shit a brick! *Ringhals*! It's a *ringhals*!" Thus was made the positive identification of the snake that I wanted. Mario's approach was rather less impulsive. He took hold of the snake, examined it, and went on to confirm Derek's histrionic diagnosis.

Derek refused to return to his empire of operations until the snake was securely placed back inside its sack. Thereafter he lost no time in venting his spleen on me for introducing such a dangerous creature to the internal hallows of *Badu Kidogo* Motors. His advice to me, which he expressed with feeling, was that I should take the snake and myself out of Mwadui as soon as possible, preferably immediately.

Ringhals was the Afrikaans name for the ring-necked spitting cobra (*naja nigricollis*). On that basis the *Mchawi*'s gift to me didn't lack punch. The snake was, I learned, highly venomous. Its *modus operandi* consisted not so much in biting as in "spitting" venom at anything on two or four legs that it perceived as a threat. In practice the venom was expelled in fine jets from its two upper fangs. In the manner of a shotgun discharge, the jets spread with distance travelled from source to ultimately form a poisonous circle of mist. The maximum range of spitting to guarantee on-target accuracy was reported to be about six feet.

Derek's reaction, although it shouldn't have been entirely unexpected, put a definite damper on my enthusiasm to own a *ringhals*. Unfortunately I felt duty bound, not to say intimidated by thoughts of incurring the *Mchawi*'s displeasure, to hold onto it. When I was back in camp I tipped the snake out of the sack on to the ground in front of my hut, hoping that it would choose to go away of its own accord as it had tried to do when the *Mchawi* brought it to me. If it wanted to go I was resolved not to attempt to stop it.

My uncertainty as to its future must have communicated itself to the *ringhals*, as it adopted a standard defensive posture. It reared up with hood spread and suddenly fired two shots of venom at me from fangs that weren't, according to the *Mchawi*, supposed to exist. Conventional wisdom said that a *ringhals* always directed its venom at the eyes of its target, but in my case either the snake's aim was off or I was at the limit of its effective range as the broadening circlet of venom droplets struck my shirt at mid-chest level. I both felt and heard the venom hit me in a single liquid splat.

A wave of genuine terror instantly gripped me. I didn't doubt that the *ringhals* was picking up the scent of my fear on its flickering tongue. Presumably believing that it had me on the run, it glided towards me, head up and mouth open with an obvious pair of long fangs extended.

My shotgun, customarily loaded for emergency purposes stood on its butt leaning against the inside wall of my hut just to the left of the entry portal. It was within easy reach. I reacted instinctively by jumping towards the portal and grabbing up the shotgun which I pointed at the advancing snake while pulling the trigger. The snake's progress was halted in spectacular fashion by virtue of its head and at least a foot of its upper body being blown to pieces.

At the sound of the shot, a small group of *watu* led by Efrem came running towards my hut in an evident state of alarm. Having ascertained to their satisfaction that the fun was over they went back to their camp, taking the remains of the *ringhals* with them. I assumed, probably correctly, that they ate it.

My initial sense of relief was quickly tempered by a nagging worry that the *Mchawi* was not going to be very happy about the destruction of his gift, let alone the means of its elimination. As if to confirm that my concerns were not unjustified, I was shocked by a great clap of thunder that came from darkling clouds above Bubiki. I heard the reverberations rolling off into the distance. It was as if the heavens were sending me a message from the *Mchawi*. The shooting of the *ringhals* was a precursor to bad luck. From then on, little would go well during the rest of the time that I remained in Tanganyika. The bad luck began that evening when the rains came.

19

Njia ya kutoka

The exit road

The rain arrived not in showers, not even in sheets, and for that matter not even in a semblance of cats and dogs (*mapaka na mambwa*). It collapsed on Bubiki and the surrounding area in the manner of an almost solid welter of water that seemed capable of drowning anyone caught out in it who attempted to take a deep breath.

The thatched roof of my hut immediately exhibited a host of imperfections. Call them legion for they were many. The roof was incapable of resisting the cascading onslaught of rain from above. Inside the hut there was no dry corner in which I could cower out of the reach of the multitude of instant leaks. The inundation continued all through the night and onwards into the next day. There was no doubt in my mind that the *Mchawi* was exacting tribute by rain as a consequence of my imprudent shooting of the *ringhals* he had gifted me. A pervasive gloom covered the land. The pounding rain was as dark and as shiny as the dorsal scales on the recently expired *ringhals*.

We were forced to suspend our sampling traverses. We huddled under the limited cover that was available as we sought to survive the downpour. The rain bounced off the *koppies* like sea-spray and ran away down-slope towards the camp in torrential sheets. Through the constant swish of the rain both on and through the thatched roof of my hut and its hammering beat on the ground outside I heard the nearby sound of a meaty thump. I dodged between drips and dribbles and went to the hut's portal from where I looked out to discover that the mud-brick walls around my shower and latrine had entirely collapsed. The lower course of the mud bricks had soaked up the water running by on the ground to become too weak to bear the weight of their mud-brick superstructure. The demolition of the walls was total. It was only fortunate that no one was inside the facilities at the time of collapse. The mud brick constructions made for the kitchen went the same way shortly thereafter, interring many of the utensils that were too close to escape the collapse.

Two days later during a temporary respite from the rain, the *fundi* who built the mud-brick walls on the *Mchawi*'s recommendation came along to my hut, which was still damp inside but which by then had the roofing thatch at least partially covered by an impermeable tarpaulin, to ask for payment of what he was still owed for services rendered. Given the circumstances, he had chosen a singularly inappropriate moment to turn up with his hand held out. I took him to inspect the foundered ruins of what he built and asked him why he thought he deserved to be paid anything at all for such defective workmanship. He declared that his work was good. He told me that he wasn't responsible for the rain. He implied that the collapse of the walls was *shauri ya Mungu*, said in a way that all too clearly implied a belief that *mavi anatukia* (shit happened). I agreed with him, but I thought it wasn't unreasonable of me to suggest that an expert in mud-brick constructions ought to know how to place some kind of dry course at the base of a wall to counter the effects of the wet season. All the same, there was no getting away from the fact that what we were experiencing was no ordinary start to a wet season.

Across the way, it seemed that the mud walls of the fair village of Bubiki had all survived their first battle with the current wet season. I knew that the *fundi* had had a hand in building a number of those walls, and I asked him why they had held firm whereas mine hadn't. I stretched my arm out and pointed towards Bubiki, whereupon a great length of mud-brick wall situated just to the right of the *Mchawi*'s green-fringed compound instantly keeled over and crashed flat. A muffled thump reached our ears a moment later. It was as if in my gesture I had cast a spell at the wall and made it disappear. The *fundi* was horrified, although perhaps not as much as I was. We slogged across to Bubiki together through cloying silt to survey the damage and to determine, most thankfully, that there were no casualties. The *fundi* gave me an "I told you so" look when I paid him his dues. More than anything else as the money changed hands, I wished to have nothing to do with mud-brick constructions ever again.

As for the rain, it kept going steadily for almost a week. Sometimes it fell hard, sometimes it was even harder, and now and then it eased to a mere drizzle. There were no genuinely dry breaks. After the week downpours were more sporadic, although they were intense enough when they came. We made several attempts to continue with sampling traverses only to end up floundering in a morass of black cotton soil slurry. We struggled out, got ourselves bogged down, and clawed our way back to camp in a spirit of abject surrender. The great *mbuga* was a vast slough of despond that it was virtually impossible to set foot on. Thick black mud attached itself both to us and to our gear and we sank to a halt in its clutches.

It was evident that we were all banging our heads against a failing mud-brick wall as far as the pursuit of sampling was concerned, leaving us with no alternative other than to consider abandoning operations for the duration of the wet season.

*

Once we managed to work the Land Rover out through the mud around Bubiki to reach the Shinyanga to Mwanza road, I went down to Mwadui to explain our mud-bound circumstances to someone in authority and to request further instructions. By then the inventory of mud-brick walls that had gone down in Bubiki village was substantial. For reasons unexplained, the *Mchawi*'s property was unaffected. The witch doctor's art was long. The medicine that he dispensed was obviously powerful stuff. I bitterly regretted the *ringhals* incident and saw it increasingly as being at the root of a cause and wet-season effect scenario.

When I got to Mwadui I was lucky to find that Gus, the Chief Geologist, was available to see me. He appreciated the situation at once in a way in which his deputy Trevor might never have done. Gus instructed me to close down the camp, to abandon the sampling programme, to clean up the campsite to the best extent that that was possible under the circumstances, to bring all the camp gear and sampling equipment back to Mwadui, and to discharge the *watu* as far as was necessary. He said that there were a number of open options in the bush elsewhere in Tanganyika that I could be reassigned to, although I noticed that he made no mention of my being offered a position in detailed work.

Gus then went on to tell me that quite by chance a request had only just come through to him from head office in Johannesburg for the secondment of a WDL Field Geologist to fill a vacancy in diamond exploration activities in the Bechuanaland Protectorate, more familiarly known as the BP, within two weeks. He offered me the position if I wanted it but gave me little time to think about it as he needed a decision right away.

I wasn't keen to leave Tanganyika, where I was feeling fully at home in the bush environment and becoming increasingly attached to the people I was working with. Nevertheless, it might have been that my spirits were at low ebb as a result of the excessive rain, as almost against my better judgement I found myself accepting the assignment to the BP there and then. Immediately afterwards I experienced a feeling that my acceptance of the assignment was a completely selfish act. The saddest aspect of it was that I would have to disband and lay off all the *watu* with whom I had shared so much through so many shades of both good and ill. I frankly had no idea of how to set about discharging them.

During the return to Bubiki from Mwadui in the Land Rover I talked to Efrem who had come along with me for the ride. My deepest regrets were that I would be parting company with him and other "inner circle" *watu* like Taji, Idi and Hamisi. I tried to coat what to me was a very bitter pill to offer the *watu*, let alone to have them swallow, by implying that although I was leaving, I trusted that I would come back before too long. Efrem probably knew as well as I did that my return was improbable. He said that he would, in his capacity as headman, inform the rest of the *watu* as to the way events were moving.

I planned to pay them all through to the end of the then current month (November) or to the completion date of their existing *kipande*s if that latter date fell later than the end of the month. On that basis the average period of notice would be at least a month, and in addition repatriation and travel allowances would be paid in accordance with regulations as published in the *GFM*. It wasn't an over-generous arrangement, but on the other hand it wasn't in any way mean-spirited.

I was ready to discuss any extra claims on a person by person basis and to make any consequent accommodations (or not) as fairly as I could.

An hour or so after I got back to camp I was sitting down in my hut trying to work out a scheme to extricate the camp from the mud when Efrem came to see me. He said that the news concerning the camp closure and loss of work hadn't been at all well received by a majority of the *watu*. As if to emphasise Efrem's words, a clamour of voices punctuated by an angry shout or two coming from outside the front of my hut created a strong impression that mutiny was in the air.

I thought it prudent to make sure that my shotgun was loaded and leaning in its accustomed position just inside the portal of the hut, and with that done I stepped outside to greet and not be greeted by a small mob of disgruntled *watu*. Their faces were certainly as sullen and perhaps a little more threatening than the clouds that hung heavily above us all.

Thoughts of *Et tu Brute?* entered my mind. I hated confrontations and always tended to shy away from them whenever I could. However, in this instance I felt quite calm. It was as if I were playing the classic part of a sheriff facing down a lynch mob in a Western film. There was even a supporting role for a shotgun on the side, although on the side was where that particular implement was going to remain. I thought that all I needed to do was be steadfast in dispersing the members of the mob. The said members were unfortunately not familiar with Wild West melodrama, and what they actually did was move towards me and form a half circle that effectively penned me against the hut's side.

My greatest disappointment was that the ring-leaders of the mob were Hamisi and John Simon. I hadn't expected that, but it seemed that when push came to shove what once seemed to be loyalties no longer counted for much. A mutter that sounded not unlike *uhuru na kazi* came from one side of the mob. As a (presumably elected) spokesman, John Simon told me that the *watu* he represented felt hard done by. That was fair enough and I didn't blame any of them for it. In their position I would probably have felt exactly the same—just as I did in my own position as well. The fact that the wet season was a *shauri ya Mungu* event meant nothing at all when the chips were down.

The *watu*'s demands were relatively simple. They wanted to be paid through to the end of December; to be fully compensated for repatriation; to be individually provided with letters of recommendation to future employers; and to be apportioned equal shares of all remaining rations that were held at the time in the store up alongside the *koppies*, assuming that the edibility of the same wasn't too depressed by wet and mud. It seemed to me that none of these demands were asking too much from WDL. I would be glad to write a letter of recommendation in respect of anyone who merited it; the rations could be shared out with a blessing on the recipients added in for luck; and all of the *watu* being laid off were guaranteed a statutory right to repatriation expenses. What it wasn't possible for me to agree to there and then, however, was the *watu*'s demand for an extra month's pay. A decision on that was outside my authority and would have to be taken up with the powers that were based in Mwadui.

Since my personal problems associated with the cashbox stolen by Saidi had not gone away, I didn't want to complicate the situation any more by agreeing to demands which exceeded regulations only to find myself liable to cover the excess. There was nothing for it but that I should make a second trip of the day to Mwadui to request a ruling on the maximum amount of pay in lieu of notice that I could dispense to the *watu*, given that the circumstances surrounding their loss of work were not of their own making. At the *watu*'s request (if not at their insistence) Hamisi and John Simon came down to Mwadui with me to ensure fair play (their words not mine). I told them that their ability to influence events would not be great as they weren't authorised to enter the gates of Mwadui, but they were undeterred. Efrem remained in camp to start up the dismantling process as best he could. I didn't expect that very much would happen in my absence, and as it turned out I was right.

I reached Mwadui, dropped my passengers outside the gates, and drove in to consult with the authorities. Gus was unfortunately no longer available for this second time of asking. Instead, I was shown into the office in which Trevor eked away the hours of his working days to meet Trevor face to face across the uncluttered expanse of his handsome desk. Trevor busied himself with shuffling a few sheets of paper in order to keep me waiting for long enough to let me know that he was the boss. He then deigned to listen to my story. The sole question at issue as I gave it to him was whether or not I could obtain permission from him to pay the *watu* that I had to lay off through to the end of the year.

Trevor's response was to cite rules and regulations that I hadn't previously heard of and to speak of the imprudence of creating precedents outside of the hard-won statutes that all WDL men out in bush camps were obliged to follow. He discoursed at such length that I was half expecting shoes and ships and sealing wax to enter his monologue. I accepted the philosophy behind what he was telling me, but that didn't help to answer my question. All I wanted to know from Trevor was yes or no to an extra month's pay. Trevor appeared unwilling to come down on one side or the other of the fence. If I had ever doubted that humming and hawing was not his stock in trade I set those doubts aside for ever.

He then put on a realistic performance of someone who had just been struck with a brainwave. He instructed me to go down to the government offices at Shinyanga and get someone in the Labour Department office to clarify what the letter of the law said regarding my paying off the *watu*. I wasn't at all happy with this, but it was clear that it was all I was going to get out of Trevor. The *watu*'s legal entitlements were not the question—what needed to be settled was how much extra pay they were to be given, and on that subject I imagined that the law couldn't have cared less.

I returned to pick up Hamisi and John Simon at the Mwadui gates, let them know what Trevor had told me to do, and drove down to Shinyanga to arrive at the government offices not long before the appointed hour of their closure for the day. With thoughts of the first of a series of cold beverages in mind, the officials were less than willing to take any interest in receiving a new supplicant. And so it came to pass that the official I met told to come back tomorrow. It was his *uhuru* from *kazi*, and not my problem with *kazi* that preoccupied him.

I fell back on putting into Shinyanga's famous port in a storm, otherwise known as the Diamond Fields Hotel. In that haven, with the sun already over the yardarm, I knew I would find my friend the inspector of police (who at that time had yet to show me his turncoat colours) seated in his customary position at the bar. There he was, busily nursing an almost empty glass and lying in wait for someone like me to come in and arrange for the contents of his glass to be replenished. I hastened to oblige him.

We discussed the matter of final payment for the *watu* over two bottles of beer apiece. The inspector's single-beer opinion did not favour paying laid-off *watu* for an extra month. With a second beer (IPA, what else?) in his hand he saw fit to change his mind and advised me that the best option for everyone involved on all sides of the question was for WDL to comply with the *watu*'s demands, pay up and have done with it. I asked him if he would be able to provide me with a written version of this opinion. He wasn't willing to go quite that far (no surprise there) but he gave me permission to quote him if I was required to do so, which was good enough for me.

It is probably just as well that I was not subsequently called on to quote the inspector's words, as that might have put him into a position where he would have had to deny what I said he said. Without a good measure of beer sloshing around under his shiny belt the inspector might not have risen to show rectitude. When my deliberations with him were complete I returned to where Hamisi and John Simon were waiting for me, not very patiently, on the back of the Land Rover. I told them that their demands were all accepted and I left it to them to inform the *watu* whom they were representing back in camp. I didn't know what Trevor's reaction to it would be, but as I also didn't care any more, I considered that I had done all I could and the case was closed. From what I knew of Trevor I was sure that he had dismissed my problem from his mind at the instant when I closed the door behind me on leaving his office.

The big lay-off payout was made three days later. Three days was how long it took us, given the mud and further lengthy falls of rain, to get all the camp gear (tents, oil drums, cooking utensils, personal effects, tarpaulins, sampling equipment and so on and so forth) collected, inventoried and ferried in stages up to the main road for loading into a five-ton truck sent up from Mwadui.

I obtained the necessary cash from the Shinyanga branch of the Standard Bank, paid each *mtu* his exact dues and left it to the *watu* as a group to divide up the comestible spoils that featured in the agreement. It was interesting that for at least a couple of hours before we quit the Bubiki campsite for the last time, large numbers of local residents gathered around its fringes, looking like vultures ready to flap in and scavenge for any pickings we might be leaving behind.

I wasn't able to follow the Lake Mianje camp protocol by setting fire to the hut that I lived in, as the hut didn't belong to me. However, so much rain had permeated and penetrated through the roofing thatch and into the walls that I doubted that any single wisp of the hut would have been capable of catching fire anyway.

*

With the exception of Efrem, Idi and Taji, the rest of the *watu* faded away following the final pay settlement. I knew where each one had received expenses to go to, but I didn't know at all where they actually went. They presumably went down to Mwadui on one or other of the trips by the five-ton truck and from there onwards to the railway station at Shinyanga by bus. The whole break-up of the camp and its people seemed so genuinely sad. It left a sorry feeling of anticlimax in its shadow.

I didn't see the *Mchawi* before I left—when I looked in on his compound to say goodbye he was not there. I assumed he might be off travelling with a few of his hyenas in search of dry ground. I ought to have been sorrier to miss him than I was, but with the prospect of more painful partings immediately ahead I had bigger things to worry about.

Of the two camp dogs, Jack was still with us but Shen had disappeared. Efrem said that he thought Shen had gone off with one of the locally hired former employees. I wasn't so happy about that as I had seen all too often how badly dogs tended to be treated in tribal villages. I was reluctant to leave Jack to that kind of fate. If Efrem had wanted to take him I supposed I would have felt happy enough, but Efrem either couldn't or wouldn't have Jack and so the dog was left with me. I expected that I would be able to get a Mwadui-based *mzungu* to adopt him. It was a bridge to be crossed when I came to it.

Efrem, Idi and Taji caught a train that left Shinyanga on the following night. They were headed ultimately for Mbeya. There was a grim sense of loss and utter finality in the air as I stood with Jack at the railway station and watched their train puff away down the line. Steam trailed behind the train like a grey banner in the damp night then vanished like the last dregs of hope.

I returned to Mwadui and the Pink House.

*

A highlight of the following day was a meeting that I had with the WDL Chief Warehouseman for the purpose of turning in and signing off on my inventory of camp gear. It was not a pleasant meeting. The Chief Warehouseman was furious at the quantity of black mud found adhering to various areas of tent canvas and directed a string of red-faced bellows at me for permitting such fouling of company property to occur. The realities of life out in the bush somehow seemed a long way removed from the Chief Warehouseman's sanitised demesne in which a small gang of *watu* was kept perpetually busy in sorting, scouring, buffing, tidying and polishing throughout every livelong day. I made an attempt to explain to him how hard we had been hit by the wet season up at Bubiki, where the mud had overwhelmed us and forced us to abandon our work. The Chief Warehouseman wasn't interested. He asked me if I knew of any good reason why I shouldn't be made to pay the cost of cleaning the tent canvas. I could think of a few reasons, not the least of which was that there was no blood left to be got from that particular stone, but as I knew that discretion was the better part of valour I restricted my reply to making an offer to carry out the cleaning personally. That also didn't interest him.

I left him to mumble to himself. He had done much to confirm my jaundiced view of Mwadui's *wazungu* club society. The needlessly sour note that he struck made me think that the *Mchawi*-inspired ripples centred on the shooting of the *ringhals* were continuing to spread. Be all of that as it might have been, I managed to complete all of my final reports together with the essential formalities related to my pending BP assignment without any hitches. With that done, there were three days left to go to a set date on which I would depart on the Dakota for Nairobi to pick up a scheduled flight connection to Johannesburg.

The one remaining question was what was to be done with the dog Jack. I didn't see his disposition as a problem as I was fairly confident that one or other of the *wazungu* of Mwadui would be glad to have him. Jack was a decent dog, friendly and even-tempered, which was a lot more than could be said for the Chief Warehouseman.

To my growing concern I could find no *mzungu* willing to accept the dog, and moreover no one who claimed to know of any other *mzungu* either in or out of Mwadui who might be willing to oblige in giving him a good home. *Wazungu* were *wazungu* and African dogs were African dogs, and it seemed that never the twain should meet. With time slipping away far too rapidly I found myself in possession of a dog that I could neither keep nor bring myself to abandon.

I received much advice from some *wazungu* that I approached to the effect that Jack should be put down. That was the very last thing

I wanted to have happen. The curious thing was that a few of them expressed a willingness to destroy Jack for me. I wondered what that said about them. My sense of disillusionment grew.

Following a night of soul-searching and heartache I reached the dreadful conclusion that Jack had no future. Indeed, putting him down was the only feasible option, and the responsibility for doing it was mine.

In the early morning of the day before I was due to take the Dakota to Nairobi, I loaded up my shotgun and with it slung over my shoulder I took Jack out of the Pink House. He wandered around happily, oblivious to my distress. I must have sighted the shotgun at the back of his head a score of times or more, but on each occasion I was incapable of pulling the trigger. When I did eventually fire the shot it seemed to be such an involuntary act that it was as if it was carried out by someone else. Jack was tugging at a stalk of grass when it happened. He was gone in an instant. I fell onto my knees alongside him and wept long tears. It took a huge effort for me to regain my feet.

The shooting of Jack was a last throw of the dice. It was the ultimate action of the shotgun in my hands. Perhaps it also marked an end to the flow of misfortune that commenced with that other fatal shot at the *ringhals*. A death for a death must have satisfied the *Mchawi*.

I wrapped Jack up carefully in a clean sheet that I got from the Pink House, placed his shrouded body in a stout canvas bag that was closed up with a draw string, and took him out of Mwadui in a Land Rover, up to the crest of a rise on the Mwanza road, where I dug his grave beneath a patch of bush and buried him. With that duty done, I drove down to Shinyanga where I handed my two firearms in to the police for secure keeping pending the promised issue of a licence for their eventual export to the BP. I didn't know that I would never see the guns again.

On my way back to Mwadui I felt as if a weight was lifted from my shoulders. I bore a wealth of memories both good and less good. Thoughts of a Book of Common Prayer confession that I formerly recited regularly during my church-going days in Cornwall came into my head with reference to the past year or so—I had erred and strayed from the ways like a lost sheep and had followed too much the devices and desires of my own heart; I had left undone those things that I ought to have done and had done those things that I ought not to have done. It was, however, prudent that I should stop short of reckoning that I was a miserable offender in whom there was no health.

I had done my best, for most of the time anyway, to fit into the ways of the bush and for the most part I believed I had succeeded. I learned to speak Kiswahili reasonably well and had made very many friends as a consequence. Although I had as such no real enemies that I knew of, I was not unaware that there were a few people here and there around Tanganyika who wouldn't be too sorry about the prospect of never seeing me again.

My job had been a life-forming experience of absolutely unique proportions and on that basis alone I thought I was coming out ahead of the game with a lot more confidence than I had had when I first arrived. There was still so very much for me to learn about Africa and its people, but my feet were on the ground and there was a road stretching out ahead that was full of promise, and no doubt littered with many more hurdles for me to stumble over and certain mistakes for me to make.

20

Kwa heri

Good bye

The Dakota that took me from Mwadui to Nairobi carried no more than half a dozen passengers. Nobody waved goodbye as I boarded. One of the passengers was a tubby, lightly bearded, greying South African. He was clad in a khaki safari suit and on his head sat a matching broad-brimmed hat. The style and tilt of the hat in the company of its owner's heavily accented assault on the English language, suggested to me that airing the topic of the Boer War within his hearing would be a bad idea.

He asked me where I was going. I told him that I was first of all heading to Nairobi (a needless comment really, since Nairobi was the scheduled destination of the Dakota) and that thereafter I would travel on to Johannesburg. He looked at me wistfully and, shaking his head a little, he exclaimed, "So you're going to Joburg!" Thereafter he kept on glancing at me during the flight while mumbling the same thing over and over again like a mantra, "So you're going to Joburg!" It was as if he were visualising me following a yellow brick road to a City of Gold and regretting that he wasn't off to see the wizard as well.

He wasn't entirely reluctant to avoid making a reference to politics as he made it plain in subsequent comments that South Africa's recent departure from the British Commonwealth found favour with him, as also did the rock-hard obduracy of Dr Hendrik Verwoerd, the then

South African Prime Minister who was the prime architect of the Commonwealth exit strategy and champion of South Africa's policy of "separate racial development" (otherwise known as *apartheid*). There was no need for anyone to worry about any outrageous nonsense like *uhuru* down in South Africa, I was told.

I began to wonder about just how magnificent a place Joburg was going to be. As someone who was on his way to becoming one of that great city's familiars, it seemed reasonable that I should start thinking of it right away as Joburg rather than Johannesburg.

Once we were disembarked from the Dakota at Nairobi's Embakasi airport my fellow passenger and his obsession with my going to Joburg both went their separate ways. I wasn't at all sorry to see them go.

An agent of WDL met me and whisked me and my luggage away out of the airport to a waiting car for transfer into the city. The agent was Belgian by nationality and jolly in manner, although given his nationality I wasn't sure what he had to be jolly about.

He took me to the Norfolk Hotel where I was to spend a single night prior to my "going to Joburg" on the following day. At the Norfolk I had the comfortable feeling of treading on known ground and I moved through its hallowed halls as if I had been to the manor born. It seemed as if I was being borne along on a cushion of euphoria. For a while I could have believed that I was the equal of any white hunter who was in residence between *safaris* and about to make a full frontal attack on the Norfolk's stock of cold beer.

In the early morning of the following day, which was a Sunday, the Belgian agent came to the Norfolk to collect me to return to the airport to catch my flight to Joburg. On the way to the airport he stopped at the building in which his office was situated and took me in with him to pick up my ticket for the flight. As we entered, one of a number of black minions hanging around the front of the building asked him, "*Bwana*, what will you give us for our *uhuru?*"

"*Uhuru?*" he responded in a tone of querulous indignation. "*Uhuru?*" he repeated with a rising inflexion. "What will I give you? What will I give you? Not a penny, not a sou!"

It was the firmest statement of political intent that I heard voiced in East Africa. It was issued with the kind of disdain that possibly characterised the remarks of aristocrats riding in tumbrels on their way to the guillotine in French revolutionary days.

*

The BOAC aircraft that took me to Joburg was a new De Havilland Comet, a jet-propelled airliner of breathtaking design and groundbreaking performance. The problems with metal fatigue that dogged the Comet's future, damaged its reputation and cut short its career were unknown quantities (to me at least) when I boarded the flight. Such irregularities were also kind enough not to make themselves known to me in between Nairobi and Joburg, as the flight plus its passengers all arrived intact at Joburg's international airport. For me it was an auspicious landing.

The passengers on the Comet were all *wazungu*, as indeed was everyone who moved with any appearance of freedom around the airport's concourses. The black South Africans that I saw seemed to be there to serve in a wholly menial capacity.

White men in uniforms were much in evidence. The uniforms were symbols of power, waves of which exuded freely from the immigration officers, the supervisors of labour in the baggage hall and the police patrolling the arrivals area. I judged that Afrikaans was the tongue of ultimate command since within my hearing all such officials used the Afrikaans language exclusively between themselves.

Most of the white officials appeared to favour wearing their hair close cropped against the skull. They exhibited sliver-thin moustaches and a military-styled bearing enhanced by starched khaki shorts and shirts, polished Sam Browne leather belts, caps that were as securely levelled as they were crisply peaked, far too many holstered guns on hips, and a virtual forest of long wooden truncheons slapping against palms.

They oversaw a black labour force that was also uniformed, although not quite as crisply as its white masters were. The black labour uniform dress code consisted of loosely fitting shorts and tunics dyed a deep blue colour. It was not possible to avoid drawing a comparison with prison garb, my impression of which was emphasised by the consistently aggressive attitude of the white officials who snarled frequently while barking orders and shouting out commands.

In making my way through the airport I witnessed three separate instances of uniformed whites yelling at groups of blacks. On one occasion the white supervisor was swinging his truncheon in a threatening manner that looked to be full of a desire to use it for the purpose for which it was intended. He was clearly enjoying what he was doing. My guess was that he would be sure to lay his truncheon across at least one black skull before he considered his day to be complete. It was a bewildering sight. I was distressed that there was nothing that I could do about it. Incoming passengers moved by without either batting an eyelid or turning a hair. Tanganyika suddenly seemed a long way away, and not only in terms of distance.

I collected my luggage and travelled from the airport into Joburg on a South African Airways transit bus. The air terminal building was located close to the main railway station just north of the city's downtown area where the great buildings of a shiningly modern city rose to greet me. I could easily have imagined myself to have arrived on another planet.

My itinerary called for me to proceed from the air terminal to a hotel named the Victoria, where I was to be accommodated. As it was on a Sunday afternoon, I wouldn't be able to report to the De Beers offices located in Joburg's Main Street to receive the details of my onward assignment until the following morning.

I approached a standing taxi and asked the driver, who was white, if he could take me to the Victoria Hotel, only to be told by him that the hotel was within easy walking distance of the spot where I was. He was kind enough to give me directions. I walked to the hotel lugging my suitcase. There was not a single black person in sight.

After I checked in at the hotel another white man carried my suitcase up to my room on the second floor. Conditioned by East African hotel experiences, I found the concept of a white porter almost impossible to grasp. But there he was, a white porter larger than life and an Afrikaner to the core.

He entered the room ahead of me, put down the suitcase, took a step over to the side of the bed, flipped a knob set into one side of the headboard, and from a loudspeaker on the wall above the bed the popular *Esme and Mervyn* Sunday afternoon record request programme on South Africa's Springbok Radio flooded into the room. The requested number on offer was a version of "Full Moon and Empty Arms", based on a theme from Rachmaninoff's second piano concerto.

The white porter asked me where I came from. I told him that I had just arrived from Nairobi after fifteen months of working in Tanganyika. He shook his head and gave me what appeared to be a look of sympathy.

"Well," he said, "You're in God's own country now!"

I didn't know what to think about that, because my mind was currently exercised with what I should do about tipping him. How much did I have to give a white man for a tip?

I didn't really have to worry of course, as one of the effects of South Africa's recent exit from the Commonwealth had been the introduction of a new unit of currency known as the rand, and I didn't have any rand with me to hand over in any denomination.

I didn't even have an English sixpence.

And that, I thought, was where I came in.

Down in the jungle
Living in a tent.
Better than a prefab—
No rent!.

Stand Easy—THE CHARLIE CHESTER SHOW (BBC)

Glossary

Kiswahili and Afrikaans words used in the text

A
Alikuwa	He was
Andika	Write
Apartheid (*Afrikaans*)	Social and political development based solely on racial considerations
Asante	Thank you
Askari	A soldier, or a soldier ant
Asubuhi	The morning

B
Baada	Afterwards
Badu	Not yet
Badu Kidogo	Sometime, but not soon
Bahati	Luck
Baraza	A formal tribal gathering or meeting
Baridi	Cold
Barra barra	Road; track
Bibi	Wife
Bila	Without
Biltong (*Afrikaans*)	Dried or jerked meat
Blanketi	A blanket
Boma	An encircling fence, often of cut thorn bush; a district government HQ

Bwana	Sir; Boss
Bweha	A jackal
Bweha masigio	A bat-eared fox

C
Chakula	Food
Changamfu	Cheerful, jolly
Chinja	Kill
Choo	A latrine
Chui	A leopard
Chumba	A room (as in a hotel)
Chumvi	Salt

D
Dagaa	Dried sprats
Damu	Blood
Dawa	Medicine
Debe	A five-gallon can of light metal containing food or cooking oil
Dikidiki	A dik-dik
Doumi	A bull
Dudu	An insect
Duka	A shop; a trading outlet

E
Elfu moja	One thousand
Elfu tatu	Three thousand
Elimu ya mawe	Geology (lit. science of rock)
Endesha	Drive (a motor vehicle)

F
Fedha	Money
Fikiri	Think
Fisi	A hyena
Fisi maji	An otter
Fundi	A recognized expert (usually in manual skills)
Funga	Open

Fungua — Close; shut
Funo — A red duiker

G
Gari — A motor vehicle (car)
Granti — A Grant's gazelle

H
Hakuna — None
Halal — Islamic ceremonial slaughtering of animals or birds for culinary purposes
Hapa — Here
Hapana — No
Hata kidogo — Not at all
Hatari — Danger
Hela — Money
Herufi — A letter (alphabetic)
Hodi? — May I come in?
Homa — Malaria; fever
Huyu — He, him

I
Iko — There is
Iko? — Is there …?
Ishirini — Twenty

J
Jambo — Hello
Jembe — A hoe; a flat bladed tool for chopping soil
Jiwe — A stone
Jua — To know
Juma pili — Sunday
Juma tatu — Monday
Juu — On top of

K
Kabisa — Absolute

Kaffir (*Afrikaans*)	Highly disparaging term for a black African
Kaffir beer	Native beer
Kale, (a Kale)	Old
Kali	Fierce; angry; pungent
Kalikiti	Cricket
Kamba	A rope (of bark or rawhide)
Kambi	Camp
Kampuni	A company
Kanga	A guinea fowl
Kanzu	An all enveloping robe, usually white
Karani	A clerk
Karibu	Come in
Kazi	Work
Kiboko	A hippopotamus, or a whip made of hippo hide
Kichocho	Bilharzia
Kichwa	A head
Kidogo	Small; little
Kidonda	Tropical ulcer
Kifaru	A rhinoceros
Kilele	A peak, summit
Kilima	A hill
Kipandi	Monthly contract of work
Kipepeo	A butterfly
Kisonono	Gonorrhea
Kiswahili	The East African lingua franca
Kitabu	A book
Kofia	A hat
Kohoa	A cold; a cough; influenza
Kongoni	A hartebeest
Koppie (*Afrikaans*)	A small hill
Korongo	A roan antelope
Kuku	A chicken
Kula	To eat
Kule	Over there
Kumi	Ten
Kumi na mbili	Twelve

Kupa	To give
Kundu	Backside (ass)
Kunywa	To drink
Kura	A vote
Kuro	A waterbuck
Kutoka	To leave or go out
Kutukia	To happen
Kwenda	To go
Kwa Heri	Goodbye
Kwanza	The first

L

Laager (*Afrikaans*)	A camp fortified around its perimeter with wagons
Lakini	But

M

Macho	An eye
Mafaa	Utility; generic
Mafuta	Oil
Mafuta ya kupika	Cooking Oil
Mafuta ya taa	Lamp oil
Magonjwa	Sick; ill
Mahindi	Maize
Maji	Water
Malima	Hills
Masikia	An ear
Matata	Trouble, mischief
Matumbu ya mnyama	Intestines, offal
Matunda	Fruit
Mavi	Excrement (shit)
Mavini	In the shit
Mbaya	Bad
Mbele	Ahead; in front
Mbili	Two
Mboga	Vegetables
Mbuga	Poorly drained and lightly vegetated open ground underlain by black cotton soil

Mbwa	A dog
Mbwa mwitu	An African wild hunting dog
Mchawi	A witchdoctor
Mchicha	Spinach
Mdogo	A small man (disparaging)
Mheshimiwa	Excellency; Exalted one
Mia moja	One hundred
Mingi	Many
Miombo	Open bush with scattered trees
Mishkaka	A kebab of unspecified provenance
Mjomba	Uncle
Mkate	A loaf or a cake
Mke	A woman
Mkojo	Urine
Mkubwa	Big; great
Mlaya	A European
Moja	One (number)
Moshi	Smoke, or clandestinely distilled village alcohol
Mpishi	A cook
Msaidizi	An assistant, a helper
Mshenzi	An uncivilized man; a rural hick
Msingida	A species of tree
Mtama	Millet
Mtoto	A small boy; a kitchen assistant
Mtu	A man (black)
Muhanga	An aardvark
Mungu	God
Mwanasiasa	A politician
Mzee	Elderly man (term of respect)
Mzungu	A white man
Mzuri	Good

N

Na	And
Nafasi	A chance; an opportunity
Naiba	To steal
Nauma	Pain

Nane	Eight
Na tosha	Enough
Nchi	Country
Ndani	In; inside
Ndege	A bird; an aeroplane
Ndio	Yes
Ngoja	To wait
Nguru	A large fish
Nguruwe	A warthog
Nini	What
Nje	Out; outside
Njia	A pathway. a track
Njugu	Peanuts
Nsya	A common bush duiker
Nyama	Meat; game animal
Nyamera	A topi
Nyani	A baboon
Nyati	A buffalo
Nyeupe	White, fair
Nyika	Savannah bush
Nyoka	A snake
Nyota	Star
Nyumbu	A wildebeest

O

Onyesha	Show (display)

P

Paa	A blue duiker or suni antelope
Paka	A cat
Pamoja	Together
Panga	Long bladed cutting implement; a sword
Pimbi	A rock hyrax
Pofu	An eland
Pole pole	Slow; slowly
Pori	The bush
Porini	In the bush
Pombe	Beer; native beer

Pongo	A bushbuck
Posho	Maize porridge
Puku	A puku
Punda malia	A zebra

R

Ringhals (*Afrikaans*)	A black spitting cobra
Rondavel (*Afrikaans*)	A small circular dwelling, normally with a thatched roof

S

Saa	Hour; time of day
Saba	Seven
Saba saba	The seventh of July – Tanganyika's Independence Day
Safari	A journey
Saidia	To help
Samaki	A fish
Sana	Very much; a lot
Sanduku	A box
Shamba	An area of cultivated ground
Shamba wabibi	A game reserve
Shauri	Fault; responsibility
Shauri ya Mungu	The will of God
Shenzi	Uncivilised
Shida	A necessity
Shilingi	A shilling (unit of currency)
Siafu	Safari ants
Sijui	I don't know
Siku	A day
Siku kuu	A very important day
Simba	A lion
Sindano	An injection; vaccination
Sisi	Us, we
Sjambok (*Afrikaans*)	A rawhide whip (infamous)
Skokiaan (*Afrikaans*)	Supercharged native beer (famous)
Sola topee	A pith helmet
Sukari	Sugar
Sungura	A hare
Swala pala	An impala

T
Taa	A lamp
Tafadhali	Please
Taka	Want
Tanga	A sail (as on a dhow)
Taya	An oribi
Tayare	Ready
Tego	Syphilis
Tembo	An elephant
Tisa	Nine
T'lapi	Tilapia (fish)
Tohe	A reedbuck
Tomba	Fuck
Tomi	A Thompson's gazelle
Tondoro	A steenbuck
Tumbili	A vervet monkey
Tumbo	Stomach; bowels
Tundu	A hole
Twiga	A giraffe

U
Ugali	Stiff unsweetened maize porridge
Uhuru	Freedom; independence (political)
Uji	Thin sweetened maize gruel
Ulaya	Europe
Unakwenda	You go
Upele	Scabies
Upesi	Quickly
Usiku	Evening; night; after dark

V
Velskoon (*Afrikaans*)	Soft leather ankle length boots, sometimes crepe-soled
Vipandi	Plural of kipandi
Voortrekker (*Afrikaans*)	South African pioneer of Afrikaans extraction

W
Waharabu	Arabs
Wahindi	Indians

Wanafasi	Tricksters or chancers
Wanawake	Women (black)
Wandorobo	Tsetse flies; nomadic bush dwellers
Wapi	Where
Warafiki	Friends
Wasinga singa	Sikhs
Wasusu	Tapeworms
Watembeaji	Walkers; pedestrians
Watoto	Children, small boys
Watu	Men; tribesmen (black)
Waza	An idea
Wazi	Open
Wazungu	White men
Weka	To put
Wewe	You

Y

Ya	Of
Yako	Your
Yangu	Mine
Yetu	Yours

Lightning Source UK Ltd.
Milton Keynes UK
UKOW04f0229180114

224844UK00012B/506/A